Intellectuals
and Public Life

Intellectuals and Public Life

BETWEEN RADICALISM AND REFORM

EDITED BY *Leon Fink*
Stephen T. Leonard
Donald M. Reid

Cornell University Press ITHACA AND LONDON

Copyright © 1996 by Cornell University

First published 1996 by Cornell University Press.

Library of Congress Cataloging-in-Publication Data

Intellectuals and public life / edited by Leon Fink, Stephen T.
   Leonard, Donald M. Reid.
        p.   cm.
   Based on the work of an interdisciplinary graduate seminar
sponsored by the Program in social theory and cross-cultural studies
at the University of North Carolina.
   Includes bibliographical references (p.   ) and index.
   ISBN 0-8014-2794-0 (cloth : alk. paper)
   1. Intellectuals—Political activity.   2. Intellectual life.
I. Fink, Leon, 1948–   .   II. Leonard, Stephen T., 1954–
III. Reid, Donald M.
HM213.I5456   1995
306.4′2—dc20   95-35620

Printed in the United States of America

 ♾ The paper in this book meets the minimum requirements of the
American National Standard for Information Sciences—Permanence
of Paper for Printed Library Materials, ANSI Z39.48-1984.

This book is dedicated to the University of
North Carolina's Program in Social Theory and
Cross-Cultural Studies (which first
brought us together) and to the spirit of
interdisciplinary inquiry for which it stands.

Contents

Preface

This volume had its inception in an interdisciplinary graduate seminar sponsored by the Program in Social Theory and Cross-Cultural Studies at the University of North Carolina. Stimulated by conditions as diverse as the publication of Russell Jacoby's *Last Intellectuals* and new activism among the intelligentsia of Eastern Europe and China, students' dissatisfaction with "ivory tower" history and social science, and our own frustration with the usual "unbiased" mode of teaching within our disciplines, we sought to bring together a variety of scholars who could both clarify the historical positions of twentieth-century intellectuals and problematize the category itself. In diverse ways the lectures and discussions that constituted the seminar sought to denaturalize "the intellectual" while destabilizing the stubborn ideological divisions (academy/world, scholar/activist) that have informed its North American history. The chapters of this book both reflect this project and considerably enlarge its scope.

We are indebted to the individuals and organizations that made this ambitious undertaking feasible and enjoyable. The enthusiastic sponsorship and logistic support of the Program in Social Theory, especially as provided by Craig Calhoun and Rekha Mirchandani, were fundamental. A generous grant from the Office of the Provost was supplemented by additional support for visiting speakers by the departments of History, Political Science, and Anthropology; the Women's Studies Program; and the curricula in African and African-American Studies; American Studies; East Asian Studies; International Studies; Latin American Studies; Peace, War, and Defense; and Russian and Eastern European Studies. The University of North Carolina's Institute for Research in the Social Sciences and the Institute for the Arts and Humanities also contributed funds and logistic support. For all this invaluable assistance we are most grateful.

Not all the scholars who contributed to this project are represented in this volume. Susan E. Estroff, Ezekiel Kalipeni, James Kloppenburg, Elizabeth Fox-Genovese, Steven Vincent, Ronald Inden, Tani Barlow, and Derek Sayer all made important presentations to the seminar and considerably enriched our discussions. An engaged group of students both occasioned the seminar and clarified its limits with their intellectual and political lives. Judith Farquhar played a vital role in the creation and long gestation of this manuscript. We regret that in the end she chose not to continue as an editor, but we respect her decision. Finally, we express appreciation to Peter Agree and Barbara H. Salazar of Cornell University Press for their patience and professionalism in seeing this project through to fruition.

L. F.
S. T. L.
D. M. R.

Intellectuals
and Public Life

1

Introduction: A Genealogy
of the Politicized Intellectual

Stephen T. Leonard

> . . . a word never—well, hardly ever—shakes off its etymol-
> ogy and its formation.
>
> —J. L. AUSTIN
>
> Concepts, like individuals, have their histories, and are just as
> incapable of withstanding the ravages of time as are individuals.
>
> —SØREN KIERKEGAARD

FROM HEAVENLY ANGELS TO POLITICAL AGENTS

"The intellectual heaven is the angel; and the angels are called heaven
because they are like to the highest heaven by reason of their dignity and
excellence." Thus did the thirteenth-century Italian teacher Jacobus de
Voragine, in his popular *Legenda sanctorum* (Golden legend), record what
must have been a widely held understanding of "intellectuals." Citing
Dionysius's *Book of the Names of God*, Jacobus describes the intellectual
angels as having "godlike minds" and "a being above all other beings and
a life above all other things that live, and their intelligence and knowledge
are above sense and reason, and more than any other being they desire
the beautiful and the good, and participate therein."[1]

I thank my co-editors, Leon Fink and Donald Reid, for their assistance in organizing
the direction of this chapter and for reading and criticizing earlier drafts. Special thanks
also to Stephanie Hoopes, whose seminar paper on the history of the concept of intellectuals
provided me with much food for thought (and texts for consideration).

1. Jacobus de Voragine, *The Golden Legend*, translation and adaptation of *Legenda sanctorum*, (1275) by Granger Ryan and Helmut Ripperger (New York, 1969), 291. My characterization of Jacobus's conceptualization of "intellectual" as a popular one is grounded in
the fact that over 500 manuscript copies of the original still exist, and that within the
first 100 years of its publication, more than 150 translations and editions were produced
(ibid., vii).

These passages are at once familiar and strange. Intellectuals, according to many of our contemporaries, are—or should be—characters of dignity and excellence, enjoying the highest forms of temporal existence because they desire and participate in the beautiful and the good. Here the virtues of the life of the mind, its advantages over the life of physical toil and day-to-day existence, and its status as a higher form of existence are assumed. Here the transcendental nature of truth and justice are implied. Here the authority of the intellect finds its grounding. The familiarity of these notions is a sure testament that "intellectuals" has come to us, in J. L. Austin's apt phrase, "trailing clouds of etymology." "Intellectuals," it seems, has been unable to shake off its etymology and its formation; it still seems (to some people) to embody "the old idea"—or rather ideas—that were associated with its earlier meanings.[2]

But while some dimensions of Jacobus's understanding of "intellectuals" seem to resonate even today, others seem strange. His references to intellectuals in association with angels (not human beings), heaven (not earthly existence), godlike minds (not developed human ones), and intelligence and knowledge above sense and reason (a sure reference to the limitations of human capacities for understanding) sound odd to our contemporary ears. For many of us, the intellectual is a human being who has specific earthly tasks because of his or her capacity for understanding. Thus while the meaning of "intellectuals" today may indeed retain some of "the old ideas," it also appears that the concept has been unable to "withstand the ravages of time," to use Kierkegaard's phrase.[3]

All of this implies a crucial interpretive principle. If we fail to note the ways in which our concepts embody a history or histories, if discontinuities and transformations are not also taken into account alongside continuities and similarities, our understandings of others—and ourselves—

2. J. L. Austin, "Plea for Excuses," in his *Philosophical Papers* (1956) (Oxford, 1979), p. 201.

3. Søren Kierkegaard, *The Concept of Irony, with Constant Reference to Socrates* (1841), trans. L. M. Capel (New York, 1966), 47. The relationship and distinction between "words" and "concepts" is drawn in James Farr, "Understanding Conceptual Change Politically," in *Political Innovation and Conceptual Change,* ed. Terence Ball, James Farr, (New York, 1989), 27n. As Farr puts it, "our language is so richly developed that most of our concepts—especially our political concepts—express themselves with matching words which name them explicitly and uniquely. This is not always so, of course, for someone may possess a concept without (yet) possessing the matching word ('I love my country' says the young girl before 'patriotism' enters her vocabulary); some words express different concepts (as when we 'bear' arms to fend off the menacing grizzly 'bear'); and some concepts may be expressed in different words (perhaps 'liberty' and 'freedom' in modern political discourse, though I am very reluctant to forward this as my own view precisely because of their very different histories)." Farr makes clear that so long as a word continues in use, the concept it identifies may undergo such radical change that earlier and later—or even two contemporary—expressions of it may entail very different concepts.

may suffer. "Intellectuals," like most social and political concepts, is constituted by a history of changes in which attempts to define and identify its instances involves an ongoing process of conceptual transformation, expanding, contracting, bending, breaking, establishing, and reestablishing meaning.

Moreover, we should be attentive to the political implications of conceptual changes. Put simply, conceptual change is a moment of political change: the vigor with which social and political concepts are contested is usually a pretty good barometer of social and political pressures; the substantive content of these disputes often provides a useful set of standards for grasping contending political interests; and how we view the continuity and discontinuity of conceptual change over time can serve to ground the conceptual resources we use in understanding, assessing, and participating in the shaping of social and political life.

What disputes, then, does the concept of the "intellectual" reflect? The chapters of this book provide some examples. But their shared concerns, and the concerns of most contemporary discourses on intellectuals, focus on the relationship of intellectual activity and political life. And the substantive content and political stakes of these concerns are in large part functions of those conceptual changes that make Jacobus de Voragine's understanding of "intellectuals" both familiar and strange. Fully substantiating this argument would of course require a much larger work that this one, but a few crucial points of continuity and change may shed some light on the character and content of modern disputes about what we might call "the politicized intellectual."

As Hannah Arendt (among many others) has suggested, a sharp distinction between the life of the mind and that of day-to-day existence has been a characteristic feature of Western thought from its earliest moments.[4] In its concern with inquiring into and contemplating what was eternal, beyond the reach of human achievement, and unchanged by human actions, the life of the mind served as a compelling ideal in which the demands of the body and the needs of mortal existence might be left behind and the possibility of participating in the realm of transcendence realized.

---

4. Hannah Arendt, *The Human Condition* (Chicago, 1958), chap. 1. Of course this distinction is not exclusively Western (see Talcott Parsons, "'The Intellectual': A Social Role Category," in *On Intellectuals: Theoretical Studies and Case Studies,* ed. Philip Rieff [New York, 1970], esp. 4–12). Nonetheless, the conceptual history sketch I provide here does attend exclusively to the Western distinction, if only because it is this Western conceptual history that serves as the background to the discussions in this volume. What's more, it may be said (and as the chapters in Part IV suggest), it is Western conceptualizations of the life of the mind that have come to dominate modern discourse on intellectuals, although I advance this claim with a reminder that historical and cultural particularities produce distinctive forms of this discourse.

The problem with this ideal was that because men—even philoso-phers—are also mortal human beings, they may be called upon to justify themselves in respect to the concerns of other mortals. Over time, these concerns expanded as people who had been excluded from the community of "men" (slaves, men of meaner status, minorities, women) made their voices heard.[5] But the roots of these conflicts were established early on. Some people have maintained that the death of Pericles and the Pelopon-nesian War marked the moment when the path of persons committed to this ideal of the life of the mind began to diverge from the path of those committed to the life of action.[6] And it was with the birth of Western political thought, crystallized in the conflict between Socrates and the citizens of Athens, that the potential tensions between what the Greeks would call the *bios theoretikos* and the *bios politikos* were realized. Speaking out against those teachers of "mere" practical wisdom, the Sophists, Soc-rates played a crucial role in transforming the main concerns of the life of the mind from physics to ethics. The effect, of course, was to make philosophy a far greater threat to the powers that be than it had been previously—a problem the citizens of Athens temporarily resolved by making the world safe *from* philosophy by forcing the execution/suicide of Socrates.[7] But a potential for conflict had nonetheless been established, and although future advocates of the life of the mind (Plato and Aristotle, among others) would continue to defend the *bios theoretikos* as the highest form of human existence, it was not until the advent of Christendom that their hopes were made good. For what Christendom embodied was a resolution of the tension between contemplation and action that effec-tively turned the life of action into a servant of the life of contemplation.

The conditions that enabled the establishment of this hierarchy were

5. At this point I should note that much of the Western discourse on the life of the mind is shot through with racial, class, and gendered presuppositions. Perhaps the most serious challenge to the distinction between the life of the mind and the life of the action has come from feminists, many of whom have argued that the dichotomous presuppositions of much Western intellectual discourse (such as mind/body, knowledge/feeling) are both inadequate and politically exclusive, particularly in light of the fact that the identities of excluded and marginalized groups are usually defined in terms of the "lower" side of the dichotomies. One aim of this genealogy is to suggest how these dichotomies have been constituted, transformed, and challenged. The contributions of Ellen C. DuBois (Chapter 9), Thomas C. Holt (Chapter 10), and Roberto S. Goizueta (Chapter 11) are particularly sharp reminders of how these issues have been addressed.

6. F. M. Cornford, *The Unwritten Philosophy and Other Essays* (New York, 1950), 54; also Arendt, *Human Condition,* 17.

7. Although most Western political thinkers have assumed that the execution/suicide of Socrates was a tragic event, this view is not universally accepted. Perhaps the most interesting example of an interpretation that sees the execution of Socrates as an attempt by the citizens of Athens to prevent the erosion of their democracy (however limited it may have been) by "intellectuals" such as Socrates is I. F. Stone, *The Trial of Socrates* (Boston, 1988).

no doubt facilitated by Julius Caesar, who strove to make Rome not only the political but the "intellectual" capital of the empire.[8] By enticing learned men to emigrate to Rome with the offer of citizenship, Caesar may have intended to strengthen the centralization of his empire. But he also created a group whose identity was cosmopolitan in character, and whose interests therefore went beyond those of the empire. With the fall and subsequent reestablishment of the empire in the form of Christendom, the life of the mind (now embodied in and defined by the clergy) could reassert the classical understanding of the "proper" relationship between mind and body, which also now spilled over into the relationships between clergy and laity, church and polity. The *bios theoretikos* and the *bios politikos* no longer existed in an uneasy tension, for through the Christian reconceptualization that distinguished the *vita contemplativa* and the *vita activa*, the life of the mind was not required to serve the needs of worldly existence; rather, worldly existence was seen to be the servant of the life of the mind. To modify the description I used earlier: What Christendom did was make the world safe *for* philosophy. If the classical thinkers sought to do so but failed, the ruling elite of Christendom sought to do so and succeeded.

Here Jacobus de Voragine reenters our narrative. For Jacobus ought to be seen as a representative figure of the mindset of Christendom. His understanding of "intellect" certainly reflected elements of what I have called the classical model of the relationship of the life of the mind and the life of action. In their use of the Latin *intellego* and its cognates (such as *intellectus, intelligens, intelligentia*), Jacobus and his contemporaries referred to the act, power, or faculty of discernment, understanding, or comprehension.[9] Moreover, this capacity was associated with the highest, most developed part of the human soul. But these classical roots also supported specifically Christian growths; intellect was seen as a capacity superior to reason and sense, and it was attributed to those beings who had, as Jacobus suggested, "a life above all other things that live." Here the angels, Aquinas's *intelligentiae*, constitute the intellectual class (if an anachronism be allowed) by virtue of their ability to "know things in themselves," whereas mere mortals know by "reason" or "rationality." In

---

8. Antonio Gramsci, *Selections from the Prison Notebooks of Antonio Gramsci* (1949), trans. and ed. Quintin Hoare and Geoffrey Nowell Smith (New York, 1971), 17–18.

9. For the etymological reconstruction in the next few pages I have drawn heavily on *The Oxford English Dictionary* (Oxford, 1971) and E. A. Andrews, *Harper's Latin Dictionary* (New York, 1907). I have used English examples exclusively, for two reasons: first, the English case represents what I think is the first clear example of the emergence of what would become "modern" conceptualizations of the life of the mind; and second, it may be argued that the widespread use of Latin in English philosophical, theological, and political discourse means that the conceptual changes in English discourse reflected, and reflected upon, conceptual changes taking place elsewhere in the Western world.

short, Christendom had alienated to the heavenly host what was, on the classical model, a specifically human (even if nearly godlike) capacity, and inasmuch as life had to be as witness to the glory of God, guided by the church, the life of action was made to serve the life of the mind.

What is remarkable about these changes is that Christendom's reconceptualization of the virtues, rewards, and authority of the life of the mind constituted one barrier by which Christendom's *temporal* authority was insulated from challenge. But even if Christendom's temporal authority proclaimed itself to be nothing more than the vehicle for understanding the character and demands of the transcendent truths of God, the simple fact of the matter was that *as a temporal authority* it embodied specific worldly interests. And in the wake of the Renaissance and the Reformation, it became increasingly difficult to sustain the conceptual framework that enabled the temporal authority of Christendom, with its institutional pursuit of a *vita contemplativa,* to maintain itself.

Eventually the political structures and conceptual grounding of Christendom eroded to the point where human beings could recover (the German *aufgehoben* is perhaps better here) those capacities that had been "alienated" to the heavenly host, but such changes took time, and some of the historical residue of Christendom continued (and still continues) to filter discussions of the relationship of the life of the mind and the active life.[10] Indeed, into the seventeenth and eighteenth centuries, it was apparently common to conceptualize "intellect" and "intellectuals" as heavenly entities.[11] As Tibor Huzar suggests, it was not until much later that the term "intellectual" and its cognates were used in reference to particular human beings: "Before the nineteenth century there are references to scribes, learned people traveling from place to place and earning a living from their knowledge or reading or writing, philosophers, poets or lawyers—but they consistently described one another as philosopher, lawyer or poet, never using the term "intellectual.""[12]

Here, then, we finally arrive at what separates us from Jacobus de Voragine: an extended moment of change in which modern intellectuals are being discursively and practically constituted. Although we certainly find many of our contemporaries defining the concept of the intellectual in ways that resonate with traditions Jacobus himself had drawn upon, we also find that the idea of the life of the mind had been given (what

10. Chapter 11 of this book serves as a reminder of the residual effects of Christendom on orthodox Christian theology.

11. See, for example, Thomas Spencer, *The Art of Logick* (1628) (Menston, 1970), 8; or Bishop George Berkeley's *Alciphron, or The Minute Philosopher* (1732), in *The Works of George Berkeley,* ed. A. A. Luce and T. E. Jessop (London, 1950), 3:166–68.

12. Tibor Huszar, "Changes in the Concept of Intellectuals," in *The Intelligentsia and the Intellectuals,* ed. Aleksander Gella (Beverly Hills, Calif., 1976), 79.

we might call) a *sociological* location; that is, "intellectual" had become available for use as a social category. But this sociological relocation also carried with it the conceptual resources that made for wider disputes, for the *kind* of philosopher, poet, or lawyer one was and the *kind* of philosophy, poetry, or law one practiced also became defining concerns for calling individuals "real," "pseudo," or particular "types" of intellectuals.

These changes were certainly complex, but there is good evidence that they can be located in the period around what many historians have called the first "modern" revolution—the English Civil War. In this period there are conceptual elements at once old and new, but the changes wrought eventually changed the contours and character of disputes about the content and purposes of the life of the mind and the persons who engaged in it. The consequence, as Marx wryly put it, was that "Locke supplanted Habakkuk"[13]—or as we might put it, the authority of the secular intellectual supplanted the temporal authority of Christendom.

It appears that by the late sixteenth century, the process of recovering the capacity of "intellect" as a specifically human attribute was already well under way. Thus could Shakespeare, in *Love's Labour's Lost* (1598), intelligibly say that "it rejoyceth my intellect, true wit"; and a half century later (1651), Hobbes was able to refer to "the VERTUES commonly called INTELLECTUAL; and their contrary DEFECTS."[14] It may well be argued that this understanding recalled a classical attribution of "intellect" as a specifically human capacity, but neither should we lose sight of its radical departure from the understandings embodied in Jacobus's *Legenda sanctorum*.

Sir John Davies's (1599) elegy for "humane knowledge" provides an opening that permits some perspective on the implications of these changes. Against the kind of "humane knowledge" that was "with fond, fruitless curiosity" sought "In books profane," Davies called on his readers to seek "through Eye and Eare" the "dying sparkle" of "*Reasons* lampe." By this means, Davies believed, human beings might approximate the condition of "the first parents" (Adam and Eve), whose "reasons eye was sharpe and cleer" and who "approach't th'eternal light as neer, as the intellectual Angels could have done."[15]

Davies's articulation of a conceptual space in which human beings are seen as potential intellectuals was, then, simultaneously an attack on the hierarchy of intellect presupposed in Christendom. Calling upon his readers to seek knowledge "beyond all books, Or all the learned *Schooles* that

13. Karl Marx, "The Eighteenth Brumaire of Louis Bonaparte," in *The Marx-Engels Reader*, ed. R. C. Tucker (New York, 1978), 596.
14. William Shakespeare, *Love's Labour's Lost* (1598) (New Haven, 1925), 67; Thomas Hobbes, *Leviathan* (1651), ed. C. B. Macpherson (New York, 1968), 134.
15. John Davies, *Nosce teipsum* (London, 1599), 2, 3, 1.

ever were," Davies leveled a charge that Hobbes would later repeat when he denounced "the Philosophy-schooles, through all the Universities of Christendom," and "the deceived Philosophers, and deceived, or deceiving Schoolemen."[16] In short, it had now become possible for each individual, not simply "some politic Bishop, or Dr Ignorant University Man, or knave poet," to achieve the status of "one of Natures litle kings," akin to the "intellectual Angels."[17]

Such an achievement, moreover, was authorized by a shift reorienting what we might call the *epistemic* dimension—the objects and methods—of intellectual activity. The objects of this activity had become worldly, not supernatural. "Nosce teipsum"—know thyself—was what Davies (and later Hobbes too) argued *true* "humane knowledge" demanded. Or as Francis Bacon argued in 1605, it was now necessary "to descend from spirits and intellectual forms to sensible and material forms."[18] The methods of knowledge were also transformed: reason and sense (or, as Davies put it, "reasons eye") were becoming sufficient for acquiring the knowledge that would make us like the "intellectual Angels"; as the objects of intellectual activity changed, it was no longer necessary to posit a form of understanding "above reason and sense" as a necessary condition for understanding "things in themselves."

Finally, these sociological and epistemic shifts were accompanied by a changing understanding of the goals or ends of intellectual activity. Whereas Christendom had taken the ends or purposes of the life of the mind to be a glorification of the eternal mysteries of God, a specifically earthly knowledge and the intellect had been made over to meet a *moral* task: to eliminate "Those wretched shapes of *Miserie* and *Woe*, of *Nakedness*, of *Shame*, of *Povertie*."[19] Only when "contemplation and action may be more nearly and straitly conjoined and united together than they have been," says Bacon, will we achieve "that which will dignify and exalt knowledge." To be sure, this new understanding did not necessarily preclude the glorification of creation, but since much of that glory was to be found here on earth, true knowledge served simultaneously as "a rich storehouse for the glory of the Creator and the relief of man's estate."[20]

With these reconceptualizations much of the conceptual groundwork for modern disputes about intellectuals was being laid. By relocating the capacity for "intellect" in individual persons or groups, by making man

16. Ibid., 7; Hobbes, *Leviathan*, 86, 99.
17. William Walwyn, "The Compassionate Samaritane" (1644), in *The Writings of William Walwyn*, ed. Jack R. McMichael and Barbara Taft (Athens, Ga., 1989), 103; Davies, *Nosce teipsum*, 8.
18. Francis Bacon, *The Advancement of Learning* (1605) (London, 1973), 37.
19. Davies, *Nosce teipsum*, 2.
20. Bacon, *Advancement of Learning*, 35.

and nature the objects of knowledge and human "reason" its method, and by casting "the relief of man's estate" as the end or purpose of knowledge, Western thinkers were erecting a new framework for understanding the relationship between the life of the mind and the life of action. Now any attempt to make the world safe *from* philosophy was required to answer the claim (as Hobbes put it) that "*Reason* is the *pace,* Encrease of *Science,* the way; and the Benefit of man-kind, the *end*" of "the Light of humane minds."[21] And attempts to make the world safe *for* philosophy had to contend with claims such as David Hume's, that "the *mere* philosopher is a character, which is commonly but little acceptable in the world, as being supposed to contribute nothing either to the advantage or pleasure of society."[22] In other words, the life of the mind and the life of action were no longer necessarily at odds—but if the English Civil War, and later the Enlightenment and the French and American revolutions, confirmed anything at all, it was that even modern men of thought disagreed about the substantive content of reason, science, the benefit to mankind, and the light of humane minds.[23] Thus was the modern intellectual brought into being as a category and character of sociological, epistemic, and moral dispute.

When the word "intellectuals" and cognates such as "intelligentsia" finally make their appearance in the nineteenth century as nouns referring to particular persons or a category of persons, they reflect in their various uses both the "trailing clouds of etymology" and the "ravages of time" wrought by the historical vicissitudes I have sketched. In Great Britain, that bastion of hardheaded (and Whiggish) empiricism, "intellectuals" acquired a distinctly unfavorable political connotation, such that Byron (in 1813) could comment, "I wish I may be well enough to listen to these intellectuals"—a meaning, Raymond Williams argues, that may have been the result of widespread "opposition to social and political arguments based on theory or on rational principle."[24] In mid-century Eastern Europe, especially Russia and Poland, the concept carried positive political connotations. It represented, according to Aleksander Gella, the concatenation of both a "higher" social stratum (better-educated members of the disinherited nobility) and those who were identified "principally on the left, in the service of social progress, revolution or national indepen-

21. Hobbes, *Leviathan,* 116.

22. David Hume, *An Enquiry Concerning Human Understanding* (1758), in *Essential Works of David Hume,* ed. R. Cohen (New York, 1965), 46.

23. Chapter 2 of this book helps further situate some of the disputes about the "appropriate" aims and content of intellectual activity that have emerged in the modern West.

24. Raymond Williams, *Keywords: A Vocabulary of Culture and Society,* 2d ed. (London, 1983), 169–70.

dence."[25] And in late-century France, the debate over *les intellectuels,* immortalized in Julien Benda's polemic *La Trahison des clercs,* embodied both positive and negative meanings, depending on the particular political position one took in *l'affaire Dreyfus.*[26] As "a Janus term, facing both towards the study and towards the street,"[27] it came into common usage after a statement titled *Manifeste des intellectuels,* attacking the state's conviction of Captain Albert Dreyfus, was published. Signed by the self-described "intellectuals" Daniel Halévy, Emile Zola, Anatole France, Lucien Herr, and Léon Blum, *intellectuels* was, for these men, a badge proudly worn. Yet it quickly became a term of disapprobation that conservative opponents (such as Ferdinand Brunetière and Maurice Barrès) called an attempt to designate "men who live in laboratories and libraries" as "supermen" and "aristocrats of thought," "poor boobies who were ashamed to think like simple Frenchmen."[28]

In these examples, the sociological, epistemic, and moral dimensions of the concept of the intellectual all make their appearance in disputes over the political role and responsibilities of the life of the mind. On what kind of knowledge claims did so-called intellectuals base their authority? For what purposes did they carry out their activities? What place in the social fabric did they occupy? On the answers to these questions the modern discourse on the intellectual turns. On these answers the modern uneasiness regarding the relationship between the life of the mind and the political life is articulated. "Trailing clouds of etymology" and showing "the ravages of time," the discourse on intellectuals has come down to us in a form in which the mere mention of the word invokes unavoidably politicized conceptual disputes.

WAYS OF SEEING

By the beginning of the twentieth century, the sociological, epistemic, and moral dimensions of the concept of the intellectual had become so thoroughly intertwined and contested that it has become difficult to ad-

25. Aleksander Gella, "An Introduction to the Sociology of the Intelligentsia," in his *Intelligentsia and the Intellectuals,* 12–15.

26. Julien Benda, *La Trahison des clercs* (Paris, 1927), published in English as *The Treason of the Intellectuals,* trans. Richard Aldington (New York, 1928). In addition to Benda's classic, a useful overview of the Dreyfus affair, as well as an enlightening discussion of the concept of "intellectuals," may be found in Ray Nichols, *Treason, Tradition, and the Intellectual: Julian Benda and Political Discourse* (Lawrence, Kans., 1978). I am happy to acknowledge Nichols's influence on the shaping of this chapter.

27. Nichols, *Treason, Tradition, and the Intellectual,* 13.

28. Quoted ibid., 29.

dress any one aspect of the concept without becoming embroiled in wider disputes. This legacy may be readily recognized in any number of late-modern attempts to grapple with the problem of defining and identifying the intellectual.

Consider, first, one of the most influential early attempts to make sense of the twentieth-century intellectual. When, in 1929, Karl Mannheim discussed "the difficult sociological problem of the existence of the intellectual" as "this unanchored, *relatively* classless stratum"—"the socially unattached intelligentsia"—his account presupposed both the cosmopolitan outlook of Caesar's learned men and the dissociation of the life of the mind from institutionalized interests embodied in the break with Christendom. Thus, among the reasons that animated Mannheim to define the intellectual sociologically was "one of the most impressive facts about modern life": that intellectual activity was no longer "carried on exclusively by a socially rigidly defined class, such as a priesthood, but rather by a social stratum which is to a large degree unattached to any class and which is recruited from an increasingly inclusive area of life."[29]

Such a sociological emphasis was not without its later proponents as well. Indeed, during the 1950s and 1960s prominent scholars were preoccupied with giving the concept a precise sociological grounding. Talcott Parsons, Edward Shils, S. N. Eisenstadt, Seymour Martin Lipset, and others defined "intellectuals" (in Talcott Parsons's words) as "a social role category."[30] But sociological dispositions notwithstanding, moral and epistemic considerations also slipped into view. Thus Lipset, for example, assumed a particular moral function for intellectuals when he defined them as people who "create, distribute, and apply *culture,* that is, the symbolic world of man, including art, science, and religion."[31] And Shils drew on an epistemic grounding, defining intellectuals as "a minority of persons who, more than the ordinary run of their fellow-men, are enquiring, and desirous of being in frequent communication with symbols which are more general than the immediate concrete situations of everyday life, and remote in their reference in both time and space."[32]

The purposes of which these sociologically conceived conceptualizations were offered were perhaps innocent enough on the surface. They went hand in hand with calls for "analytical abstraction" conducive to "formulating and demonstrating laws of universal validity," or perhaps

---

29. Karl Mannheim, *Ideology and Utopia: An Introduction to the Sociology of Knowledge* (1929), trans. Louis Wirth and Edward Shils (New York, 1936), 155–56.

30. Parsons, "The Intellectual," 31.

31. Seymour Martin Lipset, *Political Man: The Social Bases of Politics* (New York, 1963), 333.

32. Edward Shils, "The Intellectuals and the Powers: Some Perspectives for Comparative Analysis," in Rieff, *On Intellectuals,* 27.

less boldly, "a new type of objectivity in the social sciences."[33] Indeed, Shils even tendered a possible candidate for such a "law" when he offered up the claim that "there would be intellectuals in every society even if there were no intellectuals by disposition."[34] But the methodological needs of a social science are one thing, conceptual possibilities quite another, and the advocates of the sociological approach achieved nothing so much as verification of the difficulty of carving out a definition of intellectuals that makes no reference to the moral purposes and epistemic contents of the life of the mind, and thus of avoiding engagement in a debate over the political responsibility of the intellectual.

The advocates of the sociological approach must have known that no conceptualization of "intellectuals" was likely to win converts to their way of seeing unless other, competing conceptualizations could be disabled. This task they tried to accomplish by great feats of definitional fiat. But in doing so they revealed their own political agenda—a sanitized account of the intellectual as political agent.

In Mannheim's account, this sanitizing takes the form of wrenching the intellectual from class identification. His stated preference is for the "experimental outlook, unceasingly sensitive to the dynamic nature of society," which can be developed "only by a relatively classless stratum which is not too firmly situated in the social order." Thus it was only the true intellectuals—understood now as the "relatively classless stratum" (as opposed to those "whose class position is more or less definitely fixed" and whose "political viewpoint is already decided for it")—who "might play the part of watchmen in what otherwise would be a pitch-black night" of modern life.[35] In a similar mood, Shils sought to make the intellectual over into a useful member of modern social organization. "Intellectuals are indispensable to any society," he argued. The institutional requirements of the life of the mind may "generate a tension between intellectuals and the laity, high and low," but "the discovery and the achievement of the optimum balance of civility and intellectual creativity are the tasks of the statesman and the responsible intellectual."[36]

Other matters were on the political agendas of Parsons and Lipset. In Parsons's case it was the threat that "ideology"—"the primary instrument of the modern intellectual secular classes in their bid to be considered generally important"—posed to social science and the "pluralism" of modern (read Western liberal) societies in which social science was embedded

33. Talcott Parsons, "An Outline of the Social System," in *Theories of Society: Foundations of Modern Sociological Theory,* ed. Parsons et al. (New York 1961), 32; Mannheim, *Ideology and Utopia,* p. 5.

34. Shils, *Intellectuals and the Powers,* 29.

35. Mannheim, *Ideology and Utopia,* 154, 160–61.

36. Shils, *Intellectuals and the Powers,* 51.

that served to draw his attention to intellectuals as a "social role category." Explicitly in the closing pages of "'The Intellectual'" and implicitly throughout his discussions of intellectuals, Parsons seemed to try to shunt some "intellectuals" into a residual category of dated characters whose activities were at odds with modern needs, figures whose self-understandings were in "direct conflict with the double imperatives of the maximal . . . objectivity of science and of seeking general theoretical and empirical solutions of problems regardless of their bearing on immediate problems of action," while also establishing a conceptual and political space for other ("real," "true"?) intellectuals.[37] For Lipset, however, the problem was that there were intellectuals "in Nazi Germany and the Soviet Union who used, or still use, the tools and training associated with the *intelligentsia* in the service of anti-intellectual values." And even where intellectuals became participants in "democratic society," they still tend to identify with "institutions of the *status quo*" and to be subject to "potential transformation into apologists."[38] In these conditions, defining intellectuals as mere occupants of a social role might serve the purpose of unmasking their claims to authority as no different from those of any other social group.

Whatever its theoretical merits, then, we see that the contemporary sociological approach is shot through with political implications. We can also see lurking in the background of these accounts any number of themes drawn from the history of the concept. And much the same might be said of other contemporary ways of seeing the intellectual.

Consider, for example, Antonio Gramsci's distinction between the "traditional" and "organic" intellectual (a central theme of some of the chapters in this book). In what might be seen as a direct attack on the predominant sociological approach, Gramsci proposed a sociological approach of his own. Those who live the life of the mind, he asserted, are the organic creations of social and political interests, and they give the group whose interests they serve "homogeneity and an awareness of its own function not only in the economic but also in the social and political fields." Historically—or, as Gramsci says, "at least in all of history up to the present"—these once-organic intellectuals became increasingly specialized, taking the forms of ecclesiastics, administrators, scholars, scientists, theorists, nonecclesiastical philosophers, and so on, who then appeared as traditional intellectuals because they "seemed indeed to represent an historical continuity uninterrupted even by the most complicated and radical changes in political and social forms."[39]

37. Parsons, "The Intellectual," 23–26.
38. Lipset, *Political Man*, 333–34.
39. Gramsci, *Prison Notebooks*, 5, 7.

On reading Gramsci's alternative (and clearly Marxist) sociological account, one can also see elements of a critique of the knowledge claims and
moral aims presupposed in other conceptualizations of the intellectual.
Pressing his attack in ways that paralleled the early modern critique of
Christendom's scholasticism, Gramsci argued that the once-organic and
now traditional intellectuals see themselves and are seen by others as
"'independent,' autonomous, endowed with a character of their own," as
existing in a kind of "social utopia." But as he saw it, such assumptions
are "not without consequences in the ideological and political field," not
the least of which concerns the power these persons exercise in "the
complex of superstructures, of which the intellectuals are, precisely, the
'functionaries.'" In a profound conceptual move that had far-reaching
implications for later discussions of intellectuals, Gramsci called for recognition of "forms of new intellectualism" that were not "'specialized'" but
"'directive' (specialized and political)." And "the basis of the new type of
intellectual" must be "industrial labor, even at the most primitive and
unqualified level." In this way it might be possible to realize the claim
that "all men are intellectuals" (a claim that Jacobus could not have understood but that Davies, Bacon, Hobbes, and Hume might have), while
undermining the contemporary presumption that "not all men have in
society the function of intellectuals."[40]

Other contemporary ways of seeing appeal more directly to the moral
ideals of nineteenth-century conceptualizations. J. P. Nettl, for example,
attacked the sociological approach by claiming that "the problem of definition can get off the ground only by looking first at ideas as such," and
that "the actual definition of an intellectual must accordingly include not
only a certain type of thinking [ideas that can be put into practice, are
universal in scope, and are concerned with the quality of life in general]
but also a relationship to socio-structural dissent, at least potentially."[41]
Similarly, Lewis Coser, insisted that

> in the tasks they perform modern intellectuals are descendants of the
> priestly upholders of sacred tradition, but they are also and at the same
> time descendants of the biblical prophets, of those inspired madmen
> who preached in the wilderness far removed from the institutionalized
> pieties of court and synagogue, castigating the men of power for the
> wickedness of their ways. Intellectuals are men who never seem satisfied
> with things as they are, with appeals to custom or usage. . . . They
> consider themselves special custodians of abstract ideas like reason and

40. Ibid., 8, 7, 12, 10, 9.
41. J. P. Nettl, "Ideas, Intellectuals, and Structures of Dissent," in Rieff, *On Intellectuals*,
59, 88.

justice and truth, jealous guardians of moral standards that are too often ignored in the market place and the houses of power.[42]

In like fashion, even the title of Russell Jacoby's controversial book, *The Last Intellectuals*, suggests the pull that a moralized definition of the intellectual still exerts. Jacoby laments the relative absence of "public intellectuals"—"writers and thinkers who address a general and educated audience." Crafting a narrative in which intellectuals (especially those of radical persuasion) have retreated from their "public" responsibilities into the academy, where "the academic idiom, concepts, and concerns occupied, and finally preoccupied, young left intellectuals," Jacoby calls for a renewed commitment on the part of intellectuals "to a public world and a public language."[43]

As Jacoby's words suggest, these definitions are not without their political purposes, and these authors (like Gramsci, and unlike the sociologists) do not try to hide behind the screen of "objectivity"—even if some of those they hold up as models did (a fact that has also given rise to yet another way of seeing intellectuals, about which more shortly). In any case, these moralized accounts often seem to be driven by a perception that the oppositional "intellectual" is in decline, a fact they lament (though one that some proponents of the sociological approach apparently would welcome). The ideal of the oppositional intellectual enables Coser to argue that "an increasing absorption of intellectuals into various parts of the 'establishment'" may "spell the end of intellectuals as recent history has known them," and it is "questionable that the full integration of intellectuals is in the best interest of American society," if only because "a system that is no longer challenged is no longer capable of creative response."[44] And for Nettl, much as for Jacoby, a moralized definition (among other things) "reinforces the distinction between intellectuals and academics whose focus is on seminal diffusion of ideas to students, without any predicate for societal action," as well as a distinction between intellectuals and "mandarins," the "non-innovating bureaucrats" who are the "logical successors of the intellectuals—and especially in cases where the latter have been successful, where former dissent, which has become the new orthodoxy, has in turn to be defended against reaction, the former orthodoxy, which may constitute the current dissent."[45]

Nettl's comments bring us directly to yet another, more recently conceived way of seeing. If, to put it crudely, sociological definitions were

42. Lewis Coser, *Men of Ideas: A Sociologist's View* (New York, 1965), viii.
43. Russell Jacoby, *The Last Intellectuals: American Culture in the Age of Academe* (New York, 1987), 5, 141, 235.
44. Coser, *Men of Ideas*, 358, 359.
45. Nettl, *Ideas, Intellectuals, and Structures of Dissent*, 89–90, 93.

aimed at disabling moralized conceptualizations of intellectuals (the exception of Gramsci noted) only to draw attention to the political presuppositions of sociological categories, and if moralized conceptualizations were aimed at restoring the normative import of intellectuals' oppositional politics, and in doing so carried on the politicizing of the concept, these more recent definitions seem to draw this politicizing impetus further still by calling into question the basis of opposition itself when they focus on the epistemic grounds—the objects and forms—of knowledge claims.

One good example may be found in Allen Bloom's best-selling polemic against American higher education. Targeting the claims of "historicism," "cultural relativism," and their concomitant epistemic presumption that "truth is relative," Bloom called for a return to the time-honored search for timeless truths through "philosophy," "a solitary quest" in which one "must never look to an audience." But Bloom could not articulate his apparent desire to insulate truth-seeking from the imperatives of politics, in effect to make the world safe for philosophy and philosophers ("The real community of man . . . is the community of those who seek the truth, of the potential knowers"), without acknowledging the necessary relation between the life of the mind and the political life that is the conceptual and practical legacy of modernity. "The fate of freedom," he said, "has devolved upon our regime," and "the fate of philosophy in the world has devolved upon our universities, and the two are related as they have never been before." And the content of this relationship, not surprisingly, follows from the epistemic grounds Bloom sought to defend: philosophy has been "dethroned by political and theoretical democracy": "democracy took away philosophy's privileges"; what needs to be done now is to restore philosophy's place as an "architectonic" activity in which "the carpenters, masons and plumbers were its subordinates."[46]

As we have seen, such epistemic-cum-political pronouncements are not without their conceptual antecedents or, as Bloom intimated, their antagonists. Perhaps Zygmunt Bauman's distinction between intellectuals as "legislators" and "interpreters"—a distinction grounded in "differences in understanding the nature of the world, and the social world in particular, and in understanding the related nature, and purpose, of intellectual work"—best captures this field of debate. The "legislator intellectual" appeals to a certain kind of epistemic authority, his knowledge of the transcendent, the universal, the true and just for all. In one sense, the concept of the legislator intellectual is continuous with its premodern predecessors, but in another sense it is unique and peculiarly modern. For while the authority of the modern legislator intellectual may be derived in

46. Allan Bloom, *The Closing of the American Mind* (New York, 1987), 25, 20, 381, 382, 377.

part from his epistemic claims, it is the moral claim that he uses his knowledge to serve what Hobbes called "the Benefit of man-kind" that rounds out the justification for his intervention in social and political activities. Thus, says Bauman, those committed to this understanding of the life of the mind "felt it their moral responsibility, and their collective right, to interfere directly with the political process through influencing the minds of the nation and moulding the actions of its political leaders."[47]

Yet for Bauman the alternative ideal of the intellectual as "interpreter" does not so much undermine the intellectual's peculiarly modern legislating responsibilities as much as it calls into question their universal character. "Relativism," "pluralism," "communities of discourse": these are among the watchwords of the interpreting intellectual, who takes as his or her task "translating statements, made within one communally based tradition, so that they can be understood within the system of knowledge based on another tradition." But postmodern intellectuals-as-interpreters nonetheless "retain their meta-professional authority, legislating about the procedural rules which allow them to arbitrate controversies of opinion and make statements intended as binding."[48]

Bauman tries to disarm potential critics regarding the political implications of his epistemically grounded distinction by suggesting that "in no way am I implying that the post-modern mode constitutes an advance over the modern one, that the two may be arranged in a progressive sequence in any of the possible meanings of the notoriously confusing idea of progress." Yet his conclusions are not neutral. Bauman is none too happy about the tendency of some legislator intellectuals to retreat into pure theory ("The trouble with this response . . . is that the questions, to which it was intended to be an answer, tend to be forgotten") or metascience and meta-aesthetics ("self-centered and self-concerned"; "a recipe for frustration"), but the modern legislator intellectual, he argues, is engaged in realizing a project—the project of modernity itself— that "needs to be redeemed" against the "wrong turn" of rationalization embodied in "its actual history, as distinct from its original project" of enabling the spread of "individual autonomy and democratic tolerance." The question is whether legislator intellectuals can carry out this redemption. And as for postmodern interpreter intellectuals, they may turn their anti-universalizing inclinations to good (politicals) ends, except when they "abandon . . . the legislative ambitions altogether, and with them the long attachment to the legitimizing and foundational discourses." For while this strategy may be perfectly suited to "the autonomy and the institution-

47. Zygmunt Bauman, *Legislators and Interpreters: On Modernity, Post-Modernity, and Intellectuals* (Ithaca, N.Y., 1987), 3, 1.
48. Ibid., 5.

ally encouraged concern of academic philosophy with its own self-reproduction," it is hardly the stuff of a responsible intellectual-cum-political ethic.[49]

THE various ways of seeing intellectuals that I have mentioned here differ in many important respects, each playing on a particular aspect or aspects of what their proponents believe most clearly identifies intellectuals. But their differences should not be understood as merely *(sic!)* theoretical or abstract. Rather, the various definitions should be understood as political statements, crafted in response to a constellation of developments in which the identity of the intellectual has become a matter of ongoing social concern. Moreover, the terms in which they are crafted may be seen as outcomes of a long history of conceptual change that has constituted and reconstituted the intellectual as an entity in which sociological, moral, and epistemic issues are mutually constituted dimensions in conceptual/political struggle. In other words, the disputes they embody rise and fall with social and political conflict over the persons, practices, and self-understandings presupposed in the use of—or attempt to transform—the concept of the intellectual.[50]

Recognizing this difficulty, many thinkers will be tempted simply to abandon the attempt to define the intellectual. But proliferation and contestation of definitions is not sufficient ground for claiming, as did the editors of *Time* magazine back in 1965, that "there are so many different kinds of intellectuals . . . that the common label threatens to become meaningless" and that "the word intellectual should probably be done away with."[51] Instead, the proliferation and contestation of meanings may signal the need for continued exploration, inasmuch as disagreement and debate usually signal the existence of perplexity or confusion, a loss or erosion of shared understandings, and the rise of conflict and change. In

49. Ibid., 6, 195, 196, 191–92, 196–98.

50. I thank Geoff Eley and Jane Burbank for raising this issue, in different forms, in early drafts of their chapters in this book. Eley pointed out how interest in and approaches to the study of intellectuals had waxed and waned during the twentieth century. In addition, he and Burbank suggested two different approaches, the "sociological" and the "moral" or "phenomenological"; I have appropriated these distinctions and added another of my own ("epistemic") to characterize the predominant approaches to the study of intellectuals during the twentieth century, as well as to develop an analytical framework for discussing the dimensions of the concept of intellectuals. On the usefulness and purposes of conceptual histories, see Terence Ball, *Transforming Political Discourse: Political Theory and Critical Conceptual History* (Oxford, 1988), esp. chap. 1, and the theoretical essay by James Farr, "Understanding Conceptual Change Politically," in Ball et al., *Political Innovation and Conceptual Change*. Their arguments (and prodding) have helped to shape my treatment of intellectuals in this chapter. Both books also provide interesting examples of conceptual histories.

51. Quoted in Nichols, *Treason, Tradition, and the Intellectual*, 8.

short, they may (as I suggested at the outset) signal that the concept embodies serious political differences. "Here, as elsewhere," says Lewis Coser, "definitions, far from being neutral, have consequences."[52] "Here," says Ray Nichols,

> definitions are not external, but are internal to—part of—the subject. They are not mere words. They are not neutral. Implicitly or explicitly, they are political statements, statements of potential power and authority, weaving public webs of inclusion and exclusion, pulling matters together and sundering them, identifying possibilities and obstacles, setting *terms* for both conception and society. Language is an index to social events and processes and to social thought. More than that: it is itself a complex form of social practice, mediating between structures and beliefs—a critical matrix for the genesis, articulation, and diffusion of modes of thought and action.[53]

The chapters of this book may, then, be read as contributions to contemporary debates about who "the intellectuals" are and what epistemic and moral claims constitute the bases for their political interventions. By providing a range of examples in which discrete historical moments and culturally specific contexts issue in diverse conceptualizations of the relationship between the life of the mind and the life of action, they may serve to alert us to the strengths and weaknesses, the promises and pitfalls involved in uniting thought and action. This said, let me turn briefly to what lies ahead in this book.

EXPLORING THE POLITICIZED INTELLECTUAL

This book is organized in four sections. Each section attends a significant series of related moments, episodes, or traditions that have become part of the cosmopolitan discourse on intellectuals today.

We begin in Part I, "The Politicized Intellectual Today," by considering how the legacy of the Enlightenment has been articulated in the apparent opposition between the ideals of the intellectual as critic and the intellectual as expert. Locating the origins of this opposition in the conceptual and political changes that split the Enlightenment ideal of the intellectual as both critic and expert into two apparently incommensurable discourses, Lloyd Kramer (in Chapter 2) argues that much of the current debate about the roles of intellectuals plays off of this split yet retains, in various

---

52. Coser, *Men of Ideas,* vii.
53. Nichols, *Treason, Tradition, and the Intellectual,* 10–11.

ways, an essential ambiguity about intellectuals that has been part of the Enlightenment legacy since the eighteenth century. Using the work of Michel Foucault and Jürgen Habermas—arguably the two most influential contemporary commentators on the meaning of the Enlightenment—as foils for exploring the essential ambiguities of the Enlightenment legacy, Kramer maintains that the context of intellectuals' activity today and the self-understandings that intellectuals bring to that context may authorize an appeal to both critique and expertise. Here disputes about the moral ends of knowledge are cross-cut by both epistemic claims and sociological concerns, and Kramer presses contemporary intellectuals to dissolve the ambiguities of the Enlightenment legacy by attending the demands of both criticism and expertise.

In Part II, "European Intellectuals and the Socialist Project," our contributors offer accounts of episodes in the modern history of intellectuals and politics that seem to embody the ideal of the intellectual as critic, or what I earlier called a moralistic account of the intellectual as oppositional figure. Focusing on the European tradition of attraction between people committed to (some version of) the life of the mind and the concerns of the working classes, the chapters by James Epstein, Geoff Eley, Jane Burbank, and Donald M. Reid flesh out projects that attempt to realize a kind of Gramscian "organic" relationship between intellectual life and working-class politics.

In Chapter 3 James Epstein shows that in early nineteenth-century England the idea of a "plebeian intellectual" as a kind of organic intellectual was more than a mere hope. But he also shows that a specific understanding of the epistemic contents of knowledge may have isolated plebeian intellectuals between the elite culture they opposed and the working-class culture they sought to change and "enlighten." Committed at once to a conception of knowledge and reason as universal and to the task of empowering their class compatriots, many plebeian intellectuals were unable to reconcile the constraints of these two demands, and as a consequence became distanced from their class without quite becoming "traditional" intellectuals. Too abstract in their discourse to address their class compatriots yet too radical in their concerns to be taken seriously by their "traditional" counterparts, plebeian intellectuals were never quite the effective critics they hoped to be.

In Chapter 4 Geoff Eley further develops the possibilities of comparative insights by examining the place of "intellectuals" in the Social Democratic Party of Germany (SPD) before 1914. The formulation of ideology, culture, and liberal institution building (under Weimar) figures prominently in this narrative. As Eley sees it, before 1914 the SPD had great difficulty engaging what Gramsci called the "assimilation and conquest" of "traditional" intellectuals,[54] but it did provide a kind of institutional space, a subculture, that enabled both the cultivation of "intellectual" commitment on the part of rank-and-file members (thus producing "organic" intellectuals of its own) and the appropriation and reconceptualization of cultural resources (thus cultivating an oppositional discourse in the womb of the *Kaiserreich*). With liberalization and the advent of Weimar, the sociological locus of the opposition intellectual begins to shift, Weimar opens a new public space for oppositional discourse, and the organic intellectual disappears only to be replaced by a more "traditional" kind of opposition intellectual who is pushed by events into an ever more radical political stance. Thus did social and political change alter the sociological position and moral orientation of opposition intellectuals.

In Chapter 5 Jane Burbank takes up the problem of the organic intellectual in the Russian/Soviet context. Exploring the trajectory of change in a culture where the intelligentsia have played a crucial role in politics, she describes the connections between Soviet and prerevolutionary cultural formations. When some intellectuals among the opposition acquire state power, Burbank shows their transformation may generate a new intelligentsia who draw upon the historical and contextually situated meaning of the concept even as they redefine it.

With Burbank's narrative, as with Eley's, one can see how intellectuals are transformed while—or rather because—they help transform the societies in which they live. Sometimes they become outdated (as did the organic intellectuals of the SPD), sometimes they move from defending the status quo to opposing it (as did the traditional intellectuals in the Weimar left), and sometimes they become defenders of a new status quo that was formerly an opposition (as in Russia). But these developments do not exhaust the possibilities and fortunes of people who represent themselves as the intellectual spokespersons of the working classes, as Donald M. Reid intimates in Chapter 6.

Reid brings us up to the contemporary liberal democratic context, addressing the socialist intellectual's difficulties in societies where the culture and education industries continuously undercut the sociological and moral ground of critical intellectual activity. Illustrating these problems through the life and work of Régis Debray, Reid draws a particularly interesting picture of the oppositional intellectual in a culture where "intellectual" is more or less synonymous with "opposition," but where being an intellectual entails participation in the commodification of intellectual activity. Caught in a peculiar sociological position that effectively neuters any moral intentions, Debray suffers (or does he enjoy?) the peculiar privilege of the radical intellectual in an age in which opposi-

54. Gramsci, *Prison Notebooks*, 10.

tion is reduced to a posture, posture is sold as a fashion, and fashion is subject to the whims of a consuming public. Radical leftist today, moderate liberal tomorrow, reactionary conservative the next day—or so the "oppositional" intellectual is often read by the public he or she addresses.

Each of the chapters in Part II contributes to an appreciation of the ways in which the ideal of the intellectual as critic was articulated, modified, and transformed under the specific historical conditions and traditions of the European experience, and each demonstrates the peculiar ambiguities this ideal may entail—including ambiguities that seem to draw intellectuals into the orbit of claims to expertise. In Part III, "Intellectuals and the Dilemmas of the American Reform Tradition," our contributors turn their attention to the late nineteenth-and twentieth-century United States, where the intellectual in opposition seems more appropriately described as the conscience of the state. Claims to expertise loom large here as planning and incremental change animate American intellectuals dedicated to reform. But equally important are efforts to redefine the American experience from within its own specific frames of reference. In these narratives we may find that "American exceptionalism" need not be as narrowly construed (as "consensual") as it usually is, but the figures and movements here also show how attempts to appropriate and reappropriate the American experience on progressive grounds may lead to real dilemmas. And the models of the life of the mind these examples provide further sharpen our appreciation of the stakes involved in the myriad concerns that define what it means to be an intellectual today.

In Chapter 7, Mary O. Furner's account of how American economists were constrained by the state-centered character of their disciplinary discourse provides an interesting object lesson in the contradictions of professionalized academic reformism. Caught between corporate liberalism and democratic collectivism, academic economists deployed a variety of epistemic claims as a means of fortifying the authority of their political concerns and undermining those of their disciplinary opponents. Over time, as the imperatives of academic professionalization—or the constraints of their sociological location—moderated the claims of economists who remained in the discipline, radical political alternatives steadily subsided. Nonetheless, the special characteristics of the academy's place in American society did offer a political space that was more open to diverse perspectives (however limited they may have been) than those articulated in other national contexts. And as Furner notes, this fact may tell us more about the promise and limitations of economic discourse in the American academy than the monolithic accounts that have been offered thus far.

The Progressive labor reformers on whom Leon Fink focuses in Chapter 8 provide an interesting contrast to Furner's economists and speak directly to the issue of the tensions between the ideals of intellectual as social critic and intellectual as expert. Here calls for expanded state regulation and expertise in the administration of civil society clash with sentiments of democratic populism and a disdain for the inequalities of capitalist culture. Through the conflict between Charles McCarthy and Frank Walsh on the Commission on Industrial Relations (CIR), Fink tells a story of an intellectual ultimately undermined by its relation to the political realities it sought to transform. Unable to settle clearly how the purpose, interpretation, and addressee of the labor relations "intellectual's" work was to be understood, the members of the CIR eventually turned the commission into a politically superfluous body.

Ellen C. DuBois's examination of American women historians in Chapter 9 and Thomas C. Holt's discussion of W. E. B. Du Bois in Chapter 10 invite a fundamental reconsideration of the relationship between intellectual activity and political activism by and for people situated at the margins of American society.

DuBois addresses the potential for conflict that may arise between intellectuals who are simultaneously advocates for and participants in empowerment movements. Focusing on the way women historians have disputed and defined the meaning and content of women's history, she shows that the changing demands of partisanship and the changing character of scholarship are mutually constitutive, especially when the roles of activist and scholar are so closely fused as to be virtually indistinguishable.

Holt relates similar lessons. In his narrative of W. E. B. Du Bois's changing understandings of the identity of the black intellectual, Holt argues that Du Bois exemplifies the potential that marginalized intellectuals may have for developing a positive sense of self among their fellows, thus opening the possibility that the marginalized may contribute to "the larger purpose of saving humankind."

DuBois's account of the difficulties facing women historians and Holt's reading of the lessons of W. E. B. Du Bois's life dovetail neatly with the themes and concerns raised in Part IV, "Intellectuals and Colonizing Knowledge." Setting their sights on conceptions of the intellectual as they are applied, appropriated, and redefined in marginalized societies, Roberto S. Goizueta in Chapter 11 and Craig Calhoun in Chapter 12 call our attention to the imperialist tendencies and emancipatory potential of those thinkers who put knowledge in the service of political interests.

Goizueta's provocative account of a theology aimed at facilitating the political self-liberation of people living at the extreme ("Third World") margins of modernity speaks to a whole range of issues running through the history of the life of the mind, not the least of which is the possibility of defining a religious faith that does not recapitulate the elitist experiences of Christendom. In their attempts to define and act on the "preferential option for the poor," the liberation theologians compel us to rethink the most basic assumptions regarding the purposes, methods, and politics of knowledge. Arguing that the liberation theologians provide solid warrant for seeing that there is no politically uncommitted theology or knowledge, Goizueta invites intellectuals inside and outside the academy to reexamine their most cherished privileges and assumptions.

Craig Calhoun focuses on the imperialist tendencies of Western understandings of intellectuals. Whereas Goizueta's liberation theologians strive to distance themselves from the elitist tendencies of a Western ideal of the intellectual as a bearer of an "autonomous" and "specialized" knowledge, Calhoun shows how this ideal—in conflict with a "classical" model of the Chinese intellectual as teacher, in the bureaucratic hierarchy—enabled modern Chinese intellectuals to detach themselves from the state. Tracing the substantive content and intergenerational struggles that have shaped contemporary Chinese discourse on intellectuals, Calhoun relates these understandings to the Chinese student protest movement of 1989 and to its "democratic" ideals. If nothing else, the crisis of 1989 shows us how political hopes have at once been constrained by and transformed the confrontation between the indigenous and imported ideals of those Chinese who call themselves intellectuals.

Each of the chapters in this book suggests the myriad ways in which the concept of the intellectual has come down to us "trailing clouds of etymology" and showing "the ravages of time." Each explores the rich diversity of experiences, practices, traditions, and concerns that inform the ways in which the relationship between intellectual life and political life has been articulated. Some of these chapters focus on specific persons, others on groups, parties, or movements, and still others on philosophical systems, ideological frameworks, or perceptions of identity. Touching on discrete episodes or moments of time and place, each invites us to discover continuities and discontinuities between our own understandings and those of others.

We hope this book will help readers better understand the profound stakes involved in the discourse on and by intellectuals. Commissioned as part of a project that was sparked by renewed concern with the meaning and political responsibility of the intellectual (the university academic in particular), the contributions were initially meant to broaden the terms of discourse beyond those that dominated discussions in the United States. The import of this effort was further pressed upon us by developments that unfolded after it was well under way. In the early 1990s, in Eastern Europe, in China, and in numerous other countries—including the United States, where "multiculturalism" has become the point of disputes about the politics of intellectuals—people who live the life of the mind have taken on renewed importance in political events, and they have been praised and condemned for their leadership, meddling, or failure to effect social and political change. In these contexts, the likes of Vaclav Havel and Fang Lizhi were turned overnight into the intellectual heroes or villains of democracy.

If nothing else, these developments demonstrate the importance of recognizing both the historical and contextual specificity and the inherently political character of discussions of "intellectuals." But they also show that more is at stake in these discussions than differences about the meaning of a word. Indeed, only by attempting to define "intellectuals" and to understand the successes and failures, the presuppositions and influences of people who have tried to bring together the life of the mind and political life can we hope, as intellectuals and as citizens, to sort out the roles of people who, in Vaclav Havel's apt phrase, use "the power of words to change history."[55] Perhaps it might be easier for us to grasp the lessons of this book, and of the discourse on intellectuals more generally, if we would remember these words of another intellectual, John Maynard Keynes:

> The ideas of economists and political philosophers, both when they are right and when they are wrong, are more powerful that is commonly understood. Indeed the world is ruled by little else. Practical men, who believe themselves to be quite exempt from any intellectual influences, are usually the slaves of some defunct economist. Madmen in authority, who hear voices in the air, are distilling their frenzy from some academic scribbler of a few years back. I am sure that the power of vested interests is vastly exaggerated compared with the gradual encroachment of ideas.[56]

55. Vaclav Havel, "Words on Words," trans. A. G. Brain, *New York Review of Books,* January 18, 1990, 5. This article was Havel's acceptance speech for the 1989 Friedenpreis des Deutschen Buchhandels.
56. John Maynard Keynes, *The General Theory of Employment, Interest and Money* (New York, 1936), 383.

PART I

*The Politicized
Intellectual Today*

2

Habermas, Foucault, and the Legacy of Enlightenment Intellectuals

Lloyd Kramer

Criticisms of research universities and reductions in the public funding that supports them have provoked an important new debate about the role of intellectuals in American society and political culture. Although the social and political role of intellectuals has always been an issue of greatest concern to the intellectuals themselves, their many critics in American public culture have often expressed considerable interest in what intellectuals do and in the possible consequences of their actions. Anti-intellectual themes appear regularly in American political campaigns and shape many of the contemporary attacks on academic research, public education, and university curricula in the humanities and social sciences. This is the cultural context that leads me to the old (but still relevant) question of history, sociology, and politics: What is an intellectual?

I begin my own answer to this question with one of the broadest possible definitions: Intellectuals are people who write public interpretations of social, cultural, political, and personal realities. This generalization immediately raises other questions about the nature of reality, about people who communicate meaning in art or music, and about the various literary genres that writers use, but these are not the questions I intend to pursue here. Instead, I propose to explore my broad, preliminary definition of intellectual labor by posing two further questions: Does the work of intellectuals provide a critical, transforming challenge to the cultural assumptions and political powers of our society? Or does the work of intellectuals provide a legitimating, technical support for the cultural and political systems that define and dominate our society? In other

I thank Donald Reid and Dominick LaCapra for their helpful comments on an earlier draft of this chapter.

words, I want to move from the general claim that intellectuals are writers to specific questions about whether they function in modern societies as critics or as experts.

This sharp distinction between critics and experts never exists so clearly in the historical world of culture and politics, yet it offers an analytical entry into a debate about intellectuals which has cut across Western societies from the eighteenth century down to the contemporary works of Jürgen Habermas and Michel Foucault. Despite the fact that the word "intellectual" did not acquire its modern meanings until the era of the Dreyfus affair in late nineteenth-century France, the concept of a distinctive, literary community of critics and experts clearly emerged among the philosophes who formed a self-conscious "Republic of Letters" during the Enlightenment.[1] Staking out their critical role in the name of reason and progress, the philosophes assumed that criticism and expertise could be linked in intellectual projects such as the famous *Encyclopédie*—the massive collection of expert knowledge that was to serve the critical task of changing the world. The intellectuals' self-proclaimed roles of critic and expert thus developed more or less simultaneously in the eighteenth century, though the two themes are frequently separated in the terminology of modern historical or sociological analysis. Some analysts, for example, draw a clear line between critical *intellectuals,* who develop wideranging critiques of existing social institutions, and the *intelligentsia* of well-educated professionals and experts who serve these institutions in all modern societies.[2] This kind of linguistic differentiation may help to clarify the contrasting functions of modern intellectuals, but the original Enlightenment conception of philosophes (and its many derivatives) was broad enough to include both sides of the critic/expert dichotomy. In any case, I want to make a place for both critics and experts in the social category that we call "intellectuals."

The blurring of the critic/expert distinction in the term "philosophe" did not prevent the development of an eighteenth-century debate about what intellectuals were actually doing in modern societies. On the contrary, this debate became an important part of the differences that separated Voltaire and Rousseau as they analyzed the meanings and implications of progress, knowledge, and modern culture. Among their many contributions to European intellectual history, Voltaire and Rousseau

1. For analysis of the new "intellectuals" at the end of the nineteenth century, see Christophe Charle, *Naissance des "intellectuels," 1880–1900* (Paris, 1990); an excellent account of key themes in the Enlightenment's "Republic of Letters" appears in Dena Goodman, *Criticism in Action: Enlightenment Experiments in Political Writing* (Ithaca, 1989).

2. Zygmunt Bauman provides an insightful description of intellectuals and their evolving social roles in *Legislators and Interpreters: On Modernity, Post-Modernity, and Intellectuals* (Ithaca, 1987), esp. 1–20, 51–67, 127–48.

helped to launch a recurring argument about the impact of eighteenth-century social and cultural transformations on the development of modern societies; and from the beginning this debate about the meaning of the Enlightenment was also a debate about the social roles of modern intellectuals.

Given the importance of the Enlightenment in the emergence of modernity, we might well say that a dialogue with and about the legacy of the Enlightenment is the most general characteristic of modern intellectual history from the earliest Romantics to the latest postmodernists. The works of Habermas and Foucault (viewed in this context) are therefore only the most prominent recent expressions of this unending dialogue with eighteenth-century definitions of intellectuals, reason, and progress. Both of these influential authors emerged as prominent critical thinkers after publishing books on eighteenth-century European cultural history at almost the same time: Habermas's *Structural Transformation of the Public Sphere* (1962) and Foucault's *Madness and Civilization* (1961).[3] Curiously enough, it was the German Habermas who seemed to identify with and support the dominant Enlightenment conception of intellectuals, whereas the French Foucault seemed to question and even denounce most of the eighteenth-century intellectuals he discussed. These differences persist through most of their later works, so that for many contemporary intellectuals the debate between Habermas and Foucault has taken on the intensity that earlier generations found in the debate between Voltaire and Rousseau. Although the disagreements of Habermas and Foucault extend

---

3. Jürgen Habermas, *The Structural Transformation of the Public Sphere: An Inquiry into a Category of Bourgeois Society*, trans. Thomas Burger with the assistance of Frederick Lawrence (Cambridge, Mass., 1989); Michel Foucault, *Madness and Civilization: A History of Insanity in the Age of Reason*, trans. Richard Howard (New York, 1965). I use Habermas and Foucault to discuss contrasting views of modern intellectuals, but I shall not follow this theme into the mushrooming critical literature on these influential figures, which includes (to cite only a few examples in English): Thomas McCarthy, *The Critical Theory of Jürgen Habermas* (Cambridge, Mass., 1978); David Ingram, *Habermas and the Decline of Reason* (New Haven, 1987); Tom Rockmore, *Habermas on Historical Materialism* (Bloomington, 1989); Richard J. Bernstein, ed., *Habermas and Modernity* (Cambridge, Mass., 1985); Craig Calhoun, ed., *Habermas and the Public Sphere* (Cambridge, Mass., 1992); Maeve Cooke, *Language and Reason: A Study of Habermas's Pragmatics* (Cambridge, Mass., 1994); Alan Sheridan, *Michel Foucault: The Will to Truth* (London, 1980); Herbert Dreyfus and Paul Rabinow, *Michel Foucault: Beyond Structuralism and Hermeneutics* (Chicago, 1983); John Rajchman, *Michel Foucault: The Freedom of Philosophy* (New York, 1985); J. G. Merquior, *Foucault* (London, 1985); David C. Hoy, ed., *Foucault: A Critical Reader* (Oxford, 1986); David R. Shumway, *Michel Foucault* (Boston, 1989); Didier Eribon, *Michel Foucault*, trans. Betsy Wing (Cambridge, Mass., 1991); James Miller, *The Passion of Michel Foucault* (New York, 1993); Lois McNay, *Foucault: A Critical Introduction* (Cambridge, 1994); and Gary Cutting, ed., *The Cambridge Companion to Foucault* (Cambridge, 1994). See also the useful collection of articles by Habermas, Foucault, and others in Michael Kelly, ed., *Critique and Power: Recasting the Foucault/Habermas Debate* (Cambridge, Mass., 1994).

across a wide range of contemporary cultural issues, I shall focus on the contrasts in their accounts of the Enlightenment's contribution to the historical emergence of intellectual critics and experts. At the same time, however, I note how their writings also challenge or blur the dichotomy between critics and experts, thereby suggesting that the ambiguous link between the critic and the expert in eighteenth-century conceptions of the philosophe continues to appear in the work of the best contemporary intellectuals. More generally, I think the tension in the critic/expert identity of eighteenth-century intellectuals remains central to the ambiguous position of almost all modern intellectuals, who have now moved en masse from the salons to the universities and other public institutions of our society.

This institutional transformation of the intellectuals' social position easily obscures some of the continuities in the critic/expert roles that I am stressing here, and so I shall approach the debates of Habermas and Foucault by returning briefly to the differences between Voltaire and Rousseau. Their early responses to the emergence of Enlightenment culture can lead us back to Habermas, Foucault, and ourselves.

VOLTAIRE AND ROUSSEAU

The writings of Voltaire and Rousseau offer an inexhaustible source for analysis of Enlightenment-era themes and ideologies, but I shall limit my discussion to the views of modern intellectual life which appear in one text of each author: Voltaire's *Letters on England* (*Lettres philosophiques*, 1734) and Rousseau's *Discourse on Inequality* (*Discours sur l'origine de l'inégalité*, 1755). These books do not provide simple definitions of what we now call intellectuals, and they are by no means the only places to look for the views of Voltaire and Rousseau on modern culture. Yet these two famous works express significantly different responses to the development of scientific knowledge and to the people who introduce that knowledge into society. Voltaire's *Letters* argued that the rational critical writers of the seventeenth and eighteenth centuries were leading modern society toward reform and scientific progress; his "intellectuals" were informed critics who were steadily improving the world. Rousseau's *Discourse*, by contrast, argued that this new group of rational critical writers was leading modern society away from the virtues of nature and human equality; his "intellectuals" were misinformed experts who were forever devising new social and cultural hierarchies. The arguments were of course more nuanced than this stark opposition suggests, but Voltaire and Rousseau clearly developed competing, interacting conceptions of the modern intellectual which have remained influential for more than two centuries.

Voltaire described the achievements of modern English science and culture to show how intellectual progress could transform a society. Although his argument rested on the general claim that religious tolerance, scientific knowledge, and constitutional monarchy made England more enlightened than other societies, his specific heroes were the critical thinkers who doubted the inherited truths of their culture. "It is to the man who rules over minds by the power of truth, not to those who enslave by violence, . . . that we owe our respect," wrote Voltaire; and, as he explained it, nobody had done more for the "power of truth" than unorthodox political thinkers such as William Penn or unorthodox scientific thinkers such as Francis Bacon, René Descartes, John Locke, and Isaac Newton. These men exemplified for Voltaire the achievements that come when imaginative thinkers challenge the reigning assumptions of politics or knowledge, suffer persecution, and help others to see the truth. Refusing to accept the dictates of tradition or ancient authorities, critical thinkers made decisive contributions to every form of progress that Voltaire praised in the science and philosophy of modern English society.[4]

In addition to scientific progress, however, the English respect for rational critical inquiry (as Voltaire described it) helped to generate a flourishing literary and political culture that aroused the obvious envy of a French author who was striving to develop a critical perspective on his own society and a reputation for himself as a writer:

> In England as a rule people think, and literature is more honoured than in France. This advantage is a natural outcome of the form of their government. In London there are some eight hundred people with the right to speak in public and uphold the interests of the nation; about five or six thousand aspire to the same honour in their turn, all the rest set themselves up in judgement of these, and anybody can print what he thinks about public affairs. So the whole nation is obliged to study. One hears nothing but talk of the governments of Athens and Rome, and so . . . one has to read the authors who have dealt with them, and this study leads naturally to literature.[5]

Voltaire's (idealized) account of eighteenth-century English culture thus provides one of his most concise descriptions of an enlightened society and its intellectuals. In a lively public culture of debate and political ex-

---

4. Voltaire, *Letters on England,* trans. Leonard Tancock (Harmondsworth, 1980), 57, 34, 58–59, 63–64, 69–70, 72.
5. Ibid., 101.

change, critical writers played a leading role in the search for truth and the "judgement" of government policy that characterized what Habermas has called the "public sphere" of eighteenth-century society.

Rousseau also recognized that new forms of knowledge and new groups of writers had appeared in the seventeenth and eighteenth centuries, but he did not see this historical evolution as an example of human progress. On the contrary, his account of the increasingly complex divisions of labor and uses of power in modern societies suggested that "progress has been so many steps in appearance towards the improvement of the individual, but so many steps in reality towards the decrepitude of the species." Building his argument on a clear distinction between natural and civilized human beings, Rousseau questioned the optimism of philosophes who believed that reason and scientific knowledge were leading to a better-informed critical understanding of people or societies. Whereas Voltaire praised the critical rationality of Descartes and Newton, Rousseau emphasized the passions and instincts that lay concealed in all intellectual claims for rational knowledge. Amid the "mass of knowledge and errors" that characterized modern societies, argued Rousseau, "we discover only the false clash of passion believing itself to be reasoning." It was therefore false to claim that the use of reason could improve human society or that the advocates of reason (i.e., intellectuals) could play a special role in shaping a better social system. "It is reason which breeds pride and reflection which fortifies it," Rousseau explained; "reason which turns man inward into himself; reason which separates him from everything which troubles or affects him." In short, Rousseau rejected Voltaire's optimistic view of the analytical method that critical rational intellectuals were using to describe and enlighten the modern world. Though they might want to promote an accurate, liberating knowledge of human beings, Rousseau strongly doubted that much critical insight came from their work. "The more we acquire new knowledge," he complained, "the more we deprive ourselves of the means of acquiring the most important knowledge of all [i.e., knowledge of natural man]; and, in a sense, it is through studying man that we have rendered ourselves incapable of knowing him."[6]

Rousseau's description of modern intellectual culture thus emphasized its alienating effects rather than its critical functions. In the terms of my own guiding dichotomy, Rousseau saw intellectuals working as experts rather than as critics, and he suggested that they were ultimately more concerned with power and reputation than with freedom and critical analysis. In fact, Rousseau argued, modern civilization produced a type

6. Jean Jacques Rousseau, *A Discourse on Inequality*, trans. Maurice Cranston (Harmondsworth, 1984), 115, 67, 101.

of person that was unknown to the natural people of primitive societies: the government official, who represented the interests and expertise of the modern social system. Such persons serve other people instead of themselves, they manipulate language, and they deceive themselves as well as the society they control. One finds in this class of people "much indifference to good and evil coupled with . . . beautiful talk about morality" and languages of "philosophy, humanity, civility, and . . . sublime maxims" which are only deceptive "facades." All these qualities appear in that "class of men who attach importance to the gaze of the rest of the world," a social phenomenon that no natural man could ever comprehend because the modern world of judgments, hierarchies, and status had entirely replaced a primitive world in which people lived freely and for themselves: "Such is, in fact, the true cause of all these differences: the savage lives within himself; social man lives always outside himself; he knows how to live only in the opinion of others, it is, so to speak, from their judgement alone that he derives the sense of his own existence."[7] Rousseau does not refer to specific individuals, institutions, policies, or scientific disciplines. What he does provide in his *Discourse on Inequality* is a critique of the definitions of progress, rationality, and modern "man" which shaped so much of the philosophes' conception of the Enlightenment project. Like Foucault in our own century, Rousseau complained that modern, civilized people learned to define themselves according to the categories, judgments, and expertise of others. When "man" became an object of knowledge and expert research, the critical possibilities of Voltaire's rational critic gave way to the hierarchical power and language of experts in the service of government. The language of intellectuals, in other words, could serve power as well as contest it; and the experts, blinded by their own "maxims," could be remarkably unselfconscious about what they were actually doing.

Habermas and Foucault do not simply repeat the arguments of Voltaire and Rousseau, but they clearly go back over some of the same themes in that continuing modern debate over the meaning of the Enlightenment. Much like their eighteenth-century predecessors, Habermas and Foucault were highly aware of each other and of the intellectual differences that their works expressed. In fact, the dialogue that developed through their contrasting accounts of reason, progress, and the eighteenth century (among other issues) led finally to a memorable personal meeting in Paris in 1983. Significantly, the key memory of that meeting for both men referred to the role of intellectuals in politics. Habermas wrote later that he was most impressed by "the tension" in Foucault "between the almost serene scientific reserve of the scholar striving for objectivity on the one

7. Ibid., p. 136.

hand, and the political vitality of the vulnerable, subjectively excitable, morally sensitive intellectual on the other."[8] As Habermas remembered him, Foucault embodied that complex identity of the intellectual who wants to be both an expert and a critic. Foucault, for his part, especially remembered Habermas's concern with the "problem of Heidegger and of the political implications of Heidegger's thought."[9] As Foucault described it later, Habermas's conversation focused especially on that complex link between the intellectual's work as an expert and responsibilities as a critic.

No one who has read the books of Habermas and Foucault will be surprised to find that the topic of intellectuals and politics became an important subject in their personal conversations. The theme had always been important in their writing, and they obviously shared a strong interest in the social role of intellectuals. This shared interest, however, generated equally strong disagreements about the history of intellectuals in a modern Western culture that is still debating the arguments of Voltaire and Rousseau.

HABERMAS AND THE ENLIGHTENMENT'S INTELLECTUAL CRITICS

Habermas's wide-ranging theoretical and historical works almost always return in some way to a defense of the Enlightenment's critical, intellectual contribution to modernity. Deeply influenced by the German experience with Nazism, Habermas has steadfastly advocated the importance of an open, democratic public culture that adheres to the values of critical rationality. This positive conception of the Enlightenment achievement, which emerges in *The Structural Transformation of the Public Sphere,* stresses the vital role of intellectuals in the creation and defense of a rational public debate. True, Habermas's description of this new public culture in the eighteenth century also emphasizes the shaping influence of the new capitalist market economy and the new domestic relations of the bourgeois family, but he gives special attention to the institutions and debates of a new intellectual class that created both the ideal and the partial realization of a democratic public sphere.[10] Whatever else the Enlightenment may have been in the social or cultural history of Western

8. Jürgen Habermas, *The New Conservatism: Cultural Criticism and the Historians' Debate,* ed. and trans. Sherry Weber Nicholsen (Cambridge, Mass., 1989), 173–74.
9. Michel Foucault, "Politics and Ethics: An Interview," in *The Foucault Reader,* ed. Paul Rabinow (New York, 1984), 373.
10. Habermas, *Structural Transformation,* 1–117.

Europe, Habermas clearly believes that its greatest historical importance can be found in the new conception of public culture and in the new emphasis on the liberating role of reason in politics and society. Eighteenth-century intellectuals contributed to both of these developments by creating a community of critical debaters whose work shaped a new sphere for politics as well as a new literary culture. Habermas sees this Enlightenment legacy in various forms of democratic public debate, in the public interventions of critical intellectuals, and in the use of reason to resolve social conflicts or to reform social institutions. The role of modern intellectuals has therefore been critical and progressive insofar as they have supported reason and Enlightenment rationality against the Enlightenment's many cultural and political critics.

According to Habermas, the Enlightenment-era public sphere developed in a social space between the private realm of families and the official realm of governments, though it also overlapped both of these other spheres in certain respects. As worked out by English writers in coffeehouses, French philosophes in salons, and German philosophers in reading societies, the eighteenth-century's conception of the public sphere stressed equality, open discussion of all relevant issues, and accessibility for all persons who wanted to participate in a debate in which "the authority of the better argument could assert itself against that of social hierarchy." In practice, of course, most people were still too poor or illiterate to join this new debate of rational critics, and there was not much space for women of any class or ability. "Nevertheless, with the emergence of the diffuse public formed in the course of the commercialization of cultural production," Habermas explains, "a new social category arose." The new social category consisted of critical participants in a public debate that began in early eighteenth-century discussions of literature and culminated in late eighteenth-century political revolutions. This historical transformation of public culture was linked to the expanding capitalist marketplace (which challenged tradition in commercial relations), but it was the writers who led the critical debates from art and literature into politics. "Even before the control over the public sphere by public authority was contested and finally wrested away by the critical reasoning of private persons on public issues," writes Habermas, "there evolved under its cover a public sphere in apolitical form—the literary precursor of the public sphere operative in the political domain. . . . The public sphere in the political realm evolved from the public sphere in the world of letters."[11] Intellectuals therefore played a crucial part in the evolution of eighteenth-century European societies by creating a new social category: independent critical thinkers who evaluated art, literature, theater, and

11. Ibid., 36, 38, 29–31.

political theory with rational judgments that defied the authority of kings and churchmen alike.

This challenge to tradition gained its autonomous authority from the intellectuals' defense of reason, which is for Habermas (as for Voltaire) the most distinctive achievement of this new critical class: "the results that . . . issued from the public process of critical debate lay claim to being in accord with reason; intrinsic to the idea of a public opinion born of the power of the better argument was the claim to that morally pretentious rationality that strove to discover what was at once just and right."[12] This new culture of rational debate and criticism became especially influential in France, where intellectuals led the challenge to absolute authority that would explode finally in the Revolution of 1789.

Habermas clearly respects this eighteenth-century critical achievement and the interest in public life that went with it. In fact, though he does not follow Voltaire's tendency to celebrate the intellectual heroes of earlier eras, Habermas repeatedly conveys his admiration for key figures who expressed his own conception of what intellectuals should do. His favorite eighteenth-century German intellectual, for example, is Immanuel Kant, in part because Kant defended Enlightenment theories of rationality and public opinion and in part because he wanted philosophers to go beyond the academy into the public culture of their era. Habermas pointedly stresses the Kantian commitment to a "critical craft" that "was not merely academic," thereby establishing Kant's status as an ideal-type Enlightenment intellectual. "Just as the discussion of the philosophers took place in full view of the government, to instruct it and give it things to consider, so too did it occur before the public of the 'people' to encourage it in the use of its own reason." This Kantian perspective meant that the "public sphere was realized not in the republic of scholars alone but in the public use of reason by all who were adept at it."[13] Kant's unbending respect for both the Enlightenment and public culture makes him an attractive predecessor for Habermas and a much-preferred alternative to latter-day German intellectuals such as Nietzsche and Heidegger (both of whom represent for Habermas the dangers of anti-Enlightenment thought).

Yet even Kant does not become Habermas's ideal German intellectual, because the best German defense of the Enlightenment tradition, as Habermas defines it, appeared in the nineteenth-century poetry and political commentary of Heinrich Heine. Habermas argues that it "is' the duty of intellectuals to react with partiality and objectivity, with sensitivity and incorruptibility, to movements, developmental tendencies, dangers, and

12. Ibid., 54; see also 69.
13. Ibid., 105.

critical movements;"[14] and his sympathetic descriptions of Heine suggest that no German intellectual has ever accepted this duty with more insight or ability than the feisty exile poet who lived in Paris between 1831 and 1856.

Heine saw both the political opportunities and dangers that followed upon the Revolution of 1830 in France, and he first became an exemplary intellectual by recognizing the "developmental tendencies" of his era. In contrast to most Germans, Habermas tells us, he welcomed the July Revolution as "the point at which a political public sphere emerged from the literary public sphere," and he grasped the importance of this transformation for "the poet's attitude toward his work and toward the public." At the same time, though, he realized that the resurgence of political liberalism in France fostered the further development of an irrational, Romantic nationalism in Germany, which he condemned with the scathing prose of an intellectual critic who sought to maintain a link between Enlightenment rationality and Romantic literary imagination. Heine's critical efforts should have become a model for others, but in fact he became an unpopular figure among almost every group in German culture. The Germans, writes Habermas, "have not forgiven Heine the *Romantic* for rescuing their Romantic heritage from a deadly nationalistic idealization, from false historicizing, from a transfiguring sentimentality, and restoring it to its own radical origins. They have not forgiven him . . . for liquidating . . . the opposition between Romanticism and Enlightenment."[15] Heine's witty, Parisian critique of irrationalism thus brought him the kind of hatred, scorn, and anti-Semitism in Germany which the intellectual supporters of Alfred Dreyfus would face in fin-de-siècle France. As a critic of political and cultural dangers, Heine represents both the achievements and the risks of Habermas's modern intellectual: the perceptive analyst of contemporary society who becomes also the scapegoat for the society he analyzes.

In addition to his critical engagement with nineteenth-century European political culture, Heine exemplifies for Habermas a second essential trait of modern intellectuals by insisting on the distinctions between poetry and politics. Heine's commitment to Enlightenment politics angered the German Romantics, but his simultaneous commitment to the autonomy of poetry and art within the wider culture also angered the political revolutionaries. Habermas therefore draws on Heine to stress the importance of reserving a cultural space for expertise and knowledge which should not be subordinated to the political struggle of critical intellectuals.

14. Jürgen Habermas, Introduction to his *Observations on "The Spiritual Situation of the Age,"* trans. Andrew Buchwalter (Cambridge, Mass., 1984), 3.
15. Habermas, *New Conservatism*, 86, 83.

Heine defended this autonomous cultural space when he claimed "that the weapons of the poet cannot be those of the professional revolutionary, or of the professional politician." To be sure, the poet, like the scholar or the Kantian philosopher, must enter the public sphere of critical debate, yet he or she must also uphold the independence of special forms of knowledge. As Habermas explains it, "the intellectual commits himself on behalf of public interests as a sideline, so to speak (something that distinguishes him from both journalists and dilettantes), without giving up his professional involvement in contexts of meaning that have an autonomous logic of their own, but also without being swallowed up by the organizational forms of political activity."[16] Heine thus understood what both activist and apolitical intellectuals often forget: writers and scholars can and should defend the integrity or standards of their special expertise even as they enter the political debates of their public culture.

The roles of critic and expert were connected in Heine through a commitment to Enlightenment conceptions of reason, the theme that gives him a third exemplary trait in Habermas's conception of modern intellectuals. Despite the variety of subjects and analytical contradictions that readers encounter in Heine's work, Habermas argues that he was essentially "the representative of a radical Enlightenment." Like his philosophe predecessors, he employed "mockery" to challenge authoritarianism in all its guises and to defend reason against all its enemies. Indeed, writes Habermas, "his fear of the dark energies of a populism that was breaking out in revolt against reason itself—this lifelong battle, fought with the weapons of the poet, was nourished by the same inspirations, the same partisan support of universalism and individualism of the Enlightenment as the *j'accuse* of Emile Zola and the manifesto of his friends."[17]

This emphasis on the liberating, universalist nature of reason in the work of Heine and other critical intellectuals is the theme that links Habermas most explicitly to Enlightenment-era writers such as Voltaire and Kant. Like most of the philosophes, he assumes that intellectuals work in a sphere of reason that allows for communication and agreement across cultures and historical periods. He recognizes, of course, that reason necessarily operates in the world under "external, situational constraints" and that it always finds expression in "dimensions of historical time, social space, and body-centered experiences." Yet Habermas insists that communicative reason enables people to reach agreement about truths that go beyond and link their various subjective, cultural, and historical experiences. "Communicative reason," he argues, "finds its criteria in the argumentative procedures for directly or indirectly redeeming claims to

16. Ibid., 89, 87.
17. Ibid., 80, 75.

propositional truth. . . . [And] it brings along with it the connotations of a noncoercively unifying, consensus-building force of a discourse in which the participants overcome their at first subjectively biased views in favor of a rationally motivated agreement." His conception of reason thus separates the Enlightenment's "communicative reason" from the various forms of "subject-centered" reason that later shaped "bourgeois subjectivity," pushed Western culture away from the Enlightenment's original project, and led to the common modern charge that the discourse of rationality conceals its own forms of domination.[18] Indeed, the new forms of "subject-centered" reason steadily weakened the Enlightenment public sphere and facilitated the rise of intellectual experts, who have now mostly displaced the critics in all modern cultures. "The sounding board of an educated stratum tutored in the public use of reason has been shattered," Habermas argues in a critique of contemporary Western society; "the public is split apart into minorities of specialists who put their reason to use nonpublicly and the great mass of consumers whose receptiveness is public but uncritical."[19]

But if the Enlightenment developed the modern social role of the intellectual critic, why have the experts and specialists become the most common representatives of the intellectual class? Habermas attributes this transformation to the modern development of capitalist institutions, bureaucratic states, the mass media, and advertising, *and* to the emergence of a theoretical attack on the philosophes' belief in normative rationality. Foucault, by contrast, goes back to the theme of expertise and specialized knowledge, which already flourished within the Enlightenment itself and which provided the conceptual framework for modern systems of power and knowledge. His eighteenth-century intellectuals created a new ordered sphere of discipline and control rather than a new public sphere of debate and criticism. Moreover, where Habermas sees a significant rupture in Western history and culture in the demise of the public sphere over the last two centuries, Foucault sees a significant continuity in the steady extension of disciplinary practices and aspirations during this same period.

FOUCAULT AND THE ENLIGHTENMENT'S INTELLECTUAL EXPERTS

Foucault's approach to modern Western history resembles the work of Habermas in its attention to the formative influence of the Enlighten-

---

18. Jürgen Habermas, *The Philosophical Discourse of Modernity: Twelve Lectures,* trans. Frederick Lawrence (Cambridge, Mass., 1987), 284, 315, 53, 55–56, 203.
19. Habermas, *Structural Transformation,* 175.

ment, but Foucault describes the historical meaning of that influence with a radically different emphasis. Responding, perhaps, to the intellectual constraints of a Cartesian rationalist tradition in France, Foucault returns to eighteenth-century texts and institutions to examine the guiding assumptions of Enlightenment theories about reason, reform, progress, and intellectual expertise. What he finds there brings him much closer to Rousseau's critique of scholarly hierarchies and the new knowledge of "man" than to Voltaire's optimism about the progress of human understanding. Specifically, Foucault shows how eighteenth-century "intellectuals" instituted new forms of social control and surveillance in asylums, prisons, clinics, schools, and armies—all of which relied on new forms of knowledge in the emerging "sciences of man." During the eighteenth century, writes Foucault, "disciplinary power became an 'integrated' system, linked from the inside to the economy and to the aims of the [social] mechanism in which it was practised. It was also organized as a multiple, automatic and anonymous power." The much-discussed reform movements of the century's enlightened writers therefore become examples of what Foucault sees as the aspiration for "a relational power that sustains itself by its own mechanism and which, for the spectacle of public events, substitutes the uninterrupted play of calculated gazes."[20] The challenge to absolute monarchy (which Habermas sees in the new public sphere) leads in Foucault's account to the new absolutism of sovereign intellectual experts; and the exemplary institutions of this transitional eighteenth-century culture (which Habermas locates in coffeehouses and salons) appear for Foucault in clinics, asylums, and prisons.

These various institutions of confinement differed in their social functions, but they all provided a realm of opportunity and power for intellectuals. Foucault thus shares Habermas's interest in the new role of writers and would-be reformers, though he sees little evidence of freedom or equality in the reformers' work. Advocates of penal reform, for example, sought "not to punish less, but to punish better; to punish with an attenuated severity perhaps, but in order to punish with more universality and necessity; to insert the power to punish more deeply into the social body."[21] Indeed, according to Foucault, the theorists and reformers who condemned traditional social or political practices effectively transformed their own social position by acquiring new knowledge and control of others. There was in this respect a certain "convergence" between the assault on old regime medical institutions and the attack on old regime political institutions in the era of the French Revolution. Theorists of

    20. Michel Foucault, *Discipline and Punish,* trans. Alan Sheridan (New York, 1979), 176, 177.
    21. Ibid., 82.

good medicine and theorists of good government agreed on the need to shape a society that would conform to their own ideas about a rational social space. "In a concerted effort," Foucault argues, "doctors and statesmen demand, in a different vocabulary but for essentially identical reasons, the suppression of every obstacle to the constitution of this new space."[22] The key feature of this new social space would be its accessibility to the surveillance of experts, who assumed the right to bring others under their own knowledgeable gaze. Enlightenment thought thus gave rise to the disciplinary dream (and partial realization) of institutions in which it would be "possible for a single gaze to see everything constantly."[23] It was this defining gaze of experts that brought knowledge as well as power to those who described and managed the institutions of an enlightened society.

As Foucault describes the changes in late eighteenth-century society, there is much significance in the fact that the new "sciences of man" emerged simultaneously with the new social institutions of disciplinary control. The object of scientific research expanded rapidly from nature to human beings during a general reorientation of power relationships that marked the development of modern states and cultures. The medical expert who diagnosed sick people and the teacher who examined students regularly narrated the lives of others as part of the disciplining process of power. "This turning of real lives into writing is no longer a procedure of heroization; it functions as a procedure of objectification and subjection. The carefully collated life of mental patients or delinquents belongs, as did the chronicle of kings or the adventures of the great popular bandits, to a certain political function of writing; but in a quite different technique of power."[24] Eighteenth-century European writers thus established the influential model of experts who categorize and define various groups of people and problems in their societies. Foucault finds plenty of moral judgment and "petty minutiae" in the categories of the early "human sciences," but he stresses that neither the eighteenth-century writers nor their successors recognized the pervasive influence of culture and power in the development of this new knowledge. Or, to return to my own organizing categories, Foucault argues that the experts in this emerging modern society were remarkably deficient in criticizing the cultural beliefs that shaped their conceptions of scientific truth. "What we call psychiatric practice," for example, "is a certain moral tactic contemporary with the end of the eighteenth century, preserved in the rites of asylum

22. Michel Foucault, *The Birth of the Clinic: An Archaeology of Medical Perception*, trans. A. M. Sheridan Smith (New York, 1973), 38.
23. Foucault, *Discipline and Punish*, 173.
24. Ibid., 192.

life, and overlaid by the myths of positivism."[25] Like other effective social myths, however, the new human sciences created heroes who resembled gods or kings by playing a special, empowering role for the society as a whole. These heroes were the new "specialists" in the human sciences. "It is thought that [Samuel] Tuke and [Philippe] Pinel opened the asylum to medical knowledge," writes Foucault. "They did not introduce science, but a personality, whose powers borrowed from science only their disguise, or at most their justification."[26] In other words, the Enlightenment that produced new definitions of madness, criminality, and knowledge also produced a new class of persons: the sovereign intellectual expert of modernity.

The concept of sovereignty runs through much of Foucault's analysis of intellectuals, suggesting both the historical displacement of earlier sovereign powers and the unassailable authority that the new experts claimed for themselves. Kings and priests gradually surrendered their power and legitimacy to the aggressive defenders of reason, but this momentous change did not bring more freedom or power for criminals, delinquents, patients, students, or madmen. "The space reserved by society for insanity," Foucault explains in one of his more concise statements of the argument, "would now be haunted by those . . . who represented both the prestige of the authority that confines and the rigor of the reason that judges." The difference between this new controlling power and the old appeared mainly in the fact that the new authority worked "without weapons, without instruments of constraint, with observation and language only." Thus the apparently enlightened reforms of the new intellectual class delivered madmen (and all other objects of surveillance) "to the authority and prestige of the man of reason." Although this new hierarchy of knowledge and authority affected almost everyone in the society, it contributed most decisively to the severing of all dialogue across the categorical boundaries of modern social institutions. Experts could subsequently observe and describe without the challenge of reciprocal observations or criticisms from the populations they controlled. "The science of mental disease," for example, ". . . would always be only of the order of observation and classification. It would not be a dialogue."[27]

Foucault's interpretation of the Enlightenment intellectual achievement thus tends to reverse almost all of Habermas's emphasis on the equality and openness of a new, eighteenth-century public sphere in which critical intellectuals challenged the reigning order of political and cultural authority. True, Foucault's intellectuals also challenged old regime social or po-

25. Foucault, *Madness and Civilization*, 276; see also *Discipline and Punish*, 226.
26. Foucault, *Madness and Civilization*, 271.
27. Ibid., 251, 253, 250.

litical policies, but the general effect of their theories and reforms was the establishment of new hierarchies and the elimination of reciprocal discussion. In fact, Foucault's exemplary intellectual figures differ from Habermas's exemplary intellectuals in their desire to exclude the public from their knowledge and judgments and expertise. This insistence on exclusionary boundaries appears throughout Foucault's discussions of Tuke and Pinel, the founding fathers and theorists of the asylum, who carefully defined the meaning of madness and the treatments that patients should receive.[28] Similarly, Foucault discovers the essential theme of the late eighteenth-century French *idéologues* in their aspiration for control over a reformed political system that would exercise power far more efficiently than the old regime.[29] Although some *idéologues* became political critics of Napoleon, their significance as Enlightenment-era intellectuals lies for Foucault in their dream of uniting power with knowledge.

This same ambition for a new power/knowledge system emerges as the central theme in Foucault's discussion of Jeremy Bentham. Foucault uses Bentham to summarize the ideas and objectives of the modern intellectual expert in much the same way that Habermas uses Heine to describe the intellectual critic, so that Bentham and Heine become the individual and symbolic expressions of the contrasting intellectual legacies that Foucault and Habermas draw from the Enlightenment. Needless to say, Bentham's exemplary status for Foucault does not come from his specific political criticisms of the regimes or laws of early nineteenth-century England; rather, it is Bentham's conceptions of a well-ordered society and his famous plans for a "panopticon" in social institutions that give him a special place in Foucault's discussion of the new intellectual class. Foucault actually finds several overlapping assumptions in Bentham's "panopticism," each of which reveals part of the modern intellectual's aspirations.

In the first place, Bentham proposes to replace the traditional sovereignty of monarchs with a new hierarchy of social relations that subordinates bodies to a central, anonymous disciplining system. The panopticon (which is to be a central tower of observation in institutions of confinement) would thus establish the physical and symbolic structure for a social system in which the power of kings will be dispersed to multiple controlling processes of observation and categorization. "Panopticism," Foucault explains, "is the general principle of a new 'political anatomy' whose object and end are not the relations of sovereignty but the relations of discipline."[30] This new disciplinary work will not require a king, but it

28. Ibid., 241–78.
29. Foucault, *Discipline and Punish,* 102.
30. Ibid., 208.

will call for experts who develop methods of organization and surveillance which keep the whole system ticking like a machine.

The dream of disciplinary control points to a second level on which Bentham represents the ideology of Foucault's intellectual experts: the search for an unimpeded exercise of power. Bentham's vision of the rational society, as Foucault describes it, assumes "a network of mechanisms that would be everywhere and always alert, running through society without interruption in space or in time." A panoptic social system would therefore rely on maintenance workers (i.e., experts) instead of critics, and it would sustain its power through constant surveillance. Indeed, the principle of permanent observation became essential to the new expert's power, though of course the observation was to run in only one direction. "Bentham laid down the principle that power should be visible and unverifiable," Foucault explains. "Visible: the inmate will constantly have before his eyes the tall outline of the central tower from which he is spied upon. Unverifiable: the inmate must never know whether he is being looked at at any one moment."[31] Panoptic surveillance thus offers new mechanisms of power that are linked from the beginning with new methods of acquiring knowledge.

Bentham's interest in knowledge as well as power leads to a third exemplary feature of his theory. The disciplinary system that replaces sovereign monarchs cannot exercise power without the new forms of information and knowledge that the new experts collect through their labors of observation. This complex link between disciplinary power and information makes the new social system highly attractive to intellectual experts, and it makes the experts indispensable for the social system. Once again Bentham's panopticon gives Foucault the key example (or metaphor) to illustrate the general social process. The "mechanisms of observation" enable experts "to penetrate into men's behaviour," so that "knowledge follows the advances of power, discovering new objects of knowledge over all the surfaces on which power is exercised."[32] This emphasis on the links between power and knowledge in Bentham's panoptic theories establishes Foucault's own conception of what most modern intellectuals do. Whereas others may stress the social benefits that accompany the new forms of modern knowledge, Foucault prefers to emphasize that new forms of information and the people who produce it have always been intimately involved with modern systems of social control. And the aspiration for more knowledge has always functioned also as an aspiration for more power.

Although Foucault repeatedly challenges Enlightenment-era concep-

31. Ibid., 209, 201.
32. Ibid., 204.

tions of reason and truth, his detailed analysis of intellectual experts and the disciplining legacy of the Enlightenment can be seen as a reformulation in less universalist terms of the *critical* strand in Enlightenment theory that he radically deemphasizes in his accounts of eighteenth-century writers. In simple terms, we could say that Foucault's critique of the Enlightenment's "sciences of man" relies on forms of reason and rationality that he questions when they appear in the works of other authors. It should be noted, however, that Foucault saw this apparent paradox and defended its critical purposes. "If intellectuals in general are to have a function," he argued, "if critical thought itself has a function, . . . it is precisely to accept this sort of spiral, this sort of revolving door of rationality that refers us to its necessity, to its indispensability, and at the same time, to its intrinsic dangers." The methods and insights of what we call rational truth thus provide a valuable system for understanding history and the world, but reason is only one form of knowledge, and it must be subjected constantly to criticism: "if it is extremely dangerous to say that Reason is the enemy that should be eliminated, it is just as dangerous to say that any critical questioning of this rationality risks sending us into irrationality."[33] There is, finally, a commitment to criticism and even to rationality in Foucault's work which takes it closer to Habermas than the dichotomies of contemporary intellectual life may suggest. The experts, after all, are still subjected to criticism; and the critics still make their cases with the learning and knowledge of experts.

CRITICS, EXPERTS, AND ACADEMIC INTELLECTUALS

In arguing that the continuing debate over the social functions of intellectuals remains part of a continuing debate over the meaning of the Enlightenment, I have relied on several analytic dichotomies that suggest an excessively dualistic view of intellectual history: critic vs. expert, Voltaire vs. Rousseau, Habermas vs. Foucault. This analysis necessarily emphasizes the differences between these categories more than the similarities, yet I think these oppositions provide a useful structure for thinking about various definitions of intellectuals that have evolved since the eighteenth century. But these categories are by no means clear or distinct because it is also possible to establish significant connections between critics and experts or between Rousseau and Habermas or between Voltaire and Foucault. I therefore want to suggest how the tensions and fusions in my various categories point to the complexity of the intellectuals' role in society, even as I reaffirm the analytic value of the critic/expert dichotomy.

33. Foucault, "Space, Knowledge and Power," in *Foucault Reader*, 249.

Despite his strong affinities with the Voltairean strand of Enlightenment thought, Habermas may also be linked to Rousseau through several important overlapping themes. For example, Habermas's interest in achieving various kinds of political consensus on public policies may be compared to Rousseau's emphasis on the "general will." Although there is far more emphasis on the role of reason in Habermas's conception of consensus, he seems to share with Rousseau a strong commitment to some integrating process in public life, which he describes in democratic terms that are much closer to the language of Rousseau than to the elitist views of Voltaire. For Rousseau and Habermas alike, this search for an integrated political community is a serious project that calls for serious discussion instead of Voltairean wit. Habermas's prose style thus evokes the earnest purpose of Rousseau more often than the humor of Voltaire. Habermas also issues frequent warnings about the oppressive effects of instrumental reason (as opposed to communicative reason) which repeat at least part of Rousseau's early complaints about the dangers of rationality and modernization. "The encroachment of forms of economic and administrative rationality into life-spheres," writes Habermas, ". . . leads to a type of *colonization of the life-world*. By this I mean the impoverishment of expressive and communicative possibilities . . . that enable individuals to find themselves, to deal with their personal conflicts, and to solve their common problems communally by means of collective will-formation."[34] Such statements do not transform Habermas into a latter-day Rousseau, but they convey his concern with problems that Rousseau addressed far more regularly and passionately than Voltaire.

But how could Foucault be linked to Voltaire? Although Foucault repeatedly stressed that old-style "universal" intellectuals had disappeared from the contemporary world,[35] his own political and philosophical support for unpopular persons in modern France might well be compared to some of Voltaire's famous interventions in the eighteenth-century public sphere. Like Voltaire, Foucault challenged the conventions of his own era in a prose style of ironic disrespect (reminiscent, too, of Nietzsche) which undercut the serious pretensions of modern scholastics. Voltaire wrote with more wit, but Foucault shared his insistence on the need for more play and less seriousness in the discourses of social institutions and the human sciences. For all his explicit denials, there seems to be a Voltairean critical purpose and tone in much of Foucault's work: *Ecrasez l'infame!* This implicit link may become most apparent in "What Is Enlightenment?," an essay that, as Habermas notes in an appreciative commentary,

---

34. Habermas, Introduction to *Observations on "The Spiritual Situation,"* 20.
35. See Foucault's discussion of the "universal" intellectual in "Truth and Power," in *Foucault Reader,* 67–68.

suggests a personal identification with certain critical themes of Enlightenment thought.[36] Here, shortly before his death, Foucault argued that modernity should be seen as a critical attitude rather than as a body of knowledge and that the work of Kant marks the emergence of this distinctively modern theme in Western thought. The intellectual critic finally replaces the intellectual expert in Foucault's sympathetic description of the Kantian project:

> I have been seeking, on the one hand, to emphasize the extent to which a type of philosophical interrogation—one that simultaneously problematizes man's relation to the present, man's historical mode of being, and the constitution of the self as an autonomous subject—is rooted in the Enlightenment. On the other hand, I have been seeking to stress that the thread that may connect us with the Enlightenment is not faithfulness to doctrinal elements, but rather the permanent reactivation of an attitude—that is, of a philosophical ethos that could be described as a permanent critique of our historical era.[37]

Foucault's references to the Enlightenment in this late essay thus suggest his own respect for a critical eighteenth-century attitude that went far beyond expertise and continued to link twentieth-century intellectuals (such as himself) with Voltaire or Kant as well as Rousseau.

The overlapping concerns that connect Rousseau and Habermas or Voltaire and Foucault thus blur my analytical categories and suggest the definitional problems that have existed since the era of the Enlightenment itself. The meaning of intellectual labor remains a much-contested issue in the ongoing public and political debates about the dangers (or virtues) of criticism and the dangers (or virtues) of specialized knowledge. These debates shape and reflect the broad historical context in which those of us who work in modern universities constantly redefine or repeat perennial arguments about the social significance of what intellectuals do. We, too, face the tension of competing definitions: critics or experts. Of course we are not brought into universities to serve as critics; on the contrary, the training and hiring of persons in the university emphasize the development and exercise of expertise. But knowledge is rarely neutral, so that experts may soon find their way to the critical implications of the special information they acquire. The expert and the critic can come together in the same person or the same work.

As it happens, though, most academic intellectuals find it difficult to sustain both sides of an intellectual tradition that encompasses criticism

36. Habermas, *New Conservatism*, 173–79.
37. Foucault, "What Is Enlightenment?" in *Foucault Reader*, 42.

and conformity, contestation and professionalism. It is far easier to be an expert than to be a critic because expertise can readily align itself with the power that criticism must inevitably confront. Expertise protects academic intellectuals and gives us work in modern societies; it is our knowledge that makes us useful to others. Yet, as Foucault writes in his account of Kant's contribution to modern thought, the critical project for ourselves "has to be conceived as an attitude, an ethos, a philosophical life in which the critique of what we are is at one and the same time the historical analysis of the limits that are imposed on us and an experiment with the possibility of going beyond them."[38] Amid all the ambiguities and hostilities that surround the roles of intellectuals in our society, we may safely assume that extending the limits of the expert's knowledge will be of little or no social value unless we also extend the limits of the critic's challenge to power and reigning truths.

38. Ibid., 50.

PART II

European Intellectuals
and the Socialist Project

3

"Bred as a Mechanic": Plebeian Intellectuals and Popular Politics in Early Nineteenth-Century England

James Epstein

I.

The term "intellectual" would hardly seem to fit discussion of English popular radicalism during the first half of the nineteenth century. When we think about the relationship of "intellectuals" to movements of working-class social and political action, our attention is more usually drawn to the late nineteenth and early twentieth centuries. We think quite readily of the intellectual influence that E. S. Beesley, Frederic Harrison, and the positivists exerted within the labor movement during the 1860s and 1870s; at the end of the century we think of revolutionary socialists such as William Morris, H. M. Hyndman, Eleanor Marx, and E. Belford Bax or the circle of Fabians that included talents as diverse as those of Bernard Shaw, the Webbs, and Annie Besant.[1] Intellectuals drawn from the professional middle class clearly played prominent roles in late nineteenth-century labor and socialist politics.

This chapter is dedicated to the memory of Edward Thompson, socialist intellectual and historian, who surrendered neither to disenchantment nor to default.
   1. See Royden Harrison, *Before the Socialists: Studies in Labour and Politics, 1861–1881* (London, 1965), chap. 6; Martha S. Vogeler, *Frederic Harrison: The Vocations of a Positivist* (Oxford, 1984); Christopher Kent, *Brains and Numbers: Elitism, Comtism, and Democracy in Mid-Victorian England* (Toronto, 1978); E. P. Thompson, *William Morris, Romantic to Revolutionary*, rev. ed. (London, 1977); Stanley Pierson, *Marxism and the Origins of British Socialism* (Ithaca, 1973); Yvonne Kapp, *Eleanor Marx*, 2 vols. (London, 1976); Chushichi Tsuzuki, *H. M. Hyndman and British Socialism* (London, 1961); A. M. McBriar, *Fabian Socialism and English Politics, 1884–1918* (Cambridge, 1962); Paul Thompson, *Socialists, Liberals and Labor: The Struggle for London, 1885–1914* (London, 1967), esp. chap. 7; Peter Clarke, *Liberals and Social Democrats* (Cambridge, 1978), esp. chap. 2; E. J. Hobsbawm,

Use of the word "intellectual" in reference to a particular kind of person doing a particular kind of work dates from the early nineteenth century, although the word was not in common use in England until the 1870s.[2] This usage seems to correspond with the general rise of the professional intellectual in society. However, Harold Perkin, one of the few social historians to give serious attention to the subject, refers to nineteenth-century professional intellectuals as "the forgotten middle class," arguing that because they failed to forge a separate social (or "class") identity, they in effect "forgot themselves."[3] Nonetheless, Perkin maintains, they were a protean force, exerting influence far beyond their numbers by providing ideological service to the other major social classes of their era (i.e., aristocracy, middle class, and working class); they constituted a potential class on permanent loan. And yet these floating intellectuals of the Victorian age did not necessarily play equal roles in helping to forge the social and political identities of others; the measure of their influence varied among social groups and fluctuated over time. Thus Perkin comments that the "stream . . . of the professional apologists of the working-class ideal, was a more fugitive one, which ran underground for long distances, and flowed out unexpectedly."[4]

What is striking, however, is the relative insignificance of middle-class intellectuals in the shaping of the character of popular radicalism and labor struggle during the critical period 1790 to 1848. There are obvious exceptions. The great utopian socialist Robert Owen, together with the group of middle-class political economists usually mislabeled "Ricardian" socialists (which included Thomas Hodgskin, William Thompson, John Gray, and John F. Bray, among others), provided a strong dose of anticapitalist economics and a coherent analysis of exploitation.[5] It is important however, not to exaggerate such influences. As Iorwerth Prothero notes,

---

"The Fabians Reconsidered," in his *Labouring Men* (London, 1964). More generally, see Carl Levy, ed., *Socialism and the Intelligentsia, 1880–1914* (London, 1987).

2. Raymond Williams, *Keywords: A Vocabulary of Culture and Society* (London, 1976), 140–42; T. W. Heyck, "From Men of Letters to Intellectuals: The Transformation of Intellectual Life in Nineteenth-Century England," *Journal of British Studies* 20 (1980): 158–83.

3. Harold Perkin, *The Origins of Modern English Society, 1780–1880* (London, 1969), 252–70. Cf. R. S. Neale's classic essay, "Class Consciousness in Early Nineteenth-Century England: Three Classes of Five" in his *Class and Ideology in the Nineteenth Century* (London, 1972).

4. Perkin, *Origins of Modern English Society,* 264.

5. See J. F. C. Harrison, *Robert Owen and the Owenites in Britain and America: The Quest for the New Moral World* (London, 1969); Noel W. Thompson, *The People's Science: The Popular Political Economy of Exploitation and Crisis, 1816–34* (Cambridge, 1984); Gregory Claeys, *Citizens and Saints: Politics and Anti-Politics in Early British Socialism* (Cambridge, 1989), and *Machinery, Money, and the Millennium: From Moral Economy to Socialism, 1815–1860* (Princeton, 1987).

"too many historians share the attitude of contemporaries and see working men not as formulating ideas out of their own experience but as raw material assimilating ideas provided by outsiders."[6]

Often the support and sympathy that middle-class "intellectuals" (not a term they used to describe themselves) offered were at odds with the tone and style of radical working-class protest. In 1848, for example, Charles Kingsley and the group that became known as the Christian socialists tried to offer direction to the waning Chartist movement; but despite their humane intent, they were hopelessly out of sympathy with the movement's strategy of mass intimidation and its democratic principles. This comes across quite clearly in Kingsley's Chartist novel, *Alton Locke* (1850), which sympathetically presents the underlying motive for Chartism while finally viewing the effort as based on a delusion.[7] Spokespersons who were genuinely drawn to popular radicalism from outside the boundaries of the nascent working class tended to be mavericks, individuals increasingly detached from associations and identities beyond the movement itself. Moreover, disgruntled gentlemen—such as Major John Cartwright, Sir Francis Burdett, Arthur Thistlewood, Henry Hunt, Fergus O'Connor, Ernest Jones—rather than middle-class professionals were disproportionately prominent in such roles.[8]

It is beyond the scope of this chapter to explain the general absence of a guiding presence for middle-class intellectuals during this period. Undoubtedly it had something to do with the polarities of class formation, but sharp class divisions did not preclude a significant contribution on the part of middle-class intellectuals to the late nineteenth-century socialist cause. The experience of the French Revolution and the violent spectacle of the Irish rising of 1798 were crucial, as a generation of urban middle-class reformers retreated from political engagement and from the more radical emphases of Enlightenment thought.[9] As E. P. Thompson

6. Iorwerth Prothero, *Artisans and Politics in Early Nineteenth-Century London: John Gast and His Times* (Folkestone, 1979), 246.

7. Dorothy Thompson, *The Chartists: Popular Politics in the Industrial Revolution* (London, 1984), 322–23; Margot C. Finn, *After Chartism: Class and Nation in English Radical Politics, 1848–1874* (Cambridge, 1993), 60–61, 153–59; John Saville, "The Christian Socialists of 1848," in *Democracy and the Labour Movement,* ed. John Saille (London, 1954), 133–59; Raymond Williams, *Culture and Society* (London, 1958), 111–12, on *Alton Locke.*

8. For the role of the gentleman leader see John Belchem, *'Orator' Hunt: Henry Hunt and English Working-Class Radicalism* (Oxford, 1985); James Epstein, *The Lion of Freedom: Feargus O'Connor and the Chartist Movement* (London, 1982); Patrick Joyce, *Visions of the People: Industrial England and the Question of Class, 1840–1914* (Cambridge, 1991), 38–48.

9. For the Radical Enlightenment, see Margaret C. Jacob, *The Radical Enlightenment: Pantheists, Freemasons and Republicans* (London, 1981); John Redwood, *Reason, Ridicule, and Religion: The Age of Enlightenment in England, 1660–1750* (Cambridge, Mass., 1976); Isaac Kramnick, *Republicanism and Bourgeois Radicalism: Political Ideology in Late Eighteenth-Century England and America* (Ithaca, 1990).

comments: "The unity between intellectual and plebeian reformers of 1792 was never to be regained."[10] The retreat of the romantic poets vividly illustrates this uncoupling.[11] The political distance that had been traveled by the end of the Napoleonic Wars is captured in a letter from the poet laureate, Robert Southey, to the prime minister, Lord Liverpool, in the turbulent year 1817: "The spirit of Jacobinism which influenced men in my sphere of life four and twenty years ago . . . has disappeared from that class and sunk into the rabble, who would have torn me to pieces for holding those opinions then, and would tear me to pieces for renouncing them now."[12] Increasingly working people were left to nurture their own political culture. What is remarkable about the period is the extent to which intellectual and political direction was generated from within plebeian ranks. The strength, imaginative vision, and independence of this culture is of course the central theme of Thompson's monumental *Making of the English Working Class.*

Thus we return to the observation that there appears to be something incongruous about discussing "intellectuals" and early nineteenth-century popular radicalism. This incongruity derives from our normal understanding of the notion of "intellectuals" as a distinct social group drawn from certain sections of society involved in "intellectual" work—the clergy, writers, artists, university professors, certain professionals—and acting with a relatively high degree of independence with regard to their political and social allegiance or identification. If, however, we expand our definition of the term; if we think in a predominantly functional sense of an intellectual as someone who assumes the role of persuader, consciously producing or conveying ideas to a public, then it makes sense to discuss the role of plebeian intellectuals. Moreover, such a discussion may help to underscore the distinctive place of early nineteenth-century popular radicalism within the broader history of the modern British labor movement.

This formulation is loosely informed by Antonio Gramsci's discussion of the role of intellectuals in his *Prison Notebooks.*[13] Gramsci starts from

10. E. P. Thompson, *The Making of the English Working Class* (London, 1963), 115, and chap. 5 more generally. Also see J. E. Cookson, *The Friends of Peace: Anti-War Liberalism in England, 1793–1815* (Cambridge, 1982).

11. See Nicholas Roe, *Wordsworth and Coleridge: The Radical Years* (Oxford, 1988); E. P. Thompson, "Disenchantment or Default? A Lay Sermon," in *Power and Consciousness,* ed. Connor Cruise O'Brien and William Dean Vanech (New York, 1969), 149–81.

12. C. D. Yonge, *The Life and Administration of Robert Banks, Second Earl of Liverpool,* 3 vols. (London, 1868), 2:298–99.

13. Antonio Gramsci, *Selections from the Prison Notebooks of Antonio Gramsci,* ed. Quintin Hoare and Geoffrey Nowell Smith (New York, 1971), 5–23; also see Carl Boggs, *Gramsci's Marxism* (London, 1976), 75–79. The cues taken here from Gramsci are meant to be general and suggestive. There would be little point in attempting to impose his ideas in a

the proposition that all men and women, having the capacity for reason, are potentially intellectuals, but that they are not all intellectuals by social function. He then divides intellectuals in the functional sense into two groups: "traditional" and "organic." "Traditional" intellectuals conform more or less to what has been described as our normal understanding of intellectuals, although Gramsci argues that there is a class dimension to their position which is historically based but usually concealed by an illusion of social detachment or independence (their perceived interclass status).[14] "Organic" intellectuals are distinguished not necessarily by their occupation but rather by their function "in directing the ideas and aspirations of the class to which they organically belong." What is important here is the emphasis on the need for popular movements to draw leaders or intellectuals from within the predominant social groups or strata on which they are based. The organic relationship between leaders and rank-and-file adherents, or potential adherents, facilitates political mobilization to the extent to which it ensures shared understandings and identities. Gramsci maintains that to be truly effective, intellectuals must be integrated within the organization or culture of the movement as well as the everyday life and culture of a community. "The mode of being of the new intellectual can no longer consist in eloquence, which is an exterior and momentary mover of feelings and passions, but in active participation in practical life, as constructor, organiser, 'permanent persuader' and not just simple orator. . . ."[15]

Furthermore, Gramsci approaches the problem of the intellectual in revolutionary politics from the more general perspective of culture and ideology: what are the communicative conditions that allow the dominant ideas and cultural practices of a particular ruling order to be challenged broadly within modern society? This is not the place to enter the wide-ranging debate over Gramsci's theory of cultural "hegemony."[16] But it is worth insisting on the importance of one of his central insights—his view

---

detailed way on earlier movements, as he was working out his thoughts within a highly specific political situation. Part of their heuristic value, however, derives precisely from differences between Gramsci's and Lenin's definitions of the intellectual's role in socialist politics, particularly with regard to party organization.

14. Thus Gramsci departs from a view of intellectuals to which Karl Mannheim gave classic expression in *Ideology and Utopia: An Introduction to the Sociology of Knowledge*, ed. Louis Wirth and Edward Shils (New York, 1929).

15. Gramsci, *Prison Notebooks*, 3, 10.

16. See Raymond Williams, *Marxism and Literature* (Oxford, 1977), chap. 6; Chantal Mouffe, "Hegemony and Ideology in Gramsci," in *Gramsci and Marxist Theory*, ed. Chantal Mouffe (London, 1979), 168–204; Joseph V. Femia, *Gramsci's Political Thought: Hegemony, Consciousness, and the Revolutionary Process* (Oxford, 1981), esp. chaps. 2–4. The uses and abuses of Gramsci's thought have become a matter of historical controversy. See, for example, T. J. Jackson Lears, "The Concept of Cultural Hegemony: Problems and Possibilities," *American Historical Review* 90 (1985): 567–93; Leon Fink, "The New Labor History and

that these "permanent persuaders" must articulate a new system of social and political values within the shared language and symbolic discourse of a larger, national culture. The rhetoric of radical persuasion must be expansive, touching deep emotional chords, if intellectuals are successfully to challenge ingrained structures of understanding.[17] To combat a natural tendency toward elitism and isolation from the popular masses, intellectuals need to adopt a language and political style appropriate to "national-popular" consciousness.

II.

The conditions facing plebeian radicals in early nineteenth-century England were obviously very different from those facing the Italian Communist Party in the early twentieth century. Gramsci's theoretical musings—often elusively and abstractly expressed—cannot be merely projected back onto popular radicalism. They may, however, offer a starting point for thinking about the relationship between radical "intellectuals" and popular political culture during the early nineteenth century, specifically about Richard Carlile and the republican-infidel movement of the 1820s, the "zetetic" clubs formed to support Carlile, and his journals, the *Republican* (1819–26) and *Lion* (1828–29).

Carlile and his supporters were the inheritors of the materialist culture of the Radical Enlightenment, devotees of Thomas Paine, and advocates of free inquiry. In many respects they were archetypical plebeian intellectuals. As middle-class reformers turned away from the more radical tones of Enlightenment thought, works such as Paine's *Age of Reason,* Volney's *Ruins of Empires,* and d'Holbach's *System of Nature* became cherished texts among sections of radical artisans. In the 1790s such radicals were prominent in the ranks of the London Corresponding Society. Francis Place made the somewhat exaggerated claim that "nearly all the leading members were either Deists or Atheists."[18] The "zetetic" movement openly reengaged a tradition of rationalist political and theological thought that had been driven underground by government repression during the previous generation. The zetetics (the term was derived from the Greek word

---

the Powers of Political Pessimism: Consensus, Hegemony, and the Case of the Knights of Labor," and various responses, *Journal of American History* 75 (1988): 115–61.

17. Gramsci, *Prison Notebooks,* 418–21, for example.

18. British Library, Add. Ms. 27,809, f. 115; also see Mary Thale, ed., *Selections from the Papers of the London Corresponding Society, 1792–99* (Cambridge, 1983), xx, 306, 359n, 387, 396n; William Hamilton Reid, *The Rise and Dissolution of the Infidel Societies in the Metropolis* (London, 1800); and more generally Iain McCalman, "The Infidel as Prophet: William Reid and Blakean Radicalism," in *Historicizing Blake,* ed. Steve Clark and David Worrall (London, 1993).

for "to seek") were not only dedicated to the cause of political and religious liberty, exposing the evils of priestcraft and kingcraft in all guises; they were seekers after scientific truth.[19] They were aided in this materialist endeavor not only by the often erudite *Republican* "but by the multiplying army of peripatetic lecturers, with their globes and orrerys and oxyhydrogen microscopes."[20] One cannot fail to be impressed by the ambitious intellectualism of the zetetics. Indeed, access to a privileged form of knowledge was part of the movement's attraction for plebeian radicals who managed to combine a strain of artisan elitism with a profound egalitarianism.

Richard Carlile was among the most influential radical voices in England in the period that followed the Napoleonic Wars. Self-appointed heir to the mantle of Thomas Paine, he embraced the principles of anti-Christian reasoning and republicanism with a rationalist vigor that at times bordered on fanaticism. Above all other writers and publishers, Carlile was responsible for returning Paine to center stage of public politics. Between 1819 and 1834 he spent nearly ten years in prison for his stubborn refusal to capitulate to government censorship. His determined insistence that it was his natural rights as a citizen to publish political and religious beliefs regardless of their unpopularity with either government or "loyal" opinion won him the respect of England's plebeian radicals during the 1820s.[21]

Born in a small Devon market town in the year after the outbreak of the French Revolution, Carlile remembered from his childhood Thomas Paine being burned in effigy. Trained as a tin-plate maker, he joined the ranks of a declining artisanal trade. In 1813 he moved with his wife, Jane, to London, that greatest of artisan centers. Here he gave up tin plating for a life of politics, earning his living hawking Cobbett's *Political Register* and Wooler's *Black Dwarf* in the streets. His progress toward radicalism resembles that of so many other artisans: a commitment forged under the combined impact of the French Revolution, the hard final years of the war, and the encroachments of industrial capitalism on the vestiges of

---

19. See Richard Carlile, *Address to Men of Science . . . (London, 1821); Republican,* January 18, 1822, 79, 83–84, for the term "zetetic."

20. Gwyn A. Williams, *Rowland Detrosier: A Working-Class Infidel, 1800–1834* (York, 1965), 3.

21. This biographical sketch draws on Joel H. Wiener, *Radicalism and Freethought in Nineteenth-Century Britain: The Life of Richard Carlile* (Westport, Conn., 1983); also see G. J. Holyoake, *The Life and Character of Richard Carlile* (London, 1870); Theophila Carlile Campbell, *The Battle of the Press: As Told in the Life of Richard Carlile* (London, 1899); Guy A. Aldred, *Richard Carlile, Agitator: His Life and Times* (Glasgow, 1941). For Carlile's autobiographical reminiscences, see *Republican,* March 3, 1820, 226–28; May 30, 1823, 673–86; January 28, 1825, 97–126; July 14, 1826, 1–13; *Prompter,* January 29, 1831, 200–203; *Isis,* July 7, 1832, 341–45.

artisanal independence. In 1817 he embarked on his life's career as a journalist and publisher when he teamed up with William Sherwin to publish *Sherwin's Weekly Political Register*. It was during these years that Carlile discovered the writings of Paine and assumed the mission of making Paine's work, including the outlawed second part of *The Rights of Man* and the deistic *Age of Reason*, available to the widest public. Together with Sherwin, he brought out a series of Paine's works in the form of cheap tracts, and in time Carlile collected them into a two-volume edition of Paine's complete political works. These were the first popular editions of any of Paine's political writings to be openly published in Britain during the nineteenth century. Carlile followed by publishing *The Age of Reason* as part of a collection of Paine's theological works. By 1819 he had gained the attention of both the Tory government and the Society for the Suppression of Vice; he had also won popular recognition as a champion of free expression. Although Carlile was essentially a journalist rather than a speaker, his first tour of the industrial north found him beside "Orator" Henry Hunt on the hustings at St. Peter's Field on the fateful 16th of August 1819. Carlile managed to escape from Manchester and on his return to London he started his most famous journal, the *Republican,* in which he published his own and others' reports of the Peterloo Massacre.

In late 1819, Carlile began his first (six-year) stint in prison for the publication of blasphemous libel. At his trial he read the entire text of Paine's *Age of Reason* to the jury, a tactic hardly calculated to win an acquittal. It did, however, ensure that when Carlile published the trial proceedings, they contained the text of the work for which he had been prosecuted. In his way, Carlile now made *The Age of Reason* available at a price much cheaper than his original edition; but trial proceedings were not protected from the threat of government prosecution, as he had hoped.[22]

Despite Carlile's imprisonment, the *Republican* continued. Carlile edited the journal from prison, while his family and co-workers produced the paper from his shop at 55 Fleet Street, dubbed the "Temple of Reason." Shut down, burned down, moved up Fleet Street, subjected to harassment by the government and the Vice Society, the Temple of Reason survived the 1820s. After Jane and his sister, Mary Anne, joined Richard in prison, his shopworkers took over the crusade of rationalist publication; many of them soon found themselves in prison cells. From

---

22. *The Report of the Proceedings of the Court of King's Bench . . . Being the Mock Trials of Richard Carlile . . .*(London, 1822); *Vice versus Reason: A Copy of the Information Found against Mrs. Carlile for Publishing Mr. Carlile's Trial, and Defence against the Prosecution for "The Age of Reason"* (London, 1820). Carlile's original two volumes of Paine's *Theological Works* sold for a half guinea per volume; his trial sold for 2s/6d.

the provinces supporters traveled to the metropolis to replace their imprisoned comrades and to manage Carlile's shop. The *Republican* stood as testament to the touch culture of plebeian rationalism. The phenomenon of the *Republican* was as much the achievement of vendors, shopworkers, and readers as it was Carlile's. From the dock brave infidels such as the lacemaker Susanna Wright turned courtrooms into platforms for anti-Christian reasoning. Years later Wright could be found defending her "rational" bookstall in her native Nottingham with a loaded pistol.[23] From prison Carlile's shopworkers even published their own journal, the *Newgate Monthly Magazine* (1824–26). Carlile's intransigent supporters withstood the blast of persecution, and they won a significant victory: after 1824 no further attempts were made in the nineteenth century to interfere with the publication of the works of either Paine or Elihu Palmer, the American deist.[24]

The decade that saw Carlile and his army of republican infidels storm onto the scene was a particularly difficult one for popular radicalism. The state repression that followed in the wake of Peterloo, and in response to the unprecedented radical insurgence of 1819, effectively closed down the movement for democratic political reform. The Seditious Meetings Act (December 1819) made it impossible for radicals to hold large-scale public meetings, the major vehicle of popular mobilization during the immediate postwar years (1815–19).[25] Indeed, the zetetics were the only organized radical presence to survive the repression of the early 1820s. Under these conditions it is perhaps not surprising that Carlile repudiated the politics of mass constitutionalist mobilization, retreating into a policy of rationalist education. He insisted that the radical program must go beyond the demand for universal male suffrage: nothing short of strict adherence to full Paineite republicanism and to materialism would suffice. Anyone unwilling to conform to Paineite reasoning was, in effect, excommunicated: "The Writings of Thomas Paine, alone, form a standard for any thing worthy of being called Radical Reform. They are not Radical Reformers who do not come up to the whole of the political principles of Thomas Paine."[26]

Whatever the virtues of a policy of ideological purity, and there clearly

23. *Report of the Trial of Mrs. Susannah Wright, for Publishing, in His Shop, the Writings and Correspondences of R. Carlile* . . . (London, 1822); *Republican*, August 18, 1826, 188–89; September 1, 1826, 252–55.

24. Thompson, *Making of the English Working Class*, 728–33; Wiener, *Radicalism and Freethought*, chap. 5; William H. Wickwar, *The Struggle for the Freedom of the Press, 1819–1832* (London, 1928), chaps. 6 and 7.

25. Belchem, *'Orator' Hunt*, chap. 5.

26. Richard Carlile, *An Effort to Set to Rest Some Little Disputes and Misunderstandings between the Reformers of Leeds* . . . (London, 1821), 7; idem, *A New Year's Address to the Reformers of Great Britain* (London, 1821), 9–12.

were some during the 1820s, Carlile's position rendered Paineite republicanism a minority movement, the political culture of an embattled vanguard. Several reasons can be discussed. First, Carlile fractured the terms
of a dominant political idiom, that of popular constitutionalism. The
language of early nineteenth-century radicalism was permeated by popular
constitutionalism, not by the "counter-hegemonic" ideology of Paineite
republicanism.[27] Paine had cut through the protocols of eighteenth-
century political discourse with an irreverence that proved fundamental
to the development of popular political language.[28] He had insisted that
radicals eschew arguments that sought to derive political rights from historical precedent and drink solely from the purely rationalist fountain of
natural rights theory. For Paine there was no English constitution: there
could be no constitution without the creative force of the people's sovereign will. *The Rights of Man* remained the most widely circulated radical
text throughout the first half of the nineteenth century. Yet what is striking
about nineteenth-century political reasoning, both elite and popular, is
how rooted debate remained within a discourse about the "real" meaning
of the English constitution and constitutional history. To embrace constitutionalism was to participate in a powerful national myth structure, to
evoke the authoritative force of a master fiction of British society. Radicals
were able to refashion the vocabulary of constitutionalism, appropriating
the sage of constitutional struggle by giving it a democratic or libertarian twist.

To be a Paineite republican was to cut oneself off from this powerful
vocabulary of legitimation, to reject the emotional force of a radicalized
version of popular nationalism and patriotism.[29] After all, Paine had declared himself to be a "citizen of the world." Carlile was not interested
in evoking a radical sense of British patriotic virtue; quite the contrary,
he constantly directed attention to international republican heroes. In
1822, for example, in an article dated "Year 3, of the Spanish Revolution,"
he announced that Simón Bolívar had "eclipsed all the Republican heroes
that have gone before him." The list of recommended toasts for com-
memorating Paine's birthday, a central ritual of rationalist culture, captures the deep commitment to international liberty and brotherhood.

27. See James Epstein, *Radical Expression: Political Language, Ritual, and Symbol in England, 1790–1850* (New York, 1994), chaps. 1 and 3; John Belchem, "Republicanism,
Popular Constitutionalism, and the Radical Platform," *Social History* 6 (1981): 1–32.

28. Thompson, *Making of the English Working Class*, chap. 4; Olivia Smith, *The Politics
of Language, 1791–1819* (Oxford, 1984), chap. 2.

29. For a discussion of radical versions of British patriotism, see Hugh Cunningham,
"The Language of Patriotism, 1750–1914," *History Workshop* 12 (1981): 8–33; also see
Linda Colley, "The Apotheosis of George III: Loyalty, Royalty, and the British Nation,
1760–1820," *Past and Present* 102 (1984): 94–129, and "Whose Nation? Class and Class
Consciousness in Britain, 1750–1830," *Past and Present* 113 (1986): 97–117.

Toasts were drunk to Washington and Jefferson; Bolívar "and the Republicans to Colombia"; José Martín and "his companions in arms, with Republicans in Chili and Peru"; "Peter [Pierre] Boyer, and the Republicans of the Island of St. Domingo" ("We despise not their colour, but hail them as brothers"); "the Republicans of Spain and Portugal, and may they annihilate the last vestige of Kingcraft and Priestcraft"; "the French Revolution, and may the next be free of both a Robespierre and a Buonaparte"; and "the Greeks, if they fight for the Representative System of Government."[30] But it was as if Britain were bereft of a libertarian or radical tradition of its own; for the zetetics, as for Paine, there was no "usable" national past.[31]

Second, Carlile made it more difficult to separate Paineite republicanism from anti-Christian reasoning—a separation favored by many radical artisans. *The Age of Reason* was indeed "'a sword sent to divide.'"[32] Carlile and the more staunch zetetics refused to tolerate the uncoupling of democratic politics from theology. As Carlile wrote in 1821: "Other reforms will prove abortive, unless [they] be accompanied with an instruction that shall abolish superstition in the minds of the people."[33] Although the shape of his anti-Christian beliefs changed several times during his lifetime, the battle against religion became more important to Carlile as the 1820s wore on. Moreover, during the early 1820s, Carlile and his supporters broke formally with Paine's own theology, moving from deism to a more rigorous, scientifically founded atheism.[34]

Many working people rallied to Carlile's defense, not because they agreed with either his republicanism or his atheism but because they believed in the cause of free expression. It was less than obvious to many ultraradicals that democratic political reform could not be achieved without the wholesale destruction of Christian belief. Gwyn Williams comments that the growth of "infidelity" within the working class "was almost as remarkable a phenomenon of the 1820s as the more familiar triumphs of Methodism, evangelicalism, and 'vital religion.'"[35] Perhaps, but what seems certain is that although there was much indifference to religion

30. *Republican*, January 25, 1822, 97–99.
31. For a full discussion of zetetic culture and attitudes toward history, see Epstein, *Radical Expression*, chap. 4.
32. Thompson, *Making of the English Working Class*, 96–98.
33. *To the Reformers of Great Britain*, June 24, 1821, 11, 28; also see ibid., October 13, 1821, 18; Wiener, *Radicalism and Freethought*, 106–7.
34. *Republican*, June 9, 1820, 266–67; February 15, 1822, 196–97; May 10, 1822, 606; July 12, 1822, 219; Richard Carlile, *Observations on "Letters to a Friend on the Evidences, Doctrines, and Duties of the Christian Religion . . ."* (London, 1821).
35. Williams, *Rowland Detrosier*, 3; also see Iain McCalman, "Popular Radicalism and Freethought in Early Nineteenth-Century England: A Study of Richard Carlile and His Followers, 1815–32" (M.A. diss., Australian National University, 1975), chap. 5.

and often bitter hostility toward both the Established Church and the increasingly conservative Dissenting sects, Christianity, often in a primitive and democratic form, maintained a powerful hold on many working-class communities. As Edward Royle observes: "The paradox involved in any description of the masses who did not attend church is that, next to their infidelity, the most common feature about them was their religiosity."[36] Carlile might ridicule the Bible as an "obscene, voluptuous, false, scandalous, malicious, and seditious" text, but for many working people it remained a cultural touchstone, a shared language of moral righteousness.[37] The inversions in Carlile's own language—for instance, his announcement that he was the messiah of reason "risen again to stand before you"—and in infidel culture more generally attest to this view.[38]

The cult of reason, the march of rational progress, was no doubt an exhilarating prospect for many plebeian radicals. But the intellectualism of their political culture constituted a third force that potentially divided this vanguard from a larger working-class public. The struggle for knowledge is among the most familiar themes in the autobiographies of working-class leaders of the nineteenth century.[39] One thinks of the ambitious program of study that the shoemaker and future Chartist leader, journalist, and poet Thomas Cooper set for himself: "I thought it possible that by the time I reached the age of twenty-four I might be able to master the elements of Latin, Greek, Hebrew, and French; might well get through Euclid, and through a course of Algebra; might commit the entire 'Paradise Lost,' and seven best plays of Shakespeare, to memory; and might read a large and solid course of history, and of religious evidences; and be well acquainted also with the current literature of the day."[40] Cooper fell short of this prodigious schedule of learning, but he did master most of these languages and texts on his own, and while working as an artisan. For such working-class autodidacts the world of learning and politics was inseparable from the quest for knowledge and

36. Edward Royle, *Radical Politics, 1790–1900: Religion and Unbelief* (London, 1971), p. 9; also see idem, *Victorian Infidels: The Origins of the British Secularist Movement, 1791–1866* (Manchester, 1974), esp. chap. 1.

37. See Deborah H. Valenze, *Prophetic Sons and Daughters: Female Preaching and Popular Religion in Industrial England* (Princeton, 1985); Thomas Laqueur, *Religion and Respectability: Sunday Schools and Working-Class Culture, 1780–1850* (New Haven, 1976); Eileen Yeo, "Christianity in Chartist Struggle, 1838–42," *Past and Present* 91 (1981): 103–39.

38. Wiener, *Radicalism and Freethought,* 108, 201; also see Iain McCalman, *Radical Underworld: Prophets, Revolutionaries, and Pornographers in London, 1795–1840* (Cambridge, 1988), esp. chaps. 3, 7, and 9, for a brilliant handling of this theme.

39. David Vincent, *Bread, Knowledge, and Freedom: A Study of Nineteenth-Century Working-Class Autobiography* (London, 1981).

40. Thomas Cooper, *The Life of Thomas Cooper* (1872) (Leicester, 1971), 57.

political liberty. In many respects, the radical culture of the early nineteenth century was an intellectual culture of the self-taught.

The problem of mediating this intellectual culture, of securing radicalism's presence within a larger, "rougher," and more illiterate workingclass milieu, was a general problem of the age.[41] There was constant tension between a strain of artisan elitism and the democratic promise of a movement opened to "members unlimited." Much depended on how radicalism's presence was inserted in working-class communities.[42] As Thompson reminds us, illiteracy was no necessary bar to engaging in radical discourse; there was the underworld of cheap print and tavern ballads. Radicalism was accessible to listeners at mass meetings and at taverns where debates were held and newspapers were read aloud. The careers of the movement's great orators attest to the power of the spoken word.

The world of the zetetics was uncompromising, however, in its intellectual demands. The movement was based on humble men and women of learning; intelligent people with unrealized potential, eager to pit themselves against the world of elite learning and culture. The *Republican* was full of contributions from zetetics eager to exhibit their learning, constructing intricate materialist theories, exposing the absurdities of the Bible, composing odes to Paine. Even their rituals of conviviality were elaborately structured around the twin poles of Enlightenment reason and ridicule. At a dinner held at the Lancashire factory town of Ashtonunder-Lyne to commemorate the birth of Paine, "the Political Saviour of the World," the song "A Parson Who had a Remarkable Foible" followed the toast "May Priests be made to drink plentifully of the Cordial they so much recommended to others, namely, Patience and Long-Suffering." The radical printer and bookseller Joshua Hobson treated the party to a lengthy disquisition on the scientific basis of Paine's *Age of Reason*.[43] This was the movement of "clever" folks. As Carlile trumpeted in 1828: "It is

---

41. Thompson, *Making of the English Working Class,* 711–46; David Vincent, *Literacy and Popular Culture: England, 1750–1914* (Cambridge, 1989), esp. chap. 7; J. F. C. Harrison, *Learning and Living, 1790–1960: A Study in the History of the Adult Education Movement* (London, 1963); R. K. Webb, *The British Working-Class Reader, 1780–1848: Literacy and Social Tension* (London, 1955).

42. See McCalman, *Radical Underworld;* idem, "Ultra-Radicalism and Convivial Debating Clubs in London, 1795–1838," *English Historical Review* 102 (1987): 309–33; Richard Johnson, "'Really Useful Knowledge': Radical Education and Working-Class Culture, 1790–1848," in *Working-Class Culture: Studies in History and Theory,* ed. John Clarke et al. (London, 1979), 75–102; Eileen Yeo, "Robert Owen and Radical Culture," in *Robert Owen, Prophet of the Poor,* ed. Sidney Pollard and John Salt (London, 1971), 84–114; James Epstein, "Some Organizational and Culture Aspects of the Chartist Movement in Nottingham," in *The Chartist Experience: Studies in Working-Class Radicalism and Culture, 1830–1860,* ed. James Epstein and Dorothy Thompson (London, 1982), 221–68.

43. *Republican,* March 8, 1822, 302–7; Epstein, *Radical Expression,* chap. 5.

much to the merit of what is called Infidelity, that it is embraced by almost every clever man in the country. Go where I will, and hear of extraordinary genius, I find it above the superstition of the day."[44] True to Enlightenment tradition, Carlile believed that all men and women were capable of "genius," that it was merely lack of education that enabled superstition and tyranny to prevail, but mass ignorance loomed as a daunting fortress secured against reason and liberty.

Tremendous faith was placed on the power of the written word. Thus Carlile explained the importance of keeping Paine's *Age of Reason* in print:

> Just calculate how many persons may read one copy of the "Age of Reason," if it be taken care of. I know several persons, who have kept copies, which they purchased of me in 1819, in constant use, in the way of lending them up to this time, and instances where a single copy has gone through fifty families, all approving as they read. This is the way to calculate the power of the Printing Press. Had the "Age of Reason" kept circulating from its first appearance, as it has within these last four years, it would ere this, have undermined the Christian Idolatry of this country.[45]

This was a profoundly text-bound political culture. At his trial Carlile provided the jury with twelve copies of both the Bible and *The Age of Reason* so that jurors might compare the two texts and follow his commentary. Exhaustive textual exegesis, often stultifying in its literalmindedness, was a common practice among such plebeian philosophes. Zetetics took great pride in acquiring books and mastering texts, particularly the works of Paine.[46]

Carlile's own autobiographical sketch, written in 1820, offers insight into how someone "bred as a mechanic" (Carlile's description) might aspire to the world of texts.[47] He relates: "I had received all the education that a small borough in Devonshire . . . could afford me, at the early age of twelve years; it was confined to a knowledge of writing and arithmetic, and sufficient latin to read a physician's prescription." Through the auspices of a friend the young Carlile found employment at a druggist's shop in Exeter. "Being so very young," he explains, "I was called on to do many things that I conceived to be derogatory to my dignity as a scholar able to read physicians' prescriptions: so I left the shop . . . in four

44. *Lion,* January 4, 1828, 26.

45. *Republican,* November 1, 1822, 710; also September 13, 1822, 495.

46. See, for example, *Republican,* April 5, 1822, 445, for the account of William Perry, a Stockport republican and one of Carlile's imprisoned shopworkers. For a full discussion of this aspect of zetetic culture, see Epstein, *Radical Expression,* chap. 4.

47. *Republican,* March 3, 1820, 673–86.

months." At the request of his mother, who ran a small retail shop—his deceased father had been an exciseman—Carlile agreed to be apprenticed "to a business which I never liked, that of tin-plate working." He describes his apprenticeship of seven years and three months as 'a most painful one,'" claiming that he was derided by his friends "for being a slave and the master depicted as a negro driver" for the tight control his master kept over his hours.

> I soon began to shew a disposition to lay claim to, not the "Rights of Man," but the rights of apprentices, which my master professed to be ignorant of. . . . So that the whole of my apprenticeship consisted of nothing but conspiracies, rebellions and battles. On being relieved from that worse than seven years imprisonment, I made up my mind to follow that business no longer than I should be compelled: my ambition was to get my living by my pen, as more respectable and less laborious than working 14, 16 and 18 hours per day for but a very humble living.

For seven years Carlile worked as a journeyman tin plater, but unable to make a living to support his young family and being "fired with ardour by the political publications of the day," in the spring of 1817—the government having suspended habeas corpus—he moved into the dangerous world of radical Grub Street.

Some striking paradoxes appear in Carlile's account. He deeply resented working as a druggist's assistant, which was beneath his "dignity as a scholar"; he regarded his apprenticeship as "worse than seven years imprisonment"; he apparently gained no satisfaction from working as a journeyman artisan. His ambition was to escape the drudgery of long hours and low wages in order "to get my living by my pen, as more respectable and less laborious." Yet Carlile was to spend nearly ten years in a real prison; he was known to work extraordinarily long hours as a political journalist, and his efforts rarely yielded him more than a "humble living." As for becoming "more respectable," he was one of the most excoriated public writers of his day. One senses an intense desire for independence, a strong streak of anti-authoritarianism, and a driving ambition for individual self-improvement. If he does not express outright contempt for his trade, he takes no pride in the status or skills of his craft. Dignity is conferred by scholarship, not by manual labor. Independence and equality are achieved through learning, through liberation from work. Thus Carlile reflected on having rescued himself from his trade: "Never a Negro slave obtained his freedom with more joy than I quitted the mechanic's bench for a situation in which I could better improve my mind." Extrapolating from his own experience, he later observed:

The progress of knowledge affords to every man the means to educate himself, and it is by education alone that the majority can be brought out of a state of servitude to the minority. . . . But as yesterday I was a journeyman mechanic, subject to many oppressions; today I feel, that I am the equal of, and independent of, every man in the world. Education alone has made this change; for I am neither better clothed, nor better fed, than I was *occasionally* as a journeyman mechanic, and possess but little more of what is called property.[48]

Carlile left the workshop, but he explicitly sought a working-class readership, refusing to adapt his literary style to more learned tastes: "It has been said to me by more than one person: 'Let us write in the style of Hume and Gibbon, and seek readers among the higher classes.' I answer no; I know nothing of the so-called higher classes but that they are robbers; I will work towards the raising of the working class above them. . . . I as a mechanic will allow no class to be higher than myself."[49] His sense of class identification, however, did not guarantee a wide popular audience for his writing or journals.[50] Moreover, a sense of social displacement may have figured as prominently in Carlile's motivation, and in the appeal of rationalist culture, as strong feelings of collective or corporate social identity. Perhaps, as Jacques Rancière argues in respect to some French artisans and their self-appointed spokesmen in the 1830s and 1840s, the marginality of such trades as shoemaking, tailoring, and tin plating created alienated artisans who, rather than extolling the virtues of their trade, turned from the monotony and insecurity of their work to visionary worldviews and sought recognition as intellectuals.[51] In his study of London's Spencerean radicals, Iain McCalman comments: "Paradoxically, marginality might also in some instances have acted as an inducement to the pursuit of intellectuality or self-improvement."[52] The Spencean social-

48. Carlile, *New Year's Address*, 15; *Republican*, May 21, 1824, 648.
49. Richard Carlile, *Jail Journal: Prison Thoughts and Other Writings by Richard Carlile*, ed. Guy A. Aldred (Glasgow, 1942), 18–19.
50. Although weekly sales of the *Republican* had perhaps reached as high as 15,000 in autumn 1819, they fell off so dramatically by 1820 that the journal became unprofitable. It was kept alive by financial contributions from Carlile's supporters. See *Republican*, May 30, 1823, 678–80.
51. Jacques Rancière, "The Myth of the Artisan: Critical Reflections on a Category of Social History," and the responses of William H. Sewell Jr. and Christopher Johnson, *International Labor and Working-Class History* 24 (1983): 1–25. Also see Jacques Rancière, *La Nuit des prolétaires* (Paris, 1981), published in English as *The Nights of Labor: The Workers' Dream in Nineteenth-Century France*, trans. John Drury (Philadephia, 1989).
52. McCalman, *Radical Underworld*, 48–49, and also 153. Also see Chris Waters, *British Socialists and the Politics of Popular Culture, 1884–1914* (Stanford, 1990), 158–65, on the sense of alienation of the worker-intellectuals of the late nineteenth-century socialist movement.

ist Thomas Preston, who only narrowly escaped the gallows for his part in the Spa-Fields riots of December 1816, wrote about his trade of shoe-making in terms very similar to Carlile's: "I was . . . bound to the profession of which I have been since the victim and the slave."[53] The republic of radical letters might offer a measure of personal autonomy and control that no longer could be found at work. The act of writing itself, as Rancière suggests, constituted a "symbolic rupture," empowering such plebeian intellectuals in the cause of liberty but simultaneously distancing them from the world of the artisan's workbench.[54] Social displacement or marginality may also help to explain the appeal of Carlile's materialist and antihierarchical reasoning to some members of the lower professions, representatives of what Gibbon Wakefield called the "uneasy class": surgeons, out-of-work attorneys, apothecaries, preachers, and teachers.[55] These were people who in the first instance may well have felt that their class had forgotten them.

The cult of reason also had a powerful appeal for some women of both working-class and middle-class backgrounds.[56] Although women were a minority presence in the movement, female republican societies in Manchester, Blackburn, Ashton, Bolton, and Bath were among the *Republican*'s most zealous correspondents and subscribers. To an extent, zetetics merely expanded the postwar movement's innovative inclusion of women in the formal politics of radicalism: voting at meetings, forming associations with female officers, holding their own meetings, presenting addresses.[57] As a movement, however, postwar radicalism made no claims for women's political rights per se; popular constitutionalism, with its appeal to historical precedent, was unpromising for people who wished to make claims for female citizenship. Demands for equal social and political rights for women were most persuasively grounded on strictly rationalist premises. Women concerned specifically with a democratic reordering of gender relations gravitated toward republican-infidel circles and the

53. Thomas Preston, *The Life and Opinions of Thomas Preston, Patriot and Shoemaker* (London, 1817), 5.

54. Rancière, "Myth of the Artisan," 13. On the theme of social displacement within the republic of letters, see Robert Darnton, "The High Enlightenment and the Low-Life of Literature," in his *Literary Underground of the Old Regime* (Cambridge, Mass., 1981), 1–40.

55. See McCalman, "Popular Radicalism and Freethought," chap. 3, for the social composition of the Carlileites; also see Neale, "Class and Class Consciousness."

56. See Iain McCalman, "Females, Feminism, and Free Love in an Early Nineteenth-Century Radical Movement," *Labour History* 38 (1980): 1–25.

57. For the role of women in 1819, see Epstein, *Radical Expression*, 86–92; more generally, see Dorothy Thompson, "Women and Nineteenth-Century Radical Politics: A Lost Dimension," in *The Rights and Wrongs of Women*, ed. Juliet Mitchell and Ann Oakley (Harmondsworth, 1976), 112–48.

Owenite cause.[58] During the 1820s, zetetics also distanced themselves from a "rougher" artisan milieu, a male-centered culture often dominated by heavy drinking and sustained absence from the home.

The invitation to free inquiry and free expression could be profoundly liberating for women. Mary Gregory, a London supporter, described how reading the *Republican* had changed her worldview. Formerly she had retreated from the room when her husband began to read the *Republican*, "terrified" at being exposed to Carlile's religious views, but no longer: "The case is altered, for the moment your book comes into the house, I am anxious to read it. . . . Had I never read your 'Republican,' I should always have been miserable and in fear of everlasting torment for sins committed on this earth. . . . Sir, I hope there is not a married man who takes your 'Republican' but reads it to his wife. I fear they do not for if they did I think they would have come forward before this." She went on to argue that there would have to be "a great reformation in husbands, as well as government, before we can obtain our rights in free discussion with them or our sons."[59]

In 1825, Carlile dedicated the *Republican* "To Woman, Man's Equal," proposing not only that all matters should be open for discussion equally among men and women, but maintaining that wedded happiness depended on gender equality. "Be not told, with acquiescence, that there are matters unbecoming of your inquisitiveness, or that there are useful stations in human society which you are not qualified to fill. Such is not the case, if you will but quality to fill them. Your aim should be that quality with mankind. . . . Whilst you have less knowledge than your husbands, you will have less power, you will serve rather than assist; and, in the absence of equality, there cannot be wedded happiness."[60] Carlile was a pioneer advocate of birth control; he believed that women should be allowed the same kinds of sexual choices as men and should be able freely (although within marriage) to satisfy their sexual needs. He also supported divorce at the instigation of either party.[61]

Most dramatic was the conversion of Eliza Sharples. After the death of her father, Sharples left a comfortable middle-class home to follow Carlile, and in the early 1830s, she became his "moral wife." Unhappily married for many years, Richard and Jane Carlile had separated some years before. In 1832 Sharples lectured regularly at the Rotunda, the center of radical free expression during the period of the reform crisis. "The Lady of the

58. See Barbara Taylor, *Eve and the New Jerusalem: Socialism and Feminism in the Nineteenth Century* (London, 1983).

59. *Republican*, November 29, 1822, 843.

60. Ibid., Preface to vol. 11, 1825, iv.

61. "What Is Love?" ibid., May 6, 1825, 545–69; Richard Carlile, *Every Woman's Book; or, What Is Love?* (1826) (London, 1833).

Rotunda," as Sharples was known, presented the alarming spectacle of a woman who publicly denounced Christian belief as superstition and as the original cause of secular tyranny.[62]

The motivations of female zetetics were complex. During the early nineteenth century, however, such women as Mary Gregory, Susannah Wright, and Eliza Sharples may well have shared an intensified sense of displacement or marginality that underpinned their radical commitment. As Barbara Taylor writes, the early nineteenth century was a highly unstable period in male/female relations.[63] But it is also probable that most working-class women were not intent on remodeling the institution of marriage along lines of greater informality or flexibility, but rather sought increased protection against their husbands' and lovers' possible neglect of marital and familial responsibilities. Moreover, the language of women's protest typically drew legitimacy from claims associated with female responsibilities within the family and community, often invoking a rhetoric of Christian compassion. Grounding women's social and political claims on purely rationalist or liberal concepts of individual right undercut a moral vocabulary whereby women's power to protest against injustice was based on their place within the family and community and cast in terms of their roles as providers within those contexts. It was therefore their position outside the world of self-interested politics that gave power to women's speech on behalf of disinterested human welfare.[64]

Finally, it should be noted, at least in passing, that there was an ambivalence to the zetetic commitment to science, particularly at points where the "neutral" principles of social science were brought to bear on reforming working-class behavior. Carlile's open advocacy of birth control, for example, failed to win much popular support in his own day. His work held too strong a hint of the Reverend Thomas Malthus for the taste of most working-class radicals; they suspected that arguments for population limitation were disguised attempts to control the lives of working people and to rationalize lower wages in the name of iron laws

62. See Wiener, *Radicalism and Freethought*, chaps. 9 and 10; R. S. Neale, "Women and Class Consciousness," in Neale, *Class in English History, 1680–1850* (London, 1981), 205–15. In *Battle of the Press* Theophila Carlile Campbell (daughter of Richard and Eliza) reproduced many of her parents' private letters, which reflect a complex and often difficult relationship.

63. Taylor, *Eve and the New Jerusalem*, esp. 192–205; also see Anna Clark, *The Struggle for the Breeches: Gender and the Making of the British Working Class* (Berkeley, 1995).

64. See Ruth L. Smith and Deborah M. Valenze, "Mutuality and Marginality: Liberal Moral Theory and Working-Class Women in Nineteenth-Century England," *Signs* 13 (1988): 366–87; Temma Kaplan, "Female Consciousness and Collective Action: The Case of Barcelona, 1910–18," *Signs* 7 (1982): 345–66; Sally Alexander, "Women, Class, and Sexual Difference," *History Workshop* 17 (1984), esp. 135–46.

of labor supply and demand.[65] Indeed, Carlile's views on political economy were influenced by the laissez-faire writings of Bentham, Ricardo, and James Mill. His support of phrenology as an "infidel science" was radical both in its materialist thrust and in its egalitarian tone. Yet Carlile rejected Robert Owen's request to consider socialist cooperation on the "scientific" grounds that "phrenological inequalities of human disposition rendered any principle of general co-operation for equality . . . apparently impracticable."[66] The mental universe of rationalist politics is impressive for its diversity, but it was always contradictory, often assuming individualist and elitist tones and advancing views that remained difficult to secure within a broad-based movement of working people.

We are left, therefore, with the difficult question how to place Carlile and the rationalist culture of the zetetics. Certainly Carlile shared important concerns with large numbers of working-class radicals, male and female. His freethinking on religious matters, his interest in natural science, his democratic political views, and his strong streak of individualism had much in common with a certain type of self-improving artisan. The demand for equality between men and women struck a responsive chord among sections of the radical movement. The sheer audacity of the rationalist assault on the twin fortresses of established authority—aristocratic privilege and Christianity—left its mark on radical culture. Indeed, many plebeian intellectuals who cut their teeth on the republican-infidel cause during the 1820s went on to become key leaders in their local communities in the 1830s, when the political tide turned and mass radical agitation again became the order of the day. On the other hand, Carlile's attachment to bourgeois political economy, his views on divorce and population limitation, his emphasis on individualism over collective self-help, and his political and religious sectarianism were not particularly representative of artisan political culture. Nor could the style and discourse of Carlileite politics rival the emotional or intellectual appeal of either popular constitutionalism or radicalized Christianity. And yet perhaps it is because Carlile and these plebeian intellectuals resist neat categories that they are relevant to discussions about the relationship between intellectuals and political action. It is only with hesitancy that they can be considered

65. See, for example, discussions of population control in *Trades Newspaper, and Weekly Mechanics Journal,* July 17, 24, 31, August 21, and September 11, 1825. Carlile also favored the dissection of human corpses for anatomical research, and left his own body for dissection at his death in 1843. Such scientific commitments offended popular beliefs about the body. See Ruth Richardson, *Death, Dissection, and the Destitute* (Harmondsworth, 1989), 168–71, for Carlile.

66. *Lion,* February 29, 1828, 257–62; Roger Cooter, *The Cultural Meaning of Popular Science: Phrenology and the Organization of Consent in Nineteenth-Century Britain* (Cambridge, 1984), chap. 7.

bearers of a distinct class ideology or culture, although their importance to the democratic movement of their age is without question. In certain respects they may be considered "organic" intellectuals. But they often stood on the margins, radical autodidacts proud of their learning, embattled bearers of enlightenment culture, separated by their very status as philosophes manqués.

4

Intellectuals and the German Labor Movement

Geoff Eley

Assessment of the tragic twentieth-century history of the German labor movement must reckon at some point with the character of its intellectual leadership. In particular, purported tensions between intellectuals and workers, as exhibited both in institutional structures and in a cultural clash between the movement's formal ideologies (socialism and communism) and the everyday logic of working-class life, figure prominently in discussions of both the prewar decades and the Weimar Republic. Here I attempt to review these issues with special concern for the multiple meanings we impart to the term "intellectuals" and for the radical shifts in the German scene in those years.

DEFINING INTELLECTUALS

As a basic guide I prefer a simple materialist approach that locates intellectuals as a particular component of the new middle class, the one that performs cultural, ideological, and mental functions in the complex division of labor of a capitalist society, on the basis of qualifications acquired in higher education; as Eric Hobsbawm puts it, "anyone who earns or looks forward to earning his [or her] living in an occupation which is chiefly recruited from those who have passed a certificate of some kind of academic education or its equivalent."[1] This idea seems preferable to Alfred Weber's *freischwebende Intelligenz* (free-floating intelligence) or

---

1. Eric Hobsbawm, "Intellectuals and the Class Struggle," in *Revolutionaries* (New York, 1973), 245.

Karl Mannheim's "social groups whose special task is to provide an interpretation of the world for [their] society," for this kind of definition tends to be circular ("intellectuals" are those people who behave like intellectuals).

We can push the issue of the "intellectual function" a little further, however, and here I find Antonio Gramsci's thinking on this subject, with its attempt to conceptualize that function in relation to the needs, interests, and dynamism of dominant and subordinate social forces (i.e., classes, Gramsci being a Marxist), particularly useful. In general the role of intellectuals for Gramsci is to shape and organize the cohesion and self-awareness—the culture—of a particular social group, but as is well known, he also distinguished between "organic" and "traditional" intellectuals in this sense: *organic* intellectuals are the indigenous products of a social group, who perform tasks essential to its reproduction or to the reproduction of the society in which it is dominant (thus, in the case of capitalism, managers, technicians, and engineers, as well as the range of professional and administrative occupations more generally; or, in the case of the labor movement, the worker who becomes a trade union official or a political activist); *traditional* intellectuals are those who hold established social positions with long traditions, often specific to an earlier social formation and dating from an earlier historical period, which allow them far more latitude and autonomy in their cultural pronouncements and political identification (in a capitalist society this category would include priests, professors, and artists). Any social group that aspires to cast or recast society in its own image must be capable of generating its own organic intellectuals capable of exercising moral leadership and of winning over a significant proportion of existing traditional intellectuals; for otherwise the dominant meanings and understandings in society can't be contested.

In addition, for our purposes here, three specific issues should be kept in view. First is the specific institutional space available in a society for "free intellectual activity", defined in terms of freedom of the press and speech, degree of university autonomy, and so on. Such freedom affects both the ability of a rising social and political force to attract the allegiance of traditional intellectuals and the ability of its own organic intellectuals to build strong bases for themselves in society and raise strong oppositional challenges to the dominant culture. The second issue is the specific conditions of artistic/cultural production in a society, together with the relation of the artist to patronage, the market, and the public purse. Finally, we must consider the particular policies, practices, and attitudes toward intellectuals prevailing in the labor movement at any one time.

INTELLECTUALS AND THE SPD BEFORE 1914

The mainstream historiography of the Social Democratic Party (SPD) draws a sharp distinction between the formally revolutionary character of the official program and rhetoric and the reformist reality of the movement in its practical relationship with the working class. On one side is the Marxist revolutionary ideology of the intellectuals and part of the leadership (including the centrism of the later Karl Kautsky); on the other side are the essentially humble, practical, and economistic concerns of the rank and file. Into the space between them are then inserted the "practical men" of the movement, the local functionaries and trade union officials, the real soul of the SPD and the keepers of its effective mission, who got on quietly improving the lot of the workers, publicly indulgent but privately scathing about the inflammatory and maximalist rhetoric of the revolutionaries.[2] In this view, the radicalism of the German labor movement was an artificial and unnatural development imposed by its isolation from the rest of the political system between the 1860s and World War I: first the dogmatism of the German liberals forced the break of the 1860s which initially constituted the socialist movement as an independent actor; and then the repression of the Antisocialist Law between 1878 and 1890 drove the party and unions into virtual illegality. Even after the law's abolition in 1890, the Wilhelmine system continued to close itself against the SPD, restricting its development, harassing it, depriving it of allies, and essentially confining it to a subcultural and political ghetto. Left to itself—and given the political option—the labor movement would have taken its natural place as the democratic wing of a pluralist national consensus, arguing for radical measures within the overall framework of a constitutional state, something like the role of organized labor in Gladstonian liberalism in Britain or the Lib-Lab politics of the 1900s.

Even so, the growth of the movement carried a practical logic of long-term social and political integration. In Gerhard Ritter's view this logic tended inexorably to the future acceptance of labor as a legitimate factor in the decision-making structures of a developed capitalist society, realized through the mechanisms of liberalized industrial relations and the welfare state; this was an ultimate destiny that neither repressive employers, reactionary governments, nor revolutionary firebrands could hope to ob-

2. Gerhard A. Ritter, *Die Arbeiterbewegung im Wilhelminischen Reich, 1890–1900* (West Berlin, 1959); Suzanne Miller, *Das Problem der Freiheit im Sozialismus* (Frankfurt, 1964); Eric Matthias, "Kautsky und der Kautskyanismus: Die Funktion der Ideologie in der deutschen Sozialdemokratie vor dem ersten Weltkriege," *Marxismusstudien,* 2d ser., 1957: 151–97; Guenther Roth, *The Social Democrats in Imperial Germany: A Study in Working-Class Isolation and National Integration* (Totowa, N.J., 1963); Hans-Josef Steinberg, *Sozialismus und deutsche Sozialdemokratie: Zur Ideologie der Partei vor dem I. Weltkrieg* (Bonn, 1967).

struct. Measured against this process of practical integration, Ritter argues, the SPD leadership's obsession with "correct" revolutionary strategy was so much hot air, "theoretical humbug" that got in the way of sensible reformism and its inevitable triumph. The real substance of the movement was in the dogged pragmatism of the trade unions, the service activities of the labor secretariats, and the moderate parliamentary socialism of the party's South German sections. On these bases by 1900 the SPD had become "essentially a practical labor party with a few revolutionary phrases that were no longer taken seriously."[3]

This kind of approach aggressively downgrades the importance of the labor movement's official Marxist ideology. In fact, German Marxism, the great pride of the Second International, was in this view a quite artificial creation. It acquired its hold on the SPD under the exceptional circumstances of the Antisocialist Law, when the suspension of the party's normal life allowed the clique around August Bebel to impose what they took to be Marxism as the movement's official creed. The latter was then codified into the Erfurt Program during the return to legality in 1890–91, which became the fixed point of the SPD's strategic vision in the pre-1914 decades, defended against right and left alike. Moreover, for the party leadership this Marxism became a necessary "ideology of integration"—"Kautskyism," as Eric Matthias dubbed it[4]—which was capable of holding heterogeneous tendencies within the same party and of providing a source of ultimate solidarity during the frequently bitter political debates.

Aside from Ritter, Matthias, and other classics of the SPD's general history, the foundations of this argument were laid in the work of Werner Conze and his students, which focused on the early years of the labor movement, particularly the 1860s and 1870s. Conze stressed the divisive effects of bourgeois anxieties about the emergence of a separate workers' interest during industrialization, the tensions between liberals and radical democrats in the movement for national unification, and the long-term consequences of the rift of the 1860s—the "separation of the proletarian from the bourgeois democracy," in Gustav Mayer's famous phrase.[5] Once again: there was no irreducible contradiction between capital and labor (as Marxist theory postulated) and no firm structural basis for the revolutionary politics the emergent SPD leadership imputed to the working class; there was only the *political* rupture of the 1860s and a verbal radicalism that the leadership could graft onto the movement in the abnormal

3. Ritter, *Die Arbeiterbewegung im Wilhelminischen Reich,* 127, 187.
4. Matthias, "Kautsky und der Kautskyanismus," 151–97.
5. Gustav Mayer, "Die Trennung der proletarischen von der bürgerlichen Demokratie in Deutschland, 1863–1870," in *Radikalismus, Sozialismus und bürgerliche Demokratie* (Frankfurt, 1912/1969), 108–78.

conditions of the Antisocialist Law and because of the SPD's ghettolike isolation from the rest of German society and the political system, an isolation then perpetuated by the authoritarianism of the government and the major employers. Being spurned by its potential liberal allies, the German labor movement retreated into revolutionary rhetoric and class-based self-sufficiency (by contrast with, for example, its counterparts in Britain, the Low Countries, and Scandinavia, where socialist politics acquired a far more moderate and reformist profile). The SPD's Marxist tradition was the mirror image of the backwardness and authoritarianism of the official system.[6]

This scenario has been applied with particular force to the Social Democratic subculture, which is perhaps the *locus classicus* of the argumentation. On the one hand, the subculture has seemed a striking achievement, which extended the reach of the SPD beyond the more immediate means of trade union membership and party affiliation to a much broader sense of class identification by servicing workers' wider social and cultural needs. It reduced SPD supporters' dependence on and vulnerability to the authoritarianism of the dominant culture; it promoted workers' collective self-reliance; and it built a sense of pride and confidence in working-class cultural capacity. It provided everything from newspapers, lending libraries, educational services, and artistic associations to sporting opportunities, gymnastic clubs, choruses, cycling societies, special sections for women and youth, legal advice, welfare services, consumer cooperatives, and burial clubs. In theory the SPD subculture gave the working class a protected environment imbued with socialist values, which culturally and institutionally was the real materialization of the Marxist ideal of class solidarity. But at the same time, it is claimed, the subculture was mainly defensive and in its substance profoundly unrevolutionary. Following Guenther Roth, most historians have stressed the hollowness of the SPD's revolutionary rhetoric and the party's actual inability to present a genuine alternative to the dominant culture and its prevailing social and political values—its tendency, that is, simply to reproduce the given features of bourgeois culture beneath a militant but defensive gloss of laborist independence. The usual procedure has been to juxtapose the formal and rhetorical claims of the SPD's Marxist intellectuals with the "reality" of the movement's actual behavior: attitudes toward internationalism and nationalism, views of the monarchy, the reading habits of party members,

6. Werner Conze, "Vom 'Pöbel' zum 'Proletariat': Sozialgeschichtliche Voraussetzung für den Sozialismus in Deutschland," *Vierteljahresschrift für Sozial-und Wirtschaftsgeschichte* 41 (1954): 33–64; idem, "Der Beginn der deutschen Arbeiterbewegung," in *Festschrift für Hans Rothfels,* ed. Waldemar Besson and Friedrich von Gaertringen (Göttingen, 1963), 323–38; Werner Conze and Dieter Groh, *Die Arbeiterbewegung in der nationalen Bewegung* (Stuttgart, 1966).

the repertoire of socialist choruses, the socially integrative function of sporting and recreational clubs, the orthodox and "traditional" character of SPD cultural politics, and in general the movement's conventional morality—all these are held to illustrate the "thinness" of the SPD's revolutionary character, which was the property of a restricted group of theorists and intellectuals out of touch with the real outlook of the ordinary worker.[7]

Where does this leave us? That is, how do these observations relate to our immediate theme of the labor movement and the intellectuals?

The dominant view reflects underlying assumptions about how "ideology"—or, more accurately, the formal, public, and programmatic outlook of a movement and the specialists responsible for formulating and reproducing it ("intellectuals")—functions in the life of a social movement. A movement's ideology, in this view, particularly the more it is based on complex and mentally exacting philosophical, economic, or other justifications, and particularly if it's radical (e.g., Marxism in the socialist movements before 1914, or feminism in the West since the late 1960s), is mainly the concern of "middle-class intellectuals." A movement's theory or coherent philosophy has a tangential or tenuous relation to the lives of its ordinary supporters, it is thought, whose needs and interests lie elsewhere. In fact, the behavior and attitudes of the working class (or any other subordinate class, such as the peasantry) show a remarkable continuity and resilience in the face of political efforts to shape or change them, it is argued: it is notoriously hard to effect value change via policy, and when attitudes shift, they do so as a result less of conscious political interventions than of long-term structural change, particularly in the standard of living. More specifically, what we now call "traditional working-class culture" was originally shaped by the processes of urban industrialization and state formation between the late nineteenth century and World War II, and when it began to decompose, it did so in response to the new experiences of the postwar boom. In neither case, it is thought, were the strategic visions of the socialist movement formative influences on the process, and from the vantage of the late twentieth century, the European socialist parties are increasingly represented (and not only by their enemies) as uncomprehending and irrelevant, speaking for a class constituency that has already moved on, behind principles that have definitively had their day.

The Marxist theory of the SPD, then, programmatically embodied in

---

7. Apart from Roth, *Social Democrats in Imperial Germany,* see Vernon Lidtke, *The Alternative Culture: Socialist Labor in Imperial Germany* (New York, 1985), and Dieter Langewiesche, "The Impact of the German Labour Movement on Workers' Culture," *Journal of Modern History* 59 (1987): 506–23.

the Erfurt synthesis of immediate and fundamental goals, was largely external to the working class. Ideology in this sense appears only as some system of formal belief generated outside the day-to-day experience of the SPD's ordinary supporters and with dubious relevance to their lives. It could take hold only because of the peculiar circumstances of the Antisocialist Law and the reactionary Prusso-German state, and was absorbed by workers only in "abnormal" moments of crisis (such as the German Revolution), and then only crudely and simplistically, spongelike, with little dialectical interaction.[8]

Against this line of argument we must insist on the value of a more sophisticated notion of ideology. In the above usage "ideology" is still taken to refer to formal systems of belief, normally codified into party doctrines (SPD Marxism), which are then contrasted to a social or economic "reality" (the "real" attitudes of the German working class). The political then becomes confined to a more or less separate sphere, which from time to time makes an ad hoc junction with working-class realities. Implicitly, ideology becomes something that happens (or perhaps fails to happen) inside people's heads, with traces to be found mainly on the printed page. By contrast, we need to remind ourselves that ideology is also a dimension of human transactions in general as well as being localized in various kinds of formal statements, and is bound up with questions of identity and subjectivity. In that sense the ideological is every bit as real as the social, the cultural, and the economic, to which it is often counterposed. Ideology is materially and continuously embodied in institutions, practices, and social relations—in what people do and in the structured context in which they do it. Ideology is constantly at work on our everyday experiences in all sorts of ways—direct and mediated, visible and less visible, conscious and unconscious. Here, for instance, is Paul Willis on a similarly foreshortened conception of culture that juxtaposes it to work:

> This view is wrong not because it mistakes the nature of work, but because it mistakes the nature of *culture*. Culture is not artifice and manners, the preserve of Sunday best, rainy afternoons and concert halls. It is the very material of our daily lives, the bricks and mortar of our most commonplace understandings, feelings and responses. We rely on cultural patterns and symbols for the minute, and unconscious social reflexes that make us social and collective beings: we are therefore most

---

8. This view has its counterpart in the idea that a socialist consciousness can be brought to the working class only by political activists—intellectuals by function, who are free of the day-to-day material pressures and practicalities of the class struggle. This view is most frequently attributed to Lenin, but it was held also by Kautsky and other leading theoreticians of the Second International.

deeply embedded in our culture, when we are at our most natural and spontaneous, if you like, at our most "work-a-day".[9]

Ideology is to be similarly extensively understood.

Two points follow if we accept this argument. First, the dichotomy between ideology and everyday experience, where the former means "an intellectual system imported into working-class ranks by an outside intelligentsia" and the latter means the immediate or "spontaneous" culture of the working class itself (or "a set of perceptions and values into which individual workers are socialized through innumerable agencies, through their backgrounds, work and home environment"), makes no sense, because ideology is also completely implicated in the structures and processes of everyday life if we accept the broader understanding of ideology I have proposed. The everyday culture of the working class may seem naive, but in practice it is continuously shaped, shifted, and reproduced by complex interactions with all manner of agencies coming from "outside," including churches, charitable and philanthropic organizations, employers, hucksters, entrepreneurs, police, schools, state welfare, commercial entertainment, parties, voluntary societies, and—of course—trade unions and the Socialist Party. There is no reason why we should exclude the SPD and its subculture from the range of influences (the "innumerable agencies") that act on the native culture of the working class in this sense.[10]

But second, the transmission lines between the SPD rank and file and the party ideology were far more numerous and densely variegated than the mainstream approach allows, particularly if we adopt the extended, Gramscian definition of intellectual. "Intellectuals" in this notation were not just the leading theoreticians, such as Kautsky, or its communicators, such as the journalists and full-time speakers and agitators, but all the officials, functionaries, and agitators that made the subculture tick, and indeed any self-educating, improving working person who found a home in the movement. These were the "organic intellectuals" of the working class in Gramsci's interesting sense, and they certainly included the "practical men" of the trade union and party apparatuses whom such historians as Ritter, Hans-Josef Steinberg, and Matthias raise up against the unrepresentative purveyors of the official Marxist theory (the "intellectuals" in the narrower sense).

9. Paul Willis, *Learning to Labour: How Working-Class Kids Get Working-Class Jobs* (Farnborough, 1977), 120.

10. The quotations are from Dick Geary, "Identifying Militancy: The Assessment of Working-Class Attitudes towards State and Society," in *The German Working Class, 1888–1933,* ed. Richard J. Evans (London, 1982), 241, and Geary's *European Labour Protest, 1848–1939* (London, 1981), 52.

The SPD's attitude toward "culture"—and here the assumptions were largely common to right and left—was conventional and nonsubversive. It was certainly consciously oppositional (if only because the efforts of the state to censor and illegalize the movement's cultural activities left it no choice), and the belief in the liberating power of knowledge and the desire to overturn existing monopolies on academic education were extremely radical in a society predicated on extreme inequalities in these respects. But the goal of the SPD was avowedly the "civilization" and "cultural improvement of the working class" *(Veredelung des Arbeiters)* in the sense of the established "high culture" and the reception of existing (bourgeois) cultural goods. The main purpose of the educational and cultural arms of the movement was to bring its working-class supporters "up" to the level of the educated middle class. In consequence, the ability of the SPD subculture to offer some kind of counterhegemonic alternative to the official values of the *Kaiserreich* remained stymied, and the striking cultural potential of its broader community-centeredness became subsumed in an extremely conventional conception of education. There were two main dimensions to this stance:

First, the SPD's cultural politics was positively disposed toward existing "high culture," whether in the formal arts in the form of classical literature, theater, art, and music or in the broader area of taste, morality, and sensibility. In this sense the workers were expected to be serious consumers, as opposed to amateurish autodidacts. The progressive political outlook aligned the party's cultural experts broadly with the Naturalists of the 1880s (especially Ibsen, Strindberg, Zola), and this orientation encouraged suspicion and distance in relation to the cultural radicalism and experiment of the later artistic avant garde. Even representatives of the SPD's left tended to take up conservative aesthetic positions in this respect. The conflicts in and around the Freie Volksbühne in the early 1890s and the role of Franz Mehring are a good example of this effect.[11]

Second, at a fundamental cultural/ideological level, this approach allowed old values to go unchallenged and an existing structure of assumptions to be replicated. As Adelheid von Saldern says: "The party activists wanted to live worthy, upstanding, moral, moderate, and disciplined lives: on the one hand, to show the workers who were not yet organized a good example; on the other hand, to show bourgeois society that one was up to all tasks, that one deserved good standing and respect."[12] Quite apart from the uncritical relationship toward existing morality and cultural values this stance encouraged, it also stigmatized certain aspects of

11. Cecil W. Davies, *Theatre for the People: The Story of the Volksbühne* (Manchester, 1977).
12. Adelheid von Saldern, *Auf dem Wege zum Arbeiter-Reformismus: Parteialltag in sozialdemokratischer Göttingen* (Frankfurt, 1984), 235.

"rough" and disorderly working-class culture, out of which workers were to be "enlightened."[13] In this respect, the SPD's oppositional cultural politics was potentially compromised by a heavily conservative cultural sensibility, which incorporated everything from attitudes toward hierarchy and authority, the use of military language, and the fetishizing of order and discipline to the latent patriotism and patriarchal views of the family, child raising, and the place of women.[14]

What about the intellectuals in the immediate, harder sociological sense? Given the transformation of the intelligentsia, in which the rise of "the new middle class" relativized the social position and prestige of the traditional educated stratum (those with academic qualifications, *Bildung* in its German connotation of education combined with culture) through the growth of the service sector, new white-collar divisions of labor, and processes of feminization and proletarianization, it makes sense to proceed sequentially. In the early period of the socialist movement (1860s–1890s) there were clearly individual recruits from the existing *Bildungsbürgertum* (e.g., Wilhelm Liebknecht, Georg von Vollmar), who found their place in the movement as full-time cultural functionaries—usually as journalists and parliamentarians in leading positions in the party. At this early stage such leading personalities were often lionized as a charismatic "regal" alternative to the present ruling elite: Ferdinand Lassalle is an obvious case, but Wilhelm Liebknecht and August Bebel received this treatment too.[15] By the period of consolidation (from the 1890s and the lifting of the Antisocialist Law, however, such hero worship was less central to the SPD's political culture. By 1914 the expansion of the movement was already enabling it to generate its own cadres, epitomized by Friedrich Ebert, who rose through the ranks to become one of the secretaries on the national executive in 1905 and later co-chairman, a new type of machine politician. By 1914 there were some 150 to 200 full-time party officials, another 800 to 850 managers and journalists employed by the party press, and some 3,000 officials in the trade unions.

The party's expansion necessarily affected the social profile of its leadership: only seven of the twenty-five men (there were two women) who held office on the national executive between 1890 and 1933 were from professional white-collar occupations, and all were either parliamentari-

13. See Geoff Eley, "Labor History, Social History, *Alltagsgeschichte:* Experience, Culture, and the Politics of the Everyday—A New Direction for German Social History?" *Journal of Modern History* 61 (1989): 297–343, for further discussion of this point.

14. See also Brigite Emig, *Die Veredelung des Arbeiters: Sozialdemokratie als Kulturbewegung* (Frankfurt, 1980).

15. Carl Levy, "Socialism and the Educated Middle Classes in Western Europe, 1870–1914," in *Intellectuals, Universities, and the State in Western Modern Societies,* ed. Ron Eyerman, Lennart G. Svensson, and Thomas Söderquist (Berkeley, 1987), 167–68.

ans, party journalists, trade union officials, or party officials at the time of their election; to take a middle-tier leadership group, the members of the reorganization commission of 1911, only four of the nineteen members with known original occupations were not workers.[16] One group *not* present in the movement's formal positions, interestingly enough, were academics, artists, and literary intellectuals (by contrast to their counterparts in Italy, say, who were highly visible and prominent). Moreover, if we move further away from the professionalized core of the movement to its wider penumbra of influence, we find that the phenomenon of the fellow traveler—the intellectual in the academic or artistic world who broadly sympathized with socialism as the coming vehicle of modern ideas and progressive reform—was also not visibly present; we find no equivalent of Fabianism or radical bohemia. Such a development was essentially precluded before 1914 by the centralistically repressive political and intellectual culture of official Germany, and by the practical impossibility of holding a civil service appointment or academic position as a socialist. Despite some signs of limited change in this respect in the 1890s, German academics identified with socialism at the expense of their careers: "More than 30 percent of the SPD's editors were academicians suffering interruptions of their first careers."[17] Socialist thinkers had no choice but to make their careers inside the movement, in the press and such institutions as the party school, in isolation from wider intellectual exchange. The contrast with Italy here is instructive: in 1903, of the 33 Socialist parliamentarians in the Gruppo Parlementare Socialista (GPS), 29, or 88 percent, were university graduates, including a significant group of nobles and haute bourgeois, as against only 13 of the 81 SPD Reichstag deputies, or 16 percent; among the GPS graduates, 9 were also professors, three times the total for the entire German Reichstag.[18]

If we formulate this situation in terms of Gramsci's distinction between organic and traditional intellectuals, we may say that the SPD had very little ability before 1914 to detach traditional intellectuals from their existing political/ideological allegiances, which were sustained by the *Kaiserreich*'s antisocialist political culture and certain hard realities of professional survival. When the party did manage to win such intellectuals, the

16. W. L. Guttsmann, *The German Social Democratic Party, 1875–1933* (London, 1981), 251–59.

17. Levy, "Socialism and the Educated Middle Classes," 166; Sven Eric Leidman, "Institutions and Ideas: Mandarins and Non-Mandarins in the German Academic Intelligentsia," *Comparative Studies in Society and History* 18 (1986): 119–44. Also Fritz Ringer, *The Decline of the German Mandarins: The German Academic Community, 1890–1922* (Cambridge, Mass., 1969), and Konrad Jarausch, *Students, Society, and Politics in Imperial Germany* (Princeton, 1982).

18. Levy, "Socialism and the Educated Middle Classes," 168.

latter sacrificed their conventional place in society and were absorbed into the movement apparatus in a way that perpetuated the gulf between the two.

On the other hand, the SPD had created an institutional and "subcultural" environment in which large numbers of organic intellectuals could be produced. Despite the subculture's frequently described political ambivalence and its tendency simply to ape the dominant culture, the development of its own intellectuals amounted to a considerable organizational and ideological achievement. It made a very big difference, for example, that the manifold activities of the subculture were conducted and coordinated within the frame of a single national movement and articulated within a coherent and radical political perspective, rather than being decentralized and fragmented around innumerable sectional and local loyalties, as in Britain. Moreover, the party now had an institutional basis for negotiation, for confronting the dominant culture on the egalitarian and democratic issues of access and participation, and for the transforming assimilation of elements of bourgeois ideology and culture. In other words, the autonomous strengths of the subculture gave the movement's organic intellectuals a greater possibility of appropriating the dominant culture for their own purposes, rather than simply vice versa.

The subculture gave organic intellectuals what was precisely lacking in the conventional society—that is, a free and protected space for the pursuit of ideas and an intellectual freedom that inadequate guarantees for civil liberties had denied in society at large (e.g., in the universities). In the SPD the movement looked after its own in this sense. Friedrich Ebert is usually presented as the archetypal "machine man," but he was also a classic example of the skilled-worker organic intellectual whose opportunities for self-education and political activity were created by the party's protected enclave—whom the party "made" as a political subject/actor, in fact. Originally a saddler by trade, who became a baker and thence politically active through the local bakers' union, trades council, and party press commission, he worked as a reporter on the local SPD paper and operated a licensed inn while running the Bremen party before rising to the national executive in 1905. Which particular political direction Ebert took was less important than the basic context that produced him.

Carl Levy usefully distinguishes between two types of organic intellectuals before 1914 in this sense: on the one hand, "a certain gray area of former workers, would-be journalists, and skillful machine men who might have working-class roots but who were born late enough to enter the first wave of new white-collar workers"; on the other hand, the trade union officials, who would also have had working-class origins. The former were "quintessentially social mediators," who from 1900 played a disproportionately key role in shaping the leading profile of socialist politics. But their prominence also presupposed a division of labor with the "practical men" of the unions, who knew how to handle the rank and file—"They possessed a knowledge of industrial conditions and working-class life in that intimate way that the 'grays,' the lower-middle class, or the university socialists could never hope to acquire."[19]

Finally, an organic intellectual was also any working-class autodidact who found his or her way through the subculture to political activity— what Levy calls "the self-educated, the new men and women of socialism's voluntary associations, those who most keenly felt the demands of both manual and mental work," and resolved their frustrations through an "existential break" that brought them into the "white-collar world": "The party or trade-union organizer's salary (even if initially modest and accompanied by legal and physical dangers) replaces the precarious wage packet; work-time discipline is modified dramatically (even if long hours remain the rule); and perhaps most importantly one experiences geographical mobility and new circles of friends and colleagues."[20] This type, often but not always from a skilled craft background, was crucial to the culture of socialism before 1914. But while such men (and sometimes women) remained in evidence in the revolutionary years after 1917–18, the phenomenon of autonomously (and usually idiosyncratically) self-educated worker-intellectuals increasingly subsided before the newer phenomena of party-trained functionaries, state-educated upwardly mobile workers, and university academics, who now came to form the emergent left intelligentsia.[21]

What Changed under Weimar?

The shifts in this period occur on several levels, which I can address here only with brief, rather telegrammatic suggestions.

The most familiar feature of the Weimar landscape from our point of view was the radicalization of the artists (i.e., creative intellectuals in literature, theater, painting, and architecture), most dramatically (and ineffectually) represented from a political point of view by the Rat Geistiger Arbeiter (Council of Intellectual Workers), formed in the midst of the German Revolution on November 10, 1918. Over the longer term large numbers of intellectuals gravitated toward either the SPD or the German

19. Ibid., 174–75.

20. Carl Levy, "Introduction: Historical and Theoretical Themes," in *Socialism and the Intelligentsia, 1880–1914*, ed. Levy (London, 1987), 23.

21. See esp. Stuart Macintyre, *A Proletarian Science: Marxism in Britain, 1917–1933* (Cambridge, 1980), together with Jonathan Rée, *Proletarian Philosophers* (Oxford, 1984).

Communist Party (KPD), but the febrile cultural radicalism of the Weimar Republic was much larger than that party-oriented opinion, producing both the formal innovations that distinguished the period in the arts and a new intellectual public for democratic politics. Most biographical evidence indicates that the shock of the war was the crucial radicalizing experience in this respect.[22] At the same time, most discussions of this phenomenon place it in a surrounding context of modernism, and a related argument is also often made regarding the artist's changing place in society (i.e., structurally speaking in relation to the market, private patronage, and the state). In both cases, obviously, the argument goes back before 1914, and in the German context the self-conscious emergence of a radical literary-artistic intelligentsia claiming a voice in politics certainly can be found by 1911 (e.g., when *Die Aktion* was launched). Yet most work is still remarkably impressionistic, focused either on individual biographies, on textual analysis, or on wide-ranging cultural criticism, as opposed to the sociological type of approach.[23]

The questions for our purposes are: What were the parameters of the experience that produced this radical intelligentsia (in conjunctural and generational terms)? And what were the material (institutional, sociological, economic) conditions of its existence? It is distressing that we still lack a sociology of the Weimar intelligentsia in this sense, as opposed to a library of indifferently grounded cultural histories.[24] Briefly, I suggest the following:

Although we shouldn't underestimate the restrictions and repressiveness of the Weimar legal system against the left (the harassment and banning of agitprop-style activity, the censorship of film, and the general policing of culture, quite apart from the repression unleashed against

22. For one of the best examples, see Hans Hess, *Georg Grosz* (London, 1974), and Uwe M. Schneede, *George Grosz: His Life and Work* (New York, 1979); and, more generally, Robert Wohl, *The Generation of 1914* (Cambridge, Mass., 1979).

23. Until such serious social history begins to be produced, stimulating conceptual frameworks can be found in Raymond Williams, *The Politics of Modernism: Against the New Conformists* (London, 1989), and Perry Anderson, "Modernity and Revolution," *New Left Review* 144 (March–April 1984): 96–113; reprinted in *Marxism and the Interpretation of Culture*, ed. Cary Nelson and Lawrence Grossberg (Urbana, 1988), 317–33, with Discussion, 334–38. For the changing social context of the art market, see Robin Lenman, "Politics and Culture: The State and the Avant-Garde in Munich, 1886–1914," in *Society and Politics in Wilhelmine Germany*, ed. Richard J. Evans (London, 1978), 90–111; Robin Lenman, "Painters, Patronage, and the Art Market in Germany, 1850–1914," *Past and Present* 123 (1989): 109–40; and Peter Paret, *The Berlin Secession: Modernism and Its Enemies in Imperial Germany* (Cambridge, Mass., 1980).

24. The best are still the works of John Willett: *The Theatre of Bertolt Brecht* (London, 1959); *The Theatre of Erwin Piscator* (London, 1978); and *The New Sobriety, 1917–1933: Art and Politics in the Weimar Period* (London, 1978). See also Roy Pascal, *From Naturalism to Expressionism: German Literature and Society, 1880–1918* (London, 1973).

political and industrial militancy), one basic reason for the flourishing of a left intelligentsia was the stronger constitutional guarantee (and to a significant but varying extent public subsidy) of freedom of expression. The democratizing of the Constitution and strengthening of civil liberties was the obvious precondition for an atmosphere of cultural experiment, while the relaxing of the old controls and conformities in public employment also extended the boundaries of legitimate opinion. Thus Heinrich Schulz, the SPD's educational and youth expert before 1914 and in many ways the moving spirit behind the party's education committees and the party school, had had no choice but to abandon his hopes of a teaching career and to make his life inside the protected space of the movement. Under Weimar he was secretary of state in the Ministry of the Interior (1919–27), with a much broader societal and public arena available. Furthermore, his counterparts now had the option of placing themselves at the service of the movement without automatically sacrificing conventional careers.[25] To some extent the universities also now provided some autonomous space for critical intellectual work, at least for a semi-independent enclave such as the Institut für Sozialforschung in the relatively new University of Frankfurt.

In the few years before 1914, there was a definite quickening in the discourse of the "artist/intellectual and society," in which "intellect" or "the spiritual" *(Geist)* was invested with a special mission and responsibilities for the national well-being in a time of massive social change and diminished bearings. This development was a commentary both on the sociocultural consequences of metropolitan industrialization and on the specific indeterminacy of the artist's social situation—"a symptom of unease issuing from the realization by intellectuals that such a supposedly elevated and free agency as intellect should in fact be enchained by something so base and expedient as money."[26] Such a discourse produced a wide spectrum of articulations before 1914, whose polar extremes were the apolitical aestheticism of the Stefan George circle and the political messianism of *Die Aktion*. The latter was crucial to the radicalism of many artistic intellectuals in the revolutionary conjuncture of 1918–23, before what seemed to be normal life briefly resumed. The paradigmatic contrast is in the career of Bruno Taut, between the Taut of the *Gläserne Kette* in 1919, spinning his crystal castles in the air, and the Taut of *Die neue Wohnung* in 1924, settling down to the famous public housing projects of Frankfurt and Berlin. Of course, this transformation too has its material

25. Wilfried van der Will and Rob Burns, "The Politics of Cultural Struggle: Intellectuals and the Labour Movement," in *The Weimar Dilemma: Intellectuals in the Weimar Republic*, ed. Anthony Phelan (Manchester, 1985), 180–82.

26. Ibid., 167.

context, because while Taut was chief architect to the SPD city of Magde-
burg during 1921–23, economic conditions were such that only one of
his major buildings was built.[27] Again: some systematic social history of
the artist in society is badly missing from the literature.

It was certainly the war that brought the cultural unease of the intellectuals in the narrower artistic sense to a political head. The horrors of the
front galvanized a critique of the old governing order in Central Europe,
until the popular radicalizations and anticipated military collapse of
1917–18 brought individuals to a perhaps unanticipated moral political
choice. Thus Béla Balázs pondered the prospects of a revolution: "I *would
not* participate . . . (I would participate only in a revolution of the
soul). . . . But if, by accident, the battle reached me on the barricade, I
would no longer run away. The question is this: Where does the barricade start?"[28]

However we conceptualize the coordinates of this radicalization, the
years 1911/14–1917/18 produced for the first time a dissenting artistic
intelligentsia that was broadly sympathetic to the left—the category of
the fellow traveler, whose existence was effectively precluded before 1914.
In characterizing this phenomenon, we might distinguish three separate
left-intellectual milieux, once the turbulence of 1917–23 had died down.
First, many of the most radical cultural innovators gravitated toward the
KPD, partly under the inspirational impact of the Bolshevik Revolution,
partly through disillusionment with the SPD, partly through antibour-
geois cultural militancy in impatience with what seemed a shoddy compromise republic; in this sense, one road led directly from Berlin Dada
in 1917–18 to International Workers' Aid (IAH) and the beginnings of
the Münzenberg machine in 1922. A second, more amorphous milieu
extended from unaffiliated or non-Marxist leftists of various stripes to left
liberals and sympathizers of the SPD, who took their stand primarily on
the new but unfinished democratic legality of the Weimar Constitution.
This critical democratic milieu was typified by the journal *Die Weltbühne*
and its circle.[29] A final milieu was more institutionally embedded in the
universities, and is best represented by the Frankfurt School and what is
often viewed as a withdrawal from politics into the academy.[30] In fact,
the disengagement was a good deal less complete than such a verdict

27. Ian Boyd Whyte, *Bruno Taut and the Architecture of Activism* (Cambridge, 1982);
Willett, *Theatre of Erwin Piscator,* 92.

28. Joseph Zsuffa, *Béla Balázs: The Man and the Artist* (Berkeley, 1987), 58.

29. Istvan Deak, *Weimar Germany's Left-Wing Intellectuals: A Political History of Weltbühne and Its Circle* (Berkeley, 1968).

30. Martin Jay, *The Dialectical Imagination: A History of the Frankfurt School and the
Institute of Social Research, 1923–50* (London, 1973), 3; Perry Anderson, *Considerations on
Western Marxism* (London, 1976).

might imply, and the specifically university milieu also shaded into areas of professional/administrative activity that return us to the broader domain of intellectual activity in the extended definitional sense. Here the construction of a putatively social democratic state during the 1920s, particularly in the overlapping areas of housing, welfare, education, and public health, defined the political space. Hans Speier, who pioneered research on white-collar workers in the late Weimar years, is a perfect example of this imbrication. On finishing his university studies he became a model member of the left professional intelligentsia in Berlin—editor for a large publishing house, affiliated with the Deutsche Hochschule für Politik (another quasi-university institution), the SPD's Labor Education program, and the city social service apparatus, and married to a municipal pediatrician in Wedding.[31]

It's impossible to leave this question of intellectual radicalization without mentioning the sense of forward movement, of opening into a new future, and of having burned one's bridges. The road to the future was not assured because it had begun with one catastrophe (the Great War) and continued through another (the revolutionary turbulence and the inflation). As Hobsbawm says of his own background, "the Jewish middle-class culture of Central Europe after the First World War" was defined "under the triple impact of the collapse of the bourgeois world in 1914, the October Revolution and anti-Semitism." In the circumstances—"catastrophe and problematical survival," existential indeterminacy, and passionately polarized political options—the revolutionary future seemed the only one that worked.[32] John Willett makes the same point, referring to a broadly political "sense of direction . . . based on the creative artist's conscious involvement with a new society—new both in its structures and in its material resources—that had arisen out of the horrors of the First World War . . . [and] founded . . . on a generally sympathetic alertness to what was going on in the new Soviet Russia."[33] Ultimately it was this sense of historical *movement,* the exceptional urgencies of the conjuncture of 1914–23, that sprung intellectuals loose from the pathways they would more likely have followed in, say, 1910.

In terms of the Gramscian schema, therefore, the labor movement had acquired incomparably better opportunities for detaching "traditional" intellectuals from their established positions and allegiance; and while divided itself, it managed to become a powerful pole of attraction for the artistic and professional/administrative intelligentsia, in both its Social

---

31. See Hans Speier, *German White-Collar Workers and the Rise of Hitler* (New Haven, 1986); and for more on this milieu, see Atina Grossmann, *Reforming Sex: The German Movement for Birth Control and Abortion Reform, 1920–1950* (Oxford, 1995).

32. Hobsbawm, "Intellectuals and the Class Struggle," 250–51.

33. Willett, *Theatre of Erwin Piscator,* 225.

Democratic and Communist fractions, in their very different ways. But what of the "organic" intellectuals? Most obviously, the old subculture was to a great extent duplicated once the KPD stabilized its own organization after 1923: during the revolutionary years the national party splits and factions still bore an uncertain relation to local working-class cultures, which still managed an impressive degree of nonsectarian solidarity, particularly in the workplace, and the unitary organization persisted until the end of the 1920s in areas of the subculture (notably the sporting and musical movements); but by the mid-1920s the political culture of the working class was definitively divided against itself.[34] Moreover, the sociology of the SPD/KPD difference is also well known, with a younger, less "aristocratic," less securely employed (if they were employed at all), and nonbureaucratic (in the sense of officeholding before 1914) sector of the working class entering the KPD.

Second, more than just being split, the labor movement now incorporated two fundamentally different systems of political socialization, each increasingly bureaucratic and centralist in its way. Third, the number of people holding office in the SPD continued to grow. By 1925 the party had 417 full-time employees (as opposed to 150 to 200 in 1914), some 1,500 journalists and managers were employed by the party press (as against 800 to 850 in 1914), and by 1930 the trade unions employed 6,575 people (some 3,000 in 1914).[35] But fourth, the distance between the constituted apparatuses of the two parties (particularly at the national level) and the rank-and-file support was also growing, and the gulf was replicated in a more serious disjunction between the official culture of the labor movement (particularly in its older established Social Democratic and trade union subcultural form) and the everyday culture of the working class as a whole. Moreover, the more the actual diversity of the "working class" is acknowledged (along dimensions of gender, skill, age, white collar/blue collar, type of industry, employment/unemployment, and so on), the truer this observation becomes.

The most familiar discussions of this question focus on the bureaucratization of the SPD and its unions, cued by Robert Michels' classic critique,[36] together with the equally familiar processes of Stalinization in the KPD. Yet this doesn't really get to the heart of the issue, and the most

34. See James Wickham, "Social Fascism and the Division of the Working-Class Movement: Workers and Parties in the Frankfurt Area, 1928–30," *Capital and Class* 7 (1979): 1–34, and "Working-Class Movement and Working-Class Life: Frankfurt am Main during the Weimar Republic," *Social History* 8 (1983): 315–43; and Hartmann Wunderer, *Arbeitervereine und Arbeiterparteien: Kultur-und Massenorganisationen in der Arbeiterbewegung (1890–1933)* (Frankfurt, 1980).

35. Guttsmann, *German Social Democratic Party,* 246–47.

36. Robert Michels, *Political Parties* (New York, 1959).

sensitive research has shown that there was a good deal more reciprocity between apparatus and grass roots (particularly via the local and middle-level cadres) than this received wisdom suggests.[37] Particularly when we consider the question at the cultural level we need to find other ways of conceptualizing this disjunction between the working-class movement and the working-class culture it claimed to express; and while Adelheid von Saldern deals with this matter extensively,[38] there are two points I want to make.

First, some awareness of the opposition "rough/respectable" in the cultural formation of the working class is strongly implanted in British historiography, and the British influence has led to some useful airing of this issue in the German field.[39] More recently various West German historians have tackled it with the methods and perspectives of *Alltagsgeschichte* (history of everyday life), postulating a profoundly disabling gap between "the arena of formalized politics and large-scale political organization," into which the politics of the labor movement were increasingly subsumed, and the everyday culture of the workers "in the factory or the office, in the tenement house and on the street," where the "private" economy of needs and desires was really expressed.[40] Ultimately, it is the consistent inability of the labor movement to engage this everyday culture—and indeed its tendency to distance and look down on it, as something to moralize, discipline, and improve—that the discussion of working-class culture needs to address. Second, this problem of the culture gap was increasingly overdetermined by the growth of the new commercialized culture of mass entertainment and leisure, which powerfully impressed itself on socialists' consciousness in the 1920s. As the left was acutely aware, the labor movement now faced entirely new competition

37. See esp. Eve Rosenhaft, *Beating the Fascists? The German Communists and Political Violence, 1929–1933* (Cambridge, 1983).

38. Von Saldern, *Auf dem Wege zum Arbeiter-Reformismus;* "Arbeiterkulturbewegung in Deutschland in der Zwischenkriegszeit," in *Arbeiterkulturen zwischen Alltag und Politik: Beiträge zum europäischen Vergleich in der Zwischenkriegszeit,* ed. Friedhelm Boll (Vienna, 1986), 29–70.

39. Notably Evans, *German Working Class.*

40. See esp. Alf Lüdtke, "Organizational Order or *Eigensinn?* Workers' Privacy and Workers' Politics in Imperial Germany," in *Rites of Power: Symbolism, Ritual, and Politics since the Middle Ages,* ed. Sean Wilentz (Philadelphia, 1985), 303–33; Alf Lüdtke, "Cash, Coffee Breaks, Horseplay: *Eigensinn* and Politics among Factory Workers in Germany, circa 1900," in *Confrontation, Class Consciousness, and the Labor Process,* ed. Michael Hanagan and Charles Stephenson (New York, 1986), 65–95; Alf Lüdtke, ed., *Alltagsgeschichte: Theorien zur Rekonstruktion historischer Erfahrungen und Lebensweisen* (Frankfurt, 1989); Franz-Josef Brüggemeier, *Leben vor Ort: Ruhrbergleute und Ruhrbergbau, 1889–1919* (Munich, 1984); Lutz Niethammer and Alexander von Plato, eds., *Lebensgeschichte und Sozialstruktur im Ruhrgebiet, 1930–1960,* 2d ed. (Bonn, 1986); and for a detailed commentary Eley, "Labor History, Social History, *Alltagsgeschichte.*"

in the recreational and cultural sphere, because the new accessible technologies—"film, radio, gramophone, photography, travel, traffic, bicycle"[41]—proved immensely exciting, not least to working-class youth.

Now, there have been two opposing responses to this situation from a left cultural-political point of view. On the one hand, the 1920s may be said to have inaugurated a familiar left critique of mass culture and popular taste with the notion of commodity fetishism, a pessimistic response elaborated most completely by the Frankfurt School. And indeed, the new apparatus of the "culture industry," from the razzmatazz of the cinema and the burgeoning mass entertainment media to the growth of spectator sports, the star system, and the machineries of advertising and fashion, proved remarkably successful in servicing the "private economy of desire" in the 1920s, and arguably occupied precisely the human space of everyday life the labor movement had so badly neglected to fill. Significantly, once the labor movement's institutional infrastructure had been smashed after 1933, this "private" recreational domain was also the scene of the fascist state's most effective cultural activity.[42] As perceptive observers such as Ernst Bloch saw, fascism was not just the instrument of antidemocratic terror; it harnessed psychic needs and utopian longings that the left neglected at their peril. And by the same argument, the emerging popular culture was not simply an empty and depoliticized commercial corruption of traditional working-class culture; it also possessed a democratic authenticity of its own.[43]

On the other hand, therefore, this was precisely the dimension on which another section of left intellectual opinion fastened—the exciting potentials of both new technologies/media/forms of communication and new audiences, which defined the activity and thought of Walter Benjamin, Bertolt Brecht, Erwin Piscator, John Heartfield, George Grosz, and so on. The current resonance of this more affirmative response to the "mass culture" phenomenon is very impressive. Finally, the subject/addressee of this discourse was as much the new middle class as the proletariat in the traditional sense, and this orientation also finds its echoes in the late twentieth-century left's preoccupation with the politics of consumption and style ("designer socialism").

41. Von Saldern, "Arbeiterkulturbewegung in Deutschland," 59.

42. See Tim Mason, "The Workers' Opposition in Nazi Germany," *History Workshop Journal* 11 (1981): 120–37, and "Die Bändigung der Arbeiterklasse im nationalsozialistischen Deutschland: Eine Einleitung," in *Angst, Belohnung, Zucht und Ordnung: Herrschaftsmechanismen im Nationalsozialismus*, ed. Carola Sachse, Tilla Siegel, Hasso Spode, and Wolfgang Spohn (Opladen, 1982), 11–53; Victoria de Grazia, *The Culture of Consent: Mass Organization of Leisure in Fascist Italy* (Cambridge, 1981); and Luisa Passerini, *Fascism in Popular Memory: The Cultural Experience of the Turin Working Class* (Cambridge, 1987).

43. See Ernst Bloch, *Erbschaft dieser Zeit* (Frankfurt, 1962).

The formal discourse of "Weimar culture," in respect to the literary-artistic intellectuals whose ideas and legacies describe that conceptual space (e.g., the individuals who form the subjects of the works of Peter Gay and Walter Laqueur), was almost exclusively a male discourse. This fact is worth drawing attention to, given what we now know about the salience of "biological politics" in the interwar years in Germany, and given the importance of the "new woman" to the social and cultural history of the Weimar years and to the broader sociological phenomenon of the intelligentsia *qua* new middle class.[44] In fact, what we are now learning about the centrality of gender to such areas as employment, social policy, and public health in the Weimar Republic reemphasizes the desirability of revisiting the conventional notions of "Weimar culture" in this light.

Finally, it's impossible to leave this theme without pointing to the coherence of a distinctive Central European intelligentsia in the first three decades of the twentieth century. Now, whereas the boundaries of this intelligentsia were those of the historic German-speaking culture zone (which was limited to the official cultures of the Hohenzollern and Habsburg states and the literate culture of the educated, as opposed to the richer mosaic of the non-German ethnicities that also inhabited the region), there was perhaps relatively little interpenetration between the German and Austro-Hungarian intellectual circuits until the turn of the century. Arguably, the collapse of the Habsburg state in 1918, together with certain associated events (such as the defeat of the Hungarian Revolution in 1919, which created a major Hungarian left-intellectual diaspora in Vienna, Berlin, and Moscow), was necessary before the Central European intelligentsia in its full sense cohered.

Despite the inexorable encroachment of exclusive identities among the non-German nationalities of the Habsburg empire during its period of disintegration, there was still in 1900 a significant living legacy of cultural pluralism, which was most active at the level of a certain cosmopolitan intelligentsia. Here, for example, is the playwright Odon von Horvath's self-description: "If you ask me what is my native country, I answer: I was born in Fiume, grew up in Belgrade, Budapest, Pressburg, Vienna and Munich, and I have a Hungarian passport; but I have no fatherland. I am a very typical mix of old Austria-Hungary: at once Magyar, Croatian, German and Czech; my country is Hungary, my mother tongue is German."[45] We're more familiar with the paradoxes of language, culture, and nationality from the earlier nineteenth century—the well-known fact, for

44. E.g., Renata Bridenthal, Athina Grossmann, and Marion Kaplan, eds., *When Biology Becomes Destiny: Women in Weimar and Nazi Germany* (New York, 1984).
45. Jacques Rupnik, *The Other Europe* (London, 1988), 41.

instance, that František Palacký's history of Bohemia originally appeared in German. But there's a sense in which this cosmopolitan messiness still confused certain national filiations in the early decades of this century.

If we're to put a sociological value on this persistence, then it presumably has to do with the institutionalization among the intelligentsia and the urban middle classes more generally of a specifically German ideal of *Bildung,* which extended far outside Vienna into an urban network ordered around the major capitals of Budapest, Prague, Krakow, Bucharest, and Belgrade. German remained the lingua franca of Central European intellectual and artistic exchange.

To a great extent, the continuing reproduction of this cosmopolitan Central European culture had by 1900 devolved onto the shoulders of an enlightened Jewish bourgeoisie, particularly in Budapest and Prague. It's impossible to read Georg Lukács's oral memoirs, for instance, or the accounts of his early life by Michael Löwy and Mary Gluck, without being impressed by the salience of this bourgeois Jewish literary, academic, artistic, and dissenting Habsburg milieu.[46]

Another major tributary of this German-speaking cosmopolitan cultural stream was provided by pre-1914 Social Democracy. One of the most impressive features of Second International socialism in its Central European heartland was the facility with which major figures could move among Austria, Switzerland, Galicia, Bohemia, and Germany—whether we think of Karl Kautsky, Rosa Luxemburg, Rudolf Hilferding, or others. Moreover, there's a sense in which Austro-Marxism became a major life-support system for what remained of the Habsburg empire's cosmopolitanism—as the old joke had it Austrian Social Democracy was the most stable institution of the imperial order. The stability of the Austrian party mustn't be exaggerated, of course, because the party was riddled with its own greater-German assumptions. But nonetheless, the more principled elements of the pre-1914 party fought a very interesting long rear-guard action against the encroachment of a nationality-based politics.

Finally, as a result of the experiences of war and revolution between 1914 and 1921, this older socialist culture was thrown together with the radicalized younger generation of Jewish intellectuals, not least through the extrusion of the Hungarian radicals after the suppression of the Hungarian Soviet of 1919, to form the final coherent embodiment or manifestation of the distinct Central European intellectual culture before the Nazis obliterated it. By this I mean the generous-minded and highly intellectual radicalism we encounter in the memoirs and intellectual autobiog-

---

46. Georg Lukács, *Record of a Life: An Autobiographical Sketch* (London, 1983); Michael Löwy, *Georg Lukács: From Romanticism to Bolshevism* (London, 1979); and Mary Gluck, *Georg Lukács and His Generation, 1900–1918* (Cambridge, Mass., 1985).

raphies that have appeared in recent decades. Firmly bounded by the German-speaking culture zone of the nineteenth century, textured by the latter's traditions of *Bildung,* and turning around a Berlin-Prague-Vienna axis, this culture was shaped by the catharsis of war and revolution, as the bloated complacencies of imperial Europe collapsed in the consuming turbulence of 1917–18. It was also to a striking extent Jewish, although its post-1945 survival mainly in the émigré circles of London and New York has perhaps done something to exaggerate this impression. The uprooting and dispersal of this vibrant left-wing culture—and of course its brutal physical extermination—was one of fascism's lasting tragic achievements, given further impetus by the Cold War, the Stalinist purges, and the division of Europe. The very idea of Central Europe was banished from practical discourse, and has been revived only by the complex political effects of the late 1980s.

5

Were the Russian *Intelligenty* Organic Intellectuals?

Jane Burbank

As with so many phenomena in recent days and in the past, the term "intelligentsia" appears to have been a Polish contribution to Russian politics, a word that made its entrance into Russian in the mid-nineteenth century.[1] But it was Russian culture and particularly the Russian revolution of 1917 that gave the intelligentsia back to world history as a category to be taken seriously. For some in Western Europe and America, the intelligentsia meant danger—the specter of communism transformed into a recognizable, educated enemy; for others, the intelligentsia meant new horizons—the engaging promise that intellectuals could change the world; for still others, our predecessors in social science, the intelligentsia was simultaneously a moral and a theoretical dilemma—what was the place of the intelligentsia in historical processes, and how could it be defined, contained, or nourished, and to what purpose?

It was no accident, as Russians like to say, that the role of intellectuals became a problem in European culture simultaneously with the establishment of a socialist state, or, more accurately, with the unexpected survival of a government that declared itself to be building socialism. For Bolshevism after 1917 and into the 1920s put socialism into history in a new embodiment: intellectuals at the head of the "vanguard party" took upon

I am grateful to William Sewell and Barbara Walker for their readings of a draft of this chapter and to the organizers of and participants in the Seminar on Intellectuals and Social Action at Chapel Hill in 1989, for which the chapter was written.

1. The word was in use in Polish political literature in the 1840s: Andrzej Walicki, *Philosophy and Romantic Nationalism: The Case of Poland* (Oxford, 1982), 176–77, 396n. Russians, however, trace its origin to the 1860s and the literary works of Petr Boborykin, a minor Russian novelist. This claim to Russian roots was made by R. V. Ivanov-Razumnik in the first decade of the twentieth century (see his *Ob intelligentsii*, 2d ed. [St. Petersburg, 1910], 6) and has made its way into Western convention.

themselves the task of constructing a workers' state. It was this apparently real alternative to capitalist organization and to waiting for a workers' revolution that gave intellectuals a new kind of power, and thus made them a subject of political and scholarly discourse in the West. By the late 1920s this first confrontation with the concrete prospect of a different, noncapitalist future constructed under the guidance of intellectuals had produced a brilliant cluster of theoretical statements. Julien Benda's *La Trahison des clercs* (1928), Karl Mannheim's *Ideology and Utopia* (1929), the essays published in Georg Lukács's *History and Consciousness* (1919–22), Antonio Gramsci's commentaries later published as the *Prison Notebooks* (1929–35)—all written within a few years of each other—mark the historical specificity of this concern for intellectuals, their origins and functions, and their significance for the modern project.[2]

As Stephen Leonard's introduction to this volume suggests, the relation between the life of the mind and life in the world had long been a problematic of Western thought; what was different in the early twentieth century was the sharply politicized divide over how to describe and understand the intellectuals themselves. Western analyses at this time expressed the strong tension between theories based on ideas and theories based on society, a fundamental divergence that has continued in various guises to generate controversies in the social sciences. For those theorists who began with ideas, the essence of intellectuals' activity—what demanded description, explanation, and attention—was what they had to say, in particular the normative statements they brought to the shaping of the future. Thus Benda's seminal book accepts, indeed extols, the category of intellectuals as individuals "not of this world," whose reason for living is knowledge and creation; the "treason" that he decries is turning this "pure" knowledge into politics.[3] This approach could be taken from any political position—to attack or support intellectuals' ideas, to expose their fallacies or strengths in their own time or ours; what it took for granted was that ideas themselves provide the meaningful category for examination and are the defining essence of intellectual activity.

One consequence of the Russian Revolution with its apparent vindication of late nineteenth-century Marxism, however, was to revitalize materialist analysis and thus to focus inquiry concerning intellectuals on questions of class and social position, not ideas. But intellectuals, despite

---

2. Julien Benda, *The Treason of the Intellectuals* (1928), trans. Richard Aldington (New York, 1969); Karl Mannheim, *Ideology and Utopia: An Introduction to the Sociology of Knowledge*, ed. Louis Wirth and Edward Shils (New York, 1936); Georg Lukács, *History and Class Consciousness* (Cambridge, Mass., 1971); Antonio Gramsci, *Selections from the Prison Notebooks of Antonio Gramsci,* ed. Quinlin Hoare and Geoffrey Nowell Smith (New York, 1971).

3. Benda, *Treason of the Intellectuals,* 43–45.

their new power or potential power in modern politics, had no easily defined class place. From this puzzle emerged a different kind of investigation: who were the intellectuals, and what did their social position mean for politics? Here Mannheim's *Ideology and Utopia* provided a classic model of the attempt to situate intellectuals in society, both as an explanation of how they act and as a justification for their privileged place in a new "scientific" politics. For Mannheim, intellectuals were not a class but a "stratum" in bourgeois society, distinct from capitalists and workers through the possibility of possessing nondetermined and superclass perspectives.[4]

Mannheim's effort to retain a class-based history and to find a place in it for unconstrained and all-encompassing knowledge was one example of the opening of Marxism to a concern with consciousness in this period of expansive social inquiry. The most salient of these new directions in the postrevolutionary years, the one with the most resonance today in the typologies of intellectuals, was that taken by Antonio Gramsci. Gramsci, like Mannheim, recognized the power of knowledge to influence politics: from this vantage (and from his experience in Italy and Russia) emerged his notion of "hegemony" and the importance of cultural ascendancy to a revolutionary project.[5] Unlike Mannheim, Gramsci shunned a social grounding for intellectuals as a distinct entity or stratum; he instead connected intellectuals back to class, but in a differentiated way. Each class creates its own intellectuals, in Gramsci's fundamental challenge to the linkage of all intellectuals to a single class position,[6] and these "organic intellectuals" carry the organizing knowledge of their class and its particular interests. But organic intellectuals are not the only intellectuals in capitalist societies, Gramsci argued; there are others who bear the class interests of the past and whose consciousness is formed by the historically dominant culture. Moreover, these "traditional intellectuals"—priests, scholars, administrators—gain a certain freedom of thought and action by virtue of their privileged position in society. The import of this analysis for revolutionary politics was that the defense of working-class interests was not exclusively a task for proletarian intellectuals; the party of change had to capture the allegiance of traditional intellectuals who dominate the institutions of civil society. Thus Gramsci's writings, like Mannheim's, strayed creatively from a class-grounded view of intellectuals as a group, and provided an account—based on politics and culture—for why some

4. Mannheim, *Ideology and Utopia,* 156–63.

5. Hegemony was not a novel concept in Marxist discourse of the time; for an example, see Iulii Martov, *Obshchestvennye i umstvennye techeniia v Rossii, 1870–1905* (1910) (Leningrad/Moscow, 1924), 57.

6. That is, each class except the peasants, in a massive and elitist exception to Gramsci's generous notion that everyone can be an intellectual: Gramsci, *Prison Notebooks,* 6.

traditional intellectuals, born to dominant classes, might join the workers' cause. In addition, his concept of hegemony showed why the transformation of elite culture was essential to the success of socialism.

Postrevolutionary European theorists thus reflected the creative dissonance between different modes of analysis in their studies of intellectuals, and their considerations of ideas, class, and the politics of culture were prominent in many later theoretical disputes. Gramsci's attempt to bridge the highly charged gap between idealist and materialist perspectives anticipates in some respects the contemporary emphasis on the "discourse" of intellectuals, which regards intellectuals as simultaneously generating and representing a cultural context.[7] One intriguing perspective on intellectuals, an exotic outgrowth from the pole of class theory, emerged from Eastern Europe in the postwar period. This is the view, first presented to the West by Milovan Djilas and later elaborated by the Hungarian sociologists George Konrad and Ivan Szelenyi, that the intelligentsia in Eastern Europe had, by virtue of their management of the state-owned economy, in fact become a class, a ruling class.[8] The apparent idiosyncrasy of this perspective from within the communist sphere points up the historical specificity of Western theory, with its firm grounding in the civil society that Gramsci postulated.[9] In the construction of theory, it matters who controls or owns the means of production; it matters who controls the state; it makes a difference when intellectuals step into power and out of the intelligentsia.

What did the Russian intelligentsia have to do with these Western theories about intellectuals, besides helping to make an unexpected revolution and thereby opening up the subject to politics and culture? Did Western analyses of intellectuals—views focused on bourgeois societies—fit the Russian case? Or was the Russian intelligentsia a different phenomenon, and if so, how does it illuminate or modify Western theory? Or does it speak against a universalizing theory altogether—against the various projections of Western abstractions upon the world—and argue instead for a radical specificity of social organizations and their possibilities?

In the Soviet Union, the official definition of the intelligentsia was functional: the intelligentsia were the group, often a "layer," sometimes a class, of people who did mental work; in American terms, white-collar

---

7. For a discussion of discourse theory see David Hollinger, "The Return of the Prodigal: The Persistence of Historical Knowing," *American Historical Review* 94 (June 1989): 610–21.

8. Milovan Djilas, *The New Class* (New York, 1957); George Konrad and Ivan Szelenyi, *The Intellectuals on the Road to Class Power* (Brighton, 1979). Leon Trotsky, *The Revolution Betrayed* (1937) (New York, 1965), is a forerunner of this analysis.

9. Gramsci, *Prison Notebooks,* 15.

workers.[10] The intelligentsia and the two basic classes—the peasants and the "workers" (blue-collar, that is)—thus accounted for the entire population of the USSR, each component defined by its kind of work.

But this functional definition was not what Soviet intellectuals meant in conversation when they used the word *intelligentsiia,* or the singular *intelligent.* Their definition was based on attitudes, not work. An *intelligent* was a person with a particular attitude and aspirations, goals and ideas, and she was identified by those ideas rather than by her profession, position in society, or income. The essence of this attitude was moral—especially moral opposition to the injustices of the existing system and, more positively, commitment to the goal of creating a better society in its place. Underlying this self-definition of the intelligentsia was the assumption—an unquestioned one—that the *intelligent* as an individual was entitled to speak for the good of the social whole, that he spoke for the people and was the knowing conscience of the nation. It was the unexamined quality of this entitlement, the deep authenticity of the intelligentsia's sense of calling, that was most striking and unnerving to Western intellectuals and that still cries out for explanation.

These dual Soviet definitions of the intelligentsia—functional and attitudinal—would easily have been recognized by Russian intellectuals before 1917, in the first decades of the century. For them, too, the intelligentsia could be defined in two ways, although before the days of sure employment the functional definitions focused on knowledge and the preparation for mental labor. All people with a higher education could be categorized as the "broad intelligentsia" *(shirokaia intelligentsiia),* in contrast to the "real" intelligentsia, defined by their moral stance, their speaking for the people against the state. Unlike the relatively simple opposition between official and unofficial definitions in the Soviet period, however, the division of the intelligentsia into two separate categories and the need to decide who belonged in which were problems generated within prerevolutionary society. In the decades before the revolution, the intelligentsia had become an "accursed question" *(bol'noi vopros)* of Russian culture, a problem rather than a fact.

The problem was connected with the new opportunities for politics and culture that for a brief period (roughly 1895–1917) gave imperial Russia the semblance of a civil society. The explosion of numbers of professional women and men, of creative endeavors in the arts, of opportunities for political organization in 1905 and after made Russian intellectuals uneasily aware of their diversity and their lack of common purpose.

---

10. A scholarly Soviet dictionary defines "intelligentsia" as "workers of mental labor, having special training and knowledge in various aspects of science, technology, and culture": *Slovar' sovremennogo russkogo literaturnogo iazyka* (Moscow/Leningrad, 1956), 5:389.

In the new world opened up by the relatively permissive press regulations and the multiple forums for civic action, the old simplicities that had defined the intelligentsia in the past began to lose their hold. The revolution of 1905 in particular seemed to smash wide open the myths of united opposition to autocracy, of "the people" against "the state," of a simple leap into a free society. Not only did the autocracy manage to regain the political initiative after its near collapse, but the clear mandate of pre-1905 politics was spoiled by the subsequent elections to the dumas: the people did not all vote alike.

These threats to the presumption of authentic representation of the people and of progress made the intelligentsia more a problem than a reality and turned Russian intellectuals' consciousness back upon themselves, or to what they thought they were after 1905. This concern was expressed in several ways, one of them in history. In a number of mammoth publications, engaged *intelligenty* tried to trace the historical course of the intelligentsia in Russia, as if in historical progress a new confidence for the future could be found. In 1902 Pavel Miliukov, prominent liberal politician and historian, reissued several articles on Russian culture and politics in a volume titled *From the History of the Russian Intelligentsia* in order to make his writings on this topic more accessible.[11] Russian Marxists turned toward the past as well; in the aftermath of 1905, Iulii Martov, Aleksandr Potresov, and other leading Social Democrats participated in a massive study of the "social movement" in Russia.[12] In 1906 R. V. Ivanov-Razumnik, a populist, produced his two-tome *History of Russian Social Thought,* an instant classic that traced the intelligentsia's path from the eighteenth century to the beginning of the twentieth. Ivanov-Razumnik's answer to the question "What is the intelligentsia?" presented a synthesis of many definitions: "The intelligentsia is, aesthetically, anti-philistine; sociologically, a nonstate, nonclass, historically continuous group, characterized by the creation of new forms and ideals and the active introduction of these into life in the movement toward physical and mental, social and personal liberation of the personality."[13]

Each component of this definition could be examined separately, but the essence of Ivanov-Razumnik's work was to vitalize the intelligentsia as a historical continuity—to establish the sense of collective, long-term mission and progressive development that had been challenged in recent years. While functionally we may regard the Russian intellectuals' concern

11. See Miliukov's Introduction to his *Iz istorii russkoi intelligentsii* (1902), 2d ed. (St. Petersburg, 1903), vii.

12. Iulii Martov, A. N. Potresov, and P. P. Maslov, *Obshchestvennoe dvizhenie v Rossii v nachale XX-go v.,* 4 vols. (St. Petersburg, 1909–14).

13. R. V. Ivanov-Razumnik, *Istoriia russkoi obshchestvennoi mysli* (1911), 3d ed., 2 vols. (The Hague, 1969), 1:12.

for their own history—their belief in themselves as an ongoing "move-ment"—as a reply to individuals' increasing isolation in their times, this preoccupation with the past is surely one of the most characteristically Russian definitions of the intelligentsia. The insistence that there is "a history" of the intelligentsia reemerged in the Soviet period both in offi-cial scholarship, with its emphasis on the "revolutionary movement," and in unofficial dissident activities, such as the chronicling of the persecutions of the intelligentsia under Stalinism. Let me turn now to the historical tradition that Ivanov-Razumnik elaborated, one that has played so strong a role in providing Russian *intelligenty* with a collectivity.

What were the main moments in the intelligentsia's past, according to today's perspectives on Russian history?[14] Here I should note that overall the historiography of Russia and the Soviet Union is still highly depen-dent on questions and analyses generated by the Russian intelligentsia in the early twentieth century. In its violent break with the expected, the revolution of 1917 both focused attention on political issues as they were defined in the revolutionary period and simultaneously blocked the push-ing of inquiry beyond the boundaries of questions as they were raised at that time. Thus, where the intelligentsia is concerned, the basic positions staked out before 1917 still mark the limits of self-definition and scholarly investigation. For better or for worse, the idea of *an* intelligentsia tradi-tion, *a* revolutionary movement, and the "continuous" aspect of social thought have structured much of Western and Soviet scholarship on this subject.[15]

The starting point for questions about the intelligentsia, as with just about everything else in Russian history, is Peter the Great and his "West-ernizing" initiatives of the early eighteenth century. Few observers suggest that Peter was an *intelligent* (leaders of the state are not allowed into the category), but Peter's introduction of—or, more accurately, his blunt demand for—Western-based education for the upper class is held to be

14. The literature on the intelligentsia is voluminous. The most influential study in En-glish is the collection of essays that appeared in *Daedalus* in 1960 and was published in book form a year later: Richard Pipes, ed., *The Russian Intelligentsia* (New York, 1961). These essays stemmed from interpretations of the Soviet intelligentsia in the 1950s, and as such they provide a fascinating contemporary source on the culture that produced the perestroika generation, particularly David Burg's contribution, "Observations on Soviet University Students," 80–100. The outstanding study in English of Russian intellectual life is Andrej Walicki's *A History of Russian Thought from the Enlightenment to Marxism* (Stanford, 1979).

15. A good example of how the "frozen" issues of the revolutionary period spoke directly to the *intelligenty* of the Brezhnev period is Boris Shragin's thoughtful introduction to a new translation of *Vekhi* (Landmarks), the cause célèbre of intelligentsia debate before 1917: Boris Shragin and Albert Todd, eds., *Landmarks: A Collection of Essays on the Russian Intelli-gentsia, 1909*, trans. Marian Schwartz (New York, 1977), v–lv.

the necessary condition for the emergence of critical social thought. What undoubtedly is important is that Russia entered the European state system as a power in the eighteenth century and that members of the Russian elite encountered, reacted to, interpreted, and exploited the culture of the West. By the last third of the century, the initial defensive responses to European styles and culture had been superseded by the discovery of "Russianness," as scholars and artists created a new vision of their country.[16] This new national consciousness—a sense of Russian virtue, Russian sensibility, Russian history—provided the basis for a patriotic consciousness in the elite. It enabled the intellectuals of the latter part of the century to engage the discourse of the Enlightenment with confidence, and to see themselves as Russian participants in an international arena of ideas. To be Russian then—or more accurately to be an enlightened member of the privileged elite—was not to be backward.

Some Russians, however, responded to Enlightenment ideas exactly as Catherine the Great, the most astute autocrat of the century, had learned to fear. Engaging seriously the spirit of the age, a few intellectuals began to worry about equality and the "rights of man." Among them were Aleksandr Radishchev, the author of *A Journey from St. Petersburg to Moscow*, a classic (if seldom read) outcry against serfdom, and his mentor, Nikolai Novikov, an indefatigable publisher, advocate of enlightened civic virtue, and eloquent defender of the humanity of Russian peasants. The historical treatment of these figures is instructive. In Ivanov-Razumnik's 1906 study, both Radishchev and Novikov are described as founding figures in the intelligentsia tradition. In the Soviet "revolutionary movement" view, however, Radishchev assumed the honors of the "father" of the intelligentsia, while Novikov, with his practical suggestions for the development of civic and family virtue and his pleas for moral reform addressed to Catherine and to people of privilege, was demoted to the secondary ranks. In their own times, both Novikov and Radishchev were persecuted by the empress, their presses closed and their publications banned. Novikov was condemned to fifteen years' imprisonment in the Schluesselburg fortress, Radishchev banished to Siberia. This harsh repression as well as their ideas made them heroic figures to later opponents of autocracy.

The appearance of these political critics in eighteenth-century Russia led one prominent American historian to propose a socially based theory of the origins of the intelligentsia at this time. Marc Raeff argued in 1966 that the reconstruction of relations between the autocracy and the noble-service class in the eighteenth century gave rise to new aspirations in the

16. The best book on this cultural development is Hans Rogger, *National Consciousness in Eighteenth-Century Russia* (Cambridge, Mass., 1960).

elite. During the course of the century, the upper class in Russia had been gradually released from its obligation to serve the state in the military or civilian ranks. In 1736 the nobles' term of service was reduced from lifetime to twenty-five years; in 1762 their obligation to enter state service was abolished. Most historians have interpreted these changes as a victory for the nobility, who were eager to "escape" their status as servants of the crown and to settle down to enjoy life on their estates. But Raeff suggested that the nobility were frustrated by the reduction of their role in state affairs; guided by a service ethic developed in the past, nobles turned to moral ideas, to philosophy, to justify their lives—a search that eventually led them into opposition to the autocracy. "A straight line of spiritual and psychological filiation connects the servicemen of Peter the Great to the revolutionaries of the nineteenth century," Raeff asserted.[17]

Raeff's thesis was subjected to severe criticism, which I will not examine here.[18] I cite his work as an extreme—Western—example of the idea of a continuous intelligentsia tradition, as well as a noble effort to connect ideas to a class and its particular circumstances. Of course, the ideas of Radishchev and Novikov were not representative of the aspirations of their class. But more important, these intellectuals, as well as the Decembrist officers who turned the customary palace coup into a plea for republicanism in 1825, did not participate in a self-conscious culture of hostility to the state. Their ideas and actions fitted more easily with the eighteenth-century notion of a partnership between the autocrat and the aristocracy in the governance of Russia than into the hostile "outsider" mentality that developed later.

That sharply antagonistic culture emerged in the second quarter of the nineteenth century, during the reign of Nicholas I (1825–55). It was in this period of political reaction against the threat of revolution and republican government that the dialectic of repression and rebellion began to shape a counterculture. Responding to Nicholas's cultivation of an autocratic nationalist ideology (under the slogan "Orthodoxy, Autocracy, Nationality") and to the harsh controls—spying, arrests, exile, censorship—on alternative ideas, intellectuals educated in the expanding university system constructed the vital institutions of an unofficial world. The salons, discussion circles, and coded language of "thick journals" became the arenas in which the proto-intelligentsia nurtured their opposition to the state. This was the brilliant period of intellectual creativity, celebrated by later Russian writers and in Western intellectual history by Isaiah Berlin

17. Marc Raeff, *The Origins of the Russian Intelligentsia* (New York, 1966), 171.
18. See esp. Michael Confino, "Histoire et psychologie: A propos de la noblesse russe au 18ème siècle," *Annales* 22 (November–December 1967): 1163–1205.

and Martin Malia,[19] when the ideas of French socialists (St-Simon and Fourier) and German idealists (Schelling and especially Hegel) gave Russian intellectuals new grounding for their social projects. The many variants of idealism informed Slavophiles and Westernizers, Aleksandr Herzen, Vissarion Belinskii, and Petr Chaadaev as they produced their great and problematic visions of a different Russian destiny. The emphasis in historical studies of this period on the exhilarating effects of idealist understanding for alienated young intellectuals is probably fair; in Martin Malia's well-turned phrase, "the suppression of the Decembrists drove aspirations to freedom not so much underground as into the stratosphere."[20]

What is important about this period for the intelligentsia tradition is its exposure of intimate connections between the counterculture and the autocracy. At the most basic level, the autocracy's expansion of the bureaucracy and education provided candidates, not always from the elite, for intellectual activities. At the same time, the harsh restrictions on expression made secrecy and subterfuge both essential and meaningful. A new insider language, dubbed "Aesopian," was deployed to avoid the censorship. But while these developments marked boundaries between the opposition and the state, the intellectuals' own world was permeated with the essential values of the dominant autocratic culture. For one thing, the opposition, despite its reading of George Sand and concern for the "woman question," never shook off the functional patriarchy of the surrounding culture.[21] But most vitally, the outstanding figures of this critical period simply arrogated for themselves the cultural prerogatives of the autocrat. They, not he, knew the best course for Russia. Autocratic politics, with its ideological assertion of "Orthodoxy, Autocracy, Nationality," its organic assumptions, its denial of other voices, was reflected in the mirror of the opposition. It is here in the 1830s and 1840s, when Russian politics departed from the unruly ventures of Western Europe, that the absence of a civil society, or even of a civil society in the making with its demotic challenges to absolutist thought, begins to be apparent in the self-confident ideological elitism of the proto-intelligentsia.

Nicholas's deep freeze on Russian politics ended with Russia's defeat in the Crimean War and the reforms of the 1860s. But by this time the counterculture had developed its own internal dynamic: a new generation of angry young men entered their chosen world by attacking the generation of the "fathers." Idealism, good intentions, and noble goals were not

19. Isaiah Berlin, *Russian Thinkers* (New York, 1978); Martin Malia, *Alexander Herzen and the Birth of Russian Socialism* (1961) (New York, 1965).

20. Malia, *Alexander Herzen*, 43–44.

21. See Barbara Engel, *Mothers and Daughters: Women of the Intelligentsia in Nineteenth-Century Russia* (Cambridge, 1983).

enough, and neither were the government's "reforms." The basic principles of the new "nihilist" camp, declared the critic Dmitrii Pisarev in a provocative manifesto in 1861, are "what can be smashed should be; what stands up under the blows is acceptable; what flies into a thousand pieces is trash: in any case, strike out to the right and to the left, it's impossible that any harm will come of this."[22] The sarcastic, mean attacks of Nikolai Chernyshevskii, Nikolai Dobroliubov, and Pisarev on Herzen and the "men of the forties" point to the actuality of an intelligentsia culture—an ongoing, hence self-contested and self-refining culture based on personal and published statements about politics. "You [Chernyshevkii] are an ordinary viper, but Dobroliubov is a cobra," Ivan Turgenev cried out in pain, emphasizing how much belonging and fellowship had come to matter in this small world of sensibility.[23]

The "men of the sixties" called for a more revolutionary politics: for a totally new society that would overcome all previous limitations on the individual. In place of idealism and art, they advocated utilitarianism and "scientific knowledge"; these, they thought, would point the way to a new, rationally organized, and therefore liberated world. This positivist attitude was shared by several revolutionary organizations that emerged in the wake of the emancipation as well as by many academics and professionals. But from the 1860s on, it becomes more difficult to elide the identities of intellectual and *intelligent*. The postemancipation period nurtured the emergence of a large professional class—lawyers, professors, scientists—and many divergent political positions, from Fedor Dostoevskii's religious nationalism to Petr Lavrov's "subjective sociology."

At this time as well, the "people," especially peasants, finally imposed themselves as a subject to be studied as part of the construction of the future. The "Going to the People" movement of the mid-1870s exposed an ominous gap between intelligentsia ideas and village reality: peasants handed young students from the city over to the police. But this debacle, rather than destroying the intelligentsia's populism, gave it a new hold on life in two variants: the determination of conspirators in the People's Will and other circles to act *for* the people through revolutionary terrorism, and the more complex engagement with the "problem" of the peasants by Nikolai Mikhailovskii and other social theorists.[24] Revolutionary populism suffered a second defeat in 1881, when the assassination of

22. From his provocative "Skholastika XIX veka" [Scholasticism of the nineteenth century], quoted in R. V. Ivanov-Razumnik, *Istoriia obshchestvennoi mysli*, 2d ed. (Petersburg, 1908), 2:89.
23. Quoted in Walicki, *History of Russian Thought*, 203.
24. See Cathy A. Frierson, *Peasant Icons: Representations of Rural People in Late Nineteenth-Century Russia* (New York, 1993), on the development of ideas of the peasant in the 1870s and 1880s.

Alexander II failed to elicit the expected popular revolution, but only a decade later the intelligentsia found a new link with a different "people" through the Russian working class.

Marxism came to Russia firmly anchored in the intelligentsia tradition. Debates within the populist movement of the late 1870s over terrorism led the "fathers" and one "mother" of Russian Marxism—Georgii Plekhanov, Pavel Akselrod, Lev Deutsch, and Vera Zasulich—to form the first Russian Marxist circle, the Liberation of Labor group, organized in Switzerland in 1883. Similarly, Lenin's first contacts with opposition culture in the 1880s were with revolutionary circles connected with the People's Will tradition; he was particularly impressed by his reading of Chernyshevskii. (Lenin's older brother was executed for his participation in a conspiracy to assassinate Alexander III.) It was in the 1890s, in a second round of debate over a "separate"—that is, noncapitalist—Russian path to socialism that Russian Marxism won the day over the theory that capitalism was an evil Russia could avoid. The appearance of a small but growing working class in the strikes of the 1890s, the apparent inevitability of capitalist development and the destruction of the peasant community (seen in the famine of 1891–92), and the brilliant polemics of a new generation of intellectuals, particularly Lenin and Petr Struve, made Marxism for a brief period the dominant current in intellectual life.

Like other movements and schools that I have mentioned, Russian Marxism was shaped by autocratic culture. Marxist theory was relatively easy to publish—*Capital* had been translated and printed in 1872 and had been used by advocates of a separate Russian path as evidence of the undesirability of Western capitalism. But like the populists before them, Marxists were punished severely for their attempts at political organization. Lenin, Martov, and Potresov were arrested and exiled for propaganda activities among Petersburg workers; the Russian Social Democratic Party was founded in secrecy in 1898, followed by the arrest of all participants; publication of Social Democratic articles was difficult and sporadic.[25] But these obstacles to publicity and organization, as I have suggested, enabled Russian Marxism, like its predecessor ideologies, to preserve the authentic voice of the intelligentsia: its confident assertion that *these* intellectuals knew the necessary way—a long and painful one— to liberation. Nowhere is this belief more evident than in Lenin's explicit discussion of the socialist party's role in *What Is to Be Done?* (1902): "There could not have been Social Democratic consciousness among the workers. It would have to be brought to them from without. . . . The theory of socialism . . . grew out of philosophical, historical and economic

25. On Marxist publications, see Richard Pipes, *Struve: Liberal on the Left* (Cambridge, Mass., 1970), 220–21.

theories elaborated by educated representatives of the propertied classes, by intellectuals."[26]

The fact that Lenin had to articulate this view can be read as a symptom of the crisis of consciousness with which I opened this discussion of the intelligentsia tradition. For Lenin's statement is an acknowledgment that the working class, let alone the "people," did not share the intelligentsia's ideas, or at least not without instruction. By the beginning of the twentieth century, and especially after 1905 and the relaxation of the censorship, this realization loomed behind the divisive politics and exuberant culture of Russian elites. And yet the intelligentsia would not give up its ideological privilege, its monopoly on social truth. This resistance to dissolving into civil society, into intellectuals without a collective place, was made explicit in the debate over *Vekhi*, a manifesto against the intelligentsia published in 1909.[27]

Vekhi (Landmarks) was a collection of articles on a familiar theme— the intelligentsia in Russia. But this time, in the aftermath of the 1905 revolution, the contributors—Petr Struve (now a convert to the new idealist current of opinion), Nikolai Berdiaev, and others—assaulted the notions that had defined the intelligentsia tradition. The intelligentsia's self-defining claim—that they spoke for the Russian people—was false. Instead through their exclusive focus on socialism, revolution, and social reconstruction, through their positivism and atheism, the intelligentsia had betrayed their moral mission. From the perspective of the *Vekhi* group, 1905 had shown that the revolutionary path had been disastrous, not redemptive. True social reform could come only from a different focus—on individuals, their personal responsibility, and their moral obligations to law, religion, and the state.

Vekhi, perhaps the most widely read book of the prewar period, was issued repeatedly, 23,000 copies in a single year.[28] For two years after the appearance of this neo-idealist declaration and its attack on the primary opposition of intelligentsia and state, both radicals and reformists—Bolsheviks, Mensheviks, Socialist Revolutionaries, Constitutional Democrats (Kadets)—defended their status, each faction in its own way. Miliukov, the leader of the liberal Kadets, rejected the book's characterization of the intelligentsia altogether. Lenin and Martov, speaking for the Social Democrats, identified the book's position with that of the liberals, and called *Vekhi*'s conclusions "counter-revolutionary liberalism." The titles of these countermanifestos give a sense of the struggle: "In Defense of the

---

26. V. I. Lenin, *What Is to Be Done?* (Moscow, 1947), 31–32.
27. Shragin and Todd, *Landmarks*.
28. Christopher Read, *Religion, Revolution, and the Russian Intelligentsia, 1900–1912* (New York, 1980), 7.

Intelligentsia"; "Where Are We Going?"; "The Intelligentsia in Russia"; "*Vekhi* as a Banner of the Times." What is significant for us is how much self-image and ideas counted among the intelligentsia. Just as Lenin had devoted hundreds of pages in 1908 (in *Materialism and Empirio-Criticism: Critical Comments on a Reactionary Philosophy*) to attacking the wave of neo-idealist philosophy that threatened to undermine his idea of Marxism, now he and Martov felt sufficiently threatened by *Vekhi*'s idea of the intelligentsia to spend their time and ink defining the intelligentsia in their own terms. As Christopher Read concludes in his excellent book on the *Vekhi* debate, "practically all the intelligentsia commentators rejected *Vekhi* and the debate revealed that, as with the autocracy after 1905, nothing in their outlook had really changed."[29]

If Russian *intelligenty* in 1910—fragmented in their politics, in their philosophical assumptions, and in their visions of the future—could still battle over the meaning of the intelligentsia tradition, defined in various ways, the intelligentsia as a phenomenon existed at least for them. Above all, in Russian intellectuals' own definitions, it was ideas that counted, not numbers and not class. Even a Marxist as consequential as Martov, who felt that there was no longer an "objective" unity in the intelligentsia, used the category "democratic intelligentsia" to define progressive thinkers.[30] This relentless insistence on the significance of the intelligentsia's values, combined with the historical location of these values in a continuous, self-transforming, and self-defining tradition, gave the Russian intelligentsia its legitimacy as a culture.

The definition of this culture by its ideas is reinforced by the intelligentsia's later history as well, for it was precisely ideas, ideas and values developed in intelligentsia culture, that came to the fore in the revolutionary crisis of 1917. When the autocratic ideology failed, what replaced it as a ruling ethos was the entitled vanguard culture of people who were prepared, ideologically, to take its place.

By this I do not mean that the intellectuals of the revolutionary period were able to put their specific plans and programs into action. The history of the revolution and the Soviet period is the story of the inability of, first, liberals in the Provisional Government, then democratic socialists (Socialist Revolutionaries and Mensheviks in the Petrograd Soviet and the Provisional Government), and finally Bolsheviks to enact their programs—"put them into life," in the language of the time. But what underlay all these unsuccessful initiatives and what structured many of the

29. Ibid., 181–83, 161. The Social Democrats' responses are discussed on 141–52.
30. For an example, see Martov's *Obshchestvennye i umstvennye techeniia*, 56–57, in which he discusses populism as providing the basis for the unity of "the whole democratic intelligentsia of the seventies."

Bolsheviks' practices in power was that culture of entitlement, of unexamined authenticity, of a moral mandate, that had been nurtured and never destroyed in autocratic conditions. In none of the revolutionary governments or would-be governments do we find a real concern for the opinions of the "people" as a whole, for liberals as much as Bolsheviks felt entitled to pursue their own kind of progress. As the right Socialist Revolutionary Mark Vishniak observed, the idea of a constituent assembly had been sometimes an "idol" but never a strong goal of the intelligentsia.[31] In this sense both the Bolsheviks and their opponents in the revolutionary years displayed the same confidence in the different revolutions they had imagined back in the days of theory and did not doubt that they were speaking for the people's good.

Nonetheless, the revolution of 1917 brought about a significant shift in the personnel and ideologies of the intelligentsia. In effect, part of the intelligentsia—the Bolshevik part—became the government. The imperatives of power transformed the Bolsheviks' relation to the intelligentsia tradition; their task was now to change the world through the agency of the state. The Bolsheviks' leap out of critical opposition into power opened up a new divide within the Soviet intelligentsia over the next decades—a divide between the rulers and the ruled. That both sides of the bifurcated intelligentsia had inherited the same culture of entitlement only sharpened the hostilities of their initial conflicts. The intelligentsia's moral mandate informed the new state system through Lenin's institutional and ideological assertion of his party's right to lead alone and to construct the future in the interests of, but uncontested by, the working class. The autocratic voice can be heard as clearly in the barrage of criticism, engaged theory, and new projections of Russia's future produced by *intelligenty* left outside the state by the Bolsheviks' exclusionary policies. Faced with a state that claimed the right to lead far more vigorously than had the autocracy in its declining years, the opposition culture revived full force. In this way, the explicit challenge of a new orthodoxy and a new repression revitalized the intelligentsia's former mission of speaking for the people against the state.[32]

Before approaching the problem of the Soviet intelligentsia and its evolving culture, I want to return to the questions of interpretation I raised at the beginning of this discussion. How well do Western theories fit the prerevolutionary intelligentsia? Or rather, what do Russian *intelligenty* say about themselves, how would they speak back to Western defini-

---

31. M. V. Vishniak, "Ideia uchreditel'nogo sobraniia," *Griadushchaia Rossiia* 1920, no. 2: 215.

32. Jane Burbank, *Intelligentsia and Revolution: Russian Views of Bolshevism, 1917–1922* (New York, 1986), 8–11. The views of the intellectual opposition to Bolshevism in the early Soviet period are the subject of this book.

tions? First, the Russian intelligentsia cannot be defined in terms of class, since *intelligenty* had, first, a variety of class origins, and second, often no secure class base once they joined the counterculture.[33] What did count, for Russians, was education: one could simply not be an *intelligent* without participating in the culture of knowledge and reason, although one could be self-taught. By the early twentieth century, the vastly expanded educational system was producing more graduates from the peasant and townspeople's estates; these shifts decreased the proportion of people from the noble estate in both the professions and radical movements.[34] But even in the 1830s the prominent figures in the construction of intelligentsia ideas had not come exclusively from the nobility.[35] As for the leaders of the intelligentsia at the time of the revolution, their origins were diverse but for the most part privileged. That they did not confront the issue of their own class position was typical of the intelligentsia mentality; here Ivanov-Razumnik's descriptions—"nonclass, nonestate"—accurately fit intellectuals' notion of what defined themselves. In Gramsci's sense, these were not "organic" intellectuals, attached to the specific interests of a class.

If the Russian intelligentsia rejected class position or even official education as essential characteristics of their identity, they embraced as their own the other pole of Western theory, which emphasizes values. Which values was another matter, for here they often disagreed; still, one common ground appeared to be dedication to the cause of progess and justice, as Potresov noted in 1918.[36] From outside, we can point to certain typical attitudes: hostility to the state, confidence in the representative qualities of one's knowledge, a sense of place in historical and national development, and, for most, belief in progress. Because these qualities were the mirror image of the assertive, monopolistic, conservative ideology of the autocracy, we might stretch Gramsci's terms to define the Russian intelligentsia as "traditional." Its ideas reflected the particular conditions and ideas of the historically dominant culture—the culture of autocracy. And it is this autocratic culture, rather than any essential quality of abstract thought or "ideology," that gave the pronouncements of the Russian *intelligenty* their peculiarly declarative and unreflectively inclusive tone.

33. Nonetheless, one historian operating outside the Russian tradition has tried to show that various degrees of radicalism within the Jewish intelligentsia can be predicted by social situation: Robert J. Brym, *The Jewish Intelligentsia and Russian Marxism* (New York, 1978).

34. On the expansion of the intelligentsia, see V. R. Leikina-Svirskaia, *Russkaia intelligentsiia v 1900–1917 godakh* (Moscow, 1981), 5–30.

35. See Herzen's memoirs for an example of the variety of backgrounds of students at Moscow University in the 1830s: Alexander Herzen, *Childhood, Youth, and Exile,* trans. J. D. Duff (New York, 1980), 92–139.

36. A. N. Potresov, "Privet *Russkomu bogatstvu*," *Novyi den'* 15 (2) February 1918.

Did the intelligentsia with its opposition to the state create a new hegemony that could transform society? As we have seen, the intelligentsia was successful in establishing a hegemonic culture for itself, in that generation after generation of educated people sympathized with and contributed to the counterculture. The revolution of 1905 exhibited the power of a negative hegemony, as the slogan "Down with autocracy!" mobilized broad segments of the population. But as the course of the Bolshevik revolution and civil war showed, no positive hegemony had appeared to take the place of the old culture. Thus socialism in Russia had to be taught or forced upon the population.[37]

And what of discourse? Did the intelligentsia provide the terms for politics? As the waves of idealism, materialism, neo-idealism, and the controversies between Slavophiles and Westernizers, populists and Marxists illustrate, the intelligentsia did produce an ongoing discourse of its own. Most important for the revolution, the intelligentsia provided the several political ideas that came to the fore when the state collapsed. But the continuity of that discourse was vitally dependent at all times on terms set by the state. Thus, after 1917, the official discourse was radically limited once again by the Bolsheviks' assertion of their course toward progress. For regardless of the opportunities offered by Soviet publications to enterprising critics at various times, public speech for seventy years continued to be framed by the assumption of a national socialist project that could be challenged only by "enemies" of the state. This harsh restriction was a critical setback for the discourse of socialism in the Soviet Union, which now appears impoverished and disarmed in the ideological controversies of our day.

Finally, what are we to make of Konrad and Szelenyi's view that the intellectuals defended their own interests as a future class? In this interpretation, the intelligentsia through its promotion of socialism prepared the way for its victory as a managerial class in Eastern Europe. One lonely voice, Jan Vaclav Machajski, proposed such a theory in Russia in 1907, warning the working class against domination by the intelligentsia.[38] Functionally, the argument has a strong appeal, but was it part of intelligentsia consciousness? Konrad and Szelenyi assert that Eastern European intellectuals, unable to secure their place in the limited private sector, were encouraged to adopt a "teleological" attachment to socialism.[39] Of

---

37. See Peter Kenez, *The Birth of the Propaganda State* (Cambridge, Mass., 1985), on the Bolsheviks' efforts to construct a socialist mentality after 1917; and William G. Rosenberg, ed., *Bolshevik Visions: First Phase of the Cultural Revolution in Soviet Russia* (Ann Arbor, 1984), for a vivid sampling of Bolshevik hopes for change.

38. Read, *Religion*, 97–98, 160–61.

39. Konrad and Szelenyi, *Intellectuals*, 85–86. The alternative was a "nationalist" teleology.

course, not all Russian intellectuals defended socialism, especially in the prerevolutionary years. But, more important, the idea of their own class power was far from overt in the intelligentsia's ideology, which focused instead on the grander notions of nation, working class, and "people." Behind all these abstractions was the unexamined notion that intellectuals with their knowledge expressed the people's wishes, and it was this more generalized assumption that privileged a portion of the intelligentsia after 1917.

Armed with the confidence of the autocratic counterculture, the Bolsheviks proceeded to build socialism. To them the discourse of civil, bourgeois society was unnecessary and dangerous, and thus the limited openings to a pluralistic, fluid politics in the decade before the revolution were closed off once again. To skip a big stage of capitalism was to skip its political developments as well. As I noted earlier, it was precisely the repression of open politics after 1917 that revived the intelligentsia tradition for those who did not join the state; and it was the absence of an openly contested politics that preserved the oppositional intelligentsia as a social phenomenon within the Soviet system. In that marginal and marginalizing sphere, one heard the same assertive tone, the same confidence in one's opinion, the same moral value attached to one's ideas that typified the intelligentsia in the distant past.

Some differences can be seen between the prerevolutionary intelligentsia and its Soviet descendant. The Soviet intelligentsia was even less susceptible to orthodox class definition than the prerevolutionary *intelligenty,* since everyone in Soviet society—intellectuals, industrial workers, peasants—was supposed to be employed by the state. But the divide between those "official" intellectuals who had mental-labor jobs in the bureaucracies and the marginalized *intelligenty* (the opposition intelligentsia) who were pushed out or fled from the Soviet establishment continued to problematize the self-definition of the intelligentsia after the revolution. In the Stalinist period this division took its most acute and mortal form in the attempt to eradicate the physical possibility of an intelligentsia opposition, but even in less vicious times Soviet intellectuals had to face a basic choice: either to work within the official sphere, with its requirements of ideological conformity and discipline from above, or to stay outside the system at an extremely high material cost. In the multiple decisions of professional lives, Soviet intellectuals transformed this stark divide between sacrificial dissidence and rewarded state service into various intermediate solutions, most of which permitted them to reject the meaningfulness of official work and to cultivate instead the intellectual significance of private, unauthorized, but usually overlooked activities. "Writing for the drawer"—that quintessential intelligentsia task of the Brezhnev period—was accomplished not just by heroic dissidents but by many individuals inside the official culture as their "real" occupation.

This privatization of meaning had ambiguous and conflicting consequences for the Soviet intelligentsia. On the one hand, an infinity of new tensions among intellectuals was introduced by their highly individualized compromises between the official world of dissimulation and the outsider culture of authenticity. But at the same time, the elevation of personal values above professional achievement preserved and reinforced the collective intelligentsia tradition. At a practical level, it allowed linkages, important to both sides, between educated people inside the system and their friends living at the margins of the official society. These circles of personal association outside professional life provided a sphere of accommodation to the postrevolutionary situation, in which the imperatives of survival and ambition were stacked in favor of the state. And in the sphere of values, the dissociation of authenticity from state service only fortified the prerevolutionary notion of the autonomous, critically thinking *intelligent*. Thus, as before the revolution, the Soviet intelligentsia could still be defined collectively by their ideals, even if people had new grounds to argue about who was in the group.

Another area of ambiguous connection between the pre- and postrevolutionary intelligentsia is that of ideas themselves. From the 1930s until the late 1980s, the intelligentsia was deprived of its own history, at least in the official sphere. Information about political and cultural developments of the early twentieth century was grotesquely distorted or eradicated from published sources, and many of the most creative artists, scientists, and political figures were turned into "useless people," "enemies," or nonpersons. Even if some knowledge of the past was preserved in unofficial contexts, this cutting off of public discussion once again enforced the privatization of intelligentsia culture and limited the possibilities for recruitment from outside the ranks and families of the initiated. The extreme xenophobia of Soviet official culture compounded this obliteration of the past by eliminating ongoing interaction with Western culture, or at least confining that interaction to such limited arenas that no integrating discourse could take place. The narrowness of the Soviet intelligentsia's contact with the West contrasts sharply with the intellectual world before 1917, when every political or professional theorist was thoroughly and publicly engaged in pan-European debates and developments. The significance of this isolation was obvious to observers of the late Soviet scene, not just in the wild enthusiasm of Soviet audiences for Western culture but also in the undiscriminating Soviet vogue for the "achievements" of Western social science—a science whose own vagaries, self-doubts, and divisions, not to speak of failures, were opaque to Soviet intellectuals.

By the late 1980s, some of this intellectual isolation was self-imposed; there are Western and Russian ideas that held little interest for most *intelligenty*, namely Marxism and Leninism. The deification of Marx and Lenin finally became as brittle as the symbolism of the imperial family for the intelligentsia in tsarist times, and after so many years of uncontested repetition, the slogans of socialist construction were as empty of meaning as Nicholas I's "Orthodoxy, Autocracy, Nationality." This widespread attitude toward Soviet socialism points to another basic similarity between the Soviet and the prerevolutionary intelligentsia: the outsider ideology was constituted to deny the official one.

But just as in the autocratic past, the Soviet intelligentsia could not escape their intimate ties to and orientation toward the official culture they despised. The pervasive didacticism of the official press, its unqualified assertion of a single truth and a single way to think were echoed around kitchen tables in Moscow by the alienated and the marginalized. Here once again was the entitlement of the knowing subject: the state told society what to think, and in turn each individual *intelligent* told the others what they ought to think. There was one fundamental change, however, in the attitude of the intelligentsia since the Bolshevik revolution: Soviet intellectuals of the 1980s lost their confidence in the "people." To the intelligentsia, the "masses," while not of the state, were its allies against the culture of knowledge. This was a striking loss of confidence from the early years of the century, a consequence perhaps of the generalized alienation and distrust in Soviet society. Thus, the marginalized *intelligenty* of the Gorbachev period really were "free-swinging":[40] they felt beleaguered by the bosses with their false knowledge and by the people with their supposed ignorance.

Western professionals were attracted to the very detachment of this culture. (And in the intense arenas of Soviet life, Westerners usually could find hosts whose degree of marginality or accommodation was some reflection of their guests' own temperaments.) Intellectuals who had given up on state service and its demands and privileges were truly "free" from professional concerns: free from the tyranny of theory; free, in the case of the marginalized, from professional ambition; free from the need to reach conclusions collectively. The world outside the Soviet professions was a world without paradigms. In some respects the disdain for convention in intelligentsia circles was liberating and creative, but it also meant that the discourse of the Russian intelligentsia was not really a discourse— no one had to listen to anybody else.

On the negative side, at least for people sympathetic to the socialist project, was the Soviet intelligentsia's absolute hostility to official culture.

40. See Mannheim, *Ideology and Utopia,* 155.

It was precisely in this arena that Gorbachev strove for a truly innovative, revolutionary transformation. Glasnost was an invitation to the outsiders to join a public sphere; it was an assertion of a civil society where one had not been permitted to develop. And it was here that the intelligentsia could play a critical role, analogous to their function in 1917. As the ruling ideology collapsed, the intellectuals once again could bring their ideas to the fore. The critical difference from the earlier revolution was that in the late Soviet period it was the rulers who were taking the initiative, who in some measure understood the fragility of their situation and reached out to the intelligentsia for new ideas.

The attempt to create a civil society or to allow it to express itself had frightening aspects for the counterculture. The alienated intelligentsia were unaccustomed to the politics of compromise, to the construction of consensus, to the modification of absolute stands, and above all to the acceptance of subjectivity, of different and hypothetical interpretations. When Gorbachev held the reins, he was not popular with intellectuals in the Soviet capitals; he was criticized both for "dictatorial" actions and for not going far enough. His revulsion at the 1989 publication of an opinion poll displaying his less than universal popularity and his attempt to fire the editor of the offending journal showed that he was not safe from autocratic tendencies.[41]

As in 1917, the intelligentsia are once again bound to the state in a struggle to set the terms for politics and to provide new ideas in a time of crisis. Both insiders and outsiders are trying to use new rules they do not understand, to replace state command with the more fluid structures of civil society. In his acceptance of contested, public politics, Gorbachev was a great exception to the autocratic and the Bolshevik traditions. He invited the intelligentsia to join him in reform before it was too late, and he took the historic initiative of introducing "free" elections into Communist politics. It is hard to say which of these two initiatives was more subversive of the tradition of the Russian intelligentsia, who defined themselves as the opponents of the state and as the entitled representatives of the people.

Gorbachev gave way to Boris Yeltsin and the struggle to create a different society in Russia continues, having taken several dramatic turns. One vital development in the last years of perestroika was the appearance of a radically expressive independent press, as intellectuals seized the opportunity to bring the engaged voices of the private domain into public circulation. A host of new newspapers broke with the dead language of official journalism and brought vibrant, daring, and combative authenticity to

---

41. The article was published in the popular journal *Argumenty i fakty*. See *New York Times*, October 24, 1989.

political analysis. In television as well, professionals pushed hard against thick walls of censorship; this assault against internalized and imposed controls led in May 1991 to the historic creation of the Russian Republic's own channel, outside the command structure of Soviet state television. Soviet viewers were entranced by the reality of alternative versions of the "news," and the leapfrog timing of the two major channels' broadcasts encouraged critical engagement with the explosive politics of what became the last year of perestroika.

These and other efforts to break through the confines of official culture acquired vital significance in the critical months after the first coup of 1991—the military attack in January on elected government and glasnost in the Baltic republics. As never before in Soviet times, a large opposition movement emerged in Moscow and Leningrad, one that asserted its right to protest and to criticize in a series of public demonstrations against the Communist leadership and its reactionary course. By the time of the putsch of August 19–21, 1991, it could be said that the public sphere had attracted all forward-looking figures away from the discredited Communist Party and that the state was in an advanced stage of withering away. Once the outsider culture of the private sphere went public, there was no point in sustaining the fake official culture, and it collapsed upon itself.

Building a new state is not the same as rejecting the old one; as in 1917, constructing a new polity has proved far more difficult than undermining the legitimacy of the previous regime. In the ongoing and necessarily protracted process of generating viable institutions and terms of governance, the intelligentsia's culture of entitlement has had multiple and ambiguous effects. On the one hand, absolutist confidence in the righteousness of one's views, nurtured for so long by the privatization of meaning in the Soviet period, empowered intellectuals to take up Gorbachev's challenge and to enter a new world of political exploration with a freedom of expression unimaginable in the self-constrained and professionally conformist discourses of bourgeois societies. To this day, the post-Soviet press displays an exuberant subjectivity, eloquence, and imagination that irk the defenders of "objective" journalism and engage readers who like to think. Yeltsin—and every other politician and would-be politician, for that matter—is fair game for cartoonists and commentators whose wits were sharpened in the underground and now have an abundance of material to work with. Although attempts to regain control over the press and television have been a major aspect of the struggle for authority in the Russian Federation, the strident, ironic voices of self-confident, clever, and literate intellectuals still contribute to a distinctive and demanding journalistic practice.

But in the years since 1991, the very boldness of the intelligentsia's claim to represent the nation has shown its antidemocratic face. A press free to express the views of intellectuals is not intrinsically a force for popular representation. The intellectuals who joined the post-Soviet political fray were in good autocratic fashion ready to assert their notions of how the state should be constructed; they were not concerned to ask for other people's ideas about how to build a new society. Despite the Russian Federation's deep need to establish administrative legitimacy and the extensive discussions of the superiority of a "legal state," the intelligentsia did not raise the question of a new constitution after the August coup. In the euphoria of apparent victory in the fall of 1991, neither Yeltsin nor any significant faction of his rivals proposed that the new occupiers of the state set aside the variously compromised and compromising decrees and constitutions of the present and the past in order to consult the "people" about their common future. Instead Yeltsin and Gorbachev negotiated a face-saving transformation of the Soviet Union into a constellation of states based on the former constituent republics, and the Russian Federation began its existence on the not so firm foundation of a new flag raised over the Kremlin on December 25, 1991.

This symbolic birth of a nation, accompanied by a flurry of resignations, renamings, and declarations, initially carried an emotive force based on the apparent unities of the revolutionary moment of 1991. Opinion polls and elections in that year generally displayed solid support for intellectuals' opposition to Communist leaders. The results of the presidential elections in the Russian Republic in June 1991, in which Boris Yeltsin won 72 percent of the votes (of a highly engaged electorate) against an array of Communist-supported candidates, created a perception of national unity that inspired resistance during the heroic days and nights of August 1991. For almost a year after the demise of the Soviet Union, elite intellectuals' insertions of their private images of the common good into a new public sphere remained relatively unchallenged by other expressions of social will. During this critical period the intelligentsia offered no strong support for a popularly elected constituent assembly that might have provided both a clean break with the past and a new, more representative legitimacy for the future. Mark Vishniak's observation of 1920 still held true for post-Soviet Russia: though *intelligenty* were willing to struggle *for* the people, they were not concerned enough about the people's right to determine the form of future government.[42]

As support for the postrevolutionary government began to unravel in 1992, the intelligentsia's inability to imagine an inclusive domain of political creation—a profound vestige of the Soviet experience—remained the

42. M. V. Vishniak, "Ideia uchreditel'nogo sobraniia," *Griadushchaia Rossiia* 1920, no. 1: 270–92.

hallmark of the various attempts to locate and gain power in the ever-shifting institutions of the central government. The battles over a new constitution that finally took place in 1993 were conducted within the political elite. Despite the bloody and disgraceful display of the fragility of all major institutions of governance in the October Days of 1993, Russia's "democratic" politicians appear incapable of learning to make their platforms intelligible and appealing to the electorate. Nowhere was the devastating legacy of the intelligentsia's culture of entitlement clearer than in the fallen faces of the reformist candidates as the results of the elections to the new Russian parliament came in on the evening of December 12, 1993. Gathered in the Kremlin to celebrate their expected victory, the self-designated leaders of Russian democracy watched morosely as the better-organized Communists and the charismatic Zhirinovskii took the lead. Here again the intelligentsia tradition was at work: in the refusal of the reformist leaders to unite pragmatically in a single party; in their inattention to the public and its critical abilities; in their confidence that declarations of commitment—their commitments—would suffice as politics.

Looking back at Gorbachev's challenge to the intelligentsia in the late 1980s, one is struck by how resistant the intelligentsia's outsider culture has been to democratic reform. The intelligentsia's entitlement to speak for the people against the state has been put to a severe test by electoral politics since 1989 and by the real opportunity for *intelligenty* to join the state. Sustained by their own convictions, those who took up the opportunity to shape the polity at a critical moment of collapse paid little heed to the contradiction between their democratic slogans and their disengagement from the "people," who at last had gained the chance to vote out their leaders. Others, witnesses to the corruption and imperfection of "Russian democracy," retreated to the safer (at least for the short term) realm of personal fulfillment, reinforcing by their absence the gulf between the rulers and the ruled. A common, if unverified, observation during the elections of December 1993 was that "the intelligentsia did not vote." To be sure, there are other tendencies in contemporary Russia—the opening up of new professional opportunities, the shrinkage of state-sponsored academic employment, the wide gulf in values between the generations, the decentralization of professional life, the new possibilities for civic and charitable engagement. These strong shifts in the political economy may in time erode the intelligentsia culture from within. But a dismaying aspect of intellectuals' adherence to their traditional culture of moralized entitlement both inside the state and in retreat from it is that this behavior increases the chances for a return to authoritarian rule. In this respect, for all the courage of those Soviet intellectuals who made ideas into politics in 1991, a break with the intelligentsia's autocratic and Communist continuities is not assured.

6

Régis Debray: Republican in a Democratic Age

Donald M. Reid

Let me confess frankly to a personal inclination for Jacobin messianism; I have always really believed that France will again bear the torch of revolution to the rest of Europe. I find the Jacobinism of 1792 and 1848 not only sympathetic but in a sense natural to me. I can conceive of no hope for Europe save under the hegemony of a revolutionary France, firmly grasping the banner of independence.

—RÉGIS DEBRAY

I'm an ascetic and an exile in comparison to [Jean-François Revel and Bernard-Henri Lévy]. In the intellectual milieu things do not depend on administrative or political power. They depend on Bernard Pivot, on television, and Bernard-Henri Lévy at les Editions Grasset. Because he is the person who decides whether a book will make 100 francs or 100,000 francs. There is a power play going on in the intellectual milieu which the intellectuals refuse to admit to. They prefer to attack power with a big P. That's to say, they attack us at the Elysée although they do not depend on us, and we exert no power over them.

—RÉGIS DEBRAY

A defining feature of the intellectual in Europe and the United States since 1968 has been a suspicion of politics and more particularly of the state as an embodiment of power and the purveyor and enforcer of social norms. Régis Debray stands out among his intellectual peers for having vigorously rejected this line of thought. Debray's critique of the dire

I thank Leon Fink, Lloyd Kramer, and Steven Vincent for their careful readings of earlier drafts of this chapter.

effects of the media on intellectual and political discourse and his condemnation of identity politics, coupled with his steadfast allegiance to the Jacobin tradition, make him an anomoly both in France and elsewhere in Europe and in the United States. His consistent rejection of the *soixante-huitard* tradition through its various transformations provides a unique perspective for assessing changing conceptions of the intellectual's relation to the state in the West.

Debray's intense relation to the *soixante-huitard* tradition is not hard to fathom, for he came out of the same milieu as many of its most ardent proponents. He was a pupil of Louis Althusser at the elite Ecole Normale Supérieure (ENS) in the early 1960s. Finding the academic Marxism taught there too distant from the world of revolutionary change, he left France for Latin America, where he became the confidant of Fidel Castro and Che Guevara. He championed their guerrilla strategy in *Revolution in the Revolution?*, published early in 1967, and was arrested by the Bolivian army while on a mission from Castro to Guevara that spring. During close to four years in a Bolivian prison and another two and a half years in Salvador Allende's Chile, Debray undertook a personal and political self-critique. He renounced revolutionary voluntarism as the inverse of the ENS's penchant for abstraction. Debray came to believe that social groups are rooted in a collective unconscious, a product of history to which intellectuals give expression in ideologies and which is the wellspring of meaningful social action.[1]

Debray returned to France in 1973 with a mission: to make socialism in France. "It is not our fault if history has made France the country of socialism par excellence"; "For now, to reinvent socialism is to repatriate it."[2] Critiquing Guevara's conception of a continent-wide revolution, he championed the idea that politics had to flow from the particular history and culture of a people. There was no richer revolutionary heritage than that offered by French republican ideology. Debray threw in his lot with François Mitterrand, whose reconstituted Socialist Party he saw as its contemporary manifestation.

During the first decade and one-half of the Fifth Republic, France experienced what is often referred to as the Second French Revolution. The institutions that had held French society together in the past—the church, the school, and the army—declined in prestige. More democratic and less hierarchical forms of communication, organization, and sociabil-

---

1. See Donald Reid, "Régis Debray's Quest: From France to Bolivia and Back," *History of European Ideas* 14 (1992): 839–62.
2. Régis Debray, *Lettre aux communistes français et à quelques autres* (Paris, 1978), 15–16.

ity took their place.[3] For many people on the left, such developments heralded a more liberated society. Yet Debray saw a dark side to these changes. They eroded faith and commitment, the republic's only bulwarks against the commodification of cultural and intellectual life under advanced capitalism. To use the nineteenth-century metaphors of energy so dear to Debray, the nation is a dynamo given life by the energy of a shared cultural myth, but perpetually threatened by entropy and dissolution. As the liberalism of Valéry Giscard d'Estaing displaced the nationalist and statist policies of Charles de Gaulle in the early 1970s, Debray rejected the general drift of Western European socialist thought—decentralizing, libertarian, *autogestionnaire*—seeing it, like Giscardian liberalism, as the fruit of the capitalist fragmentation of society and the nation-state. While bringing together the nation-state and socialism flies in the face of much twentieth-century Western European socialist theory, it reflects the history of socialist revolutions elsewhere in the world; for Debray the two projects are united by their fundamental opposition to the liberal capitalist celebration of the individual and of market-based relativism.

Debray argues that as a result of these developments, people in the West increasingly understand their identity and their relations to one another through representations conveyed by the mass media. The resulting "mediocracy," rule by production of opinion on a mass basis, challenges the autonomy of the republican state, since the latter depends on public opinion to remain in power. Intellectuals are crucial to this process: "a system of domination that works through communication works through the intelligentsia." Intellectuals' prestige is in turn increasingly determined by their access to the mass media, but only intellectuals whose thought is easily commodified and circulated through these media ascend the mediatic heights. These intellectual stars attack the institutions and ideologies of the nation and of socialism in the name of an abstract civil society. By doing so they undermine the ideology of republicanism, which gave an institutional identity to the French collective unconscious in a nation-state that offered its citizens the possibility of liberty and community. The new media-dependent intellectuals thus unwittingly clear away impediments to the triumph of neoliberal capitalism while they open the floodgates to more primitive and brutal expressions of the group psyche. A child of the 1940 defeat, Debray evokes such developments in ominous terms: "There is more than one way to occupy a country and undermine the sovereignty of a people: the least blatant is not necessarily the least effective."[4]

3. See Henri Mendras and Alistair Cole, *Social Change in Modern France* (Cambridge, 1991.
4. Régis Debray, *Teachers, Writers, Celebrities*, trans. David Macey (London, 1981), 144, 2.

To understand the society that had taken shape in his absence from France and the roles he sees the media and intellectuals play in it, Debray has embraced "mediology," the study of the ways in which the medium through which a message is transmitted structures what is conveyed and the social identity of the audience that receives it. As a mediologue, Debray puts aside conventional modes of interpreting texts by evaluating their content, truth, or logic: socialism, for example, is (or is not) the expression of the working class; socialism has lost its allure because historical experience has proved it wrong; deconstruction of socialist texts reveals repression. For Debray, the declining appeal of socialism in France can best be explained by the growing hegemony of the mass media—especially such new media as television—which undermine both the means of expression by which socialism had propagated itself and recipients' ability to recognize themselves in its language. Through mediology, therefore, Debray claims to supersede traditional content-based dichotomies into right and left: he argues that the turn-of-the-century socialist Jean Jaurès is closer to his nationalist contemporary Maurice Barrès than to a socialist leader today.[5] While Debray's initial explorations of mediology were similar to the approach of the Frankfurt School in their attacks on the mass media as forwarding the ideology of advanced capitalism, his disillusion with François Mitterrand's presidency and his desire to found a mediological science have led him in *Cours de médiologie générale* (1991) to subordinate an explicitly political agenda to a structuralism of Althusserian ancestry: he is developing the kind of theoretical and intellectual project that in his youth he abandoned for Latin America.

Even those who find Debray's celebration of the executions and exclusions of the republican tradition disturbing can admire his penetrating analyses of the bases of intellectual prestige and power and his effort to rethink the socialist project in contemporary France. Debray worked out his ideas on these subjects in response to developments in French political and intellectual life in the 1970s and 1980s: the decline of the French Communist Party (PCF); the florescence of *gauchiste* thought in the late 1960s and early 1970s; the emergence of the New Philosophers in the mid-1970s; the tenth anniversary of May 1968; the election of Mitterrand to the presidency in May 1981; the celebration of the bicentennial of the revolution and the "Islamic scarf affair" in 1989. Debray's critical evaluations of such events provide a valuable opportunity to assess the transformation of the intellectual's role and position in French political life from the heady days of Jean-Paul Sartre selling *La Cause du peuple* to the questioning and doubts of writers in the glib, glossy *Globe* today.

5. Régis Debray, *Cours de médiologie générale* (Paris, 1991), 255–98.

COMMUNISTS, *GAUCHISTES*, AND NEW
PHILOSOPHERS

Revolution in the Revolution? had offered an extreme formulation of the
New Left critique of Communist parties: they were reified, bureaucratic
structures opposed to any revolution that did not pass through them;
they wanted to destabilize capitalism, but not themselves.[6] And yet in
Fifth Republic France precisely the inverse was happening: new forms of
communication were creating a "mediological" crisis in the constitution
of the PCF's membership. The party was not threatened because its ideas
about society had proved outmoded or false. Debray's materialist conception of ideology led him to focus instead on the party's growing inability
to generate belief in its doctrine. After all, he argued, no one became a
Communist by reading *Capital;* no one left the party because they found
out that *Capital* was wrong. The PCF had weathered myriad doctrinal
shifts because its internal mechanism for generating group identity had
remained intact. "It is because there is a communist dream that there is
a communist *we,* and therefore an organized communist practice." The
"crisis of Marxism" in the 1970s was a crisis in the union and political
organizations that generated and sustained that dream. "This ideology is
in crisis to the very extent that the modes of organization, transmission,
and preservation of the 'idea' which ground it are becoming, in this part
of the world, technologically and economically obsolete."[7] Communism
was outmoded not because liberalism had shown the falsity of capitalist
exploitation but because new technologies of information had undermined the party's mechanisms for instilling its worldview, making its
claim to represent the working class increasingly untenable.

The Communists were the party of the past. Debray reserved his sharp-
est critiques for the intellectual abstractions of such *gauchistes* as the
Althusserians-turned-Maoists, many of whom he knew from his days at
the ENS. French Maoism never expressed the dream of a *we:* it was simply
"metaphor raised to the level of politics."[8] While Debray the Guevarist
had been a voluntarist in rebellion against structuralist limitations on
revolutionary action, his Althusserian classmates had been structuralists.
In prison during May 1968, Debray had embraced the structuralism of
a collective unconscious and of an ideology that undergird social action.
His former classmates pursued an inverse path. They rejected Althusser's
structuralism for a philosophy of revolutionary spontaneity. Over the next

6. Debray, *Lettre aux communistes,* 160.
7. Régis Debray, *Critique de la raison politique, ou L'Inconscient religieux* (Paris, 1981),
196, 159.
8. Régis Debray, *Les Rendez-vous manqués pour Pierre Goldmann* (Paris, 1975), 96.

two decades, Debray's defense of republican ideology and the institutions that transmitted it would shade into a social(ist) conservatism; many of his Althusserian classmates would shift as easily from spontaneity to social liberalism and postmodernism.

Debray was particularly hostile to New Left exponents of "cultural" revolution, which he saw as ultimately eroding the very historical culture on which real revolutionary change depended. An amazed Debray went to London to thank Tariq Ali and Robin Blackburn of the *New Left Review* for their efforts to win his release from prison and ended up driving in a limousine to see John Lennon and being filmed with Lennon for the *Imagine* video.[9] Debray borrowed from the Situationists the idea of the "society of the spectacle"[10] to explain that nowhere had revolution been as thoroughly commodified and gutted of meaning as in the United States.

> While it has been shown that you can mobilize people by action that offers them an *example,* to present them with action as a spectacle is a *caricature* and will inevitably demobilize them. A prime example of such "spectacle" action is to be found among the Americans with the manifestations of a certain "new left" "protest" or "yippy-ism." . . . From depicting the revolution in a cartoon strip to looking on the cartoon strip as the revolution, from writing a screenplay on a real revolution to considering the writing of screenplays as the ultimate in revolutionary activity, the distance between reality and fantasy is not great.
>
> What is such spectacle but a way of alienating the revolutionary initiative of the masses, presenting to them as a spectacle what is their own force, surreptitiously filched from them? When the dominating power, the profit-making society, passes on its own virus—the image and the fascination of the image—to the would-be spokesmen of the dominated, the infection spreads most rapidly. Revolutionary action turns into a *spectacle;* organizing it becomes *putting on a show;* presentations of propaganda become *visual montages,* theoretical statements *posters,* and leaders *personalities:* no one escapes the treatment. One need only consider the fate of the Black Panthers. The system against which they were protesting contaminated their protest by transforming it into a show, thus reabsorbing it and finally treating it as entertainment. A number of Black Panthers ended up by showing the dominant white world a mirror image of itself, its own reactions, reversed but in substance the same: hence both the ease with which they captured that

9. Tariq Ali, *Street Fighting Years* (London, 1987), 252–53.
10. See Guy Debord, *La Société du spectacle* (Paris, 1967).

world's attention, and their inevitable evanescence. The world of the show is the world of the moment. Permanence means boredom.[11]

Guevara was killed twice, Debray complained, first by the Bolivian army, "then by the millions of posters. Nothing would have exasperated him more than the symbol he has become."[12] In criticizing the phenomenon of revolutionaries giving way to those who produced and disseminated images of revolution, Debray provided an early instance of the "mediocratic" interpretation that he would later apply to French intellectual life.

Some former *gauchistes* went on to achieve great success in publishing and advertising; they mastered the communication technologies that had passed the Communists by, but used them to attack the Jacobin and socialist culture on which Debray believed the left depended. Debray saw the explosive combination of radical abstraction and intellectual commodification as fueling the meteoric rise of the one-time *gauchistes*–turned– New Philosophers in the mid-1970s. He traced a direct path from the *gauchistes'* use of language with no grounding in the social world—their incitements to violence or their self-identification as the New Resistance— to the verbal pretensions of the New Philosophers. Their explanations of the gulag as the culmination of Marxist thought struck Debray as a reiteration of the Althusserian students' fervent belief that theory dictated social reality. This intellectual sleight of hand then allowed the New Philosophers to turn the gulag from a historical entity into a myth of evil, transportable everywhere, with no need for empirical verification: "In the arsenal of our 'political sciences,' *totalitarianism* serves just about the same functions as *fanaticism* for Enlightenment thinkers."[13]

---

11. Régis Debray, *A Critique of Arms,* trans. Rosemary Sheed (New York, 1977), 112–13. "In the United States, the all-powerful nature of the media did at least as much to liquidate the student movement (and even the Black movement) as police repression. It was the media that imposed the leaders [*responsables*] on the 'movement,' choosing them from among the most irresponsible": Debray, *Modeste contribution aux discours et cérémonies officielles du dixième anniversaire* (Paris, 1978), 68–69. For a similar interpretation of the American New Left, see Todd Gitlin, *The Whole World Is Watching* (Berkeley, 1980).

12. Régis Debray, "Les Deux Morts du 'Ché'" (1977), in *L'Espérance au purgatoire* (Paris, 1980), 121. Debray was particularly exasperated by the fact that the cult of the dead Che became totally divorced from the substance of Guevara's thought and action. Among "posthumous disciples," referring to Che became a way of asserting revolutionary élan without analysis of what Guevarism might mean in practice, of "compensatory fantasizing" rather than action, or worse: "For spectators of the revolution, mentioning his name became the fashionable and up-to-date way to condemn the extremes of that proletarian socialism to which Che had dedicated his life, in Cuba and elsewhere": *Critique of Arms,* 17–18.

13. Debray, *Modeste contribution,* 76–77; *Rendez-vous manqués,* 104n; "Les Pleureuses du printemps," *Nouvel observateur,* June 13, 1977; *Le Scribe* (Paris, 1980), 8, 235; Debray and Noam Chomsky, "Narration et pouvoir: Massacres et média," *Change* 38 (October 1979): 111; Debray, *Critique de la raison politique,* 22 (quote).

At the core of the New Philosophy was an attack on intellectuals as propagators of ideology—the cause of all evils—and servants of the state, the instruments of ideology. Debray saw this string of condemnations as the revenge of abstract rationalism on itself. He held that all societies are predicated on some collective belief system and require intellectuals to give voice to it.[14] The choice for intellectuals was not between power and antipower, but which power to serve. The New Philosophers' error was to condemn ideology while ignoring their own. They did so because they adopted the classical Marxist idea of ideology as ideas and ignored the way ideology functioned (for Debray) as an organizational process, whether or not the ideas that could be extracted from it were true or false.

Debray was particularly critical of the New Philosophers' refusal to see their own pronouncements as the ideological expressions of Giscardian liberalism. The New Philosophers embraced the "rights of man" in defense of the pure, powerless plebe against "Power," especially that of the state.[15] The avowed antipolitics of the humanitarian movements that displaced political activism in the late 1970s troubled Debray. When his old friend Bernard Kouchner, founder of Médecins du Monde (and one-time secretary of state for humanitarian affairs), said that he always wanted to be with those who received bombs rather than those who launched them, Debray responded that he wanted to be on the side of justice, whether or not it could be conceived as the locus of anti-Power. Debray trotted out his favorite example: In 1944 would Kouchner have tended to wounded *milice* or *résistants?* For his part, Debray remained loyal to the anti-Kouchner Che Guevara, the physician who put aside his stethoscope to pick up a rifle.[16]

Debray focused his critique on two elements of the New Philosophers' politics of human rights. First of all, it struck him (as it had struck Sartre) as an ideology of the West in the most classic sense: it was a new universal to impose on others. He argued that the exercise of human rights in the West was based on material abundance and more particularly on the West's exploitation of the non-West: "the first condition of the exercise of human rights in the West is that they don't exist elsewhere." (André Burguière refers to Debray's oddly "mercantilist" approach to rights as fixed in quantity.) Equally important, Debray denied the New Philoso-

---

14. Debray, *Le Scribe,* 67.
15. Ibid., 301. The New Philosophers' vocabulary owed much to Michel Foucault. Though Debray doubted the possibility of a Foucauldian politics, he reserved his scorn for exegetes who wrenched his concepts from their historical context (152).
16. Régis Debray, *Que vive la République* (Paris, 1989), 183–84, 206. When Kouchner organized a project to rescue Vietnamese boat people, both Raymond Aron and Jean-Paul Sartre backed it, but Debray refused to sign a petition in support. See Melinda Camber Porter, *Through Parisian Eyes* (New York, 1986), 236.

phers' premise that the state was solely a source of oppression. In their demystifications of the state (André Glucksmann) and the nation (Bernard-Henri Lévy), the New Philosophers were simply furthering the capitalist production of atomized individuals who know each other only as objects on the market or through representations in the media. For Debray, human rights are predicated on the existence of a state that is both the source and the guarantor of its citizens' rights. A stateless society is not utopian; it is barbaric.[17]

In *Le Pouvoir intellectuel en France* in 1979, Debray placed his analysis of the success of the New Philosophers in historical context. He identified three institutions that had controlled entry into the high intelligentsia (intellectuals with access to the means of mass communication) in France during the last century: the university from 1880 to 1930; the leading publishing houses from 1920 until 1968; and the mass media since 1968. Debray looked back nostalgically to the era when republican professors had triumphed over the church, the literary intelligentsia, and the press during the Dreyfus affair; and before higher education had been made subordinate to the needs of advanced capitalism. Recalling Paul Nizan's savage attack on these *universitaires* in *The Watchdogs,* Debray, the Nizan of his own class at the ENS, wrote that were Nizan "alive today, the odds are that he would be defending the watchdogs."[18]

While professors had served the republican state, the authors who dominated the high intelligentsia in the decades after Nizan's *Watchdogs* appeared were subject to a new set of masters. "It is the natural reflex and the vocation of the intellectual to be on the side of those who own the papers (and/or the microphones, screens, concert halls, galleries . . .)." Thus, to use a particularly resonant example in Debray's personal universe, "until 1943, the Germans and their collaborators could count on the support of almost all of the high intelligentsia of France." These writers accepted the occupation authorities not out of political sympathy but "because the material and administrative means of communication were in their hands.[19]

It was in this second period that Debray detected the emergence of elements of the contemporary mediocracy. Debray made André Malraux—the intellectual to whom Debray himself is most often compared—a fundamental figure in this transformation. Malraux, he argued, was the first of a new genre of writers who invented an authorial image (the *engagé* for Malraux): "the notoriety comes less from what we know of

17. Debray, *Que vive la République,* 197; "Il faut des esclaves aux hommes libres" (1978), in *L'Espérance au purgatoire,* 69 (quote); *La Puissance et les rêves* (Paris, 1984), 252; André Burguière, ed., *Le Tiers Monde et la gauche* (Paris, 1979), p. 66; Debray, *Le Scribe,* 213–84.
18. Debray, *Teachers, Writers, Celebrities,* 57.
19. Ibid., 143.

their work than from what we think we know of their life. . . . We buy them not to read a work but to absorb a privileged existence."[20]

Whereas certain professors or authors had previously controlled entry to the high intelligentsia through the selection and publicizing of individual texts, intellectuals lost control of this sphere in the Fifth Republic to a small world of "mediocrats": "Forty mediocrats (at the very most) have the power of life and death over 40,000 authors."[21] No "mediocrat" was more important than Bernard Pivot, for years the host of the popular television show *Apostrophes*, on which he interviewed authors. Ever the iconoclast, Debray dismissed the accolades given Pivot for raising the level of intellectual life in France and attacked him instead for exercising "a true dictatorship over the book market."[22]

With the mediocratic colonization of the world of culture, media-made celebrities displaced true intellectuals in the public sphere. For Debray, no further proof was necessary than the sudden stardom of the New Philosophers after a media blitz in the press and on *Apostrophes* in 1975 and 1976. In the past, a group of intellectuals would have had to organize themselves into a school or start a review; their work would have been debated among professors or read by authors before being presented to the public. Needless to say, Debray believed that the New Philosophers could never have passed such tests. The New Philosophers did not develop a school of thought; they were solely personalities—Malraux taken to the limit. As intellectual production increasingly became a commodity, the nostrums of old were more rapidly packaged as new philosophies.[23] The simplicity of the New Philosophy rendered it perfect for mediatic presentation in terms of dichotomies such as democracy/totalitarianism and humanism/terrorism. "If the magic discourse of the Rights of Man had not existed, the society of spectacle would have invented it."[24] The trumpeting of the "rights of man" proved to be "the best mediatic strategy" because its universal acceptability guaranteed a maximum audience, while its lack

20. Régis Debray, "André Malraux, ou L'Impératif du mensonge" (1977), in *Eloges* (Paris, 1986), 115. In signing a petition for Debray's release from jail in 1967, Malraux explained that Debray had done what he had done as a youth. See Jean Lacouture, *André Malraux*, trans. Alan Sheridan (New York, 1975), 457. Debray has gone to some lengths to differentiate himself from Malraux: he claims to think of himself as more like the fascist Pierre Drieu de La Rochelle. See Debray, *Les Masques* (Paris, 1987), 174.

21. Debray, *Teachers, Writers, Celebrities*, 119. Debray was not alone in his concern over the effects the media were having on intellectual life in France. For Foucault's worries, see Didier Eribon, *Michel Foucault (1926–1984)* (Paris, 1989), 312.

22. Porter, *Through Parisian Eyes*, 234. On Pivot, see Hervé Hamon and Patrick Rotman, *Les Intellocrates* (Paris, 1981), 172–92. Debray made his comments while a member of the Mitterrand government. They created such an uproar that he was forced to retract them.

23. See Debray, *Teachers, Writers, Celebrities*, 111n, on the intellectual fads of the late 1970s as repetitions of past work.

24. Debray, *Que vive la République*, 180.

of content ensured that it could not become the basis of effective political action.[25]

INTELLECTUALS AND POLITICS IN THE
MEDIOCRATIC AGE

From his time in prison in Bolivia, Debray had been critical of the student
revolutionaries of May 1968.[26] The theatrics of the Gauche Prolétarienne,
followed by the appearance of the New Philosophers, confirmed his belief
that the "'society of spectacle' had found its apotheosis" in the May
events.[27] On the tenth anniversary of May 1968, Debray wrote a scathing
tract in which he portrayed the *événements* as a cultural revolution necessary to enable American-style capitalism and social life to sweep away the
impediments in education, culture, and values to its complete triumph in
France.[28] A real "French ideology" (not that of New Philosopher Lévy)
that had preserved "the idea of *nation* and independence and the idea of
the *working class* and revolution" expired at precisely the point at which
their purported proponents thought they were asserting them.[29]

Gauchistes who reflected on May 1968 thought only of the defeat of
the students and workers, but Debray was equally concerned with the
ensuing Gaullist reaction. That reaction too was a victim of a ruse of
Reason: the manifestation of an endangered nationhood that ironically
prepared the way for further denationalization of economic and political
life in the hands of new liberals such as Valéry Giscard d'Estaing. "The
people of May thought they were burying capitalism, when in fact they
were seeing the last of their socialist illusions. The people of June thought
they were burying the anti-France, when in face they were turning French
government over to the Trilateral Commission." The very things that
soixante-huitards worked for in the 1970s—decentralization of political
and economic power and affirmation of the individual and the rights of
minorities—were most developed in the archcapitalist United States; it
was a natural progression from the antistatist ideology of 1968 to the

25. Debray, *La Puissance et les rêves*, 251.
26. Régis Debray, "Time and Politics" (1969), in *Prison Writings*, trans. Rosemary Sheed
(London, 1973), 114.
27. Debray, *Rendez-vous manqués*, 125.
28. A portion of Debray's *Modeste contribution* was translated in *New Left Review* 115
(May–June 1979): 45–65. In the same issue (66–71) Henri Weber criticizes Debray for
blaming May 1968 for developments in the 1970s which were the result of the movement's
defeat. The difference between the two is that what Weber sees as centers of resistance to
capitalism, Debray sees equally well as centers of resistance to the only possible bulwark
against capitalism: the socialist nation-state.
29. Debray, *Modeste contribution*, 39.

libertarianism of the New Philosophers—and the liberalism of Giscard d'Estaing.[30]

For Debray, television had not simply recorded the specter of revolution in May 1968; it had created it. "In May '68, the media *made* history 'live' for the first time ever; the fate of the country was decided on the radio and acted out on TV."[31] He saw this phenomenon as a harbinger of a mediatic democracy in which news professionals make events and spectacle supersedes the substance of politics. In a politics built on consensus rather than principle, the search was not for the best way to communicate an idea but for the idea that communicated best.[32] Everyone recognized the domination exercised by Communist states over civil society; for that very reason, this domination was weaker than that exercised in the West, where the state was subject to the power of the media.[33] The New Philosophy had its counterpart, both ideologically and in respect to its relations with the media, in Giscardian liberalism. The victory of Giscard d'Estaing over Mitterrand in 1974 had been the victory of Marshall MacLuhan over Gutenburg.[34] In an acerbic rewriting of Marx, Debray explained:

> In 1871, of the 38 million French, 24 million lived in the countryside. As the fields emptied little by little, swelling the more "dangerous" urban classes, the female electorate for awhile picked up the baton from the peasant electorate in the service of the dominant class. But dechristianization, the freeing of mores, the growth of the female labor force soon risked creating a dangerous void. It was then that television . . . recreated in industrial France the material and psychological conditions of *rural* atomization. In front of the television, we are all peasants with our little plots; we want a Bonaparte and will end up having one.[35]

"In transforming public life into a quasi-private affair, opposing not classes and ideas but individuals and temperaments, television tends, in fact, to depoliticize the political itself."[36] "A consensual society is a dead

30. Ibid., 43–44 (quote), 50, 54.
31. Debray, *Teachers, Writers, Celebrities*, 89.
32. Debray, *Que vive la République*, 99. "By eliminating any exterior referential to the message, the system of commercial communication has deduced . . . that the spectacle value of news is rigorously independent of the value of the truth of its terms": *Rendez-vous manqués*, 135. "For the media, the objective world—the thing there is something to speak of—is what the other media are saying": *Teachers, Writers, Celebrities*, 118.
33. Debray and Chomsky, "Narration et pouvoir," 116.
34. Debray, *Rendez-vous manqués*, 111–13.
35. Debray, *Lettre aux communistes*, 39.
36. Debray, "Sa Majesté la Télé" (1978), in *L'Espérance*, 60.

society." Making people spectators of a political match without an engagement in principles ultimately benefitted conservatives.[37]

Given the concentration and the personalization of power and the individuation of reception in "the Bonapartist organ" of television (and in the constitution of the Fifth Republic), Debray believed that the left would have to unite behind Mitterrand as the only figure who could bring it victory without succumbing to the small screen.[38] In fact, Debray championed Mitterrand because he embodied old-fashioned, distinctly bourgeois values at risk in the age of television: "By his origins, his culture, his disdain for money, his sense of principles placed above techniques, [Mitterrand] belongs to a French social, political, and *moral* class that will not survive."[39]

Few French intellectuals rallied to Mitterrand's campaigns or to his government after the Socialist victory in 1981; Jean Daniel has suggested that Debray's theory of intellectuals' subservience to the media comforted Mitterrand in his disappointment.[40] Debray characterized this disengagement, like that promoted by television, as essentially rightest. "French intellectuals don't want to have anything to do with the state," he remarked in 1983, "for the state is the *mauvais objet*, to go back to a Maurrasian expression."[41] While common wisdom would have it that intellectuals who took on responsibilities in the state increased their power, Debray claimed that his entry into the government as an adviser to Mitterrand had an inverse effect: "An intellectual increases his power in opposing power, lowers it in compromising with it. I betrayed the family of my youth—the left of petitions—which lived on failures and succumbed under victory."[42]

Debray saw participation in the Socialist government as the best opportunity to wrest France from its slide into spectacle and consensus. "I had this feeling in 1981, that France would disappear in banality, and anonymity, let's say, in an attitude of liberal chic. And I wanted to work on foreign policy, which seemed to be the key to the singularity of my

---

37. Debray, *Que vive la République*, p. 110 (quote); "Sa Majesté la Télé," 61.

38. Debray, *Le Scribe*, 133 (quote); *Lettre aux communistes*, 76–79. Debray participated actively in the preparation of Mitterrand's 1974 television appearances. See Olivier Duhamel, *La Gauche et la Vᵉ République* (Paris, 1980), 276–77n.

39. Debray, *Lettre aux communistes*, 79. See *Que vive la République*, 22–23, on Mitterrand as the providential man "à cheval sur la fin de l'Ecrit et le début de l'Image."

40. Jean Daniel, *Les Religions d'un président* (Paris, 1988), 87. Debray made an emotional appeal for intellectuals to support Mitterrand in 1981: "Le Temps du respect," *Le Monde*, January 25, 1981.

41. Philippe Boggio, "Le Silence des intellectuels de gauche," *Le Monde*, July 28, 1983.

42. Debray, *Les Masques*, 202. Ali complained that Debray "had become a pompous and shifty functionary of the French state": *Street Fighting Years*, 260.

country."[43] He believed that the mediocracy was sapping the French state of its special mission in the world: the effect of consensual politics was even more pernicious in foreign than domestic affairs. In response, Debray took as his inspiration de Gaulle, whose far-reaching foreign policies had frequently been attacked by the press.[44] In treatises on foreign relations he wrote while in government service, Debray expressed two basic ideas: Socialists would have to forgo a foreign policy based on abstractions; and in the particular context of the Second Cold War of the early 1980s, France should not let itself be subsumed in the "West" in the name of such principles.

Debray criticized long-time Socialist precepts in the realm of foreign policy (arbitration, collective security, disarmament, pacifism, human rights, etc.) as manifestations of an Enlightenment idealism that saw in history the working out of an immanent Reason. Socialists should abandon moral and political crusades as guides to action, and should not enroll in those of other nations. Debray called instead for a "realpolitik of the left," which would be based on an idea of the nation not in terms of geographical borders but as a complex of global military, economic, cultural, and communication systems, and on the goal of reducing others' means of acting on the nation—through force (nuclear arms), persuasion (telecommunications), and so forth.[45] The aim of such a strategy was not autonomy but independence.[46] In turn, it should be French policy to respect the interests of other nations as long as they did not challenge those of France.[47] In practice, this approach incorporated a degree of continuity from Debray's years in Latin America in its support for nationalist movements (i.e., the Afghan rebels and the Sandinistas) against hegemonic powers. The lesson of the Cuba of Debray's youth became that a movement against a local oligarchy (generally tied to one superpower) must be supported by nations such as France to prevent it from being driven into the arms of the other superpower.

Yet France itself could learn a lesson from non-Western nations' striv-

43. Quoted in Porter, *Through Parisian Eyes,* 225.

44. Debray, *La Puissance et les rêves,* 196–99. In particular, Debray argued that the French media's fixation on American events and perspectives made it difficult for France to undertake an independent foreign policy. No longer, he wrote, could a Frenchman so vilified by the American press as de Gaulle was in the 1960s be a major political leader in France: *Les Empires contre l'Europe* (Paris, 1985), 118–20, 123.

45. Debray, *La Puissance et les rêves,* 126, 132, 146–47.

46. Debray later reprised these arguments with respect to Europe, arguing that "Europe 1992" was a commercial entity, not a sacred symbolic heritage for which citizens would lay down their lives. European nations should maintain independent control of their foreign policies and armed forces, and coordinate their foreign policies rather than simply follow the American lead: *Tous Azimuts* (Paris, 1989).

47. Debray, *La Puissance et les rêves,* 119.

ings for independence of the superpowers' cultural and economic power. France and other European countries had to resist efforts by the United States to impose its interests on them through invocation of "the West."[48] The temptation was particularly strong in France, where the triumph of liberalism in social thought had its counterpart in a rampant, pent-up denunciation of Communist totalitarianism ("the East") at precisely the time when the Soviet empire was crumbling. The media, increasingly American in technique, conveyed an overwhelmingly pro-Atlantist message. Debray reiterated to all who would listen that American cultural hegemony posed a much greater threat to France than the fragmented Communist world: "There is more power in rock music, videos, blue jeans, fast food, news networks and TV satellites than in the entire Red Army."[49]

THE FRENCH REVOLUTION, SCHOOLS, AND SCARVES

For Debray, the nature of the foreign policies France would pursue and the French state's willingness to execute them were directly related to the nation's ability to wrest itself from a culture of meaningless signs and commodified signifiers. It was natural therefore for Debray to participate in the planning of the bicentennial of the French Revolution. Debray had always had a special personal relation to the revolution. The nation he embraced was a matter not of geography but of history—a history that began in 1789 and lived on in the myth of the republic. On Debray's first trip to Cuba in 1961 he had imagined himself an envoy from the Convention; he took the name Danton when he associated with guerrillas in Latin America.[50] Debray always stood firm against leftist denigrations of the revolution. "It was our good fortune to have a revolution—despised nowadays as merely national-democratic—which created everything best about this country and its history."[51]

Until the late 1970s, the historiography of the revolution had anchored

48. This is the central theme of *Les Empires contre l'Europe*. Debray is particularly critical of summit conferences, which he denounces as media events in which—as in domestic media politics—the goal is consensus rather than frank affirmation of difference and agreement.

49. Debray, *Tous Azimuts*, 117n; "From Kalashnikovs to God and Computers," *New Perspectives Quarterly* 5 (Fall 1988): 43 (quote).

50. The Convention because he felt an affinity with Victor Hugues, a character in Alejo Carpentier's *Le Siècle des lumières:* Debray, *Les Masques*, 48; Danton because of Buchner's portrayal of Danton as sensual and impulsive in *The Death of Danton*: Debray, *Journal d'un petit bourgeois entre deux feux et quatre murs* (Paris, 1976), 78–79.

51. Régis Debray, "Marxism and the National Question," *New Left Review* 105 (September–October 1977): 39–40.

the division between left and right in France. Socialist and Communist historians had accepted Georges Clemenceau's pronouncement that the revolution was of a piece: the Terror had been necessary to secure the revolution against its enemies. Historians on the right, such as Jacques Bainville and Pierre Gaxotte, had approached the revolution as antirepublican counterrevolutionaries. For both sides, the continuing conflict over the meaning of the revolution was a contest over the nature of the French polity. François Furet's proclamation that "the French Revolution is over" in his influential *Penser la Révolution française* (1979) marked a break with this tradition.[52]

Debray interpreted Furet's dictum as the culmination of the ongoing effort to repudiate the Revolution's Jacobin heritage. He compared Furet's obituary for the revolution to Philippe Pétain's in 1940, adding that at least Pétain had offered his "National Revolution" as a replacement. For Debray, the myth of the revolution constituted the French republican tradition he had embraced in prison. It was the revolution, to use Debray's terminology, that made the French a *we*. Debray interpreted Furet's work as a response to the mass media's demand for a consensual interpretation of the revolution and saw it as contributing to the "mythologic anorexia" that was dissolving the French collectivity into individuals united only by mediatic representations—the image of a national community.[53]

Debray accused Furet of meeting the needs of a "postmodern democracy" by following the Anglo-American practice of splitting the revolution into the good (the Declaration of the Rights of Man) and the bad (the Terror). The divisive idea of fraternity that had fueled the *we* of the republican nation—"that which does not divide does not cement"—was abandoned for the fête of May 1968, to which all were invited. Debray denounced preparation of a bicentennial that made the Declaration rather than the nation-state the major accomplishment of the revolution.[54] As he saw it, the Declaration was predicated on the existence of a state and of citizenship, not against the state, as contemporary theorists would have it. Their invocation of the Declaration obscured the fact that it had survived only because the Jacobins—like *résistants* during the war and Third World revolutionaries today[55]—had made choices that homilists of human rights would be totally unprepared to make: "in 1792, it was either

52. François Furet, *Interpreting the French Revolution,* trans. Elborg Forster (Cambridge, 1981).

53. Debray, *Que vive la République,* 18, 20, 56, 121 (quote).

54. Ibid., 58, 59, 87, 90 (quote).

55. Debray explains to Mitterrand: "You took the side of a minority spurned as fanatical outlaws, odious to the majority of French people, who made blood flow, and not always that of the guilty": ibid., 68.

the terrorists and the Committee of Public Safety or Brunswick's army in Paris."[56]

Debray looks to the public school as the institution that must carry on the revolutionaries' mission of instilling civic virtue and national sentiment in contemporary France. Its primary function should not be to prepare students for entry into the economy; it should instead give youth the tools of reasoning and criticism necessary to fulfill their duties as citizens in a mediocratic world hostile to such activities.[57] Debray is quite aware that his faith in schooling goes against the grain of a general post-May critique of power. He defends an opposing tradition in which freedom of thought is based on fixed identities, exclusions, and hierarchies. These things are necessary for the inculcation of a radical ideology; the alternative is the false freedom of isolated individuals brought together in the media spectacle:

> [O]ur Western societies are more and more "dissipated" (little studious), "unruly" (resistant to teaching). . . . [A]n "undisciplined" society (one in which it is not good to be a disciple) is hardly likely to lead to "socialism." Not because "socialism is the barracks." But because it is school, and it is true that the barracks are the institutional unconscious of school (for example, in France, formation in the lycée). . . . The barracks, we know, is always the others' school. If state television were to bring the barracks into the home, of the two evils we would have to choose the lesser.[58]

Debray's intervention in the "Islamic scarf affair" in 1989 reveals the implications of his conception of the republican school in contemporary France. The Jacobin France that Debray conjured up in his Bolivian prison cell had in fact long been a land of immigration; in the 1950s and 1960s, France was transformed by the arrival of large numbers of North African workers, many of whom have settled in France and raised families. Since Debray's return to France in 1973, the French have been racked by the issue whether they could accommodate these immigrants in French society and culture. The leading mechanism for deculturation and acculturation in France since the nineteenth century has been the republican school. The demand of female Islamic students in France to wear their traditional scarf to school in 1989 precipitated a crisis and nationwide debate over multiculturalism in French society.

The post-*soixante-huitards* whom Debray had long derided defended

56. Debray, *Critique of Arms*, 287. In the 1981 elections, Debray had the French choosing between the republic and the émigrés: "Le Temps du respect."
57. Debray, *Que vive la République*, 32.
58. Debray, *Critique de la raison politique*, 363.

Islamic women's right to affirm their identity against the norming role of the school in terms of "the right to difference." Not surprisingly, Debray rejected this position. He co-wrote a letter to the minister of national education which referred to it as "the Munich of the republican school" and affirmed that in order to create an independent republican citizenry, public school had to give students the opportunity to "forget their community of origin"; they would not be able to do so if they were allowed to display signs of a belief that affirmed an a priori difference among students before they ever entered the classroom.[59] All societies, Debray believes, are threatened by the irruption of a social unconscious of an essentially religious nature: in France, where the commodification of intellectual life has eroded the republican institutions in which Enlightenment rationalism could flourish, the public school remained the last bastion against the resurgence of atavistic fanaticism.[60]

The scarf controversy reveals clearly how Debray's sense of a French essence under attack connects him to a nineteenth-century republican socialist tradition deeply mistrustful not only of clericalism but of the spread of the market and of "cosmopolitan" challenges to an indivisible French republican culture as well. Debray discounts the extent of racism in French society and denies that antiracism could be more than another exercise in feel-good consensus.[61] In a long follow-up essay to the public letter, Debray used the scarf controversy to reiterate his view of the conflict facing France in terms of the classic debates over republican virtue. France could choose to be its republican self: lay, centralized, constituted by a state that is the source of the citizens' liberties. Or it could become an American democracy: accepting of difference, decentralized, a civil society bound together by the market, governed by contracts rather than the law, in which image triumphs over idea and oral expression over writing.[62] A year later, Debray framed this debate in terms of the dual legacy of the resistance to the Fifth Republic: de Gaulle embodied the true symbolic heritage of France while overseeing the nation's modernization; Mitterrand, a disappointed Debray lamented, was presiding over the demise of the last republican stronghold, the schools.[63] While it is a commonplace on the left to speak critically of Mitterrand's self-fashioning

59. Elisabeth Badinter, Régis Debray, Alain Finkielkraut, Elisabeth de Fontenay, and Catherine Kintzler, "Profs, ne capitulons pas!" *Nouvel Observateur,* November 2–8, 1989, 30–31. The issue was particularly disturbing for feminists, who interpreted the wearing of the scarf in school as acquiescence by the republic in the subordinate position of women.
60. Debray, *Cours de médiologie générale,* 354–55.
61. Debray, *Que vive la République,* 28–29.
62. Régis Debray, "Etes-vous démocrate ou républicain?" *Nouvel Observateur,* November 30–December 6, 1989, 49–55. See Jacques Julliard's reply: "Ou est-elle, votre République?" December 7–13, 1989, 50–51.
63. Régis Debray, *A demain de Gaulle* (Paris, 1990), 120.

into a new de Gaulle, the structuralist Debray claims that mediological changes since 1968 have made this transformation virtually impossible: Mitterrand is de Gaulle's opposite, the image of de Gaulle.

Like ethnicity, gender plays a crucial role in Debray's differentiation of his republican ideal from "American democracy."[64] The hands of all republicans are still damp with the blood of the murdered Father in 1793. It is this act that makes them "brothers," that is to say sons of the republic, "the Mother of us all." The citizen of the republic is implicitly a male whose forbidden passion for Marianne is directed toward the nation: "one must love the Republic, but the love of laws is hardly erotic. It is the nation that feminized duty; *la personne France* renders the general interest an individual matter; gives the universal flesh, color, and perfume." (Debray used the same analogy to explain why allegiance to a young Europe could not now replace allegiance to an aging France among virtuous citizens: "This unhappy interval constrains us to unhappy *civic celibacy*. We can no longer love the one because she is too far along in years and the other is still a featureless child. A return to the individual as the supreme end. Narcissism, generalized onanism.")[65]

If republican citizenship is masculine in Debray's account, its antithesis, postmodern democracy, is coded feminine. In mediological terms, the shift from one to the other took place largely between the time Debray entered the ENS and the time he returned to France: "1959–1969: it is no longer the reign of the telegraph (a vertical, virile, public, republican technique of transmission); it is not yet that of the telephone (feminine, horizontal, private, and democratic)."[66] Of the contemporary discomfort with French revolutionaries, he wrote, "The 'male accents' of the times and the lives in peplum bore us, and for good reason: we are more Greek. To us, so feminine, the 'virile' seems very funny"; "Homo republicanus has masculine faults; Homo democraticus has feminine qualities."[67] Democracy has no room for the "great men" who incarnate the symbolic heritage of the nation and are willing to challenge a politics of opinion polls.[68]

Debray characterized his political activity in similarly gendered terms.

64. In Debray's life and oeuvre, independent women are often duplicitous. He blamed his capture in Bolivia on a female double agent. (See Georgie Anne Geyer, *Guerrilla Prince* [Boston, 1991], 314–15.) *Les Masques* chronicles how a woman with whom Debray was involved for a decade used the personal traits that had allowed her to elude Pinochet to deceive him—and the devastating effect her deception had. He wondered if it was "because for so long he had been the oppressor-oppressed in love that [he] wanted to 'liberate people'" (133).
65. Debray, *Que vive la République*, 20, 82, 91, 125, 84 (quote).
66. Debray, *A demain de Gaulle*, 44.
67. Debray, *Que vive la République*, 78; "Etes-vous démocrate ou républicain?," 53.
68. Debray, *A demain de Gaulle*, 60.

He explained that in leaving Latin America—the world where Che was attempting to create the "New Man"—he had renounced a "certain fraternity." Though he was never a member of the Socialist Party, Debray credited it with providing "the very rare moments of fraternity and euphoria I have experienced in France." Yet in France he has few male friends because men cannot develop fraternity except in combat, an increasingly rare commodity in the consensual world of post-1968 France.[69]

Debray sees the left heritage in France as that of public institutions that preserve the republican culture of the revolution against consumerist disintegration and religious *intégralisme*. Rather than through the market and the media, as in contemporary liberalism, he contends, it is through the myth of the republic—coded male and unicultural—that the French people should realize themselves and their aspirations. The institutions that foster this myth are threatened by a new feudalism in which private interests control all means of production, communication, and exchange, while the public school system is attacked by a renascent clericalism.[70] Debray's fear is that if the nation is, as Benedict Anderson suggests, an "imagined community," the medium in which that imagination can flourish is being subordinated to new media antithetic to the dream.[71] Stripped of its republican heritage, France will lose its systems for establishing meaning and eventually will fall prey, like the non-West, to new fanaticisms more destructive than the ideologies of old, while abandoning its sovereignty to stronger powers in foreign relations.

ROUSSEAU AND MACHIAVELLI

Debray occupies a liminal yet illuminating place in French intellectual life, akin to Rousseau's place in the Enlightenment. Like Rousseau, Debray discovered the virtues of his native land through long journeys and separations from home. He portrayed the guerrilla in *Revolution in the Revolution?* in what he termed a *vision à la Rousseau*.[72] Later Debray returned to his *faux frère* Rousseau, praising him for seeing the divinity as necessary to give laws to men, and making Rousseau's origins of civil society the model for his own study of the foundation of politics.[73] Both Rous-

---

69. Debray, *Les Masques,* 36–37, 183 (quote), 184. Not surprisingly, the United States represents a very different form of male bonding for Debray. One of his most traumatic memories—Debray refers to it as a "birth"—was of finding himself among copulating men in a New York YMCA shower on July 4 during his first visit to the United States (47).

70. Debray, *A demain de Gaulle,* 130–31.

71. Benedict Anderson, *Imagined Communities* (London, 1983).

72. Régis Debray, *Revolution in the Revolution?* trans. Bobbye Ortiz (New York, 1967), 113–14.

73. Debray, *Les Masques,* 243 (quote); *Le Scribe,* 131; *Critique de la raison politique,* 23.

seau and Debray were loners who analyzed the forces of social cohesion that held groups together. Rousseau drew inspiration from reading about the peoples encountered in the New World, and Debray saw his experiences in the New World of his day as serving the same purpose: whatever in his work would stand up to actual practice, he attributed "to his excursions among the savages of politics, on the 'state of nature' side of collective existence."[74] Debray's status as an intellectual outsider, what Jean Daniel refers to as Debray's *difficulté d'être;*[75] his self-description as an intellectual who takes a moral stance by going against the optimal conditions for communication;[76] his rejection of today's salon philosophers; and his critiques of the deficiencies of Enlightenment rationalism, of the feminization of culture, and of the mediatic corruption of civil society in France (reminiscent of Rousseau on theater in his native Geneva) in the name of the nation and of civic virtue have arguably made him the contemporary French Jean-Jacques.

In an era when opposition politics has generally meant opposition to politics, Debray takes the position that intellectuals always serve power: every denunciation hides an affirmation. To be *engagé* is not to announce a principle but to embrace a cause, with all the risks it entails. Debray's roles as mouthpiece, confidant, and adviser to men in high office, from Fidel Castro and Salvador Allende to Mitterrand, have made him not only today's Rousseau but a modern-day Machiavelli as well, the failed activist intellectual seeking to cut through the thickets of received wisdom to instruct princes in service to revolutionary ethics and republican virtue. This effort has led him to pen jeremiads that sound to his contemporaries increasingly like the denunciations of aging veterans of the revolution (and the First Empire) during the July Monarchy. To be a republican in a democratic age is difficult, but perhaps no more difficult than jump-starting a recalcitrant history with Che in the Bolivian wilds, and not very different.

74. Debray, *Critique de la raison politique*, 29.
75. Jean Daniel, *L'Ere des ruptures* (Paris, 1979), 285.
76. Debray, *Critique de la raison politique*, 70–71.

PART III

Intellectuals and the Dilemmas of the American Reform Tradition

7

Social Scientists and the State: Constructing the Knowledge Base for Public Policy, 1880–1920

Mary O. Furner

A potent indicator of the relationship between intellectuals and power is the influence that intellectuals in specific historical contexts exercise over the deliberations and policies of states. Influence is obviously a complex phenomenon that cannot be reduced to a simple cause-and-effect relationship in which public officials act directly in response to recommendations of particular thinkers, or intellectuals head parties, hold office, and wield power directly. Although both these kinds of influence occur, by far the more characteristic and significant pattern is the one in which intellectuals succeed in bringing policy makers to inhabit, in some sense, the same mental world that they do—to adopt the modes of analysis and explanation that experts have constructed, and thus to define problems and envisage policy alternatives similarly. Rather like the processes of "suscitation" and "permeation" that S. E. Finer attributed to the British "statesmen in disguise" who promoted Benthamite ideas during the 1830s and 1840s, this reconstruction and transference of political vocabularies is often so subtle and gradual that it goes undetected; the indebtedness of a new policy regime to specific intellectuals is unacknowledged, as in Lord Keynes's oft-cited reference to unwitting politicians taking credit for wisdom first articulated in the scribblings of a dead economist.[1]

Nor can intellectuals exert the same degree of influence all the time.

I am indebted to Leon Fink, Stephen Leonard, William Leach, A. W. Coats, John L. Thomas, and Allen Kuliloff for helpful criticisms and suggestions.

1. S. E. Finer, "Transmission of Benthamite Ideas, 1820–1850," *Studies in the Growth of Nineteenth-Century Government*, ed. Gillian Sutherland (London, 1972); John Maynard Keynes, *The General Theory of Employment, Interest, and Money* (London, 1936), 383.

Indeed, at times in American history the relationship between intellectuals and institutional power has not been strong or fruitful, and occasionally it has been overtly hostile. In general, the need for new thinking, for new methods of dealing with situations that have been recognized as policy problems, has been greatest in periods when established theories and trusted policies have ceased to work—at times, in other words, when paradigms failed, systems faltered, and regimes seemed about to topple. Often (though by no means always) anticipated in intellectual circles, such crisis moments have provided opportunities for intellectual elites to offer advice, most effectively in the form of a new "knowledge," including explanatory models and critical theories, which promised to provide solutions for the immediate crisis and a new long-term basis for policy.[2]

Such a time arrived in the United States between the 1870s and the turn of the century, with the disturbing realization, taking hold at different moments among various social groups, that laissez-faire had failed as an authoritative system. As historians have noted, the depression of the 1870s, the Great Uprising of Labor in the 1880s, and the general crisis of the 1890s focused attention on an accumulation of strains in the nineteenth-century liberal system, involving excessive numbers of business failures, massive involuntary unemployment, the rapid rise of monopolistic corporations as the dominant business and social institutions, and the unleashing of new forms of capitalist and government power against labor unions. Recurrent depressions and unprecedented conflict between industrial classes called into question potent myths of laissez-faire, among them Say's law, which had argued that generalized overproduction was impossible, and the notion of a natural harmony between classes. Previously, it had been settled opinion among the college-educated, respectable classes that a regime of unregulated competition would ensure stability and progress, while at the same time guarding against undue politicization of the market, which would surely follow from more interventionist government.[3]

No longer. Economic distress sent farmers, workers, industrialists, and

2. On the complex idea of a "knowledge base" for policy and the possibility of "social learning," see Michael Lacey and Mary O. Furner, "Social Investigation, Social Knowledge, and the State: An Introduction," in *The State and Social Investigation in Britain and the United States,* ed. Michael Lacey and Mary O. Furner (Cambridge, 1993), 3–62; Hugh Heclo, *Modern Social Politics in Britain and Sweden: From Relief to Income Maintenance* (New Haven, 1974), chap. 6.

3. For a sense of the dimensions of the Gilded Age crisis of laissez-faire, see Sidney Fine, *Laissez Faire and the General Welfare State* (Ann Arbor, 1956); Robert Bruce, *1877, Year of Violence* (Chicago, 1970); Herbert Gutman, *Work, Culture, and Society in Industrializing America* (New York, 1966); Leon Fink, *Workingmen's Democracy: The Knights of Labor and American Politics* (Urbana, 1983); Lawrence Goodwyn, *Democratic Promise: The Populist Moment in America* (New York, 1976).

bankers in the advanced countries scurrying to the state for protection. Conversely, states, often reluctantly, assumed responsibility for economic well-being; and officials, whose reputations hinged on success in these endeavors, became increasingly dependent on reliable information regarding the condition and tendencies of the economy. These dependencies— of troubled social groups on states and of states on social knowledge— created a market for ideas, attracting intellectual energy to timely issues and opening for those with something useful to offer unprecedented access to the counsels of state.[4]

In the Gilded Age, or more accurately in a long Progressive Era, extending from the 1880s through World War I, a small contingent of talented, strategically placed social scientists seized the opportunity. Social science, and particularly economics, played a leading role in the construction of a complex, capacious, multifaceted "new liberalism" that proved, from the standpoint of its durability and flexibility, to be a worthy successor to the highly serviceable but by then outmoded fusion of individualist, antistatist liberalism and democratic republicanism that had been the dominant ideological system earlier in the nineteenth century. Just then organizing their discipline within the new university setting, in revolt themselves against classical liberalism, and compelled by repeated shocks to the economy to offer some sort of alternative, the first generation of professional economists constructed new concepts and explanations that crowded out older and rival vocabularies for describing industrial society and its problems.[5]

But precisely how, and how effectively, did American economists respond to the crisis of laissez-faire? To what effect, and by what mechanisms, did the language, analytical strategies, and ideological purposes of these particular intellectuals shape the public discourse on possible methods for bringing order to the chaos created by unregulated competition in the product and labor markets? How did their work compare with later achievements in public policy?

PROGRESSIVE Era economists (and the policy makers who adopted their terms) followed a course somewhat analogous to that of the founding

4. On the professionalization of American social science, see Mary O. Furner, *Advocacy and Objectivity: A Crisis in the Professionalization of American Social Science, 1865–1905* (Lexington, Ky., 1975); Thomas Haskell, *The Emergence of Professional Social Science* (Urbana, 1977); Dorothy Ross, *The Origins of American Social Science* (Cambridge, 1991). On the relations between economic knowledge and government, see Mary O. Furner and Barry Supple, eds., *The State and Economic Knowledge: The American and British Experience* (New York, 1990).

5. Karl Polanyl, *The Great Transformation* (1944) (Boston, 1957). On states' dependence on knowledge, see Gianfranco Poggi, "The Modern State and the Idea of Progress," in *Progress and Its Discontents,* ed. Gabriel Almond (Berkeley, 1982), 337–60; Heclo, *Modern*

generation of American intellectuals. Deeply divided, like the Hamiltonians and Jeffersonians before them, over the proper relations between state and society, economists in this new generation charted two contrasting methods for coming to terms with modernization. They developed two distinctive streams of reform thought—a "democratic statism" that historians have neglected until recently and a "corporate liberalism" that has been widely recognized as a turn-of-the-century theoretical and policy response to the breakdown of nineteenth-century liberalism. The democratic statist strand of new liberalism developed first, during the 1880s and 1890s, as social theorists began devising new roles for government in dealing with the troublesome "social question." In these proposals, spelled out initially by social scientists such as Lester Ward, Henry Carter Adams, and Richard Ely, a division of governmental power was contemplated, between a refurbished, well-informed legislature representing all segments of the new society and an expanded, competent bureaucracy staffed by experts trained in the social disciplines. This new administrative arm of government would investigate the pressing economic questions, inform the Congress, compel the corporations to operate in the public interest, and promote distributive justice by enforcing labor laws based on social investigation.

Corporate liberalism arose later, as a reaction to these tendencies in theory and policy, which important sectors of the emerging corporate and professional hierarchies considered dangerously statist. In their voluntarist, associative version of new liberalism, harmony and stability were to be achieved mainly through processes of self-organization and mutual accommodation among self-governing industrial interests and classes, under the tolerant oversight of a government prepared to enrich the climate of information in which they operated, assist in mediating their conflicts, and legitimize their necessary functions.[6]

Social Politics, 304–22; Jack Walker, "The Diffusion of Knowledge, Policy Communities, and Agenda Setting: The Relationship of Knowledge and Power," in *New Strategic Perspectives on Social Policy,* ed. John E. Tropman, Milan J. Dluhy, and Roger M. Lind (New York, 1981), 75–96; Mary O. Furner and Barry Supple, "Ideas, Institutions, and State: An Introduction," in *State and Economic Knowledge,* 3–39.

6. "Corporate liberalism" was first identified by Martin Sklar and is most fully developed in his *Corporate Reconstruction of American Capitalism, 1890–1916* (New York, 1988). I have addressed the branching of American new liberalism into distinct statist and voluntarist strands in "Liberty versus Efficiency: The Industrial Transformation and American Social Thought," colloquium paper, Woodrow Wilson International Center for Scholars, December 1982; "Knowing Capitalism: Public Investigation and the Labor Question in the Long Progressive Era," in Furner and Supple, *State and Economic Knowledge,* 241–86; and "The Republican Tradition and the New Liberalism: Social Investigation, State Building, and Social Learning in the Gilded Age," in Lacey and Furner, *State and Social Investigation,* 171–241. See also Michael Lacey's and Elliot Brownlee's chapters in both of these volumes; Ellis Hawley, *The Great War and the Search for a Modern Order,* 2d ed. (New York, 1992);

To be sure, in constructing both of these visions, new liberals had to adapt themselves to the constraints and opportunities that all American academics faced in that formative era. To the extent that policy makers in public and private bureaucracies were their intended audience, their investigations and the analyses and recommendations that resulted from them served the needs of the moment, tinged by the political agendas of participants. Thus the idea that different conceptions of a new liberalism were founded on a "knowledge base" created by statist democrats and corporate voluntarists must be employed with due consideration for the elusiveness of that concept, and for the limitations that must necessarily be placed on any sense of the completeness, coherence, or "objectivity" of social knowledge. Both versions contained elitist and antidemocratic elements that have rightly come in for criticism.

At the same time, and for better or worse, the new liberals of the long Progressive Era must be credited with providing a surprisingly large fraction of the fundamental theories and categories that scholars, policy makers, and ordinary citizens *still* rely on for comprehending the modern industrial economy. In economics (and eventually in other disciplines, most notably the law), new liberals performed a kind of didactic function, "teaching" officials and others what to define as economic and social policy problems, and how to respond to them. Absorbed into policy applications by the 1910s, these conflicting conceptions provided the basic paradigms available for defining the role and limits of state intervention, in relation to other forms of politically sanctioned collective action, in the modern corporate economy.[7]

The key to measuring the nature and extent of the economists' influence, then, lies in understanding that they did not respond monolithically to the crisis. From the 1880s onward, two conflicting bodies of economic

---

and, for a comparative perspective on social reform thought, James Kloppenberg, *Uncertain Victory: Social Democracy and Progressivism in European and American Thought, 1870–1920* (New York, 1986).

7. Terrence Ball, James Farr, and Russell L. Hanson, eds., *Political Innovation and Conceptual Change* (Cambridge, 1989), esp. James Farr, "Understanding Political Change Conceptually," 24–49. See also Raymond Williams, *Keywords: A Vocabulary of Culture and Society* (London, 1976); Daniel T. Rodgers, *Contested Truths* (New York, 1987); James G. March and Johan P. Olsen, *Rediscovering Institutions: The Organizational Basis of Politics* (New York, 1989). To fit the usage offered here, March and Olsen's definition of institutions should be expanded to include durable political and cultural traditions such as republican concerns for the public good and liberal concerns for individual autonomy. David Ward, *Poverty, Ethnicity, and the American City, 1840–1925: Changing Conceptions of the Slum and the Ghetto* (New York, 1989); and Michael B. Katz, *Poverty and Policy in American History* (New York, 1983), esp. chap. 3, provide exemplary conceptual histories. Thomas Kuhn's suggestive model in *The Structure of Scientific Revolutions,* 2d ed. (Chicago, 1970) must be corrected when it is applied to the social sciences, to allow for sustained paradigm conflict over long periods of time.

knowledge emerged. Initially the economists' controversy pitted a self-styled "new school" composed of German-trained, evangelical reformers from the republican heartland, including Henry Carter Adams, Richard Ely, Edmund James, and John Commons, who took a statist approach to the problems of labor and monopoly, against a band of "younger traditionalists," sons of a substantial commercial and professional gentry, such as Yale's Arthur Hadley and Henry Farnam, Harvard's Frank Taussig, and Cornell's (later Chicago's) J. Laurence Laughlin, who were alleged by their opponents to repudiate the newer inductive methods, defer to the likes of William Graham Sumner, and cling to laissez-faire. In a highly publicized debate over the appropriate limits of professional advocacy, both sides attracted partisans in the press, the pulpit, business circles, and the higher reaches of university administration; and for a time excessive polarization threatened to undermine the young profession's efforts to establish itself as an authoritative source of social knowledge.[8]

As the economists grappled with these problems of professional self-definition, and especially as it became obvious that their methodological differences were not entirely insurmountable, various accommodations regarding the limits and methods of advocacy were reached. At an institutional level, economists converted the overtly partisan early American Economic Association (AEA) into a more cohesive, disciplined body of professionals, capable of patrolling its boundaries, excoriating charlatans, and defending members in good standing against the more egregious violations of academic freedom as they defined it. Leaders in the profession withheld support from certain forms of activism in order to validate others, seeking to carve out a sphere of competence where responsible advocacy could be defended.[9]

In the course of wrestling with the epistemological questions raised by controversy and repression, the Americans, along with Alfred Marshall, Max Weber, Leon Walras, and others abroad, sorted out conflicting claims for viewing economics as a "positive" or as a "normative" science. In important texts of the period, such as the original AEA platform and a symposium published in *Science* that aired conflicting views, parties on both sides of the American debate recognized the contextual and historical relativism of theory. The historicist avant-garde called attention to

8. Joseph Dorfman, *The Economic Mind in American Civilization*, 5 vols. (New York, 1969), esp. 3: chaps. 7–13; Furner, *Advocacy and Objectivity;* Dorothy Ross, "Socialism and American Liberalism: Academic Social Thought in the 1880s," *Perspectives in American History* 11 (1877–78): 7–79.

9. Furner, *Advocacy and Objectivity;* A. W. Coats, "The Educational Revolution and the Professionalization of American Economics," in *Breaking the Academic Mould: Economists and American Higher Learning in the Nineteenth Century,* ed. William J. Barber (Middletown, Conn., 1988), 340–75.

culturally specific normative assumptions in the most apparently "objective" observations. For Henry Carter Adams, a precocious student of American public finance who earned the first social science Ph.D. awarded by the new Johns Hopkins University, taught at the University of Michigan and Cornell in the 1880s, and became the first professional economist to serve on the staff of a major regulatory agency, there was little point in turning economics into an engaged, socially responsible discipline if economists were then expected to deny expert assistance to governments puzzling over the crisis of laissez-faire. At the same time, to defend legitimate involvement by economists in policy discussions amidst a rash of attacks by conservative businessmen and university trustees, Ely (along with Marshall, on the British side) called on the brethren to make a good-faith effort to let the public know when they were talking science and when their personal values or biases were speaking. On the other side, even "traditionalists" conceded that truth was in some sense tested by its ability to solve the problems of a specific time and place—a failure to do so having been, after all, behind the collapse of laissez-faire.[10]

The problem of finding effective methods for exerting leverage on public questions was transformed by a momentous change in the institutional structure of policy assessment and advice. Beginning in the mid-1880s with railroad regulation and the professionalization of the labor bureaus, and proceeding at an accelerating pace during the 1890s and into the new century, new kinds of investigative agencies appeared both within government and outside, the latter including municipal research bureaus, civic federations, social surveys and reform organizations—such as the American Association for Labor Legislation (AALL)—with sophisticated investigative capacities. Created (often at the urging of experts) specifically to produce, assess, and disseminate social knowledge on industrial questions, these institutions gave economists of various ideological stripes the chance to influence policy through methods other than the direct appeals to public opinion or participation in partisan politics that had often sparked the academic freedom cases.

Whether these developments expanded or contracted the "public sphere" can be debated. What matters here is that the new forms of access—as expert witnesses, special investigators, and administrative staff

---

10. T. W. Hutchinson, *"Positive" Economics and Policy Objectives* (Cambridge, Mass., 1964). Henry Carter Adams's discussions of method are in "Relation of the State to Industrial Action," *Publications of the American Economic Association* 1 (1887): 465–549, and the *Science* "Economic Discussion," vols. 7 and 8 (1886). See also Richard T. Ely, "Past and Present in Political Economy," *Johns Hopkins University Studies in History and Political Science* 2 (March 1884); 137–202; and the AEA platform in his "Report of the Organization of the American Economic Association," *Publications of the American Economic Association* 1 (March 1886): 5–46.

for executive departments, legislative commissions, and regulatory agencies, and as consultants to the swarm of new private-sector organizations designed to represent interest groups in their dealings with the new administrative state—permitted economists with constructive ideas to express their views of what modern liberalism should look like through a process of direct engagement with the various agencies of government, often as "insiders."[11]

Although some were surely eager for career advancement, the economists who provided expertise in these new contexts cannot be counted merely as "servants of power," for what they offered was neither ideologically neutral nor patterned slavishly on the political convictions of those in power. Indeed, within limits, there was room for independence and diversity. More self-consciously theoretical and ideological than the politicians they advised, economists pursued their own agendas, often outlasting elected officials. As chief statistician for the Interstate Commerce Commission (ICC) from 1887 to 1911, for example, H. C. Adams crusaded for centralized, public administrative control of the railroad industry, and thus became an outspoken critic of judge-made law. Even alleged radicals such as Edward Bemis and John Commons, when they were purged from academic institutions, could find congenial government employment.[12]

For some, of course, the chance to exchange partisanship for expertise allowed a comfortable distance from the more visible and accountable areas of public discourse, where advocacy could occasionally end a useful academic career. Eventually, as theoretical innovations in economics showed some promise of reducing differences among experts, and as the country, enjoying renewed prosperity in the late 1890s, seemed less receptive to radical advice, the McKinley administration expanded opportunities for influence by experimenting with corporatist structures of investigation and control that demanded skilled observation and analysis. Still uncertain, Arthur Hadley, then president of the AEA, made a clumsy attempt to contain potential damage by insisting that disinterested experts should aspire to transcend class, a view that attracted hot condemnation from corporatists such as John Commons and statists such as Bemis and

11. Stephen Skowronek, *Building a New American State: The Expansion of National Administrative Capacities, 1877–1920* (New York, 1982); Jürgen Habermas, *The Structural Transformation of the Public Sphere,* trans. Thomas Burger (1962) (Cambridge, Mass., 1991); Craig Calhoun, ed., *Habermas and the Public Sphere* (Cambridge, Mass., 1992); Philip J. Ethington, "Hypotheses from Habermas: Notes on Reconstructing American Political and Social History," *Intellectual History Newsletter* 14 (1992): 21–40.

12. David Grossman, "Professors and Public Service, 1885–1925: A Chapter in the Professionalization of the Social Sciences" (Ph.D. diss., Washington University, 1973). See also the American chapters in Furner and Supple, *State and Economic Knowledge,* and Lacey and Furner, *State and Social Investigation.*

Adams, who considered class differences an inescapable element of both knowledge and policy.[13]

Progress toward professional autonomy had not in fact suppressed dissent. Yet, as the new economists reformulated the era's policy questions, it became obvious that neither side—no more Hadley than Ely—held any brief for the regime of unbridled competition, individual contract, and negative government contemplated in laissez-faire. The shallow methodological controversy of the mid-1880s gave way to much more fundamental differences over the proper response, in a liberal society, to the social question. The complex social justice and distribution issues of the 1880s and 1890s began sorting professional economists into opposing camps according to their conceptions of what kinds of theories and policies might allow them to salvage what was best, by their different lights, in liberalism.

SIGNIFICANT areas of agreement united both strands of the new liberalism. Most obviously, statist democrats and corporate liberals were in fact all *liberals,* in the sense that they saw themselves as inheritors of a philosophical tradition dating back to the Reformation, the Enlightenment, and the bourgeois-democratic revolutions that established religious, intellectual, and political liberty in the West. They were committed to private property as the basis of a necessary separation between state and civil society. But they were also, for the most part, evolutionists who understood that the new corporate forms of business organization changed the nature of property and the proper meaning and extent of property rights. Although they believed, within limits, in individual autonomy and personal responsibility, neither side any longer regarded the individual as fully autonomous in a philosophical or sociological sense, or, in considerations of method, took the individual to be the appropriate unit of investigation. The new liberals were all collectivists in the sense that they considered individualism socially, politically, and philosophically outmoded. For the most consistently statist and self-consciously historicist of them, socialism offered an attractive analysis of the dysfunctionalism of advanced capitalism and a basis of ethical comparison. Yet, to the extent that socialism would centralize power in the state and, so they thought, suppress incentives to self-reliance and creativity, it was unacceptable as

13. Hutchison, *"Positive" Economics,* 37–46. Note the difference in Arthur Hadley, "Economic Laws and Methods," *Science* 8, suppl. (1886): 46–48, and idem, "The Relation between Economics and Politics," *Publications of the American Economic Association* 4 (1899): 7–28. See also Furner, *Advocacy and Objectivity,* chaps. 5–11. For a somewhat harsher judgment of economists' motives in this transition, see Leon Fink, "'Intellectuals' and 'Workers'": Academic Requirements and the Creation of Labor History," *American Historical Review* 96 (1991): 395–421.

an ideology and a political program. For both sides in these discussions, the transition from status to contract represented a major achievement in human history, essential to progress. Thus, however much they desired social ownership of certain industries and subordination of vested rights to an ethical code, even key architects of statist new liberalism such as Adams and Ely neither expected nor desired the disappearance of private property.[14]

The statists did desire a middle way, avoiding both the inflexibility and irrationality of antistatist individualism and the bureaucratic immobilism of state socialism. Building on earlier republican precedents, on established intellectual traditions such as the liberal positivism of Lester Ward, and on the potent example of the German historical school, Adams, Ely, and their supporters put together the rudiments of a democratic collectivist discourse that proclaimed the necessity for guiding social development through the investigative and regulatory mechanisms of a more positive state. Rejecting economic individualism, they described measures for determining the conditions under which competition would operate, and for using regulation to restrain private monopolies without creating leviathan. Important elements of a statist pathway to twentieth-century liberalism had been defined by the mid-1890s and were under way institutionally in experiments such as state-level labor codes and the Interstate Commerce Commission.[15]

The associationalist strand of new liberalism arose in response to the growing threat of statism, but came together rather slowly as an alternative system. Until the late 1890s, several ingredients were lacking. The most important was nonstatist institutional alternatives to market ordering—which trade associations, trade agreements between organized employers and national unions, and mergers began to supply by the turn of the century. Also lacking was a credible theory to support the argument that voluntarism and enlightened self-interest would provide an adequate basis for social justice in the era of the trust—which applications of marginal productivity theory would eventually make possible. To some extent, also, professional loyalties and antipathies stood in the way. For the obvious careerist reasons, Arthur Hadley, a Yale instructor seeking tenure in the department of his former mentor, William Graham Sumner, refused to endorse the original AEA platform, with its overt statism and its explicit, bull-baiting denunciation of laissez-faire. Yet he acknowledged in the *Science* "Economic Discussion" the next year that the day when society

14. The similarities and differences between the two competing strands of American new liberalism are more fully explored in the sources cited in n. 6.

15. Kloppenberg, *Uncertain Victory,* is particularly useful on Ely. Dorothy Ross, *Origins of American Social Science,* surveys developments in all the social science disciplines in this period, within a framework of American exceptionalism.

could be regulated mainly through the traditional mechanism of individual contract was over. On the basis of knowledge gained in his brief
term as Connecticut labor commissioner, he was critical of the current
individualist trend in judicial reasoning, as in the recent elevation of "freedom of contract" and the pernicious "fellow servant" and "acceptance
of risk" doctrines, which, along with the spread of corporate business
organization generally, had undermined the entrepreneur's personal responsibility for decent moral standards in the conduct of business and
invited legislative intervention. Employing the potent vocabulary of evolution to promote a tolerant attitude toward innovations in business organization, Hadley noted an irresistible modern tendency to combination
in all aspects of life. He recognized individualism and a regime of unmedi-
ated competition as passing phases in the organization and management
of enterprise, to be superseded by collectivist structures and principles.
Fuller development of the potential of voluntary cooperation for cushion-
ing the shocks of industrialization awaited recognition of such initiatives
in public opinion and, more important, in public law and jurisprudence.[16]

The connection between economics and jurisprudence also preoccupied
Adams, though he understood it rather differently. Of the two, Hadley
was closer to classical roots, in the sense that he was more of a materialist
and more deterministic. He believed that social improvement came about
through a largely unconscious process of experimentation that selected
among social and business forms devised for more immediate purposes
such as profit, on the basis of their social efficiency. Adams, for his part,
mingled Christian and republican idealism with what was known in the
1880s as a telic view of evolution, comparable to Ward's analysis of the
role of mind in human progress, and to Stanley Jevons's faith in conscious, small-scale social experimentation with various ways of solving
problems, as an intelligent guide to reform. From this perspective, human
beings deliberately adapted their institutions to ethical and civic as well
as purely economic purposes, thus directing the course of social evolution.
Yet for both Adams and Hadley markets were embedded in a structure
of social and legal institutions; an abstract model of the economy was
unattainable, continued reliance exclusively on competition inadvisable,
the expectation of an autonomous natural equilibrium that produced politically and socially acceptable results insupportable, and deliberate re-

---

16. Arthur Hadley, "Competition and Combination," *Andover Review* 2 (1884): 455–
66; idem, "On the Freedom of Contract," *Science* 7, suppl. (1886): 221–25. The most
detailed account of Hadley's evolutionary outlook in print is in Martin J. Sklar, *The Corporate
Reconstruction of American Capitalism, 1890–1916: The Market, the Law, and Politics* (New
York, 1988), 57–61. See also Furner, "Knowing Capitalism" and "Republican Tradition
and the New Liberalism."

course to some purposeful coordinating agency or combination of agencies indispensable.[17]

For economists and others guided by the democratic collectivist view, the agencies of constructive change would be a reformed, scientifically informed legislature, a reformed judiciary that understood the law historically, an enlightened, expert public administration, and civic education. By contrast, those in economics, the law, and elsewhere who espoused an antistatist, associative collectivism would rely on the new corporate law, the emerging sciences of management and marketing, and the ordering possibilities inherent in the modern business corporations, the trusts, the trade unions and trade associations, and a vast array of other spontaneously arising forms of society-centered, voluntary collective action. According to the first perspective, the various agencies of government, with all their new intelligence-gathering capacities, would track the progress of social development, with the purpose of shoring up republican institutions threatened by seismic shifts in economic power and protecting the weaker members from abuse by powerful organized groups. From the second perspective, societal groups representing specialized functions, ordered hierarchically and acting in concert, would learn to adjust their differences, extending the regime of individual contract to an array of new transactions among groups that had standing as legal entities and to new forms of bargaining. In so doing, they believed, they would protect civil society and its most important institutions—individual self-determination, the market, and private investment—from being compromised by the state.[18]

It should be emphasized here once again that although these two

17. Henry Carter Adams, *Outline of Lectures in Political Economy* (Baltimore, 1881); idem, "The Position of Socialism in the Historical Development of Political Economy," *Penn Monthly* 10 (1879): 285–94; idem, "Democracy," *New Englander* 40 (1881): 752–72; idem, "Economics and Jurisprudence," *Science* 8, suppl. (1866): 15–19; and his 1896 AEA presidential address, "Economics and Jurisprudence," reprinted as *Two Essays by Henry Carter Adams,* ed. (New York, 1954); idem, "Review of W. Stanley Jevons, *The State in Relation to Labour,* in *The Nation* 35 (September 28, 1882): 270–71.

18. Woodrow Wilson, "The Study of Administration," *Political Science Quarterly* 2 (1887): 197–222, bears a remarkable similarity to Henry Carter Adams, "On the Education of Statesmen," *Princeton Review* 60 (1884): 16–35. Adams left Johns Hopkins in 1881 two years before Wilson arrived, but Wilson would have known of him from Ely's seminar and from older students who admired him, such as J. Franklin Jameson. See also Robert D. Cuff, "Wilson and Weber: Bourgeois Critics in an Organized Age," *Public Administration Review* 47 (1987): 240–44. On Hadley's early corporatism, see particularly his "On the Freedom of Contract." The study of corporate liberal politics begins with Martin J. Sklar, "Woodrow Wilson and the Political Economy of Modern United States Liberalism," *Studies on the Left* 1 (1960): 14–47; and James Weinstein, *The Corporate Ideal in the Liberal State* (Boston, 1968). See also Ellis Hawley, "The Discovery and Study of Corporate Liberalism," *Business History Review* 52 (1978): 9–20; Sklar, *Corporate Reconstruction.*

groups of economists saw the role of the state in the modern liberal order very differently, by comparison with traditional liberals they had much in common. Talk of inductive versus deductive methods lingered in the languages of both groups, not because they actually described their methods of doing science but because they served on the one hand to develop, justify, and deploy statism and on the other to defend against it. Yet in practice *all* the players on both sides—Taussig in his tariff work, Adams in his public finance work, Hadley in his railroad work, Jeremiah Jenks in his trust work, Ely in his labor union work, E. R. A. Seligman in his tax work, James in his municipal government work, and so on—joined with counterparts in the historical movements of Germany and England in studying economic institutions in their legal and cultural contexts. They discarded classical theories of competitive equilibrium; took account of other than rationalizing, optimizing motives; relied extensively, indeed predominantly, on descriptive and statistical methods; and moved beyond the unseen hand to purposeful, interventionist, collective modes of social ordering.[19]

A common loss of faith in the unregulated market left both of these discourses open to elements of marginalist thinking, and yet, significantly, unreceptive to the application of marginal utility found in modern neoclassical distribution theory. American economists were well aware of the international commotion raised by new thinking about value and pride, and made important contributions to it; but there was no consensus among them regarding the implications of this new knowledge for policy. For John Bates Clark and his followers, the value-determining capacity of the marginal increment planted the seed for a productivity theory of distribution, used to argue for the justice of the income shares determined by the price system; with allowance made for occasional disturbances of its operation. If all producers could count on being rewarded in proportion to the value they created, state interference was not required.

Others found it possible to assimilate marginalism to more critical, activist, interventionist positions. As Crauford Goodwin has argued, in this period "marginalism did not have a clear set of policy precepts attached to it." Thus it can best be viewed in the early stages of its diffusion as a bundle of related insights and techniques, distinctive because they drew attention to the role of consumer demand and the value-setting properties of the marginal increment, but ideologically neutral. Marginalism contributed to a neoclassical view of the economy as a self-

---

19. On the main works of each, see Dorfman, *Economic Mind*; Fine, *Laissez Faire*; Furner, *Advocacy and Objectivity*; Ross, *Origins of American Social Science*.

regulating, self-equilibrating machine, but also to varieties of historical, institutionalist (and for that matter socialist) thinking.[20]

One important aspect of the marginalist outlook was the attention it drew to the phenomenon of *diminishing utility*. In modern neoclassicism, this approach generated the familiar demand curves charting "individual utility functions," or the progressive satisfaction of individual desires that contributes to the making of prices. But another reading of this application of marginalism reached back to Benthamite roots, and referred to the concept of diminishing utility for society as a whole. This construction was important in the development of an Anglo-American school of welfare economists that included Ely, Commons, Seligman, Simon Patten, and Thomas Nixon Carver, as well as Alfred Marshall, Henry Sidgwick, and A. C. Pigou on the British side, who argued for redistributive policies such as progressive taxation and social insurance on the grounds that total social welfare would be maximized if income were shifted where those dollars would satisfy more pressing, life-supporting wants.[21]

By contrast, for others, including Hadley, Jenks, and Thorstein Veblen, the marginalist concept of *diminishing return* provided explanatory language for the obvious and repeated failure of glutted markets in the Gilded Age to equalize supply and demand at prices that covered the costs of average producers—and thus for capitalist crisis. Either overtly and caustically in attacks on Clark (Veblen) or implicitly through repeated apologies for managerial intervention and continued reliance on historical and institutional approaches (Jenks and Hadley), all three rejected the emerging neoclassicism.[22]

20. George Stigler, "The Adoption of Marginal Utility Theory," in *The Marginal Revolution in Economics,* ed. R. D. Collison Black, A. W. Coats, and Crauford D. W. Goodwin (Durham, N. C., 1973), 305–20; Crauford D. W. Goodwin, "Marginalism Moves to the New World," ibid., 285–304. Stigler argued that marginal utility theory was adopted slowly by American economists, and not applied systematically in published work until around 1940, because it took that long to rid American economics of amateurs and recruit able scholars who were both educationally equipped, through mastery of statistics, and sufficiently scientific in disposition to forsake policy questions for what he viewed as the purely scientific researches that marginalism made possible. Crauford Goodwin noticed a similar lag, which he attributed to German influence and the strength of historicism, although he concluded that the "marginal revolution" was succeeding in the United States by the 1890s.

21. On welfare economics, see Hutchison, *"Positive" Economics;* idem, *A Review of Economic Doctrine, 1870–1929* (London, 1953), chap. 18; Jacob Viner, "The Utility Concept in Value Theory and Its Critics, II. The Utility Concept in Welfare Economics," and Paul Samuelson, "The Foundations of Economic Analysis (Welfare Economics)," both in *Utility Theory: A Book of Readings,* ed. Alfred N. Page (New York, 1968), 299–316, 317–62; Herbert Hovenkamp, "The First Great Law and Economics Movement," *Stanford Law Review* 42 (1990): 1000–1008. On the neo-Ricardian alternative to Clark's marginal productivity theory, see Furner, "Republican Tradition."

22. Furner, "Republican Tradition"; James Livingston, "The Social Analysis of Economic History and Theory: Conjectures on Late Nineteenth-Century American Development," *American Historical Review* 92 (1987): 69–95.

MARGINALIST theory and language served in these ways as a common source for both the associative and the statist strands of new liberalism. Yet each strand had its own quite distinctive vocabulary. The key building blocks of democratic statist language were the idea of an "interregnum" between authoritative systems, which undermined traditional antistatism, and the seminal concepts of "natural monopoly" and "proprietary rights for labor," developed by Henry Carter Adams and others from the mid-1880s to mid-1890s, who outlined a new conception of relations between the modern state and civil society. By defining the public interest as long-term social and economic welfare within a framework of political liberty, as against short-term maximization by self-interested individuals, Adams challenged the core assumption of laissez-faire. Society, which should be recognized as an entity with a history and tendency of its own, rather than either the individual or the state, became the object of scientific concern and the unit of investigation.

Adams devoted the bulk of his analysis to demonstrating that the problems facing American society arose directly from an excessive, antisocial individualism and from exclusive reliance on competition to order the economy. In a regime of unfettered competition, virtue proved weaker than vice; and in sensitive areas such as industrial safety and child labor, the moral plane of competition had fallen to the level of the greediest competitor. A weak state that attracted mediocre talent to a flabby, incompetent bureaucracy had proved unable to resist being corrupted by powerful concentrations of private power. And last, amidst a general clamor for antitrust legislation that responded naturally, if ineffectually, to this imbalance between private and public power, society was losing the benefits that monopoly could offer, under adequate public supervision, in certain vital infrastructure industries.[23]

Aware that his thinking would offend antistatist liberals, Adams attempted to find precedent for a larger role for the state in American political tradition. Working historically, he drew upon his own pioneering study of public debts to recall an earlier, more statist republicanism; he detailed the extensive, beneficial involvement of state governments in economic development in the early republic, and exposed the error of the state's hasty withdrawal from financing and mixed management of internal improvements in the Jackson period. Americans now suffered from excessive privatization of functions, which could be remedied only by development of an American science of public finance and by management

23. Henry Carter Adams, "The Relation of the State to Industrial Action." On Adams's career and significance, see Furner, *Advocacy and Objectivity,* esp. 125–42; Ross, "Socialism and American Liberalism." For the argument that Civil War soldiers' pensions amounted to a rudimentary social insurance system, see Theda Skocpol, *Protecting Soldiers and Mothers: The Political Origins of Social Policy in the United States* (Cambridge, Mass., 1992).

of public utilities according to civil service principles. Reworking an older antimonopoly vocabulary, Adams hoped to teach those who still harbored Jacksonian prejudices to see the state as the defanger of monopolies, not their protector, and as a potential guardian of the liberties of laborers and consumers. At the same time, he cautioned against an extreme reaction in the direction of an excessively bureaucratic statism, which he considered as alien to American traditions and values as excessive individualism. Collectivist, in that it recognized the insufficiencies of old-fashioned individualism, the new liberalism he favored would be realized not by creation of an imperial power at the center, but through decentralized, democratic processes of investigation and control, appropriate to American culture traditions.

In his discussion of monopoly, Adams attempted to legitimate state control by pulling into the same orbit both the traditional republican principle of popular sovereignty and a modern conception of the "natural," which he associated with evolution. In his hands, the idea of "natural monopoly" served important rhetorical functions. It distinguished businesses that became monopolies by exploiting true economies of scale from the kind encountered in republican demonology, such as the tea trade under George III or the evil Standard Oil trust, which arose "unnaturally," through political favoritism, force, or fraud. Yet, despite the potential benefits of unified ownership in the infrastructure industries, big business could corrupt politics, and a republic could never tolerate monopoly in private hands. To prevent tyranny, a republican category he invoked constantly, Adams insisted that government ownership or control must be coextensive with monopoly. The growth of the state would fortunately be limited by the extent of the natural monopoly principle; in agriculture, therefore, and in manufacturing beyond a size sufficient for a reasonable division of labor, there would be no significant advantages to scale, and thus no need for public oversight, beyond some basic factory legislation.

For labor historians, Richard Ely usually takes top billing among the labor economists of the Gilded Age. But Adams was a major figure here as well, and his view of the labor question profoundly influenced the labor specialists who became the architects of the organic legislation of the New Deal. Adams's approach to labor reflected the centrality of rights in his thinking, and of "rights talk" in the labor movement of the 1880s. In an era of frequent, massive unemployment (and lacking, even for white northern males of working age, the rudiments of a social welfare state), the first issue for urban workers was access to subsistence. A strong, not unrelated second was a voice in management. Whereas labor leaders often compared the worker's lot unfavorably with chattel slavery in the South, Adams, taking a longer historical view, concluded that the average worker had been better off amidst the rude plenty of the Middle Ages than in the pernicious, mechanized insecurity of modern times. The crucial difference between the two contexts was the location of property rights among the various classes of producers, for serfs had enjoyed a customary claim to continued subsistence. As in his treatment of monopoly, Adams fully historicized property. In the new industrial system, the mythic figure of the artisan had been splintered into parts, he argued. All property in the product of industry had been awarded to capital. Modern workers retained a claim to no productive property except their day's labor and their skills.[24]

Adams adapted republican language and political sensibilities to the problem at hand, this time by calling for the creation of vested rights with standing equal to those of capital in the common law of industry, which would restore to workers a measure of job security and a voice in the conditions of their labor. At a time when hard-pressed employers insisted on the right to slash wages and workforce during depressions, he was convinced that faithful service over a reasonable period entitled employees to tenure in the job under good behavior. Drawn to several of the collectivist options under discussion in reform circles—especially profit sharing and the Knights of Labor's favorite method, cooperative ownership—he finally concluded that the practical course in the near term was the gradual, piecemeal creation of rights for wage workers through a state-promoted system of voluntary collective bargaining, which would replace the unequal system of individual contracts. In a period when unionization appeared likely to encompass quickly a large fraction of the adult male workforce, and before the chilling effect of a judicial ban on most forms of collective action by workers had set in, it seemed reasonable to expect the more advanced segments of organized labor to set the general tone of industrial relations, and thus to move all workers toward what Adams described repeatedly as an "industrial republic."

Unlike the protocorporatists of the next decade, who hoped to solve the labor question by encouraging class accommodation and cooperation, Adams understood conflict between organized interests in a free society as not only an unavoidable but a progressive force—in fact, an indispensable ingredient in human progress. He believed that most of the destructive consequences of class conflict could be eliminated through equal, independent organization of both classes, which would reorganize and reinvigorate the labor markets. As the strongest unions won protection

24. Henry Carter Adams, "'The Labor Problem,'" *Scientific American* 22, suppl. (August 21, 1886): 8861–62; idem, "What Do These Strikes Mean?" typescript with Adams to James Burrill Angell, March 25, 1886, Angell papers, Michigan Historical Collections, Ann Arbor.

through trade agreements, a gradual upgrading of social morality would cause these rights to be extended to the whole working class. The ideal method for spreading industrial democracy would be a structure of sustained adversarial relations, in which the state encouraged and facilitated collective bargaining but remained above the fray, reserving public authority to protect consumers, an important new social category, against collusion by syndicates uniting capital and labor in the new highly organized, concentrated industries. Adult male workers would have the strength and discipline to demand these rights, in Adams's typically gendered perspective. To guard their republican independence against an encroaching paternalism, direct state intervention should be reserved for protective legislation for the "dependent classes," women and children who lacked a political voice.[25]

Adams greatly influenced John Commons, and through him a host of Commons's students and associates from the 1910s to 1930s, such as Edwin Witte, William Leiserson, David Saposs, and W. Jett Lauck, who investigated industrial relations, advised unions, and drafted labor legislation. Over time, Adams's "rights" conception of the labor question broadened from matters such as the right to organize and bargain collectively to include social insurance, the living wage, unemployment compensation, and other forms of income security, as well as the general principle that every citizen had a right to a job. As the courts threw up roadblocks, statist new liberals experimented with new forms of industrial governance, following English and European precedents to some extent, but these new methods remained in touch with traditional concepts of republican independence. As Adams repeatedly put it, "there is no industrial liberty without industrial property." Preserving the republic under the conditions of mechanized production required the political creation of new forms of property.[26]

Adams, Commons, and others further down their line of intellectual descent described collective bargaining in political terms, as a system in which contractual agreements between organized contesting classes would add up in time to an "industrial constitution" governing an "industrial federation," or a labor code. As in republican thought generally, virtue—

25. Adams, "Relation of the State"; idem, "'Labor Problem'"; idem, "The Economics of Arbitration," in Chicago Civic Federation, *National Conference on Industrial Conciliation and Arbitration* (Chicago, 1894), 63–68; idem, "An Interpretation of the Social Movements of our Times," *International Journal of Ethics* 2 (1891): 1–19. On the gendered nature of Progressive Era reform, see Linda Gordon, ed., *Women, the State, and Welfare* (Madison, Wis., 1990).

26. On Commons and his tradition among labor relations specialists, see Clarence Wunderlin, *Visions of a New Industrial Order: Social Science and Labor Theory in America's Progressive Era* (New York, 1992); Furner, "Knowing Capitalism."

in this instance, distributive, justice and a decent level of social security—appeared here as the product of correct political forms. Yet in their work on the labor question, the democratic collectivists were drawn at first to a mediating role for the state, and not a coercive one such as that adopted in some parts of Europe and Australasia, where public boards empowered to settle wage disputes actually set wages. The high level of confidence these men initially placed in bargaining reflected the pervasiveness of contract as a mediating institution, but also the historical contingency of labor's situation in the Gilded Age, when American ideas regarding industrial labor relations took shape. The relevance of a collectivist version of the contract model depended on a continuation of a vigorous trend toward unionization, and particularly toward expansion of various forms of "general" unions that flourished in those years, rather than the more narrowly based craft unions that actually survived the bloody 1890s. It also required a posture of at least neutrality if not protection on the part of the state, which failed to materialize. Instead the courts developed an impressive arsenal of antistrike weapons, expanded entrepreneurial property rights, and applied the Sherman Antitrust Act to labor. The American working class was reconstituted by new immigrants, and organized employers mounted a union-busting offensive. As these later events unfolded, Adams moved in a more statist direction with respect to labor, whereas Commons, a swing figure who eventually synthesized elements of the two strands of the new liberalism, was converted in his National Civic Federation (NCF) period to a benevolent corporatism that offered some hope of legitimizing at least the skilled craft unions.[27]

Henry Carter Adams has stood in this discussion at the head of a group of historical/institutional economists who argued, contrary to the Jacksonian model of the weak state that served mainly as a mechanism for distributing public goods, that a statist society might also be more responsive to questions of social justice, and hence more democratic. This prospect, and the language and arguments that supported it, laid the basis for later experiments in statist reform during the Progressive Era, in the wartime mobilization agencies of 1917–20, and in the movement during the 1930s for an American welfare state. Between the 1890s and the

27. Leon Fink, "Looking Backward: Reflections on Workers' Culture and the Conceptual Dilemmas of the New Labor History," in *New Perspectives in Labor History*, ed. Alice Kessler-Harris and J. Carroll Moody (De Kalb, Ill., 1989), 5–29; Shelton Stromsquist, "Looking Both Ways: Ideological Crisis and Working Class Recomposition in the 1890s," paper presented at Northern Illinois University Labor History Conference, 1984; Wunderlin, *Visions;* Christopher Tomlins, *The State and the Unions: Labor Relations, Law, and the Organized Labor Movement in America, 1880–1960* (Cambridge, 1985); William Forbath, *Law and the Shaping of the American Labor Movement* (Cambridge, Mass., 1991).

1920s, it became the point of attack for an emerging antistatist strand of new liberal thinking in the economists' response to the crisis of liberalism.

THIS associative response to the crisis of competition appeared first in the early 1880s in Arthur Hadley's pioneering work on the special qualities of the new industries, including railroads and all the forms of mass production, which required long construction periods and large investments in fixed capital. Antistatist collectivism required a political economy and a policy language to support it, key elements of which Hadley undertook to provide. In an account that emphasized the devastating effects of "excess capacity," constructed during boom times and ready for production at the bottom of the next cycle, the immobility and helplessness of "fixed capital," and the resulting vicious price wars that periodically squeezed all the profit out of these industries, he departed decisively from the harmonic vocabulary of laissez-faire. His work provided scientific justification for a potent new category of "ruinous" competition that plagued a class of businesses far broader than Adams's "natural monopolies." By linking ruinous competition to social disasters extending far beyond the capitalist class, Hadley laid a theoretical basis for a sanguine view of what was from another perspective a vicious trust—in his view the socially rational, responsible "combination." In light of the threat that the industrial economy's cyclical blowouts posed to the price and investment systems, Hadley urged railroad and heavy industry owners to seek their own and society's salvation through legalized, enforceable pooling. His assumption—directly contrary to Adams's—was that the private corporate interest in the most extended market and the public interest in reasonable prices were identical; regulatory bureaucracies that would be vulnerable to political pressures and thus threaten the investment system were unnecessary.[28]

By the mid-1890s the antistatists were prepared to press the new conceptions further. In form and language, the antistatist response was partly a reaction to statist political movements gathering force in that decade, such as socialism and Populism. It was also a function of the research process itself, in relation to the appearance of new business forms, particularly the trusts. By the late 1880s it was possible for Jeremiah Jenks, an Ely student teaching at Cornell, to study in some detail the behavior of manufacturing combinations in consumer goods industries, extending

---

28. Arthur Hadley, "Overproduction," in *Lalor's Cyclopedia of Political and Social Science*, vol. 3 (New York, 1884): 40–43; idem, "Competition and Combination," *Andover Review* 2 (1884): 455–66; idem, *Economics: An Account of the Relations between Private Property and Public Welfare* (New York, 1896); Furner, "Republican Tradition"; Sklar, *Corporate Reconstruction*.

Hadley's observations. On the basis of empirical results at variance with Adams's typology, Jenks attacked the whole conception of natural monopoly, contending that substantially similar economies of scale, potentially conferring the same benefits on society, were available to all large businesses. The tendency to monopoly was inherent to any large aggregation of capital, no matter where or how employed. Thus, if state action were to be coextensive with monopoly, the natural boundary for state interference, which Adams claimed would contain the state inside safe republican limits, was illusory.

To emphasize the embeddedness of large industrial units in the technical and business processes of capitalism itself, Jenks named his new, expanded class of naturally monopolistic businesses "capitalistic monopolies." As to the political implications of the find, Jenks surmised, the new industrial giants had an inherent tendency to regulate themselves. To avoid attracting competition, they would naturally set prices only slightly above competitive levels. In exchange for slightly higher profits, their new managerial capacities would enable them to avoid overproduction, moderate the business cycle, and provide steadier employment for American labor. What was needed to make corporate capitalism self-policing? Mainly adequate publicity regarding costs and earnings, so that Clark's "potential competition," spurring owners of restless, mobile capital ever ready to set up shop in competition with a winner, could do its saving work. In place of a classical imagery that portrayed the market as a natural system guided by principles rooted in reliable tendencies of human nature, emergent corporate liberals offered an administered market. The stabilizing business of coordinating supply and demand would be the work of experts shielded by legal recognition of their vital role.[29]

This new thinking received a boost from marginalism, demonstrating an apparent if also rather deceptive linkage between corporate liberalism and neoclassical economics that set in during the 1890s. Clark's economics provided a model that claimed to accommodate the "dynamics" of the capitalist system, including business cycles and the changing business forms that Jenks and Hadley considered such creative forces, within an equilibrium system. In Clark's homely imagery, a pebble thrown into a

29. Jeremiah Jenks, "Capitalistic Monopolies and Their Relation to the State," *Political Science Quarterly* 9 (1894): 486–509; idem, "Industrial Combination and Prices," in U.S. Industrial Commission, *Report,* 19 vols. (Washington, D.C., 1900–1902), vol. 1, *Preliminary Report on Trusts and Industrial Combinations;* Carl Parrini and Martin J. Sklar, "New Thinking on the Market: Some American Economists on Investment and the Theory of Surplus Capital," *Journal of Economic History* 43 (1983): 559–78. Theories of monopoly competition that belied these hopes were later perfected by Edward Chamberlain and Joan Robinson. Historians such as Philip Scranton have described efficient methods of industrial organization that did not lead inexorably to monopoly.

tub made waves; a sudden change in methods of production might upset the market's natural tendency to fix a competitive price for every factor of production according to its marginal utility. But the tub's natural state was smooth water, and the market naturally tended to arrive at an optimum level of employment for labor and capital. Artificial interference with these forces might do more harm than good—by halting capital's restless search for better methods, for example, or by tempting capitalists to shift from labor to more capital-intensive methods to beat back union wage demands. With its homogenized, interchangeable workers and switchable units of capital and labor, Clark's image of the working economy heralded Frederick Taylor's vision, just then taking shape, of a scientifically managed factory in which an engineer held a stopwatch menacingly over "soldiering" workers.[30]

In shifting determination of the value of things from producer to consumer, neoclassical theory incorporated a recognition of the importance of desire that was cropping up in many places at the turn of the century. Conservative institutionalists such as Jenks and Hadley did not subscribe to equilibrium thinking, but they did recognize desire as an evolutionary category, subject to socially useful manipulation, and as such it entered into their business cycle and development theories. An astute strategist for corporate capitalism, Hadley (along with George Gunton and Simon Patten, in their various ways) connected the investment patterns and the job structure of the economy at a given stage in its development with the level and variety of consumption that the society supported and encouraged. In an undeveloped economy, Hadley observed, capital was invested largely in primary production; workers labored long hours for low wages, had few wants, consumed little beyond subsistence, and were highly vulnerable to cyclical unemployment and "underconsumption." The rich, unable to consume the entire surplus, became oversavers; and redundant investment led to excess production and recurrent depressions. In a more advanced society, by contrast, consumption, and thus investment and production, were more abundant and diversified; ordinary people wanted and could purchase more and better things; economic growth proceeded with fewer and less damaging interruptions; more labor was skilled or professional, employed in service occupations or diversified rather than primary production, and therefore less vulnerable to cyclical fluctuations.

Corporate liberals believed that the transition to a high-consumption economy would occur "naturally," as subsistence—a historical, evolutionary category related to the level and quality of desire—was gradually redefined, exerting upward pressure on wages. In turn, enlightened capi-

---

30. John Bates Clark, *The Distribution of Wealth* (1899) (New York, 1956); Stuart Wood, "The Theory of Wages," *Publications of the American Economic Association* 4 (1899): 1–35.

talists would recognize their own interest in mass consumption; aided by practitioners of the arts of merchandising, they would cultivate the hedonistic, secular ethic of a mass consumer culture. Added to corporate rationality, advertising, and education, the wage demands of organized skilled workers would help to speed the process, expanding the middle class by moving them into it.

Many trade-offs would naturally be required as the community progressed to a higher standard of life. But these small sacrifices were fully justified, according to defenders of the corporate system. Small proprietors might lose republican independence as the new economy converted them into salaried employees, but they would realize offsetting gains in security, affluence, and chances for upward mobility in the employ of the new corporations. Driven by necessity and its own momentum, the corporate-managerial system would stimulate innovation and reward diversity. By contrast, the redistributive state policies demanded by social democrats would impair the investment system, threaten the capacity of capitalism to sustain growth, and kill the goose that laid the golden egg. For Adams, Commons, and the democratic statists generally, capitalism was a politically constructed system capable of retaining its virtue only when it was subjected to political controls that promoted distributive equity and civic responsibility. For conservative institutionalists such as Jenks and Hadley, on the other hand, the administered markets of the emerging corporate order were capable, under the right management, of generating a continuous, socially and politically stabilizing economic expansion, fueling (but also absolutely depending on) consumption of ever more plentiful satisfying goods.[31]

CORPORATE liberals gained privileged access to the debate over industrial policy at a crucial point, when a new type of government agency, the United States Industrial Commission (USIC), conducted the first com-

31. This account of corporate liberal thinking on development relies on Furner, "Liberty versus Efficiency." Hadley's views are in "Some Fallacies in the Theory of Distribution," *Economic Journal* 7 (1897): 477–86; on the fragility of the capitalist investment system, see his *Economics*. See also George Gunton, *Wealth and Progress: A Critical Examination of the Labor Problem* (New York, 1887). Hadley's thinking contributed to the vogue of overproduction theses, which experts mobilized to explain depressions down through the 1930s. He also sowed a seed for transcending these explanations in favor of analyzing the changing composition of accumulation and investment, the shifting roles of various groups of industries in promoting or rekindling demand, and the important role of new consumer tastes in reconstructing the economy. For the later development of such thinking, see Michael A. Bernstein, *The Great Depression: Delayed Recovery and Economic Change in America, 1929–1939* (Cambridge, 1987). On the development of mass consumption, there is nothing better than William Leach, *Land of Desire: Merchants, Power, and the Rise of a New American Culture* (New York, 1993).

prehensive official investigation of the problems of the industrial economy, hoping to locate their causes and recommend legislation. The USIC added important new ingredients to a growing public investigative capacity, already reflected in the increasing depth and sophistication of the work of congressional committees, the expanding census, and the Department of Labor. Beyond coming to grips with structural changes in the economy, the USIC's immediate political purpose was to extend a kind of official meaning to the latest challenges to republican values, the great depression and bloody strikes of the 1890s, and the great merger movement, under way during its deliberations, which absorbed around three thousand businesses into some three hundred.

Reflecting the McKinley administration's interest in achieving social harmony through economic expansion and class accommodation, the USIC was corporatively organized, including members representing large capital, organized labor, and the moderate informed public. Jenks, Commons, and E. Dana Durand served as staff experts, moving back and forth between USIC and the corporatist, procorporate National Civil Federation (NCF), which employed them simultaneously as special investigators. Their efforts, and those of others they involved and consulted, injected the language and concepts of academic economics into what might otherwise have been essentially partisan proceedings.[32]

This was not the first time economists served as experts in economic and social policy debates. In the Senate's Cullom Committee hearings in advance of the Interstate Commerce Act, for example, experts such as Hadley, Charles Francis Adams, and Edmund James had attempted to persuade lawmakers to think of the railroads as "natural monopolies" eligible for some form of "combination," either through pooling, as the voluntarists desired, or under direct government supervision, as the statists preferred. When the Sherman Antitrust Bill was under discussion, however, professional opinion on the economics of the industrial trusts was not sufficiently developed to have an impact on the early stages of American trust policy. By the close of the century, with the merger movement in full swing, the corporate liberals were ready. For the first time, economists stood toe to toe with lawyers, placing the indelible stamp of the economists' discourse on the proceedings.

Under Jenks's influence, the USIC recast the social question that had preoccupied Americans since the 1880s. Earlier government investigations had focused on the political meaning of the new industrial order, and on the threat that wage labor and monopoly posed to liberty, in both its republican and classical liberal meanings. In the hearings and analytical

32. Wunderlin, *Visions;* Furner, "Knowing Capitalism" and "Republican Tradition"; Weinstein, *Corporate Ideal.*

reports of the USIC, the emphasis shifted to a disclosure and assessment of the potential benefits to be harvested from the economic efficiencies made possible by large-scale integrated production. Responding favorably, at least at the rhetorical level, to the procorporate economists' analysis, the USIC also endorsed the American Federation of Labor's recently consolidated style of national trade unionism as the basis for a new form of worker representation in industry, coming into existence as enlightened, NCF-type employers signaled their willingness to recognize the legitimacy of "responsible" unions—those that observed their contracts and controlled their members—as a basis for industrial peace.

The "USIC view" contrasted sharply with earlier discussions of the origins and nature of the corporate form. According to the "grant theory" of the corporation, which came down from the early republic and received a new birth in the democratic statist strand of new liberalism, the corporation was both the creature and the agent of the state. A purely artificial entity, it existed strictly as a public convenience, empowered to carry out limited purposes required by the public interest. It could not exceed those purposes without permission, and its investment practices and other activities warranted close monitoring.[33]

For Jenks the corporate form represented something quite different. In an era of mechanized production requiring large capital investments, it had simply evolved as the new standard form of private business, judged superior by virtue of its efficiency for amassing capital, integrating production, reducing costs, and managing distribution in new ways. Instead of denying the element of monopoly in large-scale production, a Jenks report on the pricing policies of trusts and combinations drew attention to a characteristic rise in profit margins immediately after competition ended. This monopoly gain, usually resulting from a slower reduction (not a rise) in prices than would have happened under (often ruinous) competition, was what warranted the large and risky investment, in Jenks's view. Not all mergers succeeded, after all.

The signal virtue of the combinations in this rendition was the capacity they had, under enlightened leadership, to manage capitalism, coordinating production and demand so as to prevent severe depressions. Jenks and the corporate liberals balanced the benefits that would flow to consumers from cost-saving methods and to workers from steady employment against the undoubted virtues of the dying world of proprietary capitalism and what they saw as visionary schemes for a statist direction of the new industrial order. Adopting a corporatist language of functions

33. Morton Horwitz, *The Transformation of American Law, 1780–1860* (Cambridge, Mass., 1977); Herbert Hovenkamp, "The Political Economy of Substantive Due Process," *Stanford Law Review* 40 (1988): 379–447; Furner, "Republican Tradition."

and groups in place of the "rights talk" used persistently by social democrats, the USIC promoted a pluralist vision of American society as a collection of spontaneously organizing entities, dealing privately among themselves in civil society to resolve conflicts and stabilize the economy, under minimal state supervision. The corporate form itself was credited with no inherent evil tendencies. Only bad men, who might abuse it, needed supervision. On the basis of extensive investigations of various patterns of labor relations, the USIC hailed as the preferred model not an "industrial republic" or "industrial democracy" that injected political considerations into the highly technical arena of management, but a market model of contractual arrangements between the voluntary collectives that had come to compose liberal society. The preferred form was exemplified, in the USIC report, by a "trade agreement" between a national union and a national managers' association worked out in 1900 for the machine tool industry, which embodied both a long-term wage agreement and a mechanism for preventing spontaneous walkouts during the life of the contract.[34]

In the USIC's final report Jenks condemned the trust-busting approach embodied in recent Sherman Act jurisprudence. Rejecting both republican antimonopolism and the legacy of propertied independence it expressed, he proposed federal licensing of corporations as a way of extending official recognition to the legitimacy of reasonable combination, which was the cornerstone of the merger movement. A federal licensing power was naturally open to various uses, as those who discussed the strategy over the previous decade had recognized. Senator John Sherman had argued during congressional debates on his bill that the state governments were no longer up to the task of supervising the huge manufacturing trusts, a job he proposed it transfer to the federal government. Had Sherman's view prevailed, clear-cut national authority over the sizes and uses of combinations might have short-circuited the competitive bidding between states for corporate favors that set in after the "traitor state," New Jersey, permitted companies to acquire the stock or assets of corporations in other states, producing a more timely response to the great merger movement. On the other hand, used as Jenks envisaged it, national incorporation could protect reasonable combinations from harassment, allowing the very large capital requirements of the efficient giant companies to deter destabilizing competition.[35]

34. The report was highly critical of union-busting tactics such as those uncovered in an investigation of the Chicago building trades strike. See U.S. Industrial Commission, *Report*, esp. vol. 1, *Preliminary Report*, 9–37, and vol. 19, *Final Report*, the section headed "Industrial Combinations." See also Wunderlin, *Visions*; David Montgomery, *Workers' Control in America* (Cambridge, 1979), chap. 3.

35. Montgomery, *Workers' Control in America*; Charles McCurdy, "The *Knight* Sugar Decision of 1895 and the Modernization of American Corporation Law, 1869–1903," *Journal of Economic History* 38 (1978): 631–49.

IN the aftermath of the USIC and the turn-of-the-century flowering of corporate liberalism it represented, theoretical developments called some of these approaches into question, helping to reinvigorate democratic statism. To win acceptance for the ordering capacities of the corporation, corporate liberals had to confront the issue of corporate profits as an aspect of the general subject of distribution, and the increasing disparity between rich and poor, also central to various versions of the social question. Thus their highly technical professional discussions of the nature of capital and the source of business profits flowed over into the public discourse, where the ever-increasing importance of capital in both production and society and the crowding out and cheapening of labor made the justification of profits a major issue. Among American economists, a revision of the classical meaning of capital had begun in the early 1880s, when Francis Amasa Walker defined business profits as a form of rent for the superior abilities of talented managers. Another set of observations, similar to Walker's in the sense that they stressed the special virtue of prudent, patient capitalists, were those of the Austrian school, which had a few American adherents. Their thinking based a separate share for capital in distribution and a new justification for interest on the more round-about production methods of the machine age, which required greater risk and a great deal more waiting than needful, spendthrift labor would endure. In Clark's mechanical imagery, by contrast, capital received its share exactly the way labor did, as a reward for its part in creating "utilities" desired by consumers. Increased use of capital in mechanized production contributed enormously to the productivity of labor, providing a basis for higher wages.[36]

Emerging neoclassicism failed to stifle its opposition, which rejected abstract models and stressed the legal foundations of capitalism. In Clark's cosmology, profits were strictly temporary gains due to technical or managerial improvements, which disappeared as soon as other enterprising souls could imitate new methods. By contrast, Commons attributed the exorbitant profits of the trust era to monopoly advantages (patents, franchises, favorable locations) that capitalists deliberately sought, often through politics. Responding to Jenks's discussion of the efficiency of large manufacturing corporations, H. C. Adams put forth a rudimentary theory of optimum size that denied the productive efficiency of oversized units, which survived by taking advantage of outdated laws and exploiting the state's inattention. Thorstein Veblen invented a Hobbesian language

36. Francis Amasa Walker, "The Source of Business Profits," *Quarterly Journal of Economics* 1 (1887): 265–88; John Bates Clark, "Profits under Modern Conditions," Political Science Quarterly 2 (1887): 603–19; idem, "Capital and Its Earnings," *Publications of the American Economic Association* 3 (1888): 3–69; Eugen von Bohm-Bawerk, "The Austrian Economists," *Annals of the American Academy* 2 (1891): 361–84.

in which a predatory "pecuniary society" overran and subjugated a virtuous "industrial society." While workers and engineers worried about "serviceability," greedy capitalists, obsessed by the desire to protect the "vendibility" of their endless streams of useless products, deliberately suppressed patents, "sabotaged" production, and encouraged "pecuniary emulation" and aimless, joyless buying, to maintain the price system. In Commons's scenario, unlike Clark's, the monopoly advantages that made this wasteful system possible were capitalized through the investment system, with full cooperation of the state; monopoly gains thus produced a permanent stream of income, an enduring strategic advantage, for the capitalist class.[37]

Another element of this new criticism focused on the changing composition and meaning of capital. Veblen denied that capital was any longer the product of arduous saving, as described in liberal tradition from Adam Smith to the Austrian Eugen von Bohm-Bawerk. Rather, in the modern system of industry based on loan credit, capital was borrowed money. Capitalization—literally, the credit a business could obtain and reobtain for endless cycles of production, but also, critically, the valuation placed on companies in daily Wall Street calculations—was based on the lender's expectation of profits. Such an expectation typically arose from a strategic advantage that put one entrepreneur in a position to outdo the others. Capital became a speculative thing—a flow of money values. And in the interest of protecting and enhancing monetary values, the investment system was finely attuned to detecting and rewarding monopoly advantage.

Redefining labor as a social category produced a similar deep division among economists that spilled over into the policy talk of the long Progressive era. Economists disagreed on what factors determined the rate of wages, how much trade unions could affect wage levels, what the labor question included in addition to wages, and what role, if any, the state should play in the conditions and progress of labor. Despite their differences, economists generally agreed that the legitimacy of industrial capitalism depended on the answers they could provide for the distribution question. Thus John Bates Clark tied the stability of the social order to his peculiar vision of distributive justice. "The welfare of the laboring

37. John R. Commons, *The Distribution of Wealth* (1893) (New York, 1963); Henry Carter Adams, "Publicity and Corporate Abuses," *Publications of the Michigan Political Association* 1 (1894): 109–20; idem, "Trusts," in *Papers and Proceedings of the Sixteenth Annual Meeting of the American Economic Association* (1903): 91–107; Thorstein Veblen, *The Theory of Business Enterprise* (New York, 1904); idem, "Industrial and Pecuniary Employments," *Publications of the American Economic Association,* 3d ser., 2 (1901): 190–235; John R. Commons, "Economic Aspects of the Concentration of Wealth: Its Dangers," *Independent* 54 (1902): 1040–44.

classes depends on whether they get much or little," he argued, "but their attitude toward other classes—and, therefore, the stability of the social state—depends chiefly on the question whether the amount they get, be it large or small, is what they produce. If they create a small amount of wealth and get the whole of it, they may not seek to revolutionize society; but if it were to appear that they produce an ample amount and get only a part of it, many of them would become revolutionists, and all would have the right to do so."[38]

For the statist, laborist wing of the economists' controversy, distributive justice involved more than a mathematical equivalency between effort and gain. Justice was a historical category, to be assessed in relation to the traditions and political values expressed in American republicanism. In the early, formative stages of the labor question, Ely and Adams turned the new field of labor history, which they initiated in the United States, into an important ingredient in the discussion of workers' rights, demonstrating in their accounts of the historical evolution of work, labor organization, and labor politics in the West that the work relations of industrial capitalism were in conflict with earlier traditions. On both sides of the Atlantic, late nineteenth-century economists produced a rich literature that recovered a history of customary rights and reciprocal obligations embedded in feudalism, the medieval guilds, and the decaying apprenticeship system, in which labor was protected by communal solidarity and the legal concept of a just price governed exchanges, including the wage bargain. Never having enjoyed such protections to the extent that European workers had, American artisans had at least been able to look forward to participating in the republican dream of propertied independence, owning their own shop. The patterned insecurity faced by wage laborers in the industrial system was a poor substitute, Adams argued, and workers' movements in support of industrial democracy were essentially conservative, in keeping with both liberal and republican tradition.[39]

Ely's important histories located the American labor movement in relation to similar movements in other countries, as necessarily collectivist responses to the commodification of labor. Yet, in the face of rising "social fear" in the aftermath of Haymarket, he also argued that the American pattern was distinctive. Unlike workers in France and Germany, who were

---

38. Clark, *Distribution of Wealth*, 4.

39. Adams's views were expressed in the sources cited in n. 23 above and in dozens of other articles and addresses in the Henry Carter Adams papers, Michigan Historical Collections, Ann Arbor. The most important British contributions to historicizing the concept of labor were probably those of Sidney and Beatrice Webb. Adams can be viewed as an exceptionalist only in the sense that, for institutionalists generally, economic systems are embedded in and dependent on the peculiarities of a particular legal and cultural system.

drawn by the forces of history and culture to socialism and anarchism, and despite the inevitability of class conflict, American workers remained moderate. They could be driven to revolution by capitalist intransigence and one-sided interference on the part of the state. But responsible leadership on the part of enlightened capitalists, a sympathetic clergy, middle-class experts, and responsible union leaders could channel the aspirations of American workers for cooperative ownership toward a "middle way" between anarchism and socialism that was faithful to republican traditions. To maintain American uniqueness in this regard, the right of workers to organize collectively and strike if necessary to promote their interests must be protected during the transition to cooperative forms of ownership.[40]

Also drawn to contextualism, Commons tied historical changes in the patterns of American labor organization to changing labor market conditions rather than inevitable class conflict. Interested initially in political solutions to the labor question, he began advocating in the 1890s a system of proportional representation in which economic interests, rather than geographic areas, would send their own chosen representatives to Congress. As this parliament of interests wrestled with the social questions of the day, economists would play a subordinate, advisory role, helping the various functional groups to clarify their positions. Working for the National Civic Federation at the turn of the century, Commons observed bilateral negotiations in the bituminous coal industry and thought he had finally seen an "industrial congress" in operation—a vision that invoked republicanism without requiring impossibly difficult innovations in the political state.

A swing figure between the democratic statist and corporate voluntarist strands of new liberalism, Commons developed in ensuing years a theory of collective action in which the state played largely an educational, facilitating role. Entitlements that Adams justified within a rights framework and hoped to see recognized as a new form of property Commons translated into "working rules" for industry, which capitalists and unions would hammer out among themselves, according to the evolving customs and traditions of each particular craft and industry. Arms of the state, industrial commissions and labor bureaus, would stay in touch with these constituencies, searching out problems and publicizing examples of the best practice. In this pluralist vision, which extended the imagery of contract to include all the various kinds of "transactions" that stitched a

40. Richard T. Ely, *French and German Socialism* (New York, 1883); idem, *The Labor Movement in America* (New York, 1886); idem, *Studies in the Evolution of Industrial Society* (New York, 1903). For a somewhat different assessment of Ely's exceptionalism, see Ross, *Origins of American Social Science*, 106–22.

modern society together into a working whole, benefits won through collective bargaining could no longer be viewed as extensions of citizenship. Yet, like the development of "proprietary rights" in Adams's more juristic vision of industrial relations, progress for Commons depended on the complete freedom of both labor and capital, within the bounds of criminal law and common decency, to organize and pursue their collective interests without restraint, working out their destinies in an open, democratic system of collective laissez-faire. When the courts outlawed substantially all forms of collective action by unions and the open-shop movement displaced the NCF model of labor relations, Commons and his students in the rising generation of labor specialists were forced to revisit the question of the role of the state.[41]

In the debate over distribution, progressive institutionalists such as Ely, Adams, and Commons stressed the vital role of trade unions in an American system of industrial relations able to deliver on the promise of distributive equity and revive political obligation in a disaffected working class. Conservative historicists such as Hadley, George Gunton, and Jenks saw a different purpose for unions. Inching toward a fully corporatist vision of American society, all three saw conservative unions as instruments for social stabilization, to the extent that they promoted class harmony and deflected more radical forms of labor activism. But more important, they also connected certain types of labor organizations with economic stabilization, and with the long-term survivability of modern capitalism. For Gunton, the upward pressure that organized skilled workers exerted on wages was an important mechanism for socializing the surplus product of mass-production industries. The natural evolution of mechanized industry would be encouraged, not disrupted, by a modest redistributive effect that encouraged necessary consumption. Similarly, but with more precision, Hadley formed an early segmentation theory of the labor market that divided workers into "noncompeting groups." A heightened longing for goods and a more diversified consumption, supported by the high wages of skilled workers in conservative unions, would help curtail "oversaving" and redundant investment by the rich. By the same token, denying protection to the unskilled would keep their feet to the fire and force them to upgrade both their appetites and their skills, in

41. John R. Commons, "American Shoemakers, 1648–1895: A Sketch of Industrial Revolution," *Quarterly Journal of Economics* 24 (1909): 39–81; idem, the introduction to vols. 5–10 of John R. Commons et al., eds., *Documentary History of Industrial Society*, 11 vols. (Cleveland, 1910–11); idem, *A Sociological View of Sovereignty* (1899–1900) (New York, 1965); idem, *Legal Foundations of Capitalism* (New York, 1924); and the sources in n. 37 above.

the process transforming the economy. Progress in Hadley's estimation depended on success for the talented and failure for the lazy and dull.[42]

Neither the Adams/Ely nor the Jenks/Hadley wing of the historical/ institutionalist discussion was much affected by talk of "natural" determinants of wage rates, enshrined in Clark's neoclassical imagery, where a market system, in the absence of "frictions," would automatically produce a fair distribution. Clark's was an abstract, clinical language of balances and equivalencies in which capitalist and worker were willing partners who would receive their just product—unless excessive organization on either side distorted the process. By contrast, in the USIC view, as we have seen, equal organization on both sides would be required to *override* the erratic operation of the unregulated market. Trade agreements that took wages out of competition would be a crucial element in a stabilization project built around the idea of visible hands—those of organized labor as well as capital—restricting production, supporting prices, and generally administering the markets for labor, credit, and goods.

As the USIC experience showed, participation in special blue-ribbon investigations gained economists access to the new, state-based processes of investigation and control being constructed to monitor relations between capital and labor and define the role of the state in relation to corporate business. Economists chosen to play these "insider" roles were of course selected by the political leaders in power at the moment, on the basis of reputation, previous contacts with officials, and the views they had expressed. In this instance, the economists selected by the USIC— Jenks in particular—undoubtedly delivered more or less what was expected. Yet they also had an area of free agency, advancing knowledge through their staff work, providing new language, engaging in a fruitful discourse with the corporate lawyers, and shaping the recommendations of the commission. The USIC probe came at the end of a long series of congressional committee investigations of the labor conflicts of the Gilded Age, and the widely circulated reports of the commission served as powerful antidotes to the more statist proposals offered by those committees, which had been increasingly critical of judicial interference in labor conflicts and of the doctrines of legal individualism, free contract, and entrepreneurial rights that the courts were offering to justify new protections for property at the expense of labor. Equally critical in its own way of contemporary jurisprudence, the USIC provided nonstatist, corporate

---

42. Arthur Hadley, "Some Fallacies in the Theory of Distribution," *Economic Journal* 7 (1897): 485; Gunton, *Wealth and Progress*. This account draws on an extended analysis of his development theories in Furner, "Liberty versus Efficiency."

voluntarist alternatives to such disruptive, one-sided judicial proceedings.[43]

IN the new century, in the context of a series of developments including
declining real wages among skilled workers, worsening industrial relations, and court decisions that further restricted the collective actions of
labor, conditions ripened for a resurgence of the democratic statist strand
of new liberalism. Various points of access became available for critics of
corporate liberalism, in public and private agencies devoted to reform-
ulating the labor question in light of new conditions and searching for
constructive solutions. The Department of Labor provided some opportunities, but as union membership declined under pressure from a virulent
open-shop movement, the commitment of the Bureau of Labor Statistics
(BLS) to a corporatist model of voluntary organization and collective
bargaining and its failure to track the living and working conditions of
the working class as a whole limited its effectiveness and credibility.[44]

From the standpoint of social knowledge regarding the labor question,
a kind of turning point was reached in the disclosures of the path-breaking
Pittsburgh Survey. The most important of a new genre of community
studies conducted by social scientists with foundation support, the survey
exposed the dysfunctional side of industrial capitalism. Economists in
the democratic statist tradition were much involved in designing and
conducting the study. Targeting the home city of the nation's largest
corporation, U.S. Steel, which had recently crushed its unions, the survey
revealed the dark underside of corporate industrialism. The depressing
picture included, in the words of one summary, "an incredible amount
of overwork by everybody," "low wages for the great majority," "still
lower wages for women," "an absentee capitalism with bad effects strik-
ingly analogous to those of absentee landlordism," "a continuous inflow
of immigrants with low standards," "the destruction of family life," "ar-

43. See, for example, U.S. House of Representatives, *Investigation by a Select Committee Relative to the Causes of the General Depression in Labor and Business,* House Misc. Doc. 5, 46th Cong., 2d sess. (Washington, D.C., 1879); U.S. Senate, Committee on Education and Labor, *The Relations between Labor and Capital,* 4 vols., 47th Cong., 2d sess., 1883 (Washington, D.C., 1885). "Insider learning" is a term borrowed from William Barber, "Government as a Laboratory for Economic Learning in the Years of the Democratic Roose-velt," in Furner and Supple, *State and Economic Knowledge,* 137. See also Wunderlin, *Visions.*

44. Furner, "Knowing Capitalism"; William T. Moye and Joseph P. Goldberg, *The First Hundred Years of the Bureau of Labor Statistics,* Bureau of Labor Statistics Bulletin 2235 (1985); James Leiby, *Carroll Wright and Labor Reform: The Origins of Labor Statistics* (Cam-bridge, Mass., 1960); and the bulletins, annual reports, and special reports of the BLS. The BLS employed Jenks, Commons, Roland Falkner, W. F. Willoughby, E. R. L. Gould, and W. E. B. Du Bois, among others.

chaic social institutions," and a blinding "contrast between the prosperity on the one hand of the most prosperous of all the communities of our western civilization . . . and, on the other hand, the neglect of life, of health, of physical vigor, even of the industrial efficiency of the individual" that an unregulated, amoral capitalism produced.[45]

A new uprising of labor in the distressed years between 1909 and 1913 and a changing of the political guard that brought a social scientist once schooled by Richard Ely to the White House opened the way for a second major commission study of the structure and problems of capitalism. Under the leadership of the Roman Catholic social activist Frank Walsh, the United States Commission on Industrial Relations (CIR), conducted extensive hearings and published in 1915 a nineteen-volume report that assessed the impact on American society of a permissive official attitude toward the corporate reorganization of American capitalism and the judicial assault on labor unions. As Leon Fink relates in his account of the political history of the CIR (Chapter 8 of this volume), the commission itself was ideologically balanced and deadlocked.

Meanwhile, its research staff, loaded with statist democrats, conducted a massive investigation of the social consequences of the corporate system. Young economists trained in the Adams-Commons tradition shifted the labor side of the inquiry away from unions, whose calamitous decline the commission documented, to the conditions and problems of the working class as a whole. Like the AALL, with which it shared ideas and personnel, the CIR became a training ground for the economists who were to establish industrial relations as a specialty during the 1920s. The labor historian and economist Selig Perlman did his early work for the CIR, as did Isador Lubin, Leo Wolman, Sumner Slichter, Edgar Sydenstricker, Edwin Witte, David Saposs, and William Leiserson, social scientists who would put their distinctive stamp on New Deal labor legislation. W. Jett Lauck, a Chicago Ph.D. who, like Lubin, had been influenced by Veblen, did the integrative work that positioned the CIR staff with respect to class in the United States.[46]

The CIR constructed a different view of the labor question from the

45. The quotation is from Edward T. Devine, "The Results of the Pittsburgh Survey," *Publications of the American Economic Association* 10 (1909): 209–10; Margaret F. Byington, "The Family in a Typical Mill Town," ibid., 193–206; John F. McClymer, "The Pittsburgh Survey, 1907–1914: Forging an Ideology in the Steel District," *Pennsylvania History* 41 (1974): 169–86; Paul U. Kellogg, ed., *The Pittsburgh Survey,* 6 vols. (New York, 1910–14). See also the excellent chapter by Steve R. Cohen, "The Pittsburgh Survey and the Social Survey Movement: A Sociological Road Not Taken," in *The Social Survey in Historical Perspective, 1880–1940,* ed. Martin Bulmer, Kevin Bayles, and Katherine Sklar (Cambridge, 1991), 245–68.

46. Graham Adams, *Age of Industrial Violence: 1910–1915* (New York, 1966); H. M. Gitelman, *Legacy of the Ludlow Massacre* (Philadelphia, 1988); Furner, "Knowing Capitalism."

one proposed by the USIC, giving the structures and relations of monopoly capitalism a dramatically different meaning. Whereas the USIC had assumed that corporate capitalism naturally included a progressive tendency toward unionization and general improvement in workers' incomes and conditions, CIR economists insisted, on the basis of overwhelming evidence, that no such necessary tendency existed. Whereas official policy in the McKinley era had concentrated on promoting recognition of conservative unions, the CIR focused on conditions in the largely unorganized, immigrant working class generally. CIR economists identified as serious public questions the casual labor system that was systematically exploited in major mass-production industries such as garment making and meat packing; the chronic unemployment and underemployment that afflicted virtually all workers; incomes too low to provide a decent level of subsistence to a large fraction of working-class families; the feudal conditions that prevailed in industries where workers were unorganized and unprotected; and the pernicious insecurity of life in a society that provided neither full employment nor income-maintaining social insurance.[47]

Reinvigorating the democratic radicalism of the congressional inquiries of the 1880s and 1890s, they rejected the hollow shell of collective laissez-faire. In its place, they advanced a conception of the state in which positive assistance to labor organization and redistributive policies were justified not only within the framework of an inherited rights discourse, but also, and more important, as countercyclical strategies promoting economic stabilization, in the general interest of society as a whole. In a graphic language of rights repressed and denied, CIR experts exposed a side of corporate behavior that corporate liberals had not typically shown, targeting deunionization, oppressive working conditions, and investment practices that violated the public interest in distributive equity. They located structural causes for unemployment, which would not be readily corrected by forms of private, associative action then in practice. Whereas the USIC approach to the labor question had been contained within the parameters of voluntary corporatism espoused by progressive capitalists and conservative labor, CIR economic analysis led to conclusions that were, in the American context, radically statist.

47. This account of CIR economic research is based on the fifteen microfilm reels of reports compiled by the CIR Division of Investigation and Research, located at the Wisconsin Historical Society, Madison. The most important reports for these purposes are W. Jett Lauck, "Economic Causes Underlying Industrial Unrest"; Sumner Slichter, "The Agents of Concentration"; Edgar Sydenstricker, "Conditions of Labor in the Principal Industries"; Leo Wolman, "The Extent of Organization in the United States in 1910"; William Leiserman, "The Labor Market and Unemployment"; and Selig Perlman, "Preliminary Report on Welfare Work and Social Insurance."

Unlike their predecessors in the USIC, the CIR economists saw nothing benign or progressive in monopoly. Their investigative reports linked industrial unrest generally, and particularly the violent mass protests of the 1910s, to a system of corporate enterprise that concentrated control of a large fraction of the nation's industrial workers in the hands of a few overcapitalized monopolies whose managers thought in terms of maintaining prices rather than employment. Pointing to serious structural problems that would respond to neither microeconomic nor associative solutions, they consciously rejected the neoclassical vision of self-regulating market and called for a significant extension of state responsibility and control.

A "CIR view" of what would constitute a republican response to the social question emerged from these investigations. Because of the conflict within the commission itself, reflecting its tripartite corporatist structure, the staff reports, published in succeeding years, were its foremost legacy. They mapped out an agenda for achieving economic and social democracy that included public responsibility for maintaining, redistributing, and supplementing income, increased public supervision of the investment system, a publicly financed employment service, countercyclical public works, and an elaborate, mixed public and private social insurance system, including comprehensive unemployment, old age, and sickness insurance. The commission's wholesale attack on judicial repression and legal individualism carried forward into twentieth-century policy deliberations the republican rights consciousness that had been developing in democratic collectivism since the Gilded Age. Rejecting the strategy of contrived scarcity that had become the basis of corporatist stabilization policy, CIR economists conveyed a new sense of the sources of unemployment and instability, and charted a direction in labor economics and industrial policy that contained the essentials of the modern stabilization and welfare state.[48]

MODERN American political argument originated in these debates over the content of and prospects for a new liberalism. In response to insupportable contradictions in social relations and what had previously been accepted as social knowledge, a transition in conceptual understanding occurred. To the extent that economists' categories and modes of analysis affected policy deliberations in these ways, they "economized" American political conversation. Statist and associative strands of new liberalism crowded out older thinking and traditional values, making it possible to imagine a modern liberal order.[49]

48. Daniel Ernst, "Common Laborers? Industrial Pluralists, Legal Realists, and the Law of Industrial Disputes, 1915–43," *Law and History Review* 11 (1993): 59–100.

49. For the influence of economic theory of American jurisprudence, see Herbert Hovenkamp, *Enterprise and American Law, 1836–1937* (Cambridge, Mass., 1991).

If individual economists cannot be cavalierly written off as "servants of power," their discipline was deeply implicated in the rise of the modern corporate state. New liberalism provides a vital missing piece of the story for those who attempt, erroneously, to account for an "incomplete" welfare state and a state-corporatist response to the Great Depression in terms of individualist and antistatist political traditions inherited from the nineteenth century.[50]

In fact, new liberalism, between the 1880s and 1920, had fundamentally altered inherited traditions. The new models—the corporatist voluntarism of Hadley, Jenks, and the USIC; and the democratic statism of Adams, Walsh, and the CIR—both saw a measure of fulfillment during the social and economic mobilization for World War I, which combined eclectically, under the pressure of events, elements of associative and statist direction. Subsequently, in the 1920 and 1930s and beyond, a pattern arose of cycling between the two forms, and of occasional fruitful blending of them. Yet all too often gridlock and stalemate occurred, as both the democratic aspirations of statist new liberalism and the commitment to sustained economic growth and social harmony expressed in corporate liberalism were overwhelmed by the fragmentation and institutionalized, self-referencing atavism of liberal pluralism.

Even so, it should perhaps be observed from the perspective of the late twentieth century, when the era in which politics and policy were conducted within the framework provided by new liberalism has ended, that intellectuals who constructed its major variants were an especially privileged and at the same time responsible breed, deserving a special claim on our attention. Not least, they become remarkable because, unlike many of those engaged in reinventing government and downsizing welfare today, they assumed that society as a whole somehow bore collective responsibility for the welfare of its members, and that purposeful action, through enlightened, voluntary cooperation among responsible groups in civil society or through the auspices of government, could bring about desirable results. The post–new liberal era of "rational choice," resurgent laissez-faire, talk of market solutions for problems ranging from teen pregnancy to environmental pollution, and global restructuring that shifts production between continents with little thought of local consequences is a very different time indeed.

50. As in Theda Skocpol, "Political Response to Capitalist Crisis: Neo-Marxist Theories of the State and the Case of the New Deal," *Politics and Society* 10 (1980): 155–201. Skocpol has subsequently located important precedents in the Progressive Era. See her *Protecting Soldiers and Mothers*.

8

Expert Advice: Progressive Intellectuals and the Unraveling of Labor Reform, 1912–1915

Leon Fink

President Woodrow Wilson's appointment in 1912 of a federal commission to recommend solutions to "a state of industrial war" represented an unprecedented opportunity to address the nation's most serious domestic issue. Relying as it did on several of the era's leading public intellectuals, the Commission on Industrial Relations (CIR) implicitly tested the social influence of a larger labor reform community of academics, social investigators, and political activists as well as immediate chances for a progressive policy agenda on the labor question. "If they do their work with imagination and courage," Walter Lippmann predicted, "they will do more than any other group of people in this country to shape our history."[1] Volunteering his assistance, Wisconsin's legislative librarian, Charles McCarthy, saluted the project as "the greatest work ever undertaken in America."[2]

Yet within two years a fight between the CIR's chairman and its research staff effectively split the commission into feuding camps. Unable to reach a consensus in a final report, the commission squandered much of its goodwill as well as its budgetary appropriation. Though its final recommendations may well have been, as some observers have said, the most radical social wisdom ever to emanate from an official federal authority in American history, the militant rhetoric fell largely on deaf ears.[3] Except for a few pieces of ameliorative legislation with tangential connec-

1. Quoted in Graham Adams Jr., *Age of Industrial Violence, 1910–15: The Activities and Findings of the United States Commission on Industrial Relations* (New York, 1966), 48, 50.
2. Charles McCarthy to W. J. Lauck, January 10, 1914, in Charles McCarthy Papers, University of Wisconsin, Madison (microfilm).
3. Adams, *Age of Industrial Violence*, 219–23.

tion to the commission's mission, little came of the "twenty-two months of investigation, hundreds of hours of well-publicized hearings, and thousands of pages of testimony."[4] The commission generally received a brush-off from Congress, and at best served organized labor as a propaganda tool rather than as a serious strategic ally.[5] Although the coming of World War I did indeed witness a dramatic increase in state labor regulation, the moment proved less a triumph of prewar reform fervor than an emergency measure to be jettisoned for its very coercive origins.[6] But even before outside factors such as the war came into play, the commission's internal strife had muffled its message and blunted its impact. The head of the commission's women's research division, Marie L. Obenauer, experienced the internal upheaval as "painful and disheartening beyond description." John A. Fitch, editor of *Survey,* labeled the unraveling of the commission's promise "one of the saddest spectacles of this generation." With some justification, therefore, the journal of the National Association of Manufacturers fairly crowed, "We are not disappointed with the product of the Commission's labors: nothing constructive was expected of it and nothing constructive has been produced."[7]

What went wrong with the CIR? A full answer to the question would encompass the peculiar mechanics of American politics and state reform as a whole; the issues that concern us here are the role and behavior of the labor reformers themselves. In particular, the CIR exposed competing visions of the very function of intellectual activism: What purpose did social investigation serve? In what relation to government and "the people" did investigators stand? Such queries, inextricably caught up in the contemporary conflicts of policy and personality, in the end lay bare not only obstacles to industrial democracy but key dilemmas within the social history of American intellectuals.

CONCEIVED under President Taft, chartered by Congress, and staffed by appointments of President Wilson, the CIR was a direct response to a determined campaign by a coalition of reform-minded businessmen, so-

---

4. Eugene M. Tobin, *Organize or Perish: America's Independent Progressives, 1913–1933* (New York, 1986), 58.

5. Samuel Gompers to Frank Walsh, September 15, 1915, in Samuel Gompers Papers, University of Maryland (microfilm).

6. Barry D. Karl, *The Uneasy State: The United States from 1915 to 1945* (Chicago, 1983), 46–49.

7. Marie L. Obenauer to McCarthy, March 3, 1915, and John A. Fitch to McCarthy, March 22, 1915, both in Charles McCarthy Papers, State Historical Society of Wisconsin, Madison; Adams, *Age of Industrial Violence,* 219–23; Valerie Jean Conner, *The National War Labor Board: Stability, Social Justice, and the Voluntary State in World War I* (Chapel Hill, 1983), 14.

cial workers, academics, and religious leaders.[8] Conviction of the Mc-Namara brothers for the bombing of the building that housed the *Los Angeles Times* amidst a bitter struggle over the city's open-shop policies proved a final public spur to action. In the aftermath of a presidential campaign waged in a climate of growing dissatisfaction with laissez-faire economics (in which three candidates were identified with "progressivism" and the fourth with socialism), the political climate could hardly have been more conducive to industrial reform proposals. Finally, dissatisfaction with earlier commissioned research that legislators had all but ignored persuaded the new commission from early on not merely to collect information but to "be interpretative and remedial."[9]

From the beginning, the CIR assumed a determinedly didactic posture. Structured on the model of the corporatist National Civic Federation (with its nine members equally divided among business, labor and public representatives), the commission generally followed the lead of its chairman, the Kansas City attorney Frank P. Walsh, and its most distinguished public member, Professor John R. Commons of the University of Wisconsin.[10] Appointment of these two well-known labor reformers consolidated support from both organized labor and the intellectual community. Even the ever-suspicious Samuel Gompers suspended his initial criticism of "intellectuals on a sociological slumming tour."[11]

Superficially, the alliance of Chairman Walsh's political skills with Commons's scholarly expertise offered bright prospects for the commission's

8. For surveys of the CIR's work, see Adams, *Age of Industrial Violence;* James Weinstein, *The Corporate Ideal in the Liberal State,* 172–213 (Boston, 1968); Edward A. Fitzpatrick, *McCarthy of Wisconsin* (New York, 1944), 189–206; Marion Casey, *Charles McCarthy: Librarianship and Reform* (Chicago, 1981), 102–260; Mark Perlman, *Labor Union Theories in America: Background and Development* (Evanston, Ill., 1958), 279–301. Other useful references are found in autobiographical reminiscences, including John R. Commons, *Myself* (New York, 1934), 165–81; and Mrs. J. Borden Harriman, *From Pinafores to Politics* (New York, 1923), 131–75.

9. The best survey of earlier investigations of the labor question is Clarence E. Wunderlin Jr., *Visions of a New Industrial Order: Social Science and Labor Theory in America's Progressive Era* (New York, 1992); Adams, *Age of Industrial Violence,* 73. See also William Leiserson's advice to the CIR on learning from the mistakes of the 1902 U.S. Industrial Commission; Commission on Industrial Relations (CIR), *Final Report and Testimony,* 11 vols. (Washington, D.C., 1916), 1:344–57.

10. The nine commission members included three "public" representatives: Walsh, Commons, and Florence (Daisy) Hurst (Mrs. J. Borden) Harriman, a Democratic party stalwart with ties as well to the social work community; three labor representatives: Austin B. Garretson, president of the order of Railway Conductors; James O'Connell, vice president of the AFL and director of its Metal Trades Department; and John B. Lennon, treasurer of the AFL; and three business representatives: Frederic A. Delano, railroad owner; Harris Weinstock, department store owner and real estate developer, a liberal, from California; and Thruston Ballard, a Kentucky liquor baron.

11. Quoted in Adams, *Age of Industrial Violence,* 48.

effectiveness. Both the integrity of his convictions and his energy in pursuing them recommended Frank Walsh to many people in the reform community as the perfect captain for a radical-progressive assault on the battlements of industrial privilege. The journalist George Creel, for example, lionized him as "a great lawyer, a persuasive speaker, and the most authentic liberal I have known."[12] Selected after the legal scholar Louis Brandeis declined to serve, Walsh combined extensive labor contacts with impeccable radical reform convictions. A loyal Democrat, he had organized a social-workers-for-Wilson brigade in 1912; he also enjoyed a more personal connection to the White House through Margaret Wilson, the president's daughter, who cultivated a number of Progressive reformers.[13] The one chink in Walsh's armor was perhaps a product of his very combativeness. When, in the spring of 1915, Creel jokingly addressed the CIR chairman as "Mr. Francis 'Poleon Walsh" and "Dear 'Polean the Greatest," many of Walsh's colleagues and erstwhile admirers were no longer smiling.[14]

Politically, Walsh exhibited a crusading populist spirit alongside a bare-knuckled realpolitik born of his Missouri background. Born in 1864 to a poor Irish-Catholic family in St. Louis, Walsh held a succession of laboring jobs before he taught himself law in 1889 and entered the rough-and-tumble world of Kansas City machine politics. The young George Creel (who himself had climbed from déclassé southern roots into a professional career) quickly lined up with Walsh, the brains behind the local anti-Pendergast political chieftain and chief reform strategist in corruption-ridden Missouri.[15]

Together Walsh, Creel, and a coterie of reform-minded writers and small businessmen articulated a self-styled antimonopoly politics resting on hostility to the corporations, radical tax doctrine, and generous social welfare spending. In the courtroom and out, Walsh attacked the corruption of the political parties, the railroad's influence over legislators and judges, and the shameful plight of the urban poor. A big, athletic man with a booming voice and commanding courtroom presence, Walsh regularly dueled against James A. Reed, a loyalist of Tom Pendergast, and future U.S. senator, in cases across the state, including the successful

---

12. George Creel, quoted ibid., 69.

13. Boyd Fisher, director of the New York City Efficiency Society, wrote "Uncle Frank" Walsh on September 18, 1913, that he had just stayed in the president's cottage in Vermont, where he had gone "horseback riding a good deal with Miss Margaret," and had written the president supporting Walsh's appointment to the CIR: Frank Walsh Papers, New York Public Library.

14. George Creel to Walsh, May 27, 1915, ibid.

15. Creel, *Rebel at Large: Recollections of Fifty Crowded Years* (New York, 1947), 48.

defense of Jesse James Jr. on charges of train robbery.[16] Few persons selected for federal governmental responsibility had developed a less respectful attitude toward the trappings of office or the niceties of procedure than Walsh. When legal ambiguities arose in connection with the work of the pioneering Kansas City Board of Public Welfare, for example, Walsh responded with a chuckle, "To [hell] with the law. Let us go ahead and do it and we will take care of the law later."[17] Creel characterized him as "an agitator outside," not "a plodding administrator inside."[18]

A self-styled champion of the underdog, Walsh displayed especially friendly relations with organized labor. Receiving early endorsement as CIR chair from Samuel Gompers, President of the AFL, and continuing cooperation from the commission's three moderate labor representatives, Walsh also quickly won over such radical figures as Big Bill Haywood and Eugene V. Debs and drew warm praise from Mother Jones. Perhaps Walsh's closest contact in labor circles was the militant and politically minded chief of Chicago's Federation of Labor, John Fitzpatrick, with whom he would collaborate for years to come.[19]

Walsh made no pretense of neutrality on the labor question. In correspondence with the editor of the *Christian Socialist* in 1915, he called himself a political independent, and "so far as social and economic effort is concerned . . . ready to go with any person or group traveling in the direction of human justice."[20] Awaiting congressional confirmation of the CIR panel in the summer of 1913, he listened sympathetically when his hometown friend L. A. Halbert advised that the commission seek to "give the people power over industry and not be hindered by the ancient fetish of the rights of private property." Though such a purpose could not be openly avowed, allowed Halbert, he urged Walsh to develop the "data to establish this position so that it can become the dominant ideal for all time."[21] During the same period Walsh wrote Creel that "we will call our little meeting of 'conspirators' in New York early this Fall for the purpose

16. Adams, *Age of Industrial Violence*, 69–72. The young James was reportedly so impressed by his counsel's performance that he himself became a lawyer and "clean-government insurgent" (70).

17. A. Theodore Brown and Lyle W. Dorsett, *K. C.: A History of Kansas City, Missouri* (Boulder, Colo., 1978), 156–57.

18. Creel, *Rebel at Large*, 48.

19. Adams, *Age of Industrial Violence*, 57, 62; Walsh's only qualm about working with labor representatives on the CIR came when he reflected that the railway conductors' leader, Austin B. Garretson, represented "the most conservative labor organization of the country." See Walsh to Creel, September 3, 1913, in Frank Walsh Papers, New York Public Library. On the Creel-Fitzpatrick connection, I am indebted to Steven Sapolsky.

20. Quoted in Weinstein, *Corporate Ideal*, 186.

21. L. A. Halbert to Walsh [June–July 1913], in Frank Walsh Papers, New York Public Library.

of finding out exactly what we want and going after it." Already, reported Walsh, "this Commission has put me in touch with a number of people around the country of genuine radical views and undoubted sincerity . . . I will try to establish a sort of a quarters for [our] own people . . . [With] writers for some genuine work such as we could get together, there is no telling where we would stop."[22]

Of all Walsh's early moves to set the CIR on a solid footing, none seemed more astute than his recruitment of the University of Wisconsin scholar John R. Commons as a fellow commissioner.[23] Not that the appointment was surprising. Indeed, an investigation of industrial life without a Madison imprimatur would have been more startling. Since the 1880s, the state university had championed the rhetoric of public service and aligned itself with the social gospel critique of free-market capitalism. The happy coincidence of La Follette progressivism and the social policy orientation of the university's president, Charles R. Van Hise (who was himself considered for the CIR chair), secured Madison's reputation in the early twentieth century as a laboratory for progressive legislative measures.[24] For nearly two decades, intellectual research, reform political strategy, and the drafting of legislative bills commingled as never before in American society.[25] Toward this end, Van Hise took no more important step than his acquiescence in the recruitment of the controversial labor economist John R. Commons in 1904. In addition to a distinguished reputation for social research, Commons by 1910 had inspired pioneering state legislation for civil service extension, an industrial commission, and workers' compensation. With an encyclopedic grasp of American labor history and experience on both the U.S. Industrial Commission of 1902—the last federal survey of industrial conditions before the CIR—and the path-breaking Pittsburgh Survey of 1907–9, Commons was recognized as the nation's leading authority on the problems of industrial society by the time the CIR was created. Walsh's promise to Commons "to rely heavily on such experts as you" symbolically paid tribute to (and in turn won support from) the entire sector of contemporary social service and social science professionals.[26] In concrete terms, Walsh

22. Walsh to Creel, September 3, 1913, ibid.

23. Commons clearly shared the general enthusiasm for Walsh apparent in the progressive community. The professor's college-aged son, for example, chose to feature a portrait of Walsh for a magazine-writing class based on "what I've read and heard from Dad and others": John Alvin Commons to Frank Walsh, March 10, 1914, ibid.

24. Adams, *Age of Industrial Violence*, 56.

25. John P. Henderson, "Political Economy and the Service of the State: The University of Wisconsin," in *Breaking the Academic Mould: Economists and American Higher Learning in the Nineteenth Century*, ed. William J. Barber (Middletown, Conn., 1988), 318–39.

26. On the USIC see Wunderlin, *Visions of a New Industrial Order*, 27–45; see also John F. McClaymer, "The Pittsburgh Survey, 1907–1914: Forging on Ideology in the Steel

looked to Commons to organize the commission's research work, while the chairman himself concentrated on the public hearings.

Much as it was in the world of scholarship, Commons's influence on the CIR was ultimately secured through the efforts of his students, broadly defined. His direct role was limited from the outset by an obligation to return to teaching after a two-year leave to work with the Wisconsin Industrial Commission. With only his summers available for full-time focus on the project, Commons relied on a research team composed of brilliant young students, former students, and intellectual acquaintances.[27] The early months of investigation, however, proceeded slowly. With little coordination between hearings and research and a lack of clear goals, the thirty-four-year-old economist W. Jett Lauck struggled to coordinate work on a disparate set of topics, ranging from coercion in company towns to the legal framework for collective bargaining to working women's welfare.[28] Only when Charles McCarthy answered an urgent call from Commons and Walsh to assume direction of research in June 1914 did the investigatory process really snap into shape.[29]

Charles McCarthy was already a skillful and renowned professional policy maker when he joined the CIR. Having transformed the Wisconsin Legislative Library from a mere hole in the wall into the country's first research and bill-drafting service, he had played an integral part in the progressive transformation of Wisconsin's government. Indeed, McCarthy himself popularized the state's reform legacy in *The Wisconsin Idea*— a virtual ode to the marriage of democratic idealism and administrative efficiency, commissioned by Theodore Roosevelt to aid the Progressive cause in 1912. Preoccupied with political matters in Madison, McCarthy initially fended off appeals to act in any more than a consultant role to the CIR. When he finally accepted Chairman Walsh's plea for help, however, McCarthy entered the scene with the confidence of one used to reorganizing things. Among his first communications to Walsh was a gentle chiding of the chairman for being "altogether too good-natured—you allow everybody to impose themselves upon you . . . You can't even get through your mail without interruption."[30]

District," *Pennsylvania History* 41 (1974): 168–86. On the progressive reform community and the commission, see Adams, *Age of Industrial Violence,* 46, 52, 58.

27. Commons, *Myself,* 166–67. Besides Charles McCarthy, Wisconsin students associated with the commission included F. H. Bird, Carl Hookstadt, William L. Leiserson, Selig Perlman, David J. Saposs, Sumner Slichter, Helen Sumner, and G. L. Sprague. Clara Richards and two other librarians from the Wisconsin Legislative Reference Library would assume similar duties for the federal commission.

28. Lauck, who turned thirty in 1910, had directed industrial investigations for the U.S. Immigration Commission, 1907–10.

29. Adams, *Age of Industrial Violence,* 205–6.

30. McCarthy to Sir Horace Plunkett, February 27, 1913, and McCarthy to Walsh, March 3, 1914, both in Charles McCarthy Papers, State Historical Society of Wisconsin, Madison.

Although McCarthy, like Walsh, emerged from a poor Irish working-class background—his father was a factory worker and his mother kept a boardinghouse in Brockton, Massachusetts—his ascent traversed a different geographic and educational plane and engendered a different approach to government and politics. Accepted as a special student at Brown University after following the theater circuit as a stagehand to Providence, Rhode Island, McCarthy flourished under the tutelage of the Brahmin historian John Franklin Jameson. As physically daring as he was intellectually ambitious, the wiry young McCarthy also excelled at football; he was nominated for all-American teams and was the first Brown man to score against both Harvard and Yale. His notoriety on campus was sealed in the special friendship that developed between the shoeworker's son and John D. Rockefeller Jr., his classmate and the assistant football team manager.[31]

Even collegiate fame, however, did not separate McCarthy from the burden of his humble social roots. Unlike most of his Brown classmates, McCarthy worked his way through college; indeed, in order to graduate, he required special faculty dispensation for coursework missed while working. After graduation, McCarthy coached football at the University of Georgia for two years, supplementing his income with research on southern history for Professor Jameson. Finally, he was able to enter graduate school at the University of Wisconsin, where he was attracted by both the reputation of the history department and the reform thought of the economist Richard T. Ely. McCarthy took his Ph.D. in history, economics, and political science in 1901, writing a prize-winning thesis under Frederick Jackson Turner on the Anti-Masonic Party.[32] Even with solid intellectual credentials, however, he fell short of full academic qualifications. Rough of speech, awkward in personal style and dress, and, most important, unmistakably Irish, McCarthy was apparently judged a poor social risk for a university position by both Turner and his old friend Jameson. Fortunately for McCarthy, a position as chief documents clerk for the state's Free Library Commission opened shortly after his graduation, and Turner pushed McCarthy into it with enthusiasm and relief. Professional placement coincided with personal commitment when McCarthy married his landlady's daughter, a schoolteacher of German-Protestant background.[33]

McCarthy's odyssey of hard work and modest upward social mobility equipped him at once with a thirst for cultural refinement and an abiding sympathy for those who had not enjoyed his own good fortune. Once in

31. McCarthy to Plunkett, February 27, 1913, ibid.; Casey, *Charles McCarthy*, 10.
32. Fitzpatrick, *McCarthy of Wisconsin*, 23–25.
33. Casey, *Charles McCarthy*, 21–23.

Madison, he displayed a fierce idealism about social service and social justice. Even while doggedly pursuing his dissertation travels in various eastern cities, for example, he regularly wrote his wife, Lucile, of the hardships of the working people he saw around him: "The electric went by the docks and I could see the sailors at work, the stevedores hauling and tugging, could hear loud orders, curses and all the hum and rattle and roar of business . . . What a loafer I am! What an easy time we have compared to them!" Journeying through Pennsylvania, he contrasted the "crashing of modern machinery" to the "thousands of creatures ground down and brutalized in all this."[34] McCarthy would later recall his early sense of mission: "I had an idea in my head that there was somebody needed between the great mass of workers and the educated people and I tried in every way to prepare myself to be that somebody if I could."[35]

Rather than a populist agitator like Walsh, however, the educated McCarthy emerged as a skillful technician of the machinery of government. In what one contemporary called "the accidental meeting of an opportunity and a shrewd Irish intellect," McCarthy had almost single-handedly developed the prototype for state legislative reference services. Self-consciously drawing on the examples of such earlier British reformers as Francis Place, who developed an influential private library of political tracts, and Jeremy Bentham, who insisted on a practical test for all reform ideas, the young McCarthy simultaneously answered contemporary demands for efficiency in government and growing calls for ameliorative legislation. McCarthy became a particularly valuable accomplice for activist Wisconsin governors, especially during the administrations of two progressive sons of the university, Robert La Follette (1900–1906) and Francis McGovern (1910–14). McCarthy also made a mark in national political circles, violating his declared nonpartisanship in the heady reform climate of 1912. Courted by both Wilson and Theodore Roosevelt after La Follette's candidacy suffered irreparable setback, McCarthy joined the platform committee at the Bull Moose convention and co-authored the famous antitrust plank, whose excision by conservatives from the published platform ultimately dampened Roosevelt's independent appeal.[36]

34. Ibid., 18–19.
35. Quoted in Fitzpatrick, *McCarthy of Wisconsin,* 7.
36. Casey, *Charles McCarthy,* 30, 90–95. One contemporary account estimated that more than 90 percent of Wisconsin state legislative acts from 1901 to 1921 were composed in McCarthy's "bill factory": ibid., 38. The host of measures that McCarthy christened "the Wisconsin idea" encompassed direct primaries for all state offices, establishment of state railroad and civil service commissions, creation of an extension division of the university, and then, in a tide of legislation in 1911, passage of workers' compensation, an industrial commission pioneering in health and safety regulation, protective regulations for child and female workers, continuation schools for workers on the European model, and finally, creation of a state board of public affairs with a planning capacity for a continuing reform

McCarthy's "radical progressivism," two terms he comfortably applied to his own thinking, differed in one important respect from Walsh's labor populism. On top of traditional democratic egalitarianism the "Wisconsin idea" heaped a new social welfare statism. Thus, while the Wisconsin program continued to depend for its rationale on antimonopolism—"unequal conditions of contract" over the necessities of life and industry, the swamping of individual capacity and initiative by "predatory wealth"— the remedy, suggested McCarthy, was "not so simple."[37] The "Wisconsin idea" required less an understanding of workers and farmers under capitalism (whose universal plight was assumed) than an appreciation of the experience and insight of a remarkable group of university-based reformers. The arrival of Richard T. Ely, in particular, who had studied in Germany before finishing his graduate work at Johns Hopkins, brought the "inspiration of New Germany" back to "the German university of the German state of Wisconsin." This institutional connection, combined with the social impact of a depression, facilitated a successful transcendence of liberal individualism and classical political economy.[38]

Though naive (if not a trifle racist) in its comparative sociology, McCarthy's Teutonic idealism served a rather shrewd set of observations about American society.[39] As determined reformers had discovered since the Gilded Age, neither the legislature nor the courts could be looked to as effective instruments of social welfare in the United States. Like other

---

agenda. See Robert S. Maxwell, *La Follette and the Rise of the Progressives in Wisconsin* (Madison, 1956), 74–86, 153–72.

37. Charles McCarthy, *The Wisconsin Idea* (New York, 1912), 1–4.

38. Ely "saw an empire being fashioned by men regarded in his own country as merely theorists; he realized that these Germans were more than mere theorists; that they were laying the foundations for a great insurance system; that they foresaw the commercial prosperity of the country built upon the happiness, education and well-being of the human units of the empire; that order, intelligence, care and thought could be exercised by the state": ibid., 27–28. For a more complex explanation of the subject, see David P. Thelen, *The New Citizenship: Origins of Progressivism in Wisconsin, 1885–1900* (Columbia, Mo., 1972); on the "free translation" of German social science ideas to American shores, see Jurgen Herbst, *The German Historical School in American Scholarship: A Study in the Transfer of Culture* (Ithaca, 1965), esp. 129–59; on the discrepancies between actual developments in German academic culture and American perceptions of them, see Konrad Jarausch, "The Universities: An American View," in *Another Germany: A Reconsideration of the Imperial Era,* ed. Jack R. Dukes and Joachim Remak (Boulder, Colo., 1988), 181–206.

39. McCarthy's idolization of Prussian developments appeared to rest on a combination of Bismarck's three-pronged social legislation of the 1880s (sickness insurance, accident insurance, and old-age pensions) and the fact that such measures appeared to defer in part to the agitation of the academic *Kathedersozialisten* ("socialists of the chair") around Gustav Schmoller and the Verein für Sozialpolitik. For a more skeptical view of German social welfare legislation, see J. Tampke, "Bismarck's Social Legislation: A Genuine Breakthrough?" in *The Emergence of the Welfare State in Britain and Germany, 1850–1950,* ed. W. J. Mommsen (London, 1981), 71–83.

Progressives, McCarthy placed ultimate blame on a patronage-based political system: "Good administration is impossible unless combined with ordinary business methods and the latter are not compatible with the policy "to the victors belong the spoils."[40] Nor had "nonpolitical" courts helped matters. By narrowing the constitutionality of both regulatory and welfare measures and by granting a rule by injunction in industrial relations, the judiciary had proved even more insensitive to the condition of the "man in the street."[41]

What was missing from the public sphere was the continuity—and flexibility—of dispassionate administrative authority. "Good laws," declared McCarthy, "are ineffective unless accompanied by good administration." In the circumstances, the "German model" heralded an alternate path to social democratic initiatives via administrative action. Lacking a reliable civil service structure, Wisconsin reformers led by John R. Commons had developed the public commission as an alternative administrative apparatus.[42] McCarthy was not unaware of the paradox of a philosophical radical defending a system of government by appointment. "It may seem strange," he allowed, "that the system of appointive offices meets with so much approval in a state where there is such confidence in democracy and where the direct primary election is in favor."[43] McCarthy nevertheless expressed confidence that a vigilant public could at once take full advantage of highly trained government "experts" and at the same time hold them to democratic accountability.[44]

Selectively invoking the contributions of diverse social architects—Bis-

40. McCarthy, *Wisconsin Idea*, 174. Cf. the remarkable similarity of McCarthy's reasoning with that of Ann Shola Orloff and Theda Skocpol, "Why Not Equal Protection? Explaining the Politics of Public Social Spending in Britain, 1900–1911, and the United States, 1880s–1920," *American Sociological Review* 49 (December 1984): 726–50. Cf. also Edwin Amenta et al., "The Political Origins of Unemployment Insurance in Five American States," *Studies in American Political Development* 2 (1987): 137–82.

41. McCarthy, *Wisconsin Idea*, 2–4.

42. The uniqueness of the Wisconsin idea, McCarthy emphasized, lay in the "idea of introducing experts into the administration of the law": McCarthy to Milton A. Miller, February 19, 1914, in Charles McCarthy Papers, State Historical Society of Wisconsin, Madison. In a tribute to Commons years later, David J. Saposs, who also worked on the CIR as a young graduate student, argued that Commons served government "not only as a technician. His conception of the tri-partite bodies, like the Wisconsin Industrial Commission, introduced a revolutionary means of administering laws concerned with intricate social and economic problems": "The Wisconsin Heritage and the Study of Labor: Works and Deeds of John R. Commons" (unpublished manuscript, 1960), in David J. Saposs Papers, State Historical Society of Wisconsin, Madison.

43. McCarthy, *Wisconsin Idea*, 172. Two years later, again advocating federal commissions before the CIR, McCarthy reemphasized, "I am not talking against democracy; I am talking for democracy": CIR, *Final Report and Testimony*, 1:381.

44. McCarthy, *Wisconsin Idea*, 190–93. McCarthy thus favorably compared commission regulatory authority to the jurisdiction of ordinary courts: "You can't control the ordinary

marck, the civil service, radical intellectuals, the socialists—McCarthy turned "Germany" (and occasionally other countries as well) into a veritable cafeteria for American progressive measures. "Shall we always hear the returning travellers' tale of the improvements throughout the entire world with a provincial and smug spirit and be foolish enough to believe that we can learn nothing, while right in our midst are problems which have confronted every nation at some time in its history?" Adopting the *via media* arguments of his European social democratic contemporaries, McCarthy sought to preempt an ideological rebuff: "Shall we always be deceived by the cry of 'Socialism' whenever it is necessary to use the state to a greater degree than formerly? When it comes to the attainment of any reasonable legislation for the true betterment of human beings, the only way to beat the Socialists 'is to beat them to it.'"[45]

His whole educational-professional experience imbued McCarthy with an infectious enthusiasm about the possibilities of rational reform action. Called in the first batch of expert witnesses in late December 1913 to advise the CIR, McCarthy spoke with utter confidence and perhaps a touch of insolence about extending the Wisconsin experiment to the national level: "We had this situation in Wisconsin: They had that reform movement in the state, headed by Mr. La Follette. It was a question of what should be done, just the thing that you people are up against, and a question of how they could do it, and we hit upon a way of working that thing, which might be useful to you here." Essentially, McCarthy's proposed method—one that he would soon be in a position to act upon—amounted to a national commission of applied brainstorming.[46]

McCarthy and his Wisconsin-trained staff exemplified what Commons had called "utilitarian idealism," a social-democratic faith that "constructive research" might lead to the "gradual reconstruction of society."[47] Dedication to the exacting standards of social investigation, they were convinced, went hand in hand with radical social change. In private communications they regularly referred to themselves as "radicals," penetrating critics of the social order, yet equally saw themselves as professionally respectable "experts."[48]

---

courts; you can control the commission courts, you can control the appointment of its members, you can provide for a recall of the commission by a vote of Congress, you can bring them before Congress, and in general you can do a hundred things with them that you can't do with the courts": McCarthy to Joseph Davies, December 11, 1913, in Charles McCarthy Papers, State Historical Society of Wisconsin, Madison.

45. McCarthy, *Wisconsin Idea*, 298, 300. See also James T. Kloppenberg, *Uncertain Victory: Social Democracy and Progressivism in European and American Thought, 1870–1920* (New York, 1986), 145–286.

46. CIR, *Final Report and Testimony*, 1: 379–80, 382.

47. See Commons's essays "Utilitarian Idealism" (1909) and "Constructive Research" (1907), in his *Labor and Administration* (New York, 1923), 1–13.

48. See, e.g., Helen L. Sumner to Commons, January 19, 1905, and May 20, 1914, in John R. Commons Papers, State Historical Society of Wisconsin, Madison.

Tensions between the philosophic radicalism and pragmatic reform practice of this group of labor investigators were neatly registered in the views of William Morris Leiserson. Deputy director of the Wisconsin Industrial Commission and barely thirty years old when he was summoned to the CIR as assistant research director under McCarthy, Leiserson still managed to inhabit both the idealistic world of his radical socialist youth and a more technocratic province of government administration that would define his future career. A Jewish immigrant from Estonia, Leiserson arrived in Madison in 1905 as a revolutionary socialist, but quickly tempered his views under the influence of undergraduate teachers such as Commons as well as the Milwaukee municipal socialists Victor Berger and Daniel Hoan, to whom he quickly gravitated. Even after graduation, however, Leiserson and fellow Commons students such as Ira B. Cross and David J. Saposs maintained contact with the local Socialist club. As late as 1912, Leiserson was in indirect negotiation with Friedrich Sorge about the proper translation of Marx on Henry George, and as late as 1915 he was still writing articles for the Socialist Milwaukee *Leader*.[49]

Something of the division in Leiserson's soul was apparent in his first contact with the CIR. Summoned as a witness before joining the staff himself, Leiserson, in good Wisconsin fashion, first urged the panel not to get bogged down in the general problem of unemployment but to focus on getting "something done right now." Proposing a national chain of public employment offices, Leiserson momentarily allowed that the idea "may look like dealing with palliatives that are not getting at the fundamental thing." When the labor commissioner James O'Connell pursued the issue, asking for the underlying remedy for unemployment, a revealing exchange took place:

> *Mr. Leiserson.* If you want to know how to remedy that proposition, I may state, that, for example, all industries in the country ought to be owned by the Government, and everybody ought to get a month's vacation the way I do . . . That is the fundamental remedy in my opinion. If you recommended that, where would you get? You would get nowhere.
>
> *Commissioner Delano.* We would get it in the neck.
>
> *Mr. Leiserson.* Yes; that is why I say you have got to get down to the practical proposition of what you can do now . . .

49. J. Michael Eisner, *William Morris Leiserson: A Biography* (Madison, 1967), 9–10; Saposs to Leiserson, October 17, 1915, and Carl D. Thompson to Leiserson, December 28, 1912, both in William Morris Leiserson Papers, State Historical Society of Wisconsin, Madison.

Commissioner Lennon. If you would come in every day we would all be Socialists, the first thing you know.

Mr. Leiserson. Well, I would not object.[50]

If the young Leiserson was more cavalier than most in revealing his ultimate political sympathies, his basic outlook—that is, deep-seated social democratic commitments combined with an eye for detailed and defensible policy initiatives—fitted the Wisconsin pattern. Together, McCarthy and Leiserson clearly believed they were riding a radical reform juggernaut. The adrenalin fairly flowed between them in early December 1914, for example, when McCarthy described a sleepless night from which he had profited by rereading Beatrice and Sidney Webb on the rise of British new unionism of the 1880s.[51] Convinced that if they sized up their situation properly, the pace of social progress in the United States might truly match that of Europe, the CIR directors inspired a young and ill-paid staff with a spirit of happy sacrifice.

It was not long before national versions of the Wisconsin strategy— striking social initiatives veiled by their very administrative machinery— were emanating from the research wing of the commission. Perhaps McCarthy's most far-reaching proposal was one calling for a federal industrial council, a body modeled on Wisconsin's industrial commission but considerably expanded in scope. Through the industrial commission form (justified by the welfare clause of the Constitution) reformers could achieve "what we have so often talked about in the past—the expansion of the constitution." Generated in discussions with Commons, who for years had conceived of various such plans, the idea was ultimately concretized in a bill drafted by a young commission staffer, Selig Perlman, "to bring about an approximate equality in the bargaining power of labor and capital in unorganized industries." Proposing state intervention on a scale far more massive than even later New Deal reformers ever contemplated, Perlman's plan offered basic protection for labor's right to organize and strike with an extensive list of unfair labor practices. It further stipulated that an industry in any locality which remained unorganized

---

50. CIR, *Final Report and Testimony,* 1: 345–47.

51. McCarthy, via the Webbs, saw the role of intellectual leadership in England as follows: "Here you have the federation [Trades Union Congress] becoming somewhat exclusive; the unorganized getting disgruntled; the old program discredited; then you have the coming in of the Socialists with a new program led by [John] Burns and Tom Mann. With this new program they sweep everything before them. They even . . . organized the unorganized and the result is the great dockers' strike. It seems to be more absorbing and have a new meaning now . . . I think we will miss a great deal in our view point if we do not look to the history of the trade unionism in England": McCarthy to Leiserson, December 16, 1914, in Charles McCarthy Papers, State Historical Society of Wisconsin, Madison.

six months after passage of the act constituted "prima facie evidence that employers have prevented organization" and authorized the council to "step in and fix the conditions of employment, viz: wages, hours, etc. subject to review by the courts."[52]

A sense of complementarity initially bound Walsh and McCarthy in harmony within the life of the commission. McCarthy enjoyed a relatively free hand on the research end of things, while the chairman viewed his role as conducting less a legislative research bureau than a trial before "the great jury of the American public." In dramatic and well-publicized forays across the country, the commissioners bore striking witness to the rawest scenes of industrial warfare—the attack on the Wobblies in Paterson, New Jersey; threats to the Protocol of Peace in the New York garment industry; the crushing of the shop crafts' federation on the Illinois Central Railroad; the routing of the Fulton Bag Mill employees in Atlanta; and, most dramatic, the Ludlow Massacre, which obliterated the coal miners' strike against the Rockefeller-owned Colorado Fuel and Iron Company. Altogether, the Walsh-led commission provided a continuous, blistering exposé of industrial tyranny in the United States.[53] With public advocacy his main mission, Walsh tended to look on McCarthy's research and bill-drafting responsibilities as "technical matters," a matter of "tying up" administrative ends. Still, for months he willingly deferred to the Wisconsin-led brain trust in order to surround his own convictions with the force of "scientific" legitimacy and, ultimately, added political weight. He seemed generally impressed by McCarthy's political brainstorming, such as his proposal to use the tariff laws to enforce fair labor standards on "protected" industries—"like everything else you present to me it looks good." Similarly enthusiastic about an idea to investigate the "gun men" (or private police forces) employed in industrial disputes, Walsh specified that the investigators be drawn "from among your students at Madison . . . I don't believe I would entrust it to anybody in the U.S. except yourself." His own result-oriented thinking led McCarthy, naturally, to invert the chairman's priorities; recurringly he tried to subordinate, or at least coordinate, hearings with less flashy investigations of his research staff. Yet, however peripheral he found public hearings to the concrete work of bill drafting, McCarthy also recognized their educational value, particularly under the direction of such a skillful public advo-

52. McCarthy to Walsh, "Suggestions for the Federal Industrial Relations Commission," January 1914 and February 14, 1914; McCarthy to Judson King, June 8, 1914, all ibid., Selig Perlman proposal, n.d., in U. S. Department of Labor, CIR administrative file, RG 174, Box 2.
53. Adams, *Age of Industrial Violence*, offers a compelling account of the CIR's findings.

cate as Walsh, whom McCarthy respectfully described as "a Wendell Phillips type, essentially an agitator."[54]

Outside pressure first drew their contrasting styles and skills into conflict. A rump group of largely southern, conservative congressmen who had sought to sabotage the investigation from the start forced Walsh to return intermittently to Congress for necessary appropriations.[55] As early as the summer of 1914, uncertainty of funding was producing occasional backbiting between the administratively lax and cavalier Walsh and the scrupulous and efficient McCarthy.[56] Walsh regularly waved off McCarthy's attempts to impose a stringent timetable on the project. "You have always worried too much about the finances of this Commission," Walsh insisted after McCarthy complained of dwindling funds in December 1914. "I feel almost as though I could do all I care to do without any financing from a public source. You stick to me . . . and we will come out all right."[57] But the resources were simply not sufficient to sustain such a liberal managerial approach. Proceeding unchecked on all fronts, the commission hit dire straits by February 1915. Finally forced to reckon with fiscal reality (and fearing denial of a last request from Congress), Walsh, at a Chicago meeting on February 28, ignored McCarthy's advice and ordered draconian cuts in the research budget, including wholesale staff layoffs. When McCarthy strenuously objected, Walsh effectively relieved his chief lieutenant of command.[58]

54. Walsh to McCarthy, June 5, 1914; McCarthy to Walsh, August 11, 1914; Walsh to McCarthy, August 20 and July 13, 1914; McCarthy to John S. Murdock, January 14, 1915, all in Charles McCarthy Papers, State Historical Society of Wisconsin, Madison.

55. On the commission's financial woes, see Adams, *Age of Industrial Violence,* 206–9; Casey, *Charles McCarthy,* 112. An initial CIR appropriation for $100,000 first became available in October 1913 for the fiscal year ending in July 1914. An additional "deficiency" appropriation of $50,000 was secured in March 1914. With only $200,000 appropriated for 1914–15 ($50,000 less than McCarthy calculated as minimally necessary), by February 1915 the commission was literally running out of money. In March Congress appropriated an additional and final $100,000. In a letter to Commons dated March 1, 1915, McCarthy recounted his experience of the budget nightmare: "When I came on last July, I could get no budget until October and then did not get a budget rightly itemized or an account of the expenditures rightly itemized. I was told repeatedly by Walsh not to worry about the money and Mr. L. K. Brown told me that Walsh did not want to let me have the budget. Finally, when I got the budget or some idea of it, I found we were going in the hole completely": Fitzpatrick, *McCarthy of Wisconsin,* 195–96.

56. Almost from the day of his arrival at the commission, McCarthy called (in vain) for suspension of the hearings on grounds of efficiency and financial exigency: "Cannot the Commissioners themselves be of more service working at some specific work than to be sitting up there all day listening to these speeches?": McCarthy to Walsh, June 22, 1914, in Charles McCarthy Papers, State Historical Society of Wisconsin, Madison.

57. Walsh to McCarthy, December 23, 1914, ibid.; Adams, *Age of Industrial Violence,* 208.

58. Adams, *Age of Industrial Violence,* 209; minutes of CIR Meeting, February 28, 1915, in Charles McCarthy Papers, State Historical Society of Wisconsin, Madison.

While the money question touched the raw nerve of the chairman's authority, a more insidious issue had already alienated Walsh from McCarthy before their public confrontation. A most unexpected conflict had arisen during the investigation of the Rockefeller interests in Colorado. The work of the CIR had coincided roughly with the escalation of one of the nation's most violent industrial disputes, the coal miners' strike against the Rockefeller-controlled Colorado Fuel and Iron Company (CFI) in southern Colorado. Beginning in September 1913, the strike pitted some 10,000 ethnically diverse workers' families against a virtual industrial barony. Owning the lands and homes of their laborers, controlling courts and county government, paying wages in scrip valid only in company stores, contributing to a mine death rate twice as high as that of any other state in the nation, and enforcing its rule with a heavily armed private police force, the CFI was a catalog of horrors of unregulated capitalist power. National Guard troops, initially ordered in by Governor Elias M. Ammons in late October as a strictly neutral force to quell growing skirmishes between strikers and company police, in the end only added to the company's muscle power. Billeted on company property, supplied through the company store, and freed from earlier restrictions by an intimidated governor, militia officers openly protected strikebreakers. Tragedy followed on April 20, 1914, when a machine-gun attack on the strikers' tent colony at Ludlow engulfed the entire encampment in flames. Among the fifty-three persons killed in the onslaught were two women and eleven children, who had suffocated in a dug-out tent cellar. Widespread unrest followed the "Ludlow Massacre" until the U.S. Army intervened on April 28, ending the violence and effectively crushing the strike. Walsh's good friend George Creel, who was covering the Colorado story at the time, immediately fingered the Rockefellers as "traitors to the people" and "accessories to the murder of babes." While the CIR assembled an impromptu hearing (and the Congress established a separate mediation panel), Frank Walsh determined to go after the "system" that could produce a Ludlow.[59]

For Walsh, like Creel, that system was embodied in John D. Rockefeller Jr. More than any other witness before the CIR, Rockefeller received the full force of Walsh's prosecutorial passion. Outfoxed by his subject's well-coached and evasive encounter with the commission in January 1915, Walsh pursued him again in a furious, unrelenting examination the following May.[60] His exposé of Rockefeller's complicity in the CFI's

59. Adams, *Age of Industrial Violence,* 146–61, 175; Creel, *Rebel at Large,* 128.
60. Peter and David Horowitz, *The Rockefellers: An American Dynasty* (New York, 1976), 122–23. Rockefeller, who received expert guidance from the Canadian labor reformer Mackenzie King before his initial appearance, disarmed many listeners with a declaration of good intentions: he accepted unions in principle, and allowed that "combinations of capital

elaborate and unbending antiunion campaign (utterly contradicting Rockefeller's own carefully constructed alibi of ignorance and distance from the affair) constituted for Walsh a glorious final chapter of the commission's work, dramatic proof of the populist argument that a democracy could not allow economic power to fall into too few hands.

From the beginning Walsh and the CIR staff saw the "evil" of Rockefeller power not only in its ramifications at the workplace but also in its impact on basic democratic process. For this reason, they extended considerable effort to document the direct corruption of public officials and other, more insidious forms of corporate influence-buying, including the dismissal from the state university of an outspoken anti-Rockefeller law professor.[61] Rockefeller's hiring of Ivy L. Lee, former journalist and public relations pioneer, as corporate publicity director after the massacre also came in for close scrutiny. Grilled on two extended occasions, Lee seemed to arouse special ire among the commissioners (as well as the larger progressive community), in part because he so brazenly manipulated the facts, in part, perhaps, because he employed his intellectual skills on behalf of the archvillains of the reformers themselves. Upton Sinclair, for example, rechristened him "Poison Ivy"; Carl Sandburg judged him to be "below the level of the hired gunman and slugger."[62]

---

are sometimes conducted in an unworthy manner, contrary to law and in disregard of the interest both of labor and the public." In short, according to Rockefeller, if things had gone wrong in Colorado, the problem lay in administration further down the corporate ladder. To the correspondent Walter Lippmann, Rockefeller thus emerged in his testimony as a "weak despot governed by a private bureaucracy which he is unable to lead . . . I should not believe that the inhumanity of Colorado is something he had conceived . . . there seemed to be nothing but a young man having a lot of trouble, very much harassed and very well-meaning": "Mr. Rockefeller on the Stand," *New Republic* 1 (January 30, 1915): 12–13. Even Mary "Mother" Jones was inclined to look kindly on Rockefeller the man after his testimony. See H. M. Gitelman, *Legacy of the Ludlow Massacre: A Chapter in American Industrial Relations* (Philadelphia, 1988), 75–77. Carl Sandburg, in contrast, offered the orthodox left-labor view of Rockefeller: "The Two Mr. Rockefellers—and Mr. Walsh," *International Socialist Review* 16 (July 1915): 18–24.

61. For the case of Professor James H. Brewster of the University of Colorado, see Walter P. Metzger, ed., *Professors on Guard: The first AAUP Investigations* (New York, 1977), 47–120. On Rockefeller money ties to the state's universities, see Collier and Horowitz, *The Rockefellers*, 125.

62. On corporate subversion of democratic government, see CIR, *Final Report and Testimony*, 1: 58, 78–79, 84. As part of the CFI's damage-control machinery, Lee had circulated a statement from Colorado's Law and Order League "to the effect that the death of the two women and eleven children had occurred because of their carelessness in overturning a stove in the tent, rather than because of the militia's gunfire." Sinclair and Sandburg are quoted in Collier and Horowitz, *The Rockefellers*, 119. For Lee's CIR testimony, see *Final Report and Testimony*, 8: 7897–916; 9: 8715–30, 8849–63. Lee transcended his temporary notoriety to build a whirlwind career, counting not only Standard Oil but American Tobacco and General Mills as clients, creating for the latter the immortal Betty Crocker persona and the "Breakfast of Champions" slogan for Wheaties. The life of this millionaire consultant

But it was the outwardly most benevolent of the Rockefeller "cultural" projects that most intrigued the commission, especially Walsh and McCarthy. W. L. Mackenzie King, the former Canadian minister of labor, had accepted a contract just after the massacre to undertake a "far-reaching study of industrial problems" for the Rockefeller Foundation. A new industrial relations department of the foundation, which had previously shied away from controversial social questions, was created for the occasion. Despite the general philosophical mandate for the project, King was rushed to Colorado to devise a grievance system (later unveiled as the famous "Colorado Plan" of company unionism) in lieu of collective bargaining. Although Rockefeller himself ultimately drew public praise (and even, indirectly, a kind of presidential pardon) for his industrial penance, King and the foundation's industrial relations department did not so easily pass muster before the CIR.[63]

It was McCarthy himself, it appears, who first suggested to a receptive Walsh that the commission use the King investigation to open a general inquiry into the roles of private foundations in matters of education and social research.[64] As a zealous and idealistic advocate of public education, McCarthy had for some time entertained doubts about the growing role of private philanthropies in educational matters, opposing on principle, for example, even the much-celebrated Carnegie pension program for university professors. Unless philanthropists such as Carnegie and Rockefeller presented their gifts in one great bundle, no strings attached, McCarthy worried, they would come to exercise undue influence over supposedly democratic bodies. He thus coached Walsh in October 1914 that "the world will . . . and should distrust" the great foundations. As an alternative to the foundations, McCarthy endorsed an idea popular among Madison reformers—a national research body, perhaps even a "national university," as advocated by President Van Hise.[65]

Frank Walsh required little encouragement to take on the foundations.

---

ended in infamy, however. In 1934, already afflicted with brain cancer, he was exposed before the Special House Committee on Un-American Activities for his alleged role in protecting the image of the German petrochemical firm I. G. Farben (which had entered into a cartel with Standard Oil of New Jersey) and the Third Reich. See Collier and Horowitz, *The Rockefellers,* 118, 225–26.

63. CIR, *Final Report and Testimony,* 9: 9784–85. King's recruitment to the foundation and his subsequent extended influence on John D. Jr. is particularly well documented in Gitelman, *Legacy of the Ludlow Massacre.*

64. On October 7, 1914, Walsh wrote McCarthy that he liked "your Rockefeller proposition," adding that he hoped to recommend to Congress "that the activities of this alleged Foundation be prohibited by law": Charles McCarthy Papers, State Historical Society of Wisconsin, Madison.

65. McCarthy to W. H. Allen, October 1, 1914; McCarthy to Walsh, October 8, 1914; William Leiserson to McCarthy, January 11, 1915, all ibid.

As early as 1913 he voiced support for the replacement of all privately funded social work by political action and public funding. If for academics such as McCarthy and Commons private money posed a *potential* problem for public institutions, for Walsh it was more like a gushing stream of pollutants. In January 1915, when the commission entered the second phase of its Colorado investigation, it thus turned an unparalleled investigatory light on the cultural counterparts of corporate power, ultimately devoting more than a thousand printed pages of testimony to the subject "The Centralization of Industrial Control and Operation of Philanthropic Foundations."[66]

For Walsh the hegemonic influence of the foundation suggested the ultimate, terrifying expansion of monopoly power from the material world to thought control. In words dripping with venom, Walsh would later conclude:

> Mr. Rockefeller is taking money obtained through the exploitation of thousands of poorly nourished, socially submerged men, women and children, and spending these sums, through a board of personal employees, in such fashion that his estate is in a fair way not only to exercise a dominating influence in industry, but, before many years, to exact a tribute of loyalty and subserviency to him and his interest from the whole profession of scientists, social workers and economists . . . No argument is needed to convince a sensible American of the subtle and pervasive and irresistible power that is wielded autocratically by men who control the disbursement of huge sums of money. It is a power that goes straight to our instincts, to our points of view, to the raw materials of which our opinions and judgments are made.[67]

Walsh's convictions on the subject of the foundations were so strong as to provoke a split within the progressives' ranks. *Survey* magazine, the leading contemporary exponent of reform-minded social research and an early crusader for the CIR, in an October 1914 editorial welcomed the newly announced Rockefeller Foundation initiative while at the same time offering a rather critical assessment of the industrial commission's first year of work. Lauding the "disinterested" record of Mackenzie King in labor controversies, *Survey* expressed a willingness to accept the foundation's intention "at its full face value—an attempt to take up the 'most complicated and at the same time the most urgent question of modern

66. Boyd Fisher to Frank Walsh, June 20, 1913 and Walsh to Fisher, June 24, 1913, both in Frank Walsh Papers, New York Public Library; CIR, *Final Report and Testimony*, 8: 7427.

67. Frank P. Walsh, "The Great Foundation" (1915), in Frank Walsh Papers, New York Public Library.

times,' and to grapple with it 'for the well being of mankind throughout the world.'" Contrasting the administrative autonomy of the foundation with the cumbersome bureaucratic machinery that had slowed the CIR's work, *Survey*'s editor, Paul U. Kellogg (who had earlier directed the Pittsburgh Survey for the Russell Sage Foundation), went so far as to suggest that "the limitations of a private inquiry, undistracted by divergent points of view, with unlimited resources and time, with no patronage assaults to stave off, are less obvious than those of such a public commission."[68]

The irrepressible Walsh quickly fired back. In a series of published exchanges with Kellogg, the commission chair not only defended the CIR's work against its private competitor (and paid an especially vigorous tribute to its research director) but also attacked the editorial as "cunning and dishonest," concluding that the editors must have been "compelled to publish the same . . . by your patrons and masters, and that you are ashamed of it." Walsh's shot (and another soon fired by Creel in an article titled "How Tainted Money Taints") was a clear reference to *Survey*'s endowment by the Russell Sage and Carnegie foundations.[69]

Although the particular controversy was soon muted, the *Survey* altercation set an ominous example for the intellectual reformers at the commission. With his courtroom blunderbuss Walsh implicitly opened fire on an entire generation of intellectuals, targeting them as apologists for monopolists. Financial insecurity and uncertain social standing had, in fact, brought many social scientists and social investigators of the early twentieth century into reliance on the philanthropic extensions of the great corporations as well as wealthy individuals. John R. Commons's appointment at the University of Wisconsin, for example, depended on a package of philanthropic grants and gifts, including a modest subvention from the Carnegie Foundation.[70] At the time he opened up on Kellogg, Walsh could not have anticipated how deep into his own ranks the logic

68. *Survey* 33 (October 10, 1914): 54–55. Though still hopeful with regard to the work of the CIR, *Survey* complained, "It is an open secret that for ten months following the commission's appointment it floundered badly, without a clear-cut program of work, without clear-cut division of responsibility, and with great areas of the field before it practically untouched." For the Pittsburgh Survey, see John F. McClymer, "The Pittsburgh Survey, 1907–1914: Forging an Ideology in the Steel District," *Pennsylvania Magazine* 41 (1974): 168–86. For *Survey*'s close coverage of the CIR, see *Survey* 27 (December 30, 1911): 1419–29; 29 (December 28, 1912): 385–86; 30 (July 5 and August 2, 1913): 452–53, 571–88; and 31 (November 8, 1913): 152–53.

69. *Survey* 33 (November 14, 1914): 177; Adams, *Age of Industrial Violence*, 26. Creel's article appeared in a March 1915 issue of *Pearson's Magazine:* Paul Kellogg to Walsh, February 5, 1915 in Frank Walsh Papers, New York Public Library.

70. Richard T. Ely to John R. Commons, December 16, 1903, reel 27, in Richard T. Ely Papers, State Historical Society of Wisconsin, Madison. The principal funders of Commons's initial research project at Wisconsin included V. Everett Macy and Stanley McCormick, according to Harold L. Miller of the State Historical Society of Wisconsin.

of his attack might extend. It is unlikely he would have altered his course in any case.

For McCarthy the CIR crusade against his old schoolmate, Rockefeller might have provoked conflict and discomfort from the beginning. Surprisingly, it did not. Indeed, for some months Charles McCarthy served Walsh as a willing and effective instrument of the campaign to confront John D. Rockefeller Jr. with his social responsibilities. When Walsh chose the investigation of foundations as the vehicle for hauling Rockefeller and other company officers before the CIR (perhaps because Rockefeller had already appeared before another congressional body focused more narrowly on Colorado strike issues), he looked to McCarthy for critical assistance. "I expect you can give us a lot of assistance in getting young Mr. Rockefeller and Mr. Greene [Jerome Greene, secretary of the Rockefeller Foundation] before the Commission," Walsh wrote in early October. Two days later, Walsh again pleaded with McCarthy to get Rockefeller "of all others" to cooperate. "Use all your good offices and ingenuity to bring this about." McCarthy seemed perfectly willing to do his part. Cheering on Walsh before his first encounter with John D. Jr., McCarthy agreed that there was "a great case to be won." As late as mid-December he agreed that the evidence gathered from Colorado "confirms all your program in relation to the Rockefeller matter. Inevitably abuses will come unless these big endowments are under some kind of public control. All the way through there is a confirmation of my idea about JDR, Jr. as the same man I knew, far away from people, good intentions personally but enmeshed and educated in a system which is entirely wrong."[71]

But it was precisely his direct personal contacts with Rockefeller that made things more complicated for McCarthy than for Walsh. McCarthy did not suddenly exhume an old friendship in contacting Rockefeller from his CIR position. Rather, ever since the miners' troubles broke out in Colorado, he had, in fact, conducted a frustrating private campaign to "reform" Rockefeller's thinking and behavior on industrial matters, communicating at once with the stiff and aloof Rockefeller and a small circle of old school friends and Rockefeller confidants.[72] As part of this effort, McCarthy had tried, in vain, at least since March 1914 to expand the

71. Gitelman, *Legacy of the Ludlow Massacre*, 20–21, 58; Walsh to McCarthy, October 8 and October 10, 1914; McCarthy to Walsh, December 21 and December 14, 1914, all in Charles McCarthy Papers, State Historical Society of Wisconsin, Madison.

72. The Rockefeller-McCarthy old-school network included the attorney John S. Murdock (Brown, class of '96); Everett Colby (class of '97), the Progressive chairman of the New Jersey Commission on Old Age Insurance; and Lefferts M. Dashiell (class of '97), assistant treasurer of the Rockefeller Foundation. Colby was Rockefeller's undergraduate roommate as well as captain of the football team. McCarthy actually received his degree in 1897 but always listed his class as 1896.

foundation's interests in the areas of social and industrial welfare.[73] When, after the Ludlow events, Rockefeller referred vaguely in congressional testimony to contemplation of an industrial inquiry, McCarthy encouraged him further, writing in August that "*now* would be the time for it when the Commission is in being. If you could coordinate your work with that of the Commission the result would be perhaps a sane and wise program which could be brought out a year from now."[74]

To be sure, the format and composition of the Mackenzie King project—tightly controlled by the foundation officers—were not what McCarthy had had in mind. As soon as the King venture was announced, McCarthy urged their mutual friend John Murdock to warn Rockefeller that "it is necessary to have a Democratic Organization. A Complete one." The money, he insisted, ought to be given outright to an industrial body with labor and business representation. "If that is done this money will be a great blessing." If not, it "may be a great curse." Yet Rockefeller and his emissaries turned a deaf ear to such entreaties, claiming that a thoroughly "scientific" investigation could not be comprised by mere public "opinion." Privately, McCarthy despaired that Rockefeller was "not in contact" with the real world and needed a public jolt to wake him up. Always trusting Rockefeller as a man of "good intentions," McCarthy determined to break through the "wooden" people around his old friend. Still hoping that in the heat of the Walsh hearings, Rockefeller would willingly surrender the King investigation to "popular control," McCarthy told his college friend John Murdock that "this great investigation may be the best thing that ever happened to John D. Rockefeller, Jr."[75]

73. John D. Rockefeller Jr. to McCarthy, March 16, 1914, in Charles McCarthy Papers, State Historical Society of Wisconsin, Madison. After talking with Rockefeller only days after the Ludlow massacre, Everett Colby wrote McCarthy on April 27, 1914, "The trouble with John is he thinks that controversies of this kind can be stripped to a naked principle . . . which you know is not the case" (ibid.). Disappointed, McCarthy yet insisted that it was "of the utmost importance to this country that a powerful man like J.D.R. will broaden out his life and his concepts as he grows older. Somebody must get near to him and counteract the forces which are making his life stiff . . . He probably thinks I am an idealist and I would have very little influence along that line with him": McCarthy to Colby, April 29, 1914, ibid.

74. Still, McCarthy was not about to browbeat his old friend. "Understand," he dissimulated, "that I have nothing to do with the hearings or the findings of the commission. I am a radical, at least I am called radical, and you are naturally a conservative, but whatever comes up in this world, there shall be nothing but personal friendship between us": McCarthy to Rockefeller, August 7, 1914, ibid.

75. McCarthy to John Murdock, October 10, 1914, and January 14, 1915; Rockefeller to McCarthy, October 20, 1914, all ibid. By the end of October, McCarthy betrayed a sudden impatience with his conversion mission. "Your viewpoint and your attitude," he wrote Rockefeller, "is so absolutely different from mine that I cannot hope to explain my attitude to you in this letter . . . Your institution will not do the great work which you planned for it unless it is done upon a different basis entirely . . . The years have gone by

But the errand for Walsh complicated McCarthy's task. He now took the lead in securing Rockefeller's cooperation with the government panel. Seeking a conference in early October with Jerome Greene, for example, McCarthy masked his real doubts about the Mackenzie King project behind a screen of benign curiosity: "I think it is of tremendous importance to the country. Great foundations are going into philanthropic work and other work which has a bearing on the great question of industrial unrest . . . Such a conference will be of the greatest value to you." Similarly, in encouraging a hesitant Rockefeller to meet with the commission, McCarthy emphasized the positive public relations that might come from such an appearance: "The more you keep explaining and the more approach you make to the American People . . . the better they will understand your motives." In the end, McCarthy flattered Rockefeller, the industrial project would bring him well-deserved appreciation. "It will probably be side by side with your health work and your agricultural work in the South the greatest work your institution will be known by." When his sweet talk to the Rockefeller entourage was short-circuited by a subpoena issued independently by a commission staffer to Rockefeller in Providence, McCarthy apologized profusely, distanced himself from the maneuver, and pleaded that as research director he had "nothing to do with the hearings of this kind." The apology was largely disingenuous, however, for McCarthy himself had already worked up a set of tough questions for Rockefeller to confront on the witness stand.[76]

However well intentioned, McCarthy had compromised his position with regard to the Rockefeller case. Over the course of a very few months he had acted toward the Rockefeller industrial mission alternately as promoter, tutor, and prosecutor. His own faith in his consistent effort to respect a valued friendship while at the same time serving the public interest was entirely sincere—and attested to by the deposit of all correspondence with the Rockefeller people in the CIR files. In the process, however, he opened himself (and potentially the entire commission) to the appearance of double-dealing and hypocrisy.

But who would have an interest—and the nerve—to strike at McCarthy? On January 14 McCarthy first expressed alarm that malicious rumors were circulating about him at the Rockefeller headquarters at 26 Broadway. Suspecting Jerome Greene, who he believed had never appreciated his ideas and blocked his personal access to Junior, McCarthy appealed to his old friends and Rockefeller's confidants John Murdock and Lefferts

---

and I never had a chance to see you or talk with you to any great extent upon the great economic question with which we have been struggling": October 29, 1914, ibid.

76. McCarthy to Jerome Greene, October 8, 1914, and McCarthy to John D. Rockefeller Jr., October 17, 1914, both ibid.

Dashiell to affirm his integrity. "I want those who knew me when I was a boy to know now that I am the same person with the same purposes, the same objects, the same standards that I had when I was in college." Dashiell responded by telegram: "Your fears are groundless. Friendship absolutely unaffected." Three months later, however, Murdock let slip that "John D. was very indignant at being summoned here in Providence and he laid it all to your door." On January 15, 1915, only ten days before the first Rockefeller hearing, McCarthy received an urgent summons from Walsh to come to New York. Walsh had just been told by Rockefeller that, according to the records of the foundation, "only one" outside person had encouraged them to begin a study of labor conditions, and his name was McCarthy. There was further insinuation, hinted at by Rockefeller and apparently magnified by others, that McCarthy's original interest in the Rockefeller project had been pecuniary; that is, he had applied to direct the inquiry himself. Rockefeller also produced for Walsh the early letters from McCarthy that documented his claim.[77]

Stung by the revelations, Walsh nevertheless proceeded with the Rockefeller investigation. Faced with McCarthy's strenuous and self-righteous denial of any wrongdoing (including a refusal to dignify the charges by defending himself before a special commission meeting), Walsh temporarily pocketed the issue. The hearings went as scheduled except for one particular: while focusing on the structure and activities of the foundation, Walsh all but ignored the Mackenzie King research project, with which the government's own research director might easily be linked.[78]

The proud Walsh, however, never forgave McCarthy the embarrassment his friendship with Rockefeller had caused the commission. When McCarthy dared to challenge Walsh's authority during the commission's budget crisis of February 1915, Walsh deftly turned the tables on him, making McCarthy's (rather than Walsh's) unscrupulous conduct the pivotal issue. "There is no doubt in my mind," Leiserson explained to McCarthy, "that the reason Walsh fired you was to shift the issue from the budget to you personally." Despite the protests of John R. Commons and most of the staff, Walsh won endorsement of his actions before a special CIR executive session by "foxily [trying] to show how you were treacherous to the Commission." The *Survey* editor John Fitch, who earlier had been the victim of Walsh's taunts, was outraged. "It would appear

77. McCarthy to John S. Murdock, January 14, 1915; McCarthy to Lefferts M. Dashiell, January 15, 1915; Dashiell to McCarthy, January 18, 1915 (telegram); Murdock to McCarthy, March 18, 1915; Walsh to McCarthy, January 15, 16, and 18, 1915, all ibid.

78. See CIR, *Final Report and Testimony*, 8:7763–97. Only a few vague questions were directed to Rockefeller about the industrial investigation, and these not by Walsh but by Commissioner James O'Connell (7892–95).

that he intends to scream Rockefeller at everybody who crosses his path."[79]

For Walsh, however, the Rockefeller issue served as more than an expedient tool with which to rid himself of a bureaucratic rival. It seemed to confirm a deeper suspicion of the aims and methods of the intellectuals with whom he had been making common cause. How else explain the sense of triumph with which he reported the initial dismissal of the Wisconsin brain trust to George Creel? "The most complete cleaning out . . . that the Wisconsin idea has ever received in its long and tempestuous career," he crowed, citing other research experts (besides McCarthy) "whose heads [will] fall with a distinctly dull thud within the next two weeks . . . It was the biggest intellectual victory I ever won any place."[80]

In the weeks after McCarthy's dismissal, in fact, Walsh and his friend Creel fashioned a thoroughgoing repudiation of ideas and people they had once admired. To the St. Louis publisher William Marion Reedy, for example, Walsh offered a scathing dissection of the Wisconsin idea. Its "'large, constructive programs,'" wrote Walsh, required cooperation with the "principal despoilers" of workers' rights [i.e., the Rockefellers] and involved "interminable 'bill-drafting'" and an administrative machinery "which should throw the legal profession into spasms of delight and the proletariat into hopeless despair."[81] Creel voiced even more viscerally the resentment that "independent" radicals such as he and Walsh felt for those they called the "professors." Smarting from a *New Republic* editorial critical of his earlier attack on Paul Kellogg, Creel responded with a vivid contrast between himself and his detractors:

> For fifteen years I have devoted myself to a task of agitation in politics and industry, trying always to stay close to what may be termed the

79. Leiserson to McCarthy, March 4, 1915, and John Fitch to McCarthy, March 22, 1915, both in Charles McCarthy Papers, State Historical Society of Wisconsin, Madison. In vain Commons offered a counterplan to the commissioners, reinstating McCarthy and his research priorities while abandoning future hearings. McCarthy received numerous expressions of support from people who had worked with the CIR. "If you lose out we shall all resign in a body," wrote the researcher Carl Hookstadt. But McCarthy himself counseled against anything destructive to the work of the commission. Though Leiserson and "one or two others" resigned in protest (others, including Perlman, had already been terminated for budgetary reasons), most of McCarthy's friends stayed on to complete their work. Particularly after an additional congressional appropriation came through, Chairman Walsh, ironically enough—and with the exception of his famous second grilling of Rockefeller in Washington in May 1915—basically returned to the priority on research and writing that McCarthy had counseled. See Carl Hookstadt to McCarthy, March 5, 1915; Lauck to McCarthy, January 30, 1915; McCarthy to Lauck, April 3, 1915; McCarthy to R. H. Hoxie, April 10, 1915; Leiserson to McCarthy, March 12, 1915, all ibid.; Walsh to William Marion Reedy, April 17, 1915, in Frank Walsh Papers, New York Public Library.

80. Casey, *Charles McCarthy*, 116.

81. Walsh to Reedy, April 17, 1915, in Frank Walsh Papers, New York Public Library.

"underdog." During this time I have seen oppression, exploitation, corruption, treachery and betrayal in all their forms, and it may well be that these experiences have made me less than judicial, overquick to suspect and denounce. You, on the other hand, are academic products who have come to be commentators by self-election, based upon self-valuation, aided, I believe, by an endowment fund that spares you the fear of existence. The antagonism between us, therefore, is as instinctive and inevitable as that of the house cat for the street dog.[82]

McCarthy, for his part, had lost all respect for the direction of the commission. Initially he and Leiserson believed that they could outmaneuver Walsh, who they agreed was "absolutely weak when it comes to knowledge of the subject." All they had to do, they thought, was expose his ignorance of "scientific work" before his fellow commissioners. When even the remonstrance of Commons proved futile, however, McCarthy accepted his defeat. While encouraging the young researchers who looked up to him to stay and extract "some ray of light" from the commission, McCarthy now privately judged Walsh "absolutely incompetent and untrustworthy."[83] McCarthy's role on the CIR had come to an ironic end. The man who had most idolized the state as an agent of rational and judicious social change had come face to face with the underside of bureaucratic power.

In view of such personal bad blood and recrimination within its activist core, it is not surprising that the CIR failed to reach internal consensus or effective outside support. In the end Congress shut its ears to the cacophony of the commission, manifested in three conflicting reports along with a host of individual disclaimers and supplemental opinions among the nine commissioners. The major cleavage separated Walsh and the three labor commissioners, who signed an eloquent anticapitalist and antistatist report drawn up by Basil Manly, from a loose coalition of the five other commissioners, who endorsed in principle Commons's plodding and rather dispirited version of Wisconsin idea.[84] Still shadowboxing with his intellectual adversaries (while also seeking allies among

82. Letter to *New Republic* 2 (March 27, 1915): 209–10.
83. Leiserson to McCarthy, March 2, 1915; McCarthy to Leiserson, March 3, 1915; Clara Richards to McCarthy, February 2, 1916, all in Charles McCarthy Papers, State Historical Society of Wisconsin, Madison. McCarthy privately compared Walsh to Ferdinand of Naples as George Trevelyan presented him: "While you are with him he will put his arm around you and say caressing things to you . . . Go five minutes away from him and he becomes fearful and suspicious. At once vague terrors seize him and he issues an order for your destruction": McCarthy to Lauck, April 3, 1915, ibid.
84. The three employer commissioners also felt compelled to offer a separate report attacking the commission staff for its "manifestly partisan" attitude and balancing the critique of management practices with a bill of particulars against union violence.

his fellow commissioners), Chairman Walsh tacked in the end toward a radical version of AFL "voluntarism." Seeking a British-style immunity to legal prosecution for labor unions (a proposal also endorsed by Commons), the Manly report was spare in its positive demands from government: stringent inheritance taxes, public ownership of utilities, and a confiscatory tax on unimproved land. Indeed, the "official" report warned explicitly against unnamed advocates of a "huge system of bureaucratic paternalism such as has been developed in Germany." In a supplemental statement to the Manly report, Walsh dissented even from Manly's call for a "special commission" on mediation, a much-diluted version of the Commons-Perlman plan for state and national industrial commissions with extensive administrative powers. Violating "the habits, customs, and traditions of the American people," such a "ponderous legal machinery," scoffed Walsh, would equally subject business and workers to "the whim or caprice of an army of officials, deputies, and Governmental employees."[85]

The commission's chairman did not neglect a related area of concern— the unregulated power of foundations in general and the depredations of Rockefeller money in particular. In the last of several "additional findings" submitted to Congress, Walsh and two of the labor commissioners described the $100 million Rockefeller trust as "wages" "withheld by means of economic pressure, violation of law, cunning, and violence." Excoriating Rockefeller and Mackenzie King for failing to answer questions put to them on the stand (even recommending that they be summoned for further questioning before the House of Representatives), Walsh and company called for liquidation of the foundation and expropriation of its assets for purposes "directly beneficial to the laborers who really contributed the funds." It was a grand, if largely futile, denouement.[86]

WHILE rooted in a complicated and by no means inevitable chain of events, the internal impasse on the CIR reflected a basic, built-in-dilemma for twentieth-century radical reformers. Generally operating in the absence of (or at some remove from) popular mass movements, intellectuals

---

85. CIR, *Final Report and Testimony*, 1:19, 35, 38, 91, 123–24, 156–65, 265–66, 171–230, 156–157.

86. Ibid., 81–8, 269. Though the Walsh-led offensive against the foundations failed in its ultimate aims, it did affect the future style of corporate support for social research. Instead of direct foundation sponsorship, "in the 1920s academic holding companies rooted in the discipline associations—for example, the American Council of Learned Societies (ACLS) and the Social Science Research Council (SSRC)—emerged to mediate the direct contact between wealth and knowledge exposed and denounced by the [CIR]": Edward T. Silva and Sheila A. Slaughter, *Serving Power: The Making of the Academic Social Science Expert* (Westport, Conn., 1984), 263.

played prominent roles as advocates of popular welfare and democratic rights. But how could intellectuals best "represent" the people and their interests? The alternatives sharply delineated during the CIR experience almost uncannily anticipated two dominant pathways of intellectual advocacy during the following century. On the one hand, intellectuals have posed as "agitators" or "educators" of public opinion. On the other hand, "social planners" or "engineers" have sought social deliverance less in the unruly marketplace of public opinion than in a rational discourse among themselves or at best with articulate representatives of interested parties.[87]

The CIR offered a forum for both intellectual roles: a vehicle for advocacy by agitators behind Walsh and a laboratory for rational policy formulation by Commons and McCarthy. In his CIR role Walsh, in fact, shared in the development of the arts of mass communication with contemporary friends and foes. Public relations experts such as the notorious Ivy Lee, who made the corporate image itself the subject of advertisement, effectively mediated the relationship between the mass producer and the mass market. By joining government investigation to the muckraking style of journalism, pro-labor radicals such as Frank Walsh and George Creel fashioned a counterbalancing form of mass advocacy.

Alongside these contending agents of popular persuasion—each reaching out in his own way to corral, cajole, or excite a distant public—stood another brand of intellectual activist: the planner or social engineer. No less political or partisan by inner conviction, planners trusted more to the forms of administrative agency than to the white heat of public opinion. Planners, like publicists, came in different political shapes. Mackenzie King thus served as an able social engineer within the post-Ludlow Rockefeller camp, recruiting Junior to a lifelong crusade for company unions (or nonunion employee representation plans), even as Charles McCarthy and John R. Commons perfected the same skills in public bodies for more liberal ends. Leiserson consoled Commons near the end of the commission's work: "You have no sympathy with so-called learned reports, to be stored away in libraries, but on the other hand . . . you have less respect for loud protestations against well known industrial evils . . . instead of trying to get at fundamental causes and working out permanent remedies."[88]

87. One recurrence of basic CIR divisions is seen in the split that later developed on the National Labor Relations Board in 1939 between Leiserson and the leftist Edwin Smith and Joseph Madden, with their legalistic, "adversarial" approach. See Christopher L. Tomlins, *The State and the Unions: Labor Relations, Law, and the Organized Labor Movement in America, 1880–1960* (New York, 1985), 199–213.

88. Leiserson to Commons, August 14, 1915, in Leiserson Papers, State Historical Society of Wisconsin, Madison. For an excellent elaboration on Ivy Lee's and Mackenzie King's roles in the Rockefeller enterprise, see Gitelman, *Legacy of the Ludlow Massacre.*

But for all those intellectuals who identified themselves as democrats and self-conscious agents of radical social change (and these included both Walsh and McCarthy) the limitations of their position—either as agitator or as engineer—seem, in retrospect, all too clear. None of the CIR protagonists were able to wrest from their work the results they had wanted. Frank Walsh, as David Montgomery suggests, might well have had the makings of a great social-democratic legislator, but he needed a mass following to press home his eloquent message.[89] Failing in the end to arouse the independent wrath of the workers as an alternative to bureaucratic control of industrial relations, Walsh himself became the chief agent of governmental administrative intervention during his World War I stint as co-chair of the War Labor Board (WLB). Without apparent embarrassment, he managed a disputes adjudication machinery remarkably like the one he had earlier scoffed at when it was broached by his more "academic" CIR colleagues.[90] Walsh's friend George Creel also entered wartime governmental service, but he did so by elaborating on the very techniques of popular persuasion that he had originally practiced as a journalist. The similarity of method between radical reform education and corporate advertising was perhaps never better exemplified than by the assimilation of both into Creel's Committee on Public Information, the wartime propaganda machine responsible for "unifying" a doubting public around Wilson's war aims.[91] In another sense, Creel's self-righteous moralism had simply been applied to new ends. A fellow muckraker once noted, "To Creel there are only two classes of men . . . There are skunks, and the greatest man that ever lived. The greatest man that ever lived is plural,

89. "No other figure of his time, or perhaps of any time in American history, so clearly personified the possibility and the potential character of a labor party as did Frank Walsh": David Montgomery, *The Fall of the House of Labor: The Workplace, the State, and American Labor Activism, 1865–1925* (New York, 1987), 361.

90. Indeed, frustrated by employers' resistance to arbitration of disputes during the war, Walsh was so drawn into the administrative orbit as to recommend that the board be reconstituted to impress the largest employers—including John D. Rockefeller Jr.!—into service. See Weinstein, *Corporate Ideal*, 248. On the nature of WLB machinery and its indebtedness to CIR proposals, see Conner, *National War Labor Board*, 15, 18–34. Walsh, generally speaking, seems a man less of fine distinctions than of broad commitments. Unlike his more restrained academic colleagues on the CIR, he led with his heart, not his head. For more on his personal impetuosity and flights of passion, see Leila J. Rupp, "Feminism and the Sexual Revolution in the Early Twentieth Century: The Case of Doris Stevens," *Feminist Studies* 15 (Summer 1989): 294.

91. In the years after World War I Creel continued to mix journalism and reform advocacy with intermittent use of the state apparatus of social control. Though his autobiography of 1947 lambastes Mexico's president Lázaro Cárdenas for his socialist excesses, Creel's papers show him to have been a consultant to Cárdenas in his establishment of a Mexican Ministry of Public Information and Propaganda in 1940. See Creel, *Rebel at Large*, 81–85; index of George Creel Papers, Library of Congress.

and includes everyone who is on Creel's side in whatever public issue he happens at the moment to be concerned with."[92]

Compared to such natural agitators, the intellectual engineers kept to an outwardly more consistent but inwardly more troubled course. After his commission work, Commons fell into the most severe of his periodic depressions, collapsing before the spring exam period in 1916 and not returning to his academic post until February 1917. Many years later, Selig Perlman recalled that the conflict within the commission "made a tremendous impression upon Professor Commons, it robbed him of his sleep and peace of mind." Commons would again consult for federal and state authorities about employment and other issues, but never at his prewar pace. McCarthy, for his part, recuperated from his commission experience by throwing himself into a dollar-a-year position with the wartime Food Administration. Separated from his family and living in near-penury in Washington, D.C., when he was not visiting war-torn Europe, McCarthy seemed utterly driven to patriotic service. When he died in 1921 at age forty-eight, more than one friend lamented that he had simply "burnt himself out."[93]

The painstaking plans for labor reform, advanced by both Commons and McCarthy proved to be political nonstarters, championed neither by the workers they might most have benefitted nor by public officials unwilling (outside of wartime exigency) to challenge the marketplace regulation of labor relations. In this sense the CIR project displayed the fateful isolation of intellectual activists and reformers from local and state-based political leverage, the common frustration of early twentieth-century state builders by the United States' peculiarly decentered political authority. Reformers, that is, could research and advocate all they wanted, but such activity did not necessarily swing votes or ensure tangible political influence.[94] With no way to mobilize an independent constituency for their ingenious governmental programs, social engineers such as McCarthy and Commons were captives of their reigning public patrons. Unfortunately for them, the United States had no Bismarck (and only the occasional La

92. Mark Sullivan quoted in John A. Thompson, *Reformers and War: American Progressive Publicists and the First World War* (Cambridge, 1987), 17. On Creel's latter-day self-righteousness, see Cletus E. Daniel's characterization of Creel as "patron-savior" and "authoritarian progressive" in his role as NRA regional administrator in the early 1930s: *Bitter Harvest: A History of California Farmworkers, 1870–1941* (Ithaca, 1981), 174–217. I am indebted to Cindy Hahamovitch for this reference.

93. Interview with Selig Perlman, April 13, 1950, State Historical Society of Wisconsin, Madison; Commons, *Myself*, 182, 185; Fitzpatrick, *McCarthy of Wisconsin*, 213–17. McCarthy even tried to organize a combat company of famous football players and other athletes, offering himself among 236 volunteers before the plan fell through.

94. Stephen Skowronek, *Building a New American State: The Expansion of National Administrative Capacities, 1877–1920* (Cambridge, 1982), esp. 12–14, 121–76.

Follette) who was capable of turning their intellectual handicraft into political-administrative reality. A consumer democracy may thus have bestowed unprecedented attention on a growing class of academically trained, critical intellectuals without necessarily buying their vision of public policy.[95]

95. The intellectuals' own consciousness of the limits of their public role was more evident after the war, in the spate of disillusioned commentary on the problem of "public opinion" in a modern democracy. As is evident in the writing of Walter Lippmann, one of the intellectuals' most articulate representatives, a prime concern was the difficulty of introducing experts and expertise into the consideration of public issues. In this sense the CIR might be considered a skirmish in intellectual disillusionment before the onset of the Great War. See Walter Lippmann, *Public Opinion* (1922) (New York, 1965), esp. 250–57. See also Thompson, *Reformers and War*, 279–86.

9

Making Women's History: Activist Historians of Women's Rights, 1880–1940

Ellen C. DuBois

> The impression conveyed by our text books is that this world has been made by men and for men and the ideals they are putting forth are colored by masculine thought. . . . Our text books on Civics do not show the slightest appreciation of the significance of the "woman's movement."
>
> —PAULINE STEINEM

Most of the people who wrote and promoted the history of women's rights in the years immediately after women won the vote were veterans of the suffrage movement who thought the preservation of that history would contribute to "the cause." They were not academically trained, but popular, even amateur historians. The enthusiasm and sense of political mission with which they pursued the preservation and writing of the past in the 1920s and 1930s characterizes an important phase in the missing history of the feminist movement between the decline of suffragism and the rise of women's liberation.

The activities of those historian-activists underlie the current surge in women's history. The archives they created, the books they wrote in the 1920s, 1930s, and early 1940s awaited—even enticed—feminists of the 1960s and 1970s to become historians of women. In a basic way, the modern emergence of a field of women's history was the belated realization of the mission they had begun years before. There is precious little historiography of women's history before 1970, but the few articles we have focus exclusively on academic historians, as if these women were the

I thank Ann D. Gordon for her criticisms and suggestions on this chapter.

significant predecessors of today's women's historians.[1] But for years only a handful of women entered the profession, and they—for obvious reasons—stayed away from the subject that would have drawn attention to their difference. Mary Beard has been the object of much interest, but even she has been examined in isolation, rather than as part of a larger group of former activists who were making women's history in the same years.[2]

An examination of the early, unrecognized practitioners of women's history can also shed light on larger problems: why and how political insurgence is related to the historical impulse; why a group pushing its way into civil society and political recognition becomes hungry for a history of itself and for a recognized place in the larger past. Extrapolation from this particular episode suggests a way to formulate the link between politics and history, between the past and the future. Feminist, labor, black liberation, and similar movements all rest on two postulates whose contradictions only a theory about the movement of history can resolve. On the one hand, such movements declare a past of oppression, subordination, and injustice; on the other, they assert the possibility of a future of an entirely different order—a future of emancipation or liberation. Activists committed to social change need to create for themselves a historical interpretation that can take them from one kind of past to a different kind of future. Moreover, this need for history takes on different forms during different stages in a movement's development: sometimes the purpose of history is to inspire, sometimes to sustain, sometimes to recall.

Examining the link between politics and history can help us to understand not only the history of social movements but history in general. "Memory is the thread of personal identity," writes Richard Hofstader, "history of public identity."[3] Attacks by right-wing critics on "history from the bottom up" have been particularly effective in spreading the

---

1. See Kathryn Sklar, "American Female Historians in Context, 1770–1930," *Feminist Studies* 3 (1975): 171–84; Joan W. Scott, "History and Difference," *Daedulus* 116 (1987): 93–118.
2. On Beard, see Ann D. Gordon, Mari Jo Buhle, and Nancy Schrom Dye, *Women in American Society: An Historical Contribution* (Madison, Wis., 1972), 2–3; Ann J. Lane, ed., *Mary Ritter Beard: A Sourcebook* (New York, 1977); Berenice Carroll, "Mary Beard's *Woman as Force in History*: A Critique," in *Liberating Women's History*, ed. Carroll (Urbana, 1976), 26–41; Bonnie G. Smith, "Seeing Mary Beard," *Feminist Studies* 10 (Fall 1984): 399–416; Suzanne Lebsock, "Reading Mary Beard," *Reviews in American History* 17 (June 1989): 324–39; Nancy F. Cott, "Two Beards: Coauthorship and the Concept of Civilization," *American Quarterly* 42 (1990): 274–300; and Cott, ed., *A Woman Making History: Mary Ritter Beard through Her Letters* (New Haven, 1991).
3. Richard Hofstader, *The Progressive Historians: Turner, Beard, Parrington* (New York, 1968), 3.

262216 *Ellen C. DuBois*

idea that passion and scholarship are enemies, that history cannot be "true" and argue a case at the same time. We who are practicing historians are so busy defending against these onslaughts that we have no time to investigate the relationship between partisanship and scholarship in other, less defensive ways. But impulses other than academic are important—perhaps fundamental—in the recording, writing, and interpreting of history.

Needless to say, the women's rights movement does not constitute the entirety of women's past. The historians examined here have virtually nothing to say about the history of women in the wage-labor force, but important books on this subject, dating at least as far back as the federally sponsored *History of Women in Industry* published in 1911, have helped to shape subsequent work on women workers.[4] Similarly, a historiography of African-American women reaches back to the group biographies of women worthies of color published in conjunction with the black women's club movement at the turn of the century.[5] These and other aspects of women's historical action need to be situated in their own politically informed historiography.

THE EVOLUTION OF A MASTER NARRATIVE OF WOMEN'S HISTORY

Activism for women's rights was linked to women's history even before woman suffrage was secured. Elizabeth Stanton wanted to write a book on the history of women's aspirations for emancipation as a way to develop the argument for sexual equality as early as the 1840s.[6] After a series of political defeats in the mid-1870s, her partner, Susan B. Anthony, revived the idea, and along with Matilda Joslyn Gage they undertook what they imagined would be a one-volume history of woman suffrage. To those who contended, even then, that "the actors themselves cannot write impartial history," Elizabeth Stanton responded that "a history written by its actors get[s] nearer the soul of the subject."[7] By the time Stanton

4. Helen L. Sumner, *History of Women in Industry in the United States*, vol. 9 of *Report of the Condition of Woman and Child Wage-Earners in the United States*, (Washington, D.C., 1911); similarly, Alice Henry, *The Trade Union Movement* (New York, 1915).

5. Lawson Andrew Scruggs, *Women of Distinction: Remarkable of Words and Invincible in Character* (Raleigh, N.C., 1893); N. F. Moselle, *The Work of the Afro-American Woman* (Philadelphia, 1908); Sadie Daniel, *Women Builders* (Washington, D.C., 1931); Elizabeth Davis, *Lifting as They Climb: The National Association of Colored Women* (Chicago, 1933). Thanks to Ann D. Gordon for this suggestion.

6. Elisabeth Griffith, *In Her Own Right: The Life of Elizabeth Cady Stanton* (New York, 1984), 87.

7. Elizabeth Stanton, Susan B. Anthony, and Matilda Joslyn Gage, eds. *History of Woman Suffrage*, vol. 1, 2d ed. (Rochester, N.Y., 1889), 7.

gave up the project, more than a decade later, the *History of Woman Suffrage* had reached three volumes and more than 3,000 pages; in 1922, long after all three of the original editors had died, the sixth and final volume was finished. There is nothing in the annals of American reform quite like the *History of Woman Suffrage*, a prolonged, deliberate effort on the part of activists to ensure their place in the historical record.

All six volumes situate women's demands for political equality in a larger context, not only of women's legal rights but of the long elevation and emancipation of the sex. The initial volumes are very broadly conceived, a combination of Stanton's broad philosophical range, Anthony's organizational energies, and Gage's historical sensibilities. Although the editors were not shy about their own historical interpretations (Stanton, for instance, saw women's rights in terms of the long history of individualism), they included an enormous amount of primary material so that readers could reach their own conclusions. Personal reminiscences, conference proceedings, newspaper articles, and stump speeches are linked together by a loose narrative, a lovely, long string of separate historical jewels. Anthony also insisted on expensive steel-plate portraits of women important in the struggle for women's rights, so that future generations would have counterevidence to the charge that all strong-minded women were unwomanly.[8]

Stanton wrote a great deal of the text, and her interpretation of the rise of the movement pervades the volumes. Gage supplied important supplementary essays on the history of women in the American Revolution, in the rise of newspaper publishing, and most notably on the long history of Christian misogyny and attacks on witchcraft. These essays extended the project's historical range. Anthony, to whom the project came to take on great personal meaning, was the business manager. For volume 3 she solicited an essay by a local activist in each of the states, with enormously detailed information about the growth of the movement at the rank-and-file level. "Put a request . . . asking any person who knows of any fact or any person that you have not mentioned to send it to you at once," she advised the author of the Illinois chapter. "That way you'll get everything." She hired the indexer from the *New York Tribune* to prepare a very detailed index to all three volumes, to increase their accessibility. She then sold and gave away thousands of volumes, largely at her own expense. "Every normal, high school, college and public library ought to have the books," she insisted. "It is the only place that the facts about the work done by and for women can be found."[9]

8. On these and other matters concerning the production and publication of the first three volumes, see Anthony's correspondence with Elizabeth Boynton Harbert, 1878–82, in Harbert Papers, Huntington Library, San Marino, Calif.

9. Anthony to Harbert, May 11 and April 2, 1882; June 6, 1903, all ibid.

Anthony's name also appeared on volume 4, but by this time most of the work was being done by her biographer and protégé, Ida H. Harper, who finished the last two volumes in 1922.[10] The last three volumes of the *History of Woman Suffrage* are quite different from the first three. They are a history less of a social movement than of an organization— the National American Woman Suffrage Association (NAWSA). Chapters are organized around annual conventions, lists of officers, and accounts of speeches and committee reports, so the narrative of historical transformation is notably lacking in excitement. Intra-and interorganizational conflicts were read out of the account, even as they shaped what was included and what was excluded.[11] The exclusion of all evidence of conflict or alternatives—historical, strategic, or even interpretive—made for a sense of historical inevitability rather than social struggle. Women's enfranchisement was depicted as part of the inevitable unfolding of American democracy, of women being drawn along with men into the national destiny. Oddly enough, this Whiggish tale of the steady climb of women toward collective advancement was combined with an antidemocratic suspicion of and hostility to the political impulses of the (male) masses. (The earlier volumes, by contrast, had tended to situate women's rights as part of the long march of oppressed humanity against unjust authority.)[12]

The last three volumes of the *History of Woman Suffrage* also engaged the problem of leadership—and more deeply the relation of individual to movement—in a different way from the earlier volumes. The early volumes were lavish in their appreciation of individual achievement: numerous names of female "firsts" organized the account of historical progress.[13] The final volumes gave more weight to the individual achievements of

10. Susan B. Anthony and Ida Husted Harper, eds., *History of Woman Suffrage*, vol. 4 (Rochester, N.Y., 1902); Ida Husted Harper, ed., *History of Woman Suffrage*, vols. 5 and 6 (New York, 1922).

11. See, for instance, an exchange between Carrie Chapman Catt and Harper about whether "the truth" should be told about Harriet Taylor Upton's resignation from her NAWSA office: Catt to Harper, October 14, 1921, in Carrie Chapman Catt Papers, Library of Congress. Similarly, Harriot Stanton Blatch complained that vol. 6 included an account of a 1910 meeting at which open-air agitation was discussed when in fact Anna Howard Shaw had forced her to call off the session. "So much for the accuracy of that Harper book": Blatch to Caroline Lexow Babcock, September 18, 1925, in Babcock-Hurlburt Papers, Schlesinger Library, Cambridge, Mass.

12. Contrast Harper's comments about the "prejudiced, conservative and in a degree ignorant and vicious electorate" that has "the power to withhold the suffrage from women" in *History of Woman Suffrage*, 4:xxiii, with the much more democratic treatment in Matilda J. Gage's essay "Preceding Causes" in vol. 1. In Gage's account, conservatism and fear of change are characteristics of the majority of both men and women; similarly, women's rights are part of a larger process of democratic transformation.

13. For instance, vol. 1 is dedicated to "the memory of Mary Wollstonecraft, Frances Wright, Lucretia Mott, Harriet Martineau, Lydia Maria Child, Margaret Fuller, Sarah and Angelina Grimke, Josephine S. Griffing, Martha C. Wright, Harriot K. Hunt, M.D., Mari-

fewer women. The complex history of the movement was merged into the persons of a handful of leaders, who were rendered as saints, selfless embodiments of a larger cause. Chief among them was Susan B. Anthony, who was universally recognized as the summit of the women's rights pantheon. The focus on Anthony not only tended to shut out recognition of many other leaders but set a pattern for the treatment of the relationship between private life and public achievement that was eminently Victorian. Leaders either lacked distinct private lives (Anthony lived her life in total devotion to the movement) or, as in the official version of Stanton's life, were perfect in their expression of motherly devotion and homemaker excellence.

Thus, by the last phase of the woman suffrage movement and the final volumes of the *History of Woman Suffrage,* the historical account of the women's rights movement had narrowed considerably. By 1910 or so, a considerable consensus had formed around a single, controlling version of women's rights history: that in the early nineteenth century, American women had begun to "awaken," to follow the road that lay waiting to lead them to their "advancement," through higher education and the opening up of the professions, past temperance societies and women's clubs, ultimately to arrive at the temple of political equality.[14] This frozen account of the past, a history characterized by celebration, inevitability, and canonization, as well as by a rigid separation between public achievement and personal life, constituted what might be called a "master narrative" (the patriarchal reference is intended) of women's rights.

In the years immediately before and after the ratification of the Nineteenth Amendment, the two wings into which suffragists had split waged an intense intramovement war over, among other things, the history of women's rights. Each version stressed different political virtues: the size and efficiency of the National American Woman Suffrage Association

---

ana W. Johnson, Alice and Phebe Carey, Ann Preston, M.D., Lydia Mott, Eliza W. Farnham, Lydia F. Fowler, M.D., Paulina Wright Davis."

14. Here is a version from the introduction to vol. 5 of *History of Woman Suffrage* (xvi–xvii):

> One step led to another; business opportunities increased; women accumulated property; Legislatures were compelled to revise the laws and the church was obliged to liberalize its interpretation of the Scriptures. Women began to organize; their missionary and charity societies prepared the way to clubs for self-improvement; these in turn broadened into civic organizations whose public work carried them to city councils and State Legislatures, where they found themselves in the midst of politics and wholly without influence. Thus they were led into the movement for the suffrage. It was only a few of the clear thinkers, the far seeing, who realized at the beginning that the principal cause of women's inferior position and helplessness lay in their disfranchisement and until they could be made to see it they were a dead weight on the movement. Men fully understood the power that the vote would place in the hands of women, with a lessening of their own, and in the mass they did not intend to concede it.

versus the militance of the National Woman's Party.[15] They disagreed so intensely over which wing was ultimately reponsible for passage of the Nineteenth Amendment that they read each other out of their factional versions of history. These historical skirmishes were conducted with great vehemence; in 1921, for instance, the two factions fought over who would dedicate a statue to women's rights pioneers in the Capitol rotunda.[16]

Ultimately, however, neither account diverged from the master narrative. They shared the same basic framework for their history. Both wings, for instance, apotheosized Anthony, disagreeing only on which faction was her rightful heir. Both embraced the notion that woman suffrage ultimately prevailed because it was a "single-issue" movement, from the perspective of which all other causes were competitive with women's advancement and all politics were male manifestations, equally hostile to the cause of women.[17] The dispute between factions was not over the basic content of the history of women's rights but only over who controlled its telling and which side would reap the glory of past triumphs.

Though the master narrative continued to be reproduced for many decades, from 1920 on processes worked to complicate this historical account and widen the resources with which American women's history could be written.[18] The meaning of the past began to change, against a background of general transformation in organized women's politics—especially the challenge and threat posed by the successful end to the long struggle for the vote and the replacement of Victorian norms of selfless service with modern standards of individualism and self-realization. At the deepest level, the ratification of the Nineteenth Amendment undermined the consensus about the significance of women's path through

15. For the National Woman's Party version, see Doris Stevens, *Jailed for Freedom* (New York, 1920); Inez Haines Irwin, *The Story of the Woman's Party* (New York, 1921). For the National American Woman Suffrage Association version, see Carrie Chapman Catt and Nettie Rogers Shuler, *Woman Suffrage and Politics* (New York, 1923); Maud Wood Park, *Front Door Lobby* (Boston, 1960); and, of course, vol. 6 of *History of Woman Suffrage*. Given the almost total exclusion of the Woman's Party from the final volumes of the *History of Woman Suffrage*, Harriot Stanton Blatch humorously suggested to Doris Stevens that she publish *Jailed for Freedom* in the same format and call it *History of Woman Suffrage*, vol. 4: Alice Paul to Harriot Blatch, September 30, 1920, in Alma Lutz Papers, Vassar College, Poughkeepsie, New York. Paul did not get the joke.

16. I discuss this episode in my biography of Harriot Stanton Blatch, *Generation of Power: Harriot Stanton Blatch and the Winning of Woman Suffrage* (New Haven, forthcoming).

17. Note the similarities, for instance, between Catt and Shuler, *Woman Suffrage and Politics,* and Irwin, *Story of the Woman's Party.*

18. See Ellen Carol DuBois, "Eleanor Flexner's *Century of Struggle:* Viewing and Reviewing a Feminist Classic," *Gender and History,* 1991, in which I argue that Flexner's 1959 work was the first original synthesis of the history of women's rights to break through this half-century-old narrative framework.

history. The achievement of woman suffrage ironically threatened to bring to a close the long-told history of women's steady ascent into public life. It certainly called into question the future organization and purpose of the organized women's movement, but it also called into question the meaning of the past. The winning of woman suffrage stimulated a reaction against the dominant account of women's past and started the search for themes in women's history not fully satisfied by enfranchisement.

FEMINIST WOMEN'S HISTORY

A new, more modernist approach can be detected in women's history writing beginning in the 1920s. This kind of women's history might best be characterized as "feminist," in the sense in which Nancy Cott develops the term in *The Grounding of Modern Feminism*.[19] She uses "feminism" to describe not the long movement for women's rights but a particular ideology of female emancipation and sexual justice that first appeared in the 1910s and both superseded and repudiated the Victorian "woman movement." Whereas the woman movement stood for selflessness in service to the cause, feminism stood for self-development as the route to women's emancipation. Whereas the woman movement rested on the principle of social purity, feminism went in search of female sexuality. Whereas the woman movement looked to the elevation of women collectively, feminism aspired to the liberation of individual women from social constraints, including those imposed by other women. Feminists reacted against the history associated with this older woman movement. They replaced the master narrative of women's collective advancement with the history of individual women in conflict with social norms, a history that concentrated less on the inevitability of social reform than on the triumph of the individual over narrow social restrictions.

Feminist women's history in the 1920s paralleled larger currents in the practice of history. As Peter Novick observes, in the postwar period academic historians in general were frequently eclipsed by historians who wrote for a popular audience.[20] Feminist historians were not academically trained and employed historians but rather professional writers and journalists. Like male progressive historians, they rejected the Whiggish tales of inevitable progress and national destiny. Instead, these feminists wanted to get under the surface, to push past appearances, to discover

19. Nancy F. Cott, *The Grounding of Modern Feminism* (New Haven, 1987), esp. Introduction and chap. 1.

20. Peter Novick, *The Noble Dream: The "Objectivity Question" and the American Historical Profession* (Cambridge, 1988), 193.

"the inside story." In their case, the hidden reality was more likely to be psychological and sexual than economic. Like male progressive historians, the feminist historians saw no conflict between the "scientific" pursuit of "reality" and their own convictions. They believed it was possible to look at the past both impartially and with "the warmth of the advocate."[21]

An interesting and early example of this new feminist approach to women's history is Katharine Anthony's 1920 biography of Margaret Fuller. Anthony, a University of Chicago graduate, Greenwich Village "new woman," and pioneering psychobiographer, had already written an important study of the German and Scandinavian women's rights movements, which she had praised for going beyond legal equality to address the sexual and maternal particularities of women's lives.[22] Now "that suffrage is out of the way," Anthony was looking for a representative of a "broader kind of feminism" in the American tradition as well; she found it in Margaret Fuller.[23] Earlier biographers had justified or excused Fuller's eccentricities in order to defend her literary stature, but her personal extravagances were precisely what fascinated Anthony. Unlike an earlier generation of women's historians who preferred their heroines to have harmonious domestic situations and to live in service to a larger cause, feminist revisionists such as Katharine Anthony found chaotic personal lives a source of both interest and inspiration. Although Anthony praised Fuller's writings for their anticipation of twentieth-century feminist themes, she admired Fuller's life, its turbulence and its passions, even more. As a favorable review in *The Nation* noted, Fuller was so interesting precisely because her life "is dissociated from any movement except in the broadest sense of the word."[24]

A 1927 biography of George Sand, by Marie Jenney Howe, is similar in conception to Anthony's *Margaret Fuller*.[25] Howe was a close friend of Anthony and founder of the important feminist literary and social club Heterodoxy, to which several other feminist historians belonged.[26] Howe admired Sand as "a modern woman born one hundred years too soon." Sand's modernism lay in the way she had lived her personal life ("she regarded laws and customs as ephemeral"), in her combination of masculinity and femininity into a character that was "inclusively human," and

21. The phrase is Katharine Anthony's in *Margaret Fuller: A Psychological Biography* (New York, 1920), v.

22. Judith Schwartz, *Radical Feminists of Heterodoxy: Greenwich Village, 1912–1940* (Lebanon, N.H., 1982); Katharine Anthony, *Feminism in Germany and Scandinavia* (New York, 1915).

23. Anthony, *Margaret Fuller*, v.

24. *Nation*, January 12, 1921.

25. Marie Jenney Howe, *George Sand: The Search for Love* (Garden City, N.Y., 1927).

26. Schwartz, *Radical Feminists of Heterodoxy*. Katharine Anthony, Doris Stevens, Inez Haines Irwin, and Rheta Childe Dorr were all members.

in her "generous self-revelations"—her willingness to make the complexity of her life accessible to others. "She ruined her life several times," Howe wrote admiringly, "but always crawled out from the débris and built up a new existence, until in the end she learned to adjust herself to life as it is and people as they are."[27]

In all the feminist histories of this period, sexual expression, not enfranchisement, was the redeeming goal of women's history. Women's past appeared different in light of Freudian ideas and the "scientific eroticism" of the 1920s. But whereas male modernists tended to blame women as the agents of Victorian sexual repression, feminist historians used pro-sex ideas to retrieve rather than condemn the women's rights tradition. In the case of Margaret Fuller, Anthony used Freudian tools to explore and defend Fuller's intimate bonds with other women, the implicit eroticism of which she regarded as healthy and vital. Anthony also regarded Fuller as a predecessor of the modern movement for sexual emancipation. "She was one of those who stood as sign-posts along the road which was to lead in time to a scientific view of the nature of love." In Howe's biography of Sand, subtitled *The Search for Love,* she retold Sand's life as a series of turbulent affairs, conflicts between her "desire for freedom and the need for human ties." Even Sand's intense advocacy of the revolution of 1848, which Howe regarded as the climax of Sand's life, she presented in terms of Sand's conflicting desires for transcendent love and a separate self. Howe's treatment of Sand's sex life, while deeply romantic, was nonetheless thoroughly feminist: Howe's heroine was in lifelong revolt against men's aspirations to possess and dominate women.[28]

The publication in 1927 of Paxton Hibben's anti-Victorian biography of Henry Ward Beecher made an important contribution to the feminist rereading of women's history.[29] Hibben, a war correspondent whose only previous book was a biography of King Constantine I of Greece, decided to take on Beecher, the leading Protestant minister of the 1860s and 1870s, to expose the sordid "reality" beyond his shining reputation for moral rectitude. In particular, Hibben rediscovered a half-century-old festering scandal in which Beecher had been accused of seducing Elizabeth Tilton, wife of his close friend Theodore. Hibben demonstrated conclusively that Henry Ward Beecher had been an adulterer. Hibben's research probed the secrets not only of Beecher and the Tiltons but also of women's rights. Hibben discovered that Susan B. Anthony and Elizabeth Cady Stanton were the ones who had spilled the beans, albeit inadvertently, about the Beecher/Tilton affair. Moreover, the person they had told,

27. Howe, *George Sand,* xii–xiv.
28. Anthony, *Margaret Fuller,* 36; Howe, *George Sand,* 337.
29. Paxton Hibben, *Henry Ward Beecher: An American Portrait* (New York, 1927).

who told the world, was a figure that sexually conservative women's rights leaders had been trying to suppress ever since—the notorious "free lover" Victoria Woodhull.

Within a year, two books appeared which explored the implications of Hibben's research for women's history. The more original of the two was *"The Terrible Siren,"* Emanie Sachs's biography of Victoria Woodhull (who had died the year before at the age of eighty-nine).[30] Sachs, a "new woman" and successful novelist, found in Woodhull the perfect counterheroine for a feminist rereading of women's rights history. Using Hibben's research for a start, Sachs unearthed the entirety of Woodhull's extraordinary life. Woodhull had risen from an impoverished, unlettered background to national prominence as a radical leader in the early 1870s. She was a stockbroker and a communist, a woman suffragist and a free lover. In short, she violated all of the oppositions on which Gilded Age culture was premised. Sachs celebrated Woodhull's "healthy eroticism" and her resistance to the enforcers of Victorian morality, not only Henry Ward Beecher but also other women—including his sisters—who monitored the boundaries of "true womanhood." Above all, Sachs appreciated Woodhull, as Katharine Anthony had Margaret Fuller, for her irrepressible individuality. Upon reading Sachs's book, Inez Haines Irwin, another feminist historian of the period, confessed to an embarrassed glee. Woodhull and her sister, Tennessee Claflin, "made me blush," Irwin wrote in 1928. "At the same time I could not help taking a rich and wicked joy in the way they walked rough shod, spike heeled and copper toed over the entire male sex."[31]

In 1928 Rheta Childe Dorr's life of Susan B. Anthony, *The Woman Who Changed the Mind of a Nation,* was published, the first biography to appear since the authorized version that Anthony herself had supervised in 1898.[32] With the help of Paxton Hibben, Dorr had tried to get hold of Anthony's diaries, but Anthony's literary executors resisted; it might be better to destroy the sources, they feared than to let them fall into the wrong hands.[33] Without fresh sources, Dorr drew primarily on Hibben's version of the Beecher/Tilton scandal to reexamine Anthony's life. In an interpretation that has carried over into much subsequent history, Dorr

30. Emanie Sachs, *"The Terrible Siren": Victoria Woodhull (1838–1927)* (New York, 1928). Sachs also wrote under her married name, Arling. Little seems to be known about Sachs, but how she came to write a book about Woodhull so soon after her death surely invites investigation.

31. Irwin to Maud Wood Park, June 20, 1929, in National American Woman Suffrage Association Papers, Library of Congress, reel 1.

32. Rheta Childe Dorr, *Susan B. Anthony: The Woman Who Changed the Mind of a Nation* (New York, 1928); Ida H. Harper, *The Life and Work of Susan B. Anthony* (Indianapolis, 1898).

33. Harper to Park, July 13, 1930, in Carrie Chapman Catt Papers, Library of Congress.

linked the Beecher/Tilton scandal to the political split within the woman suffrage movement that lasted from 1869 to 1890. Like Victoria Woodhull herself, this split became an embarrassment to later woman suffrage leaders, and discussions of it virtually disappeared from official movement histories. Dorr revived the history of this nineteenth-century split, in part to anticipate a second, twentieth century split of the suffrage movement, in which she was vitally involved. As a feminist historian, she also gave the nineteenth-century split an essentially sexual rather than personal or political interpretation. On the one side stood Lucy Stone and the American Woman Suffrage Association, like Henry Ward Beecher himself "as puritanically conservative as Plymouth Rock."[34] The other wing, Dorr argued, consisted of social radicals. They supported divorce, defended daring women such as Woodhull, and challenged middle-class convention. Anthony in particular she praised for her "long crusade for sex freedom." Because Dorr had broken through the control that the guardians of Anthony's memory exercised over the meaning of her life, her book caused a great stir. Ida Harper, Anthony's official biographer, publicly criticized Dorr for doing in Anthony's name what Anthony herself would not do: disclose what she knew about the Beecher/Tilton affair.[35]

In this genre of feminist history, the issue of secrets and the notion that it is the historian's job to expose them loomed quite large. In fact, the woman suffrage movement itself had been suppressing things for a long time. From the 1890s on, its leaders had become set in the habit of denying any sexual unconventionality in or around their movement. Partly, they had made a strategic decision to fit in with rather than challenge the moral convictions of American women; and partly, as the years progressed, Victorian morality became more coercive and they became more implicated in it. Nor was sexual unconventionality the only secret in the women suffrage movement. The existence of political conflict among suffragists was as strenuously denied as sexual unconventionality, perhaps because it was as much at odds with Victorian notions of womanhood. Indeed, sexual and political secrets became inextricably linked, if only by the common process of suppression. As a young suffragist in the 1890s, right after the twenty-year factionalization of the movement had ended, Carrie Chapman Catt recalled there was much buzzing about each side's sexual infractions among veterans of the split.[36]

Over the years, keeping these secrets became part of the general obligation that suffrage leaders felt to control the history of their movement in

34. Dorr, *Susan B. Anthony*, 220, 3.
35. Harper, review of *"Terrible Siren," Woman's Journal*, January 1929, 35.
36. Catt to Alice Stone Blackwell, September 8, 1930, in Carrie Chapman Catt Papers, Library of Congress.

order to serve its larger purposes. This habit of suppression contributed to the rigid quality of the master narrative. The iconoclastic feminist historians of the 1920s broke through the control that suffrage leaders had long exercised over the history of their movement. Jazz Age women's history encouraged the curiosity even of former suffragists who had always subscribed to the Victorian conviction that facts that upset people were best ignored, and thereby weakened the taboo against independent inquiry and interpretation. Anthony's literary executors made discrete inquiries about her part in the Beecher/Tilton scandal to satisfy themselves that Hibben had been wrong, only to discover that he was right.[37]

Carrie Chapman Catt is a good example of this process. When the feminist histories of the late 1920s first appeared, she objected to the exposure of old conflicts and intramovement "gossip," which she thought harmed the historical reputation of the suffrage movement. Gradually, however, she came to believe that what she owed the past was exposure rather than control. She admitted that she had always wondered about certain "mysteries" of the suffrage movement, confessed to old friends what her real feelings about nineteenth-century leaders had been, and even entertained the possibility that Anthony had been motivated by personal passions and not merely selfless dedication.[38]

Catt's changing relation to the past, like that of other aging former suffragists, reflected a larger change in the historical consciousness of women's rights. In general, the efforts of former suffragists and feminists to record and reexamine women's rights history in the late 1920s coincided with—and were a reaction against—a growing amnesia about their movement in the larger society. Throughout the early 1920s, when the passage of the Nineteenth Amendment was still a living memory to most Americans, general-audience periodicals regularly told the history of woman suffrage. But by 1930, knowledge of and interest in the women's rights past were fading, casualties of general disinterest in the cause of women's equality as participants in the movement began to pass from the scene. Even some younger activists in the organized women's movement, ignorance about the women's rights past was a problem. At a meeting of the National Council of Women in 1933, Catt suggested that the American women in attendance knew as little about the history of their own

37. Catt asked Harper "if it was true" and Harper told her Anthony herself had told her the story: ibid. Catt also thought Blatch had told Hibben: Catt to Lucy Anthony, November 8, 1928, ibid. Blackwell refused to concede Beecher's guilt in her biography of her mother.

38. She wondered if Anthony had so unceasingly promoted Stanton out of "simple affection and devotion or whether there were other reasons"; I believe she was suggesting that Anthony had been in love with Stanton. See Catt to Blackwell, September 18, 1930, in Carrie Chapman Catt Papers, Library of Congress.

movement as did their foreign guests.[39] The long habit of control exercised over the movement's written history and the excessive concern with politically correct meanings contributed to the erosion of memory. Old narratives of selfless service, the only accounts in circulation, had little meaning for the younger generation. If the history of women's rights were to stay alive, new generations had to be able to find their own meanings in the past. As interpretations of the past became less rigidly patrolled, this history took on more of the flexibility and organic quality that it needed to stay vital.

HISTORY'S DAUGHTERS

Between the exposure of suppressed secrets, the breaking of the taboo against conflicting interpretations of the past, and the creation of new interpretations that had meaning for younger women, these feminist histories of women's rights succeeded in stimulating even greater curiosity about the past. Among the women who were particularly affected by this deepening interest in women's history were Lucy Stone's daughter, Alice Stone Blackwell, and Elizabeth Cady Stanton's daughter, Harriot Stanton Blatch, both of them activists in their own right.[40] By 1930, Lucy Stone was remembered, if at all, simply as the woman who refused to take her husband's name upon marriage, and Stanton was remembered only as Anthony's sidekick, her white curls the best known thing about her.[41] As they neared the end of their own lives, both Blackwell and Blatch seem to have been seized with a deep sense of devotion to their mothers' memories and a desire to come to their defense. The opening up of the historical arena made it possible for them to act on those feelings and to record for the future aspects of the past about which they had direct knowledge. Their contributions to history were simultaneously personal and substantive.

39. Catt, "Only Yesterday," in *Our Common Cause, Civilization: Report of the International Congress of Women, July 16–22, 1933, New York, New York* (New York, 1933), p. 235.

40. Other daughters of activists also wrote history or wanted to were Julia Ward Howe's daughters, Maud Howe Elliott and Florence Howe Hall, and Katherine Devereux Blake, teacher-feminist and daughter of Lillie Devereux Blake; even Victoria Woodhull's daughter, Zulu Maud, who wanted more than anything else to prove that her mother had never been a free lover, tried to swim upstream into the feminist historical river to do so. See esp. the symposium "Glimpses of Three Pioneers, by Two Daughters and One Niece," *Woman's Journal,* December 1929, 22–23. This anti-Dorr symposium featured daughterly reminiscences of Howe, Stanton, and Anthony (by Lucy Anthony).

41. Ruby A. Black, "A Soul as Free as the Air," *Equal Rights,* December 20, 1930, 363. In an undated letter to Alma Lutz, c. 1939, Blatch complained about the excessive focus on Stanton's white curls, to the exclusion of her "unusual brain": Alma Lutz Papers, Vassar College.

Alice Stone Blackwell's 1930 biography of her mother was stimulated by Hibben's, Sachs's, and especially Dorr's books. Blackwell found it difficult to believe that Beecher, whom her parents had defended, had really been an adulterer. She disapproved of Sachs's fascination with Victoria Woodhull, whom she had been raised to believe had damaged the cause. And she was incensed by Dorr's dismissal of Lucy Stone as someone who had made no significant contribution to women's history after her marriage in 1854.[42]

In response, Blackwell wrote the first full biography of Stone. The reviewer for the National Woman's Party weekly, who had been ignorant of the magnitude of Stone's historic significance, praised the book for demonstrating the "potency and courage" of her equal rights activism.[43] Blackwell especially contributed an elaborate account, from her mother's perspective, of the 1869–90 split among suffragists. In contrast to Dorr's account, her version of the rift was genuinely political. She demonstrated that the movement had split primarily because of deep differences over "the race question and the sex question."[44] In particular, she countered Dorr's racist treatment of the post–Civil War period and recalled what a tragedy the splitting apart of black and woman suffrage was for Stone's generation.[45] When she came to the next twenty years of intramovement conflict, though, Blackwell gave as nasty as she got, responding to Dorr's insults to her mother with all the disparaging things her parents had ever said about Stanton and Anthony.[46] This part of the book had the character of a family quarrel that had stewed for a half century. Even her friend Carrie Chapman Catt urged her to tone it down. "You must remember that a whole series of unjust whacks have been given to the American side," Blackwell responded petulantly. "Could it be reasonably expected that I would not state [my mother's] side of the case, in a matter where her motives had been so much misrepresented?"[47]

Blackwell's biography of Stone, in turn, led Harriot Stanton Blatch to act on behalf of her own mother's fading reputation. Blatch had made an initial stab at documenting her mother's contribution decades before, at the time of Stanton's death. But the project fell by the wayside as more

42. Dorr, *Susan B. Anthony*, 191.

43. Black, "Soul as Free as the Air," 362–65.

44. Alice Stone Blackwell, *Lucy Stone: Pioneer of Women's Rights* (Boston, 1930), 206.

45. Dorr considered black suffrage "the most ghastly mistake of reconstruction", and described former slaves as "unclean beasts" with "savage instincts": *Susan B. Anthony*, 172, 175, 215.

46. For instance, she charged that Stanton advocated ultraradical issues because it "amused her to watch the fluttering in the dovecotes that followed," and that Anthony had accused her parents of not really being married: Blackwell, *Lucy Stone*, 219, 230.

47. Catt to Blackwell, September 8, 1930, and Blackwell to Catt, September 13, 1930, in Carrie Chapman Catt Papers, Library of Congress.

pressing matters, in particular the still unmet demand for woman suffrage, took her energies. In 1922 Blatch and her brother, Theodore Stanton, reissued Stanton's autobiography and a collection of her letters and diary entries. Both volumes were heavily edited and conformed to the standards of the master narrative, stressing Stanton's exemplary domestic life and traditional female virtues. Stanton and Blatch were also concerned that the overarching sanctification of Anthony was obscuring their mother's role in history, and by judicious cutting they downplayed Anthony's presence in the documents.[48]

Stanton's place in history was further disturbed—that is, both highlighted and slighted—by the women's rights histories of the late 1920s. As Hibben and Sachs made clear, Stanton had played a central role in the Beecher/Tilton scandal, the Victoria Woodhull episode, and the split within the woman suffrage movement. Rheta Childe Dorr essentially dismissed her as a rotund and witty foil to the steely Anthony. Even Alice Stone Blackwell, in her eagerness to rehabilitate her own mother's reputation, charged Stanton with the impulsive and destructive course taken by the Stanton/Anthony wing of the movement. There was something unavoidably competitive in the rewriting of women's history in this period: to elevate one woman seemingly was to denigrate another. Thus one reader who believed she had found in Stone a modern heroine in whom devotion to the equal rights cause was combined with an admirable marital life contrasted Stone with Stanton, who, she charged, could not really speak her mind because she was "considerably submerged by her marriage."[49] In the same spirit, Blatch wrote an angry review of Blackwell's book, calling Stone a "dessicated saint" and her mother one of the "juicy radicals" that history would ultimately vindicate.[50] The "juicy radical" Blatch portrayed was a far cry from the perfect Victorian homemaker and mother of the 1922 edition of Stanton's autobiography, and suggests the impact of new feminist standards even on Blatch's and Blackwell's images of their mothers.

Above all, Blatch deeply resented the overshadowing of her mother's memory by what she called "the advertising" of Susan B. Anthony. Blatch was particularly incensed that the National Woman's Party was crediting the woman suffrage amendment, which her mother had introduced in

48. Theodore Stanton and Harriot Stanton Blatch, eds., *Elizabeth Cady Stanton as Revealed in Her Letters, Diary and Reminiscences*, 2 vols. (New York, 1922). On Harriot Blatch's and Theodore Stanton's "tampering" with their mother's letters, see Amy Dykeman, "'To Pour Forth from My Own Experience': Two Versions of Elizabeth Cady Stanton," *Journal of the Rutgers University Libraries* 44 (June 1982): 1–16.

49. Black, "Soul as Free as the Air."

50. Harriot Stanton Blatch, "Pioneering in the Fight for Women's Rights: A Daughter's Eulogy," undated clipping in Alma Lutz Papers, Vassar College.

1878, to Anthony, for whom it had been posthumously named. "You may admire above all women Mary Queen of Scots & I Queen Elizabeth," she wrote about the elevation of Anthony at her mother's expense. "But . . . when you take off the belongings of my queen and dress your queen up in them it is a high offense."[51]

When and why Blatch became so enraged at Anthony remains to be determined by scholarship that untangles these complex and ever-changing relations between the present and the past. At the time of her mother's death, Blatch was still quite close to Anthony, but sometime after Anthony's death, certainly by 1920, her feelings about Anthony had changed radically. As angry as she was, Blatch's resentment was concentrated less on what Anthony had been than on what she had become. She asked questions about interpretation and meaning: Why had Anthony been elevated, her mother denigrated, and by whom? She came up with two answers. One was that, unlike Anthony, her mother had linked woman suffrage to various "heresies," notably free love and free thought, and that starting in the 1890s, rival leaders who wanted "a pure suffrage movement" began to "bury her alive," and remove her from history.[52]

Blatch's other hypothesis was that as a "single woman" Anthony had an advantage in memory over Stanton, the wife and mother. As in her cutting remark about the "dessicated" Lucy Stone, Blatch was using modern standards for sexual activity to rehabilitate her mother, at the expense of allegedly more Victorian and less sexual women's rights leaders, notably the unmarried Anthony. But in addition, Blatch suspected that Stanton, who had her own family, was not available for general historical appropriation; whereas Anthony, whose life was the cause, functioned as a *symbolic* mother for feminists, calling forth all the sentiment that can be invested in such figures. Thus Gertrude Stein titled her modernist yet reverent opera about Anthony *The Mother of Us All*.[53] And Dorr, in her own effort to appropriate Anthony's historical cachet, referred to the campaign for a woman suffrage amendment as "Susan's child," which subsequent NAWSA leaders had "abandonned."[54]

Stimulated by her criticisms in the Dorr and Blackwell books, Blatch came to feel that she must do even more to preserve her mother's memory. She especially wanted a "very aggressive biography . . . a stirring, fighting volume" on her mother, but was unable or unwilling to write it herself and critical of "the untrained persons" who were "making up history."[55]

51. Blatch to Lutz, n.d., in Alma Lutz Papers, Vassar College.
52. Blatch to Lutz, n.d. (probably September 1933), ibid.
53. Gertrude Stein and Virgil Thomson, *The Mother of Us All* (New York, 1977).
54. Dorr, *Susan B. Anthony*, 355.
55. Blatch to Lutz, September 2, 1934, and n.d. (perhaps July 26, 1933), both in Alma Lutz Papers, Vassar College.

So when Alma Lutz, a young member of the National Woman's Party who had previously written a biography of Stanton's teacher Emma Willard, began to correspond with her about her mother, Blatch knew she had found Stanton's biographer. By 1931 or 1932, they had embarked together on a life of Stanton. Blatch made sure to include in it every hint of sexual adventuresomeness she could find in her mother's life: Stanton's unrequited love for her sister's husband is prominently featured. Separate chapters are also devoted to "that dangerous subject, divorce," and to Stanton's role in the Beecher/Tilton scandal. Blatch also began work on her own memoirs of the final phases of the suffrage movement. Both books were published by Alma Lutz, after Blatch's death, in 1940.[56]

ARCHIVING WOMEN'S HISTORY: ENTRUSTING THE PAST TO THE FUTURE

In the late 1920s, about the time she began to imagine a biography of her mother, Blatch arranged for Stanton's papers to be deposited at the Library of Congress.[57] "How beautifully you prepared her papers for the Congressional Library and for posterity," Mary Beard wrote when she saw them some time later. "All your penned notations, all your ties, and folders touch me to the core."[58] Blatch's decision to place the raw materials of her mother's life in the public domain was a democratic archival act, in contrast to her earlier, intrusive editing of her mother's autobiography.[59] Susan B. Anthony had much earlier donated her own book collection and several scrapbooks of newspaper clippings—though not her personal papers—to the Library of Congress; the librarian of Congress agreed to her request that the books be kept separately and prominently featured, but his successor allowed Anthony's collection to be merged into the general holdings.[60] Until Blatch deposited Stanton's papers, the only significant manuscript collection in a public depository concerned with the history of women's rights consisted of papers donated by Carrie

56. Alma Lutz, *Created Equal: A Biography of Elizabeth Cady Stanton, 1815–1902* (New York, 1940); Harriet Stanton Blatch and Alma Lutz, *Challenging Years: The Memoirs of Harriot Stanton Blatch* (New York, 1940).

57. The Library of Congress "Case File" dates the initial deposit as September 1928.

58. Beard to Blatch, January 24 [1937], in Alma Lutz Papers, Vassar College.

59. The chief of the Manuscript Division of the Library of Congress wrote to Alice Stone Blackwell in 1915 for her mother's papers, but Blackwell ignored his request and the papers did not arrive at the library until 1961: Introduction to *Register of Papers in the Manuscript Division of the Library of Congress: The Blackwell Family, Carrie Chapman Catt, and the National American Woman Suffrage Association* (Washington, D.C., 1975), iv.

60. Leonard N. Beck, "The Library of Susan B. Anthony," *Quarterly Journal of the Library of Congress* 32 (1975): 325–35.

Chapman Catt to the New York Public Library in 1923. Catt was so dissatisfied with the way her papers were managed that in 1938 she sent the remainder to the Library of Congress.[61]

The lack of interest, slow pace, and outright mismanagement that characterized the archiving of the materials of women's history eventually drew the attention of Mary Beard, so often regarded as the only woman active in the development of women's history in this period. It was in Beard, with her assiduous promotion of the systematic archiving of women's history sources through the 1930s, that the first stage in the development of women's history can be said to have culminated. Beard was a suffrage activist before she was a historian. In 1933, in the midst of all the new activity and excitement about the recording of women's past, Beard's anthology on women's history in the United States, *America through Women's Eyes,* appeared.[62] The book included selections from many of the new feminist histories of women's rights: Sachs's biography of Woodhull and Blackwell's life of Stone were excerpted; many selections from the *History of Woman Suffrage* were included as well. Blatch's writings were also featured in the anthology. This book signifies the beginning of Beard's passionate project of gathering and reinterpreting women's history.

Beard's goal was to use the materials of women's history to criticize the politics of "equality." She was beginning to develop a feminist critique of the history of feminism, whether or not she fully realized she was doing so. Inasmuch as the complexities and contradictions of Beard's work continue to permeate the field of women's history, the historical context in which she labored is important to establish. Her opposition to a version of women's past that focused too exclusively on woman's subordination is related to other challenges to the master narrative of suffrage history. For all the originality of Beard's approach to women's history, her work as a historian was not sua genera but an enterprise she shared with others, who, like her, were concerned with women's past as part of their commitment to women's future.[63]

Beard's greatest contribution to the development of women's history was her leadership in the archiving of the materials of women's past. Until original documents were collected by concerned participants, deposited

61. Catt to Helen Tufts Bailey, September 29, 1927, and Catt to Blackwell, February 4, 1938, both in Carrie Chapman Catt Papers, Library of Congress. In the 1927 letter Catt mentioned that her gift to the New York Public Library filled six file cases of four drawers each; the holdings currently under Catt's name in the library's Rare Book Division are much smaller.

62. Mary R. Beard, *America through Women's Eyes* (New York, 1933).

63. I owe a debt of gratitude to Nancy Cott for stimulating discussions on many of these points.

with sympathetic archivists, and made available in public depositories, the past of the women's rights movement could never become "history"; it lacked a public dimension and the capacity to outlive the individuals who had participated in it. In the 1930s, as important figures and then their children died, a few collections of papers were deposited; the California suffragist Alice Park arranged for her papers to go to the Los Angeles Public Library, and Swarthmore College bought Jane Addams's papers. But these were drops in the barrel compared to what was out there in attics and basements, being ignored, destroyed, and otherwise lost. The demoralization of women's rights leaders combined with the public's disinterest in the cause to create a situation in which depositories neither sought out nor were offered primary source collections in women's history.

The importance of publicly available documents as an antidote for the fragility of the past and the rapidity with which memory fades can be seen in a fascinating incident concerning Blatch, Beard, and Stanton. When *America through Women's Eyes* was published, Blatch chided Beard for omitting her mother's historical contribution and the rich history of women's rights to which she was a key. But Beard, it seems, knew little about the nature and scope of Stanton's social thought, or of the political tradition within women's rights which she represented. Stanton's papers were now available at the Library of Congress, however, so Blatch was able to direct Beard to them. Beard found them a revelation. "I have longed to rush in upon you with my excitement over your mother! . . ." she wrote Blatch. "I consider your mother a basic thinker and it is genuine delight to get closer to her in the way you have made possible. . . . I was so ignorant that I feared I should not find the fundamental economic thought [in her papers]. Thank god, it is there!"[64] Exposure to the range of Stanton's thought had a positive impact on Beard's assessment of the feminist tradition. Soon after reading Stanton's writings, she wrote an article titled "Feminism as a Social Phenomenon," in which she gave an appreciative account of the early phases of women's rights.[65]

In other words, the deliberate collection and preservation of source materials was necessary to establish the contribution to public life even of a figure as well known as Stanton. Women of equivalent historical significance—Frances Willard and Charlotte Perkins Gilman—were not so lucky as Stanton; because their papers were held back until the 1960s (by organizational and familial protectors respectively), their role in history became less and less visible. Perhaps if Beard had known more of

64. Beard to Blatch, January 24, 1937, in Alma Lutz Papers, Vassar College.
65. Mary R. Beard, "Feminism as a Social Phenomenon" (1940), in Lane, *Mary Ritter Beard*.

the rich history of the women's rights movement, she might have condemned it less.

Beginning in the mid-1930s, Beard organized a feminist movement for the preservation and promotion of women's history. The Hungarian feminist and pacifist Rosika Schwimmer had originally posed the idea of a World Center for Women's Archives. Schwimmer's concerns were both scholarly and political. A European, antifascist, and Jew, Schwimmer was deeply pessimistic about what the future held for women. Archives were a way to preserve what was most inspiring about the past until such time as women would be in a position to remember it. "It is at this period of retrogression in women's rights and pacifist activities," Schwimmer wrote in 1935, "that it becomes of utmost importance to assemble the facts of women's struggle and achievements during the last century at least, so that historians of the future will find it possible to establish the truth about today."[66] Blatch suggested that Schwimmer present her idea to Mary Beard, who dedicated herself to the project from 1935 until the eve of World War II.

Beard was joined by many other American feminists and former suffragists, who needed little to convince them of the importance of collecting and preserving the sources of women's history. The hostility between Blatch and Blackwell faded, as both served as trustees to the project. As Schwimmer had sensed earlier from a European perspective, preserving women's history was a way, perhaps the only way, to serve the cause of women's equality in those years. Eventually Beard's World Center for Women's Archives fell victim to the global tragedies of the 1940s (and to lingering factional battles among former suffragists). However, what are still the two major depositories of women's history sources in the United States, the Sophia Smith Collection at Smith College and the Schlesinger Library at Radcliffe College, begun in 1942 and 1943 respectively, were spin-offs of the World Center project. As war settled on women and men alike, Carrie Chapman Catt gloomily predicted that "the women's movement will be forgotten and *almost* buried in the great tragedies that have succeeded it. So I think it is very important to put all the memorial collections available into museums and libraries while we are still alive. There may be some persons who desire to investigate in the direction of the woman movement and there should be source materials to aid them."[67]

66. Rosika Schwimmer, "A World's Center for Women's Archives," *Equal Rights,* October 5, 1935, 245; Maryann Turner, *Biblioteca Femina: A Herstory of Book Collections Concerning Women* (New York, 1978), 35–40.

67. Catt to Blackwell, September 13, 1943, in Carrie Chapman Catt Papers, Library of Congress.

AFTERWORD

It was more than two decades before Catt's hesitant prophecy was ful-
filled. With a few notable exceptions in the intervening decades, the
women's history project begun by former suffragists and feminists of the
1920s and 1930s was not resumed until the late 1960s and early 1970s.
Since then, women's history has grown into a large, thriving, and remarkably popular enterprise. Unlike our predecessors, most of us who write
and teach it are academics. This circumstance has had an enormous—and
not entirely positive—impact on the expansiveness with which we pose
our questions, the boldness with which we answer them, and our willingness and ability to recognize the contemporary concerns that underlie our
reconsideration of the past. At the same time, though it is increasingly
fashionable to condemn the taming of radical intellectual life within institutions of higher learning, the admission of women (and women's concerns) into the academy actually represents a tremendous advance. For
the first time, someone other than white gentlemen have the freedom
(and the income) to develop, teach, and write their own understandings
of the past.

But since the immediate context of most women's historians is the
university, we tend to be more conscious of academic and disciplinary
influences on our work than social and political ones. The response of
historians to the suit brought by the Equal Employment Opportunities
Commission against Sears, Roebuck in the 1980s for failure to promote
significant numbers of women to high-commission sales jobs was a good
sign: faced with an overt political conflict over the contemporary implications of women's history, most women in the field took a side and almost
none hid behind the facade of scholarly neutrality or indifference to controversial issues.[68] But much of the time, the contemporary political
meanings of our work remain subtextual, often even to ourselves. This
exercise in historiography should further quicken our political sensibilities
as women's historians. From our predecessors we may learn not to patrol
our own interpretive borders or insist on politically correct history, but
to become more politically conscious about the history we are crafting.
The more we learn about the historiography not only of previous generations of women's history but of our own as well, the more aware we will
be of the larger context in which we work.

68. See Ruth Milkman, "Woman's History and the Sears Case," *Feminist Studies* 12
(1986): 375–400; Alice Kessler-Harris, "EEOC v. Sears, Roebuck and Co.: A Personal
Account," *Radical History Review*, no. 35 (1986), 57–79.

10

The Political Uses of Alienation: W. E. B. Du Bois on Politics, Race, and Culture, 1903–1940

Thomas C. Holt

Certainly one of the most quoted passages in African-American letters is found in the first of W. E. B. Du Bois's poignant and haunting collection of essays, *The Souls of Black Folk*. Since it is the axiomatic text embracing key themes I wish to explore in this essay, I will quote it in full.

> After the Egyptian and Indian, the Greek and Roman, the Teuton and Mongolian, the Negro is a sort of seventh son, born with a veil, and gifted with second-sight in this American world,—a world which yields to him no true self-consciousness, but only lets him see himself through the revelation of the other world. It is a peculiar sensation, this double-consciousness, this sense of always looking at one's self through the eyes of others, of measuring one's soul by the tape of a world that looks on in amused contempt and pity. One ever feels his twoness,— an American, a Negro; two souls, two thoughts, two unreconciled strivings; two warring ideals in one dark body, whose dogged strength alone keeps it from being torn asunder.
>
> The history of the American Negro is the history of this strife,—this longing to attain self-conscious manhood, to merge his double self into a better and truer self. In this merging he wishes neither of the older selves to be lost. He would not Africanize America, for America has too much to teach the world and Africa. He would not bleach his Negro soul in a flood of white Americanism, for he knows that Negro

Reprinted from *American Quarterly* 42, no. 2 (June 1990): 301–23. Copyright © 1990 American Studies Association.

I am much indebted to Nellie McKay and to Leora Auslander, my colleague at Chicago, for their helpful comments and suggestions.

blood has a message for the world. He simply wishes to make it possible for a man to be both a Negro and an American, without being cursed and spit upon by his fellows, without having the doors of Opportunity closed roughly in his face.[1]

This poetic passage appeared in the essay "Of Our Spiritual Strivings," a slightly revised version of an earlier publication in the August 1897 issue of *Atlantic Monthly*,[2] which was, in turn, a reformulation of a paper presented in March of that year to the American Negro Academy (a recently formed organization of black intellectuals). Comparison of these texts suggests not only the trajectory of Du Bois's thought, but the intellectual struggle it entailed. The earliest version, "The Conservation of the Races," suggests not only the social-biological reality of race[3]—despite difficulties defining it—but also the utility of racial differences for social progress, a theme to which Du Bois would frequently return. In that essay Du Bois published his earliest (and least poetic) formulation of the paradox of double-consciousness:

Here, then, is the dilemma, and it is a puzzling one, I admit. No Negro who has given earnest thought to the situation of his people in America has failed, at some time in life, to find himself at these cross-roads; has failed to ask himself at some time: what, after all, am I? Am I an American or am I a Negro? Can I be both? Or is it my duty to cease to be a Negro as soon as possible and be an American? If I strive as a Negro, am I not perpetuating the very cleft that threatens and separates black and white America? Is not my only possible practical aim the subduction of all that is Negro in me to the American? Does my black blood place upon me any more obligation to assert my nationality than German, or Irish, or Italian blood would?

1. W. E. Burghardt Du Bois, *The Souls of Black Folk: Essays and Sketches* (Chicago, 1903), 3–4.

2. *Atlantic Monthly* 80 (August 1897): 194–98. Though the differences between "Of Our Spiritual Strivings" and "The Strivings of the Negro People" are few, they are significant. Deletions and emendations render the 1903 version more emphatic about the "gifts" and "latent genius" of blacks and more direct about American racism (for example, "the doors of Opportunity closed roughly in his face" substituted for "losing the opportunity for self-development"). The 1903 essay also has a stronger political resonance, arising less from changes in the text than from its necessarily intertextual reading with others in the collection, which challenge both the leadership of Booker T. Washington and American capitalism. Cf. Manning Marable, *W. E. B. Du Bois: Black Radical Democrat* (Boston, 1986), 48–49.

3. Anthony Appiah has provided a penetrating exploration of Du Bois's vacillation between a biological and a social-historical definition of race. While I agree with much of his analysis, I suspect—if I read him correctly—that he slights the force of social practice in constituting "races" historically without regard to biological or cultural realities. "The

This "incessant self-questioning" stifles "action," "responsibility," and "enterprise," leaving the best "energy," "talent," and "blood" of the race paralyzed, thus surrendering the field of action to "every rascal and demagogue who chooses to cloak his selfish deviltry under the veil of race pride."[4]

On the surface, both passages have as their theme the fundamental duality of black life in America, the paradox of being so intimately a part of the national culture and yet so starkly apart from it; or, as Du Bois puts it, "an outcast and a stranger in mine own house" (3). In the 1903 essay, alienation is material, cultural, and spiritual. Blacks are builders of the economic infrastructure, yet dispossessed of its fruits; creators of one of its truly original native cultures, in story and song, yet culturally demeaned and maligned; faithful adherents to the nation's basic ideals and values, yet shunned, abused, and stigmatized as if an alien people.

Yet, the contrasts between these two formulations are also interesting. "The Conservation of Races" is addressed to a black audience; indeed, it is an exhortation to the "talented tenth" for self-appointed racial leadership. It begins with an assertion of the reality of racial differences, against which it is vain to protest; blacks are of a different "blood" and are aliens in their own land. The passage quoted comes in the middle of the essay, following another that poses for black intellectuals a choice between assimilation and the affirmation of racial solidarity and group action. It is a Hamlet-like portrait in which black intellectuals are poised at a crossroads, where they must choose between racial suicide and racial solidarity; hence, the exhortation *to conserve* the race. They are admonished to put aside the self-questioning, confusion, hesitation, and vacillation that thwarts resolution and action, leaving the race vulnerable to charlatans who only exploit race consciousness. In words that very well could have come from contemporary African-American conservatives like Glenn Loury or Thomas Sowell, Du Bois rails against black immorality, the breakdown of family, and the enemy within. "Unless we conquer our present vices they will conquer us," he thunders. It is worth noting that when he wrote this warning Du Bois was fresh from his study of the Philadelphia ghetto and that his tone here is consistent with *The Philadelphia Negro*.

By contrast, *Souls of Black Folk* marks Du Bois's conscious turn toward active political engagement. It is a sustained attack both on the sterile and pusillanimous leadership of Booker T. Washington and the materialist ethos of American capitalism to which Washington's philosophy was in-

---

Uncompleted Argument: Du Bois and the Illusion of Race," in *"Race," Writing, and Difference,* ed. Henry Louis Gates Jr. (Chicago, 1986), 21–37.

4. *The Conservation of the Races,* Occasional Paper no. 2 (Washington, D.C.: American Negro Academy, 1897), in *Pamphlets and Leaflets by W. E. B. Du Bois,* ed. Herbert Aptheker (White Plains, 1986), 5.

debted. "Of Our Spiritual Strivings" sets forth the major themes to be explicated throughout the following essays. Although many of the themes of "Conservation of the Races" are present in this text, too, the tone is much different, and the paradox seems somehow deeper and more subtle. Possibly, this difference is because the essay is addressed primarily to a white audience. Yet, read against the texts and themes Du Bois would develop over the following forty years, "Strivings" also reflects a deeper, more subtle exploration of the dilemma originally posed in "Conservation," notwithstanding that only a few months separated their respective composition.

In "Strivings," blacks are not so much aliens as alienated. It is not culture difference but cultural disfranchisement that shapes their struggle. Their artisans, ministers, doctors, and artists are deprived both of the means to pursue their crafts to higher standards and the recognition of the worth of indigenous material and creativity. Although Du Bois writes of "the innate love of harmony and beauty that set the ruder souls of his people a-dancing and a-singing" (5), for the most part, African-American culture appears as the product of a special experience—in this instance slavery and a hard freedom—rather than a special providence or provenance. Thus, if the *specialness* of black culture is a consequence of the uniqueness of black experience, it follows, too, that that culture is not a fixed entity, not a system or structure, not a grammar to be decoded. It is—like race, perhaps—contingent, contested, and historical.[5]

Here, then, racial difference is more clearly a socially constructed phenomenon rather than a biological reality.[6] It is not even a given of human consciousness but must be summoned there from the social environment. The passage quoted is the third paragraph of the essay, and it follows a

5. I want to suggest here that it might help in reading Du Bois's discussion of culture if we stressed qualities of openness rather than closedness, process rather than patterns in cultural formation. This conception is one suggested, for example, by Renato Rosaldo, when he writes: "In contrast with the classic view [of anthropology], which posits culture as a self-contained whole made up of coherent patterns, culture can arguably be conceived as a more porous array of intersections where distinct processes crisscross from within and beyond its borders": *Culture & Truth: The Remaking of Social Analysis* (Boston, 1989), 20.

6. Like most Victorian intellectuals, Du Bois believed in a notion of race that conflated biology, culture, and nationality. As such, it did not imply rigid genetic determinism but, in fact, lent itself to the more modern notion that race is socially constructed. In Du Bois's mind, it was *geist* or spirit fashioned out of a common experience and struggle. In the 1950s, he would write: ". . . for race was not color; it was inborn oneness of spirit and aim and wish": *Black Flame* 2:128. Nonetheless, in his earlier writings, race appears much less socially contingent and much more a fixed, even immutable fact of identity. Cf. Appiah, "Uncompleted Argument." On the development of nineteenth-century racism, see Reginald Horsman, *Race and Manifest Destiny: The Origins of American Racial Anglo-Saxonism* (Cambridge, 1981), and Ronald Takaki, *Iron Cages: Race and Culture in Nineteenth-Century America* (New York, 1980).

description of Du Bois's *discovery,* as a child, of racial discrimination, when a young schoolmate insulted him. That insult stimulated a consciousness of his difference, and of himself in relation to his schoolmates that he had not felt before. Thereafter, the "sky was bluest when I could beat my mates at examination-time, or beat them at a foot-race, or even beat their stringy heads." He had to reconstitute his relation to his world, and in the process his consciousness of acting and being in that world. "Between me and the other world there is ever an unasked question: unasked by some through feelings of delicacy; by others through the difficulty of rightly framing it. . . . How does it feel to be a problem?" In its opening paragraphs, then, the 1903 essay frames the problematic question of how one achieves mature self-consciousness and an integrity or wholeness of self in an alienating environment. This problem would become the dominant focus—political and cultural—of Du Bois's life and work.[7]

Introduced here, too, is the metaphor of the veil, a leitmotif in Du Bois's writing that summons multiple variations on the theme of sight and insight. Falling between the white and the black worlds, the veil obscures vision—vision of self and of other. The problem shifts subtly from being a matter of what we are—a race apart—to how we are seen, and how we see ourselves. The pain of prejudice springs not only from the cold stare of whites but also from one's invisibility to them. Equally important is the capacity for self-recognition because it forms the essential basis for action and struggle. In this essay, the emphasis is less on the black immorality and venality excoriated in "Conservation" than the unfathomable endurance and strength of an oppressed people. Blacks have gifts for the world—both current and potential. The goal is not social endogamy or black nationalism but to be "a co-worker in the kingdom of culture" (4).

Neither is this essay merely a plea for tolerance and cultural pluralism. The suffering of "this historic race" gives it a claim to specialness, to have "a message for the world," and with that comes also the duty to change the world. More specifically, black intellectuals, "the talented tenth," have a special duty to their race, and the race could be the saviors of humankind. Thus, the struggle for black self-realization becomes, in turn, a struggle for all people.

Variations on these themes—suspended duality, unresolved paradox, perpetual alienation—appear throughout Du Bois's long and prolific career. His recognition of both the intractability and the efficacy of this double-consciousness is one reason that Du Bois has avoided interpretation by most scholars. His major biographers find him incomprehensible

---

7. *Souls of Black Folk,* 1–2.

and inconsistent; they portray him lurching between the antithetical and contradictory goals of black nationalism and racial integration.[8] There has been a persistent misreading of Du Bois and a misperception of the basic truths about the African-American experience that he did so much to disclose. Indeed, Du Bois's paradoxical positions may be taken as somehow emblematic of the African-American experience generally. By that I mean, African-Americans *live* a kind of paradox embodied in their very lives, which are shaped profoundly by conflicts of identity and purpose. Although this paradox of crosscutting racial and national identities articulates differently within different class strata, it marks the lives of all African-Americans because all experience racial alienation in some form— social, economic, or political.

For example, a sharecropper like Nate Shaw expounds an attachment to the American work ethic that is clearly inconsistent with his situation, one in which maximum work effort literally does not pay. He "accepts" that ideology, nonetheless, and organizes his life *as if it were true,* even as he understands that the opportunity it implies is an illusion. Shaw's "acceptance" is not a reflection of false consciousness, however, but a curious blend of pragmatism, hope, and fatalism, which has characterized the black response to an historical experience of extreme and arbitrary oppression.[9]

Pressing the logic of Du Bois's formulation suggests a radical proposition: that African-Americans should celebrate their alienation, for *it* is the source of "second-sight in this American world." Although Du Bois implies in the 1903 version of the paradox the eventual resolution of the divided self in historical time, "to merge his double self into a better and truer self," much of what he writes later suggests that African-Americans accept, even embrace, the contradiction and paradox arising from dual identities and consciousness. Because they live in two worlds at once, African-Americans possess the power to see where others are blind.[10] Alienation—raised to a conscious level, cultivated, and directed—has revolutionary potential. The insight of the oppressed is neither innate nor inherent; it must be worked for, struggled for. Once achieved, it becomes a tool for probing the deeper meanings and contradictions of experience

8. The striking exceptions among Du Bois biographers are Arnold Rampersad and, more recently, Manning Marable, both of whom generally defend Du Bois against charges of inconsistency. *The Art and Imagination of W. E. B. Du Bois* (Cambridge, 1976), esp. 163–64; Marable, *W. E. B. Du Bois* (Boston, 1986). Julius Lester also discounts such criticism in *The Seventh Son: The Thought and Writings of W. E. B. Du Bois* (New York, 1971), 1:112.

9. Theodore Rosengarten, *All God's Dangers: The Life of Nate Shaw* (New York, 1974).

10. One might compare these notions about sight and insight to the African concept of *ashè* as discussed in Robert Farris Thompson, *Flash of the Spirit: African and Afro-American Art and Philosophy* (New York, 1983).

and for creating change. For blacks, then, racial alienation can be the counterpart of class alienation, and it can serve the same revolutionary purposes.

It is not likely, of course, that Du Bois realized the fuller, more radical implications of his propositions in 1903, and certainly not in 1897. Over the following four decades, however, the proposition that double-consciousness could be both intractable and efficacious became more explicit in and central to Du Bois's thought and politics. It was an idea hammered out of intellectual and political struggles. On the one hand, he grappled with reconciling Marxian and Freudian explanations of the human condition while, on the other hand, he struggled to fashion an organizational strategy at the NAACP appropriate both to the hegemony of world capitalism and the tenacity of racial prejudice. For Du Bois, intelligence and politics, thought and experience, were necessarily interactive; his theories of race and anti-racist struggle—which many of his contemporaries and later historians have found so confusing and vacillating—evolved over a period of years out of the interaction between his intellectual and political labors. To understand him, therefore, one must endeavor to read his eloquent texts against the gritty backdrop of the organizational confrontations that simultaneously engaged him.

An analysis on these two levels approximates Du Bois's own, since he hardly distinguished between written texts and the text of experience. Indeed, his technique was almost naively reflexive, in that his own life became the text, the point of departure, for each of his major explorations of race, culture, and politics.

Much of Du Bois's value to us, certainly, is in his extraordinary responsiveness to the world around him. He lived such a long life, through periods of rapid change in the black experience, and was incredibly prolific throughout his life, especially during his quarter of a century editorship of the *Crisis,* where his responses were monthly. Thus, we literally observe Du Bois witnessing the fundamental transformation of African-American life from the mid-nineteenth to the mid-twentieth centuries, from a world lit by candlelight to the nuclear fire. It would have been strange, indeed, if he *had* remained "consistent."

Moreover, his multiple careers—historian, sociologist, poet, novelist, journalist, activist—were all crucial to his life project, providing multiple perspectives and multiple voices. Several of Du Bois's biographers have accepted, to some degree, the notion that his scholarship suffered because of his politics or that his scholarly demeanor undercut his political effectiveness; but Du Bois's life project was to develop a theory of society interactively with and through social and political practice ("work, culture, liberty") in order to achieve enlightenment *and* emancipation.[11]

11. I am thinking here of the interwar origins of the Frankfurt School and the development of critical theory, which like Du Bois drew on Marxian and Freudian thought. This theme is one that I hope to develop in a separate paper.

Du Bois's witness to the transformation in black life during the 1930s Depression is a useful period for exploring the maturing of his ideas about theory and practice that were merely implied in *Souls*. Here, one can appreciate the subtleties and limitations of his philosophy of racial uplift when tested by social crisis, the difficulties inherent to the African-American liberation struggle generally, and the systematic misreading and unresponsiveness of many of his critics.

This period was easily the most controversial in Du Bois's long life. Confronted with the Depression crisis, he argued for a fundamental shift in NAACP strategy: the fostering of independent black economic enterprises. Provocatively, deliberately, he labeled this scheme "voluntary segregation." After a heated debate over this issue in the pages of the 1934 *Crisis*, Du Bois resigned from the NAACP. Although most have recognized that other factors contributed to this rupture with the organization he had helped to found, scholars generally assert that the self-segregation issue was its fundamental cause, which, not coincidentally, was the interpretation that his antagonists at the NAACP sought to promote. For example, the Chicago branch urged the national office of the NAACP to accept Du Bois's resignation but to deliver a statement pointing to segregation as the cause of the conflict and not his economic program. Otherwise, Du Bois would "escape the burden of approving segregation," and the NAACP would be charged with "failing to rescue Negro workers and tenant farmers from their plight."[12]

Du Bois's ideas brought down upon him a firestorm of criticism from his contemporaries and dismissive judgments from some of his biographers. He was accused of reviving the Booker T. Washington "separatist" philosophy which he had done so much to scotch. From Jamaica the exiled Marcus Garvey accused him of plagiarizing his self-help scheme, a criticism endorsed by a biographer of Garvey.[13] Du Bois's biographers portray him as an old man, out of touch with reality, who had lost his way. Francis Broderick titles his chapter that treats this subject "Negro Chauvinism." There Du Bois is described as "retreating" to older formulas, "into the protective shell of his own race." Elliott Rudwick also calls Du Bois's plan a reactionary scheme and quotes the negative contemporary reaction approvingly.[14]

The irony is that Du Bois saw this period as his most creative. After a

12. Chicago Branch to NAACP, July 8, 1934; Irvin C. Mollison to Bd. of Directors, July 3, 1934, "Du Bois Controversy," Administrative Files, NAACP Papers, Washington, D.C.

13. Tony Martin, *Race First: The Ideological and Organizational Struggles of Marcus Garvey and the Universal Negro Improvement Association* (Westport, Conn., 1976), 309–10.

14. Roy Wilkins describes his and other contemporary reactions in *Standing Fast: The Autobiography of Roy Wilkins* (New York, 1982), 152–53. Francis L. Broderick, *W. E. B. Du Bois: Negro Leader in a Time of Crisis* (Stanford, 1959), 150; Elliott M. Rudwick, *W. E. B. Du Bois: Propagandist of the Negro Protest* (New York, 1978), 275–80.

half century of study and struggle along the color line, he had found the key to a theory of race relations and, thus, a program of racial uplift consistent with the paradoxes of the African-American experience. It is worth noting that in both the quasi-autobiographical *Dusk of Dawn*, published in 1940 (he was seventy-two), and the *Autobiography* of the late 1950s, shortly after which he joined the Communist Party, Du Bois remained content with much of the controversial program he had formulated in the 1930s.

The key fifth chapter of *Dusk to Dawn* is titled "The Concept of Race," which Du Bois significantly describes as not so much a concept "as a group of contradictory forces, facts and tendencies" (133). Thus, race no longer has the social-biological concreteness implied in the 1897 essay. Here, many of the themes of "The Conservation of the Races" and "Of Our Spiritual Strivings" appear again, but now reformulated in the context of Du Bois's more sophisticated understanding of human behavior and social action. The veil that once shrouded blacks from view, obscuring both their problems and virtues and their latent powers, has changed. It is now "some thick sheet of invisible but horribly tangible plate glass" sealing off a "dark cave," within which blacks are "entombed souls . . . hindered in their natural movement, expression, and development . . ." (130–31). The veil has become an imprisoning wall.

Blacks can be seen by the outside world now, but not heard. Consequently, all their gestures and expressions are incomprehensible, even absurd, to the white outsiders. After a while, the inmates begin to wonder if the outside world is real; they tend to become narrow, provincial, their interests and activities confined to the tomb; they become "inured to their experience." On the other hand, the wild and suicidal efforts of those who attempt to break through the glass (the revolutionaries, the deviants) only excite horror and terror in the outside world.[15]

From this really quite horrible parable, Du Bois concludes that outsiders—however well intentioned—cannot know the experience of those within and thus cannot speak for or lead them. Leadership can only come from among the entombed. Such leaders must be "race men," unselfish, loyal, and committed to unending sacrifice for the collective good. In chapter 7, "The Colored World Within," Du Bois restates the group economy idea, a project that cannot succeed without the dedicated and disciplined leadership of "race men."

In the final chapter of *Dusk of Dawn*, Du Bois describes the intellectual

---

15. *Dusk of Dawn: An Essay toward an Autobiography of a Race Concept* (1940) (New York, 1968), 130–33. Compare this reaction to racism with the passage in *Souls* where "their youth shrunk into tasteless sycophancy, into silent hatred of the pale world about them and mocking distrust of everything white," 3.

sources for the rethinking and reformulation of his social philosophy. During the period preceding his articulation of the self-segregation scheme and of his subsequent break with the NAACP, he had made the twin discoveries of Marx and Freud. From Marx he learned that there was a deeper structural basis for racial oppression; that it was not enough to fight for integration into a house that was inherently flawed. From Freud he learned to appreciate the irrationality of prejudice and its deep-seatedness. "I now began to realize that in the fight against race prejudice, we are not facing simply the rational, conscious determination of white folk to oppress us; we are facing age-long complexes sunk now largely to unconscious habit and irrational urge, which demanded on our part not only the patience to wait, but the power to entrench ourselves for a long siege against the strongholds of color caste."[16]

What Du Bois claimed, then, was that his program was not defensive and reactionary, but forward looking and militant. The product of a long gestation period, his plan represented a blending from eclectic, yet seminal, modern intellectual forces: Marxism and Freudianism. Furthermore, it was not a retreat to nationalism, but a recognition of the international dimensions of the racial conflict, indeed, that African-Americans could be the vanguard of an international assault on class privilege. This dimension is something that neither Booker T. Washington nor Garvey could have envisioned.

In many ways Du Bois was naive and, certainly, misread the flow of future events—but then so did many other radicals during the Great Depression. Yet, I believe it is necessary to accurately represent his thinking processes and to acknowledge the integrity of those processes as he describes them. When we examine the content and timing of his writings in the *Crisis* together with his personal correspondence during this period, his reminiscences in *Dusk of Dawn* do ring true. This period was not one of despair and withdrawal but one of intense and excited intellectual creativity. In many ways, Du Bois was not retreating to older, discredited formulas but advancing toward new formulations that might address an as yet dimly foreseen crisis.

During the late twenties and early thirties, the Marxian theme of class struggle and the Freudian theory of a nonrational, unconscious basis for human behavior were woven into Du Bois's scheme to build a separate black economy. Throughout this period there remained a clear distinction between Du Bois's analysis of the problem, which was Marxist, and his solution, which was nationalist. "I am not turning to nationalism to escape Communism," he wrote in April 1933 to George Streator, his assistant at the *Crisis*.

16. *Dusk of Dawn*, 296.

I could not have communism if I wanted it. There is no such choice before me. The only thing that I have to choose is annihilation by American capitalism peacemeal [sic] [or] racial organization in self-defense. Don't let communists or anybody else fool you into thinking that internationalism is at hand and that we have only to join it. Negro prejudice still lives.[17]

The onset of the Depression was significant in confirming his fears about the fate of blacks in twentieth-century America and in conveying a sense of urgency to his project. It was not the catalyst for that project, but rather a contributory factor, or the context for other factors. Du Bois claims to have been a socialist since before the Great War, having voted with the Party in New York City in 1912. He also had been exposed to socialist ideas during his student days in Germany. Heretofore socialist, much less Marxist, ideas had not loomed prominently in his analysis of the race problem.

Du Bois began to change after his 1926 visit to the Soviet Union, where he declared that if the Russian society he saw was the result of the Bolshevik Revolution, then he was a Bolshevik. Even this appeared to be more a reflection of Du Bois's rhetorical style than a serious commitment to Marxist-Leninist principles. Indeed, given his oft-repeated commitment to nonviolence, Du Bois appeared more likely a Fabian than a Leninist.[18]

The March 1928 issues of the *Crisis* did contain an article affirming the mutual interests of black and white workers in reforming capitalism; it also recognized that both black and white workers were blind to their common economic interests and were likely to remain so. Two months later the language was even stronger: it was "idiotic to hope that white laborers will become broad enough or wise enough to make the cause of black labor their own . . . in our day." By November 1929, Du Bois was dismissing political democracy as an ineffective form of governance because (1) "the vast majority of Americans are not intelligent," (2) they are economic slaves, and (3) the country is "ruled by organized wealth."[19]

These pronouncements seem to spring from Du Bois's basic populist sympathies; apparently, they preceded his systematic reexamination of Marxian thought. Indeed, he credits a speech at Howard University in 1930 as the catalyst for recasting his economic ideas. Interestingly, the Howard speech also has been cited as the opening gun of his campaign

17. Du Bois to George Streator, June 1933, in W. E. B. Du Bois Papers, Amherst, Mass. (microfilm copy).
18. *Crisis* 33 (November 1926): 8.
19. *Crisis* 35 (March 1928): 98 and 36 (November 1929): 374.

for the group economy/self-segregation strategy. In that speech he argued that both Booker T. Washington's program of industrial training and his own emphasis on academic education had failed, both schemes overtaken by the fundamental transformation of the American economy. But Du Bois realized that his speech was weak on practical remedies, so "he began to study Marx in earnest."[20]

By the end of that year, Du Bois—in an attack on President Herbert Hoover's policies—declared the pursuit of private profit an unsound basis upon which to organize an economy for the general good; "income [was] a social product . . . not simply the result of individual effort . . . and must be divided by human judgment." In this essay he also linked, in cryptic fashion, the pursuit of profit and the oppression of blacks: "it pays today from six to six hundred per cent to hate 'niggers' and keep them in their places."[21]

In the summer of 1932, the *Crisis* ran a symposium of black newspaper editors' views on communism and the race problem, to which Du Bois appended a recommended reading list of six books. In January 1933, he wrote Abram Harris, a black Marxist professor at Howard, requesting recommendations for additions to his own library on Marxism. "I have been re-reading Marx recently as everyone must these days." Two months later the *Crisis* published an article, "Karl Marx and the Negro," in which Du Bois declared Marx the greatest economic thinker of modern times and regretted that he had not lived to apply his "great mind . . . first hand" to the Negro problem.[22]

What is interesting about this article, however, is that while it affirms Marx's greatness, it notes the limitation of his work with respect to the race issue—simply because Marx had not addressed that issue. This, then, is the unfinished business of Marxian analysis. Marx's analysis of the problem of capitalism was sound, but the solutions as they bore on the race problem remained to be formulated. Indeed, for Du Bois, "work, culture, liberty" continued to be the keys to unlocking the paradox of race and class. "I have no faith in anything which is so scientific that it will not be swayed by perfectly human motives, and among them, race prejudice."[23] Cultural achievement would do more to break down race prejudice than anything else, he replied to a supporter, but cultural achievements of decisive scale required great economic progress.[24]

Du Bois's intellectual embrace of Marxism did not yet involve a political

20. Rampersad, *Art and Imagination,* 164.
21. Ibid.
22. *Crisis* 39 (June 1932): 190–91; Du Bois to Abram Harris, January 6, 1933, in Du Bois Papers; *Crisis* 40 (March 1933): 55–56.
23. Du Bois to Miss Martha Adamson, March 27, 1934, in Du Bois Papers.
24. Du Bois to Mrs. A. V. Williams, April 5, 1933, ibid.

embrace of American Communists, whom he regarded with utter contempt. Marx may not have known about the Negro problem, but the American Communist party of the 1930s was *willfully* ignorant. They were a group with "pitiable mental equipment," he wrote in April 1933. The only social equality their tactics would likely win for blacks was the equality of a jail cell.[25]

Notwithstanding his admiration for the Russian experiment in socialism, he asked: "What part can [American Negroes] expect to have in a socialistic state and what can they do now to bring about this realization? And my answer to this has long been clear. There is no automatic power in socialism to override and suppress race prejudice. . . . One of the worst things that Negroes could do today would be to join the American Communist Party or any of its many branches."[26]

Clearly, the source of Du Bois's contempt was the failure of the American Communists to recognize the intractability of racism among the white proletariat. At times, Du Bois argued that it was in the interests of white workers to discriminate against African-American workers. American capitalism had produced a kind of labor aristocracy whose prosperity was built on "a mud-sill of black labor."[27] At other times he insisted that racism had origins more deep seated than material interests. "White labor has to hate scabs; but it hates black scabs not because they are scabs but because they are black. It mobs white scabs to force them into labor fellowship. It mobs black scabs to starve and kill them."[28]

There was, then, a simultaneous recognition of the power of Marxian analysis of modern social ills—ills traceable to the fundamental structures of national and international capital—and of the psychological dimensions of this malady, wherein the oppressed were blinded to their true interests, wherein white workers oppressed black. The problem, then, was one of class *and* race. The solutions, likewise, had to be both internal and external to the black community.

"What is to be done?" Du Bois asked rhetorically. "There is to my mind," he wrote in a 1928 *Crisis* article,

> only one way out: Manufacturing and consumers co-operation among the major part of twelve million people on a wide and ever-increasing scale. There must be the slow, but carefully planned growth of manufacturing trusts, beginning with the raising of raw material on Negro

25. *Crisis* 40 (April 1933): 93–94.
26. "Social Planning for the Negro, Past and Present," *Journal of Negro Education* 5 (January 1936): 110–25, quoted in Julius Lester, ed., *The Seventh Son: The Thought and Writings of W. E. B. Du Bois,* vol. 2 (New York, 1971), 436.
27. *Crisis* 40 (May 1933): 103–4, 118.
28. Quoted in Lester, *Seventh Son,* 2:403.

farms; extending to its transportation on Negro trucks; its manufacture in Negro factories; its distribution to Negro co-operative stores, supported by intelligent and loyal Negro consumers.

Through such organization blacks would overcome race prejudice and monopoly capital and "insure the economic independence of the American Negro for all time."[29]

As with socialism, Du Bois had been sympathetic to the idea of producer and consumer cooperatives for more than a decade.[30] In the late twenties and early thirties, however, sympathy became commitment. Moreover, he now emphasized the power of the consumer rather than the producer. It was "a mistake to think that the economic cycle begins with production," he wrote in 1931, "rather it begins with consumption." Since America's black population exceeded that of many nations, its internal economic power as consumers should be organized. The consumer boycotts by blacks in New York City and Chicago during the early 1930s were for him proof of the latent power of consumer militancy.[31]

Du Bois's socialism saved him from a bourgeois conception of cooperation. He drew his inspiration from cooperatives he had seen in Russia and read about in Europe, not from Marcus Garvey. Nor was this plan by any means a return to the petty capitalism of Booker T. Washington. You could not build a black economy on craftsmanship and mom-and-pop stores, he argued. The American economy had been fundamentally transformed. Individual craftsmen and shopkeepers were disappearing; the old trades were "now part of highly organized combinations, financed with large capital." Concentration, consolidation, monopoly capital were the order of the day. Black labor was threatened with redundancy; it could expect help neither from big capital nor big labor. Furthermore, he wrote:

> If we simply mill contentedly after the streaming herd, with no clear idea of our own solutions of our problems, what can we expect but the contempt of reformers and slavery to a white proletariat? If we expect to enter present or future industry upon our own terms, we must have terms; we must have power; we must learn the secret of economic organization; we must submit to leadership, not of words but of ideas; we must lead the civilized part of these 12 millions of our race into an industrial phalanx that cannot be ignored, and which America and the

29. *Crisis* 35 (May 1928): 169–70.

30. Du Bois had advocated cooperatives in 1917–18 and helped form the Negro Cooperatives Guild: Rudwick, *W. E. B. Du Bois*, 195–96. See also the exchange of correspondence: Du Bois to Harry Pace, April 11, 1918; Du Bois to Elmer Cornbeck, November 4, 1918; Du Bois to James P. Warbasse, August 22, 1929, all in Du Bois Papers.

31. *Crisis* 38 (November 1931): 393 and 37 (March 1930): 102.

250   *Thomas C. Holt*

world will come to regard as a strong asset under any system and not merely as a weak and despicable liability. . . .[32]

Du Bois was equally insistent that his plan was not a return to Booker T. Washington's accommodationism. "I am convinced that the Negro has got to turn his attention primarily to his economic condition, to earning a living, and earning it in new ways," he wrote a supporter in March 1935. Yet, unlike Washington, he did not wish to make "Negro labor a part of the great industrial machine" and his plan intended "no essential change in the fight on racial segregation." He conceded that "it does mean that we have got to accept most of the segregation that we suffer today, and that there is no hope in our day or many years to come." This fact was inescapable, since *white* racial prejudice showed no sign of diminishing in the near future. "Under these circumstances, we have got to work together, and in racial groups, and if that is what my friends call Segregation, I am all for it because I have got to be."[33]

Out of such necessity could come opportunities for effective racial leadership and profound social change. A movement for economic cooperation required the leadership of "Negroes of education and intelligence who regard their education not simply as an open sesame to a privileged position, but as means of service to a disfranchised and disinherited group of workers." Thus, the "talented tenth" of 1903 was reconstituted as the revolutionary vanguard for the 1930s, who would transform a disabling condition into a creative force. Booker T. Washington's philosophy had involved "the flight of class from mass" through material accumulation, Du Bois wrote in *Dusk of Dawn,* while his own program had involved a flight of class from mass through culture. It was now clear that class and mass must unite "for the world's salvation."[34] For Du Bois, therefore, race consciousness undertook the role of class consciousness in Marxian theory: the latter was the basis for whites organizing for their liberation; the former could serve as the resource for black liberation.[35]

There was a greater chance of this occurring among blacks because of their still limited class differentiation. "We who have had the least class differentiation in wealth, can follow in the new trend and indeed lead it." In this connection, I think it is important to recognize that Du Bois was not oblivious to existing or potential class interests splitting blacks; he

32. *Crisis* 37 (March 1930): 102.
33. Du Bois to Alexina C. Barrell (Cambridge, Mass.), March 1, 1935, in Du Bois Papers.
34. *Dusk of Dawn,* 216–17.
35. Du Bois to Alexina C. Barrell (Cambridge, Mass.), March 1, 1935, in Du Bois Papers.

simply felt that such conflicts had not matured to an extent that would prevent race unity.

In a letter to a French correspondent, Du Bois contrasted the effects of Anglo-Saxon racism with the color-blind, assimilationist policies of the French colonial administration, which drew the Senegalese elite away from the masses. "The net result is rather strange. The oppressed Negro in America and in English colonies is oppressed as a group and within that group is a potential educated leadership which stands with the group and fights for it. In black France, on the other hand, the dark masses have no leaders. Their logical leaders, like Diagne, Candace and others are more French than the French, and feel, quite naturally much nearer the French people than to black Africa or brown Martinique."[36]

One of the first duties of the elite would be to reeducate the masses for the new social order, because cooperatives required "the habit and order of cooperation." The elite must establish such order and inculcate such habits:

> An economic battle has just begun. It can be studied and guided; it can teach consumers' co-operation, democracy, and socialism, and be made not simply a record and pattern for the Negro race, but a guide for the rise of the working classes throughout the world, just at the critical time when these classes are about to assume their just political domination, which is destined to become the redemption of mankind.[37]

African-Americans were specially suited, therefore, to light the way for the rest of the world. Their oppression had inured them to hardship and sacrifice; exclusion from the larger world would render the social sanctions of "the colored world within" all the more potent. Blacks could achieve greater community discipline by virtue of their oppression. "We have an instinct of race and a bond of color, in place of a protective tariff for our infant industry. We have, as police power, social ostracism within to coerce a race thrown back upon itself by ostracism without; and behind us, if we will survive, is Must, not May."[38]

Oppression bestowed more than discipline and endurance; it bestowed *sight*. The oppressed specially valued the American ideals of freedom and equality; thus, they could *see* where others could not. "Once in a while through all of us there flashes some clairvoyance, some clear idea, of what America really is. We who are dark can see America in a way that white Americans can not."[39]

36. Du Bois to Monsieur J. G. Fleury, December 1932, ibid.
37. "Does the Negro Need Separate Schools?" in Lester, *Seventh Son,* 2:416.
38. *Crisis* 40 (April 1933): 93–94.
39. "The Criteria of Negro Art," *Crisis* 32 (October 1925).

It is not difficult here to discern the continued parable of the cave. Looking through a glass darkly, neither white workers nor their black counterparts can see each other clearly. The outside leaders cannot lead the entombed. The only course open to those within the cave is to organize their inner resources—material and spiritual—to create a base from which the entire edifice can be reformed. Being black—thereby capable of gaining strength, discipline, and solidarity from their oppression—the cave dwellers are blessed "with a second-sight" into the promise *and* the broken promises of America.

> Even as you visualize such ideas [he challenged Chicago students in 1926], you know in your hearts that these are not the things you really want [referring here to American materialism]. You realize this sooner than the average white American because, pushed aside as we have been in America, there has come to us not only a certain distaste for the tawdry and flamboyant but a vision of what the world could be if it were really a beautiful world. If we had the true spirit; if we had the Seeing Eye, the Cunning Hand, the Feeling Heart; if we had, to be sure, not perfect happiness, but plenty of good hard work, the inevitable suffering that always comes with life; sacrifice and waiting, all that—but, nevertheless, lived in a world where men know, where men create, where they *realize* themselves and where they enjoy life. It is that sort of world we want to create for ourselves and for all America.[40]

Du Bois despaired of getting a hearing—much less action—on these lofty ideals and complex ideas from the NAACP leadership as it was constituted in the 1930s; and he was right. Even with the benefit of historical hindsight, Roy Wilkins—in his posthumously published autobiography, *Standing Fast*—still only saw a personal conflict between Du Bois and Executive Secretary Walter White. Even many of Du Bois's former allies saw merely a disgruntled sexagenarian. Thus, Du Bois turned for political support to the black youth—the college-bred "talented tenth," most of whom were less than half his age. Contrary to the image of an old man out of touch with reality, Du Bois actively cultivated allies in the NAACP's local branches during this period and sought to bring some of these onto the national board.[41]

These efforts began at least as early as 1932 and met with some success, but not enough to shift the balance of power within the NAACP. Six months before his resignation, Du Bois wrote to Abram Harris, one of

40. Ibid.; italics added.
41. Du Bois found strong support for his proposal to reorganize the NAACP among young people during a lecture tour through the Midwest. See Du Bois to Streator, March 21, 1934, in Du Bois Papers.

his young radical allies who fully agreed with him on the need to "purge" the NAACP leadership.[42] Du Bois complained that they were still stymied by "the opportunism of [Walter] White and the reactionary economic philosophy of the Spingarns." So far, his effort to reorganize the Board of Directors had met only limited success. Despite the addition of Harris and the support of a few others, Du Bois's faction was still "a hopeless minority within a group of elderly reactionaries." He seriously doubted that they would be strong enough "to begin a fight for the root and branch re-organization of the N.A.A.C.P."[43]

It was obvious to most knowledgeable contemporaries that Du Bois wanted to get rid of Walter White and White's alter ego Roy Wilkins. From his personal correspondence, it is clear that his friends Arthur and Joel Spingarn were targeted as well. The Spingarns were capitalists, he wrote George Streator in January 1934, and "the *Crisis,* so long as I conduct it, is going to be Socialist and Left Wing Socialist, and I am going to work out a philosophy on segregation that is going to take into account the realities of the situation in the South."[44]

Therefore, the ideological struggle over segregation took place in the context of an ongoing struggle for control of the organization. The ideological differences may have provided the occasion for debate, but its energy came from the increasingly bitter infighting, and in this, neither Du Bois nor Harris were a match for Walter White.[45] In May 1934, the Board approved a resolution barring the use of the *Crisis* to criticize the organization. Du Bois protested that he could not abide any such effort to muzzle him. He might just as well have said that the passage of this resolution signaled that he had lost his "root and branch" fight for the soul of the NAACP. In June 1934, he submitted his resignation, to be effective on July 1, 1934.[46]

42. In the letter to which Du Bois was responding, Harris, a Marxist economist at Howard University, had argued that they must purge the NAACP and that new intellectual leadership was needed to cultivate "a new set of values" among the Negro masses. He would endorse Du Bois's notion of a cooperative movement if it were connected "with the general demand for change." He could see the possibility of a consumer backlash against an increasingly cartelized industrial sector which could lead to "guild socialism." Under those circumstances, "a co-operative movement among Negroes might prove very valuable. Whatever happens it is going to take independent Negro intellectuals to furnish guidance both indirectly and directly": Abram Harris to Du Bois, January 6, 1934, ibid.

43. Du Bois to Abram Harris, January 16, 1934, ibid.

44. Du Bois to Streator, January 10, 1934, ibid.

45. The struggle apparently also involved nasty gossip about Du Bois's private life in Atlanta. George Streator to Du Bois, May 16, 1934, ibid.

46. The "gag rule" was moved by Du Bois's erstwhile ally Dr. Louis Wright in the May 14 Board meeting, which Du Bois did not attend. Of course, the full story of Du Bois's resignation would require examination of the declining fortunes of the *Crisis,* as well as the segregation issue. Certainly, there had been repeated and concerted efforts to curb Du

There was a last minute flurry of activity to find a compromise, but it was already clear to the principals what the outcome of the struggle had to be. When Du Bois—who was away from New York as a visiting professor at Atlanta University—had first heard of the Board's decision, he fired off a telegraphic message to Joel Spingarn: "My resignation is now inevitable."[47]

The events leading to Du Bois's resignation are inextricably tied to and provide a context for evaluating the evolution of his social philosophy during the late twenties and early thirties. I think it is clear that his was not the reactionary scheme of a man of failing intellectual powers, nor was it simply a defensive response to the depression. Du Bois correctly foresaw the increased concentration of American economic power, although he overestimated the staying power of 1930s radicalism. He also failed to foresee the relatively rapid and significant incorporation of blacks into many sectors of the labor movement and the New Deal. Thus, he did not foresee, perhaps even discounted, the rapid rise of a black labor aristocracy, such as that described by E. Franklin Frazier in *Black Bourgeoisie*, whose interests and values, many would argue, diverged and continue to diverge from those of the black underclass. This development undercut the notion that class forces within the black community were not as important as racial forces pressing in from without.[48]

However, he did sense that blacks would still be the last hired and first fired, and that large sectors of the potential black proletariat would never be proletarians at all, but remain outside the labor force—a permanent underclass. Because he recognized—even predicted—this development, he could not have thought that his separate economy idea could be the basis of any final solution to the race problem. These broader structural changes were issues the whole society—through the state—would have to address. The separate economy was merely a contingent, intermediate step to husband the strength of the black community for that larger strug-

Bois's independence since the magazine's first deficits appeared in the summer of 1929. All of this would necessitate another paper, however. I am convinced, nonetheless, that the resonance between philosophical differences and political animosities best explain Du Bois's decision to resign. The struggle was really for the soul of the NAACP. See "Minutes of the Board of Directors, 14 July 1930; 14 May 1934, Papers of the NAACP. Part I: Board Meetings, Annual Conferences, Speeches, and Special Reports, 1909–1950" (Frederick, Md.), microform, reel 2.

47. Du Bois to J. E. Spingarn, May 21, 1934, in Du Bois Papers. See also "Minutes of the Board of Directors," June 11 and July 9, 1934, in NAACP Papers (microform). Actually efforts to find a compromise were not exhausted until late June. As late as June 14, Du Bois expressed optimism about a solution. "Things may work out all right," he wrote his wife, Nina.

48. This failure of foresight Du Bois would recognize himself in the postwar era. See Gerald Horne, *Black and Red: W. E. B. Du Bois and the Afro-American Response to the Cold War, 1944–1963* (Albany, 1986), 224.

gle—the struggle to do away with *all* economic privilege and oppression. For Du Bois, the ultimate goal was always justice for all people. In his vision, blacks should use their unique resources to light the way for the rest of the world.

Furthermore, the organized power of black consumers was not as visionary as his critics claimed; that power would be demonstrated strongly in the Civil Rights Movement of the 1960s (and in more recent years by the Reverend Jesse Jackson's "Operation Push"). But, of course, that same Movement demonstrated the extraordinary organizational talent, dedication, and most of all, unselfish leadership necessary to mobilize that power effectively and to sustain it.

Such leadership is precisely what Du Bois assumed would be forthcoming from his talented tenth—a group he refers to in 1897 as "the first fruits of the new nation, the harbingers of that black tomorrow which is yet destined to soften the whiteness of the Teutonic today." And again in *Souls of Black Folk,* where he challenged yet again:

> Work, culture, liberty,—all these we need not singly but together, not successively but together, each growing and aiding each, and all striving toward that master ideal that swims before the Negro people, the ideal of human brotherhood, gained through the unifying ideal of Race; the ideal of fostering and developing the traits and talents of the Negro, not in opposition to or contempt for other races, but rather in large conformity to the greater ideals of the American Republic, in order that some day on American soil two world-races may give each to each those characteristics both so sadly lack. We the darker one, come even now not altogether empty-handed; there are to-day no truer exponents of the pure human spirit of the Declaration of Independence than the American Negroes; there is no true American music but the wild sweet melodies of the Negro slave; the American fairy tales and folk-lore are Indian and African; and, all in all, we black men seem the sole oasis of simple faith and reverence in a dusty desert of dollars and smartness. . . . Merely a concrete test of the underlying principles of the great republic is the Negro Problem, and the spiritual striving of the freedman's sons is the travail of souls whose burden is almost beyond the measure of their strength, but who bear it in the name of an historic race, in the name of this the land of their father's fathers, and in the name of human opportunity.[49]

Thus, in one of his earliest essays, Du Bois stakes out the main themes that mark much of his subsequent intellectual and political work. "Work,

---

49. *Souls of Black Folk,* 11–12.

culture, liberty," are key, mutually supportive values essential not only to African-American liberation, but to all humankind's effort to live a morally satisfying and useful life. They express themes of political and personal commitment, of striving for self-knowledge and a sense of self, and of the essential material and moral conditions requisite to self-realization. Yet through this passage, too, comes the continuing themes of cultural paradox: first, one must recognize and value differences in order to achieve unities; and moreover, that oppression itself valorizes and empowers its cultural products—"the wild sweet melodies," the tales and folklore, the "simple faith and reverence." Therefore, it is not only the salvation, but the duty of the oppressed to realize themselves, their powers, in order to serve the larger purpose of saving humankind. It is a visionary charge, but then, being a visionary requires that one have vision. It is helpful, too, if one has "second-sight."

PART IV

Intellectuals and
Colonizing Knowledge

11

The Preferential Option for the Poor: Liberation Theology and the End of Political Innocence

Roberto S. Goizueta

At the third general meeting of the Latin American Bishops' Conference (CELAM), held at Puebla, Mexico, in 1979, the bishops boldly proclaimed: "We affirm the need for conversion on the part of the whole Church to a preferential option for the poor."[1] In making this statement, the bishops were reaffirming the importance of the axial shift that had taken place in 1968 at Medellín, Colombia, when the Latin American Catholic Church, as an institution, had committed itself to becoming a "Church of the poor."[2] While the institutional, explicit, and public nature of this commitment signaled a new era in the history of the church in Latin America, in reality this shift reflected a dialectical retrieval of social, ecclesial, and theological movements that, in their confluence and their rootedness in Latin American history, radically transformed the traditional Christian understanding of the evangelical command to "feed the hungry" from an ethical imperative to an epistemological and theological precondition of faith.

The institutional shift represented by Medellín and Puebla accompanied the epistemological shift that reflected this sociohistorical confluence. The late 1950s and early 1960s, as Samuel Silva Gotay relates, had witnessed the "stagnation of industrialization and social development programs, which had raised the hopes of the populist movements that, in the wake of the depression of 1930, attempt[ed] to extricate themselves

---

1. John Eagleson and Philip Scharper, eds., *Puebla and Beyond: Documentation and Commentary* (Maryknoll, N.Y., 1979), 264.
2. CELAM, *Documentos finales de la II conferencia general del Episcopado latinoamericano* (Bogotá, 1969), 172–80.

from the old dependence on agricultural exports in order to substitute imports and create an internal market and a whole national economy." This crisis of liberal capitalist reform strategies in Latin America led to "a new understanding of the problem of underdevelopment as, at bottom, an understanding of the historical process of *imperialism*. This consequently yield[ed] the only possible strategy for extirpating the constant dependence of underdevelopment: liberation from the bonds to the external economy."[3] The failure of populist, reformist strategies was thus followed by the emergence and growth of revolutionary movements, many of them inspired by the Cuban revolution. At the same time, changes equally radical (in their own way) were occurring within the Roman Catholic Church. At the grass-roots level, clergy and laity were becoming involved in these social movements, and at the magisterial level (the church's teaching office), many conciliar, papal, and episcopal pronouncements seemed to encourage such involvement.

Insofar as the declarations of Medellín and Puebla represented a positive response to this sociohistorical reality (and its consequent epistemological implications), and were perceived as doing so, they could not be dismissed as more of the same naive episcopal rhetoric about the need to serve the poor and to work for social justice. While a century of Roman Catholic social teaching and especially the organic cosmology or worldview underlying the church's teaching fed this revolution, the pastoral experience of Latin American Christians engaged in the struggle for justice revealed the ambiguities inherent in that teaching. They had come to see the need to attend to the concrete, sociohistorical, and epistemological *conditions of the possibility* of the realization of a more just social order, and hence the realization of the church's self-identity as articulated in its own social teaching. In the wake of Medellín and Puebla, a commitment to solidarity with the poor (beyond working "for" or "on behalf of" the poor) could no longer be seen as an option available to people who wanted to become *exceptional* Christians, or saints; that commitment was now demanded of everyone who wanted to be Christian, period— and of the church, insofar as it claims to be Christian. In the words of Jon Sobrino, the poor can no longer be seen as "simply the beneficiaries of liberation. . . . for believers they are the historical locus of God, the 'place' where God is found in history."[4]

It is this transposition of social justice from the realm of ethics to the realm of epistemology (the conditions of the possibility of knowing God)

3. Samuel Silva Gotay, *El pensamiento cristiano revolucionario en América Latina y el Caribe: Implicaciones de la teología de la liberación para la sociología de la religión* (Río Piedras, Puerto Rico, 1983), 29, 35 (my translation).

4. Jon Sobrino, *Spirituality of Liberation* (Maryknoll, N.Y., 1988), 24.

and theological method itself (the conditions of the possibility of doing theology) that has been the real shift effected within the Latin American church and Latin American theology since the 1960s, especially in grass-roots ecclesial movements and in the liberation theology born within them.[5] As long as the struggle for social justice is viewed as merely an ethical imperative derived from or consequent to one's prior encounter with God (in prayer, say, or in one's assent to religious beliefs), one can rest assured in one's "belief," one's "knowledge of God," or one's "Christian faith," without feeling compelled to engage in action that is not seen as intrinsic to that encounter with God, which has already occurred in the act of intellectual assent, or belief. If the struggle for justice is viewed as the privileged sociohistorical locus of God's revelation, however, the place where one encounters God, then that struggle is not simply an ethical injunction that one can choose to follow or ignore while still remaining a believer and a faithful Christian (all the while, perhaps, admitting one's sinfulness and weakness); now the commitment to the poor becomes itself the criterion for an authentic encounter with God, the criterion for authentic belief in and knowledge of God. Christian faith, theology, and ethics—believing the truth, knowing the truth, and doing the good—are inseparable: to know God *is* to do justice (Jer. 22:13–17).[6]

What lies at the heart of much First World criticism of Latin American liberation theology, whether ecclesiastical or academic, is an implicit resistance to this ecclesial-epistemological shift. What is resisted is not the importance of a commitment to social justice per se but the assertion that that commitment is an epistemological precondition for Christian faith and hence for the church to be truly church, or *ekklesia*. This resistance

5. As the "father of liberation theology," Gustavo Gutiérrez is perhaps the foremost of the theologians whose theology arises out of pastoral work among grass-roots ecclesial communities; see, e.g., Robert McAfee Brown, *Makers of Contemporary Theology: Gustavo Gutiérrez* (Atlanta, 1980). An extended treatment of the relationship between liberation theology and popular ecclesial movements in Latin America is beyond the scope of this chapter, but that relationship has been examined by many liberation theologians, as well as by other scholars and social critics; see, for instance, Sergio Torres and John Eagleson, eds., *The Challenge of Basic Christian Communities* (Maryknoll, N.Y., 1981); Phillip Berryman, *The Religious Roots of Rebellion* (Maryknoll, N.Y., 1984) and *Liberation Theology* (New York, 1987), 63–95; Alfred Hennelly, *Theology for a Liberating Church* (Washington, D.C., 1989), 81–94; Raúl Vidales, "Evangelización y liberación popular," and Ignacio Ellacuría, "Hacia una fundamentación filosófica del método teológico latinoamericano," both in Enrique Dussel et al., *Liberación y cautiverio: Debates en torno al método de la teología en América Latina* (Mexico City, 1975), 209–33 and 609–35; Walter LaFeber, *Inevitable Revolutions* (New York, 1983), 219–26; Christopher Rowland, *Radical Christianity* (Cambridge, 1988), 115–49; Francisco Moreno Rejón, *Salvar la vida de los pobres* (Lima, 1986), 47–73; and Jon Sobrino, *The True Church and the Poor* (Maryknoll, N.Y., 1984), 21–24.

6. See Robert McAfee Brown, *Liberation Theology* (Louisville, 1993), 66–67; John R. Donahue, "Biblical Perspectives on Justice," in *The Faith That Does Justice*, ed. John C. Haughey (New York, 1977).

is evident, for example, in the Vatican's various responses to liberation theology. While strongly reaffirming the Catholic Church's denunciation of social injustice, Pope John Paul II remains reluctant to root that denunciation in the base communities' experience of God *within* their struggle for liberation; that is, in praxis. The Pope's condemnation of injustice continues to be derived from—and therefore a mere derivative of—the church's prior (in both time and importance) belief, as expressed in the Scriptures and Christian tradition. The Vatican's denunciations of social injustice thus suffer from an internal ambivalence that can only weaken their practical impact: the commitment to the poor is an important, central, and even critical responsibility for the believer, but not a necessary criterion for belief itself.[7]

Either explicitly or, more often, implictly, this issue has divided the Latin American church, not whether a Christian ought to work for justice (a contention very few would deny) but what the relationship is between that work and Christian belief. This division is the theological-ecclesiastical analogue of the division between liberal capitalist theories of development, which view qualitative criteria ("quality of life," education, health care, opportunities for cultural expression, etc.) as extrinsic to development ("economic growth"), and dependency paradigms, which view qualitative criteria as intrinsic to any genuine development, so that there can be no true development without them.[8] Is a country "developed" if, despite a high per capita gross national product, half of its population does not have access to adequate health care? Analogously, is a person Christian if, despite professions of orthodox beliefs, he or she is not actively working for a more just social order? The question becomes even more explosive (figuratively and literally) if "church" is substituted for "person." Hence the resistance of the Vatican to an epistemological rather than a merely ethical interpretation of the preferential option for the poor: the former represents a fundamental challenge to the reigning ecclesial model, which views the church as a pyramid, with the Christian faith being revealed to those at the top and gradually trickling down (again the economic analogy is apt) to the base. It is for this reason that the liberation theologians who have suffered most at the hands of the Vatican, such as Leonardo Boff, have been not those who most ardently embrace Karl Marx but those who challenge the pyramidal ecclesial model.

---

7. See Vatican Congregation for the Doctrine of the Faith, "Instruction on Certain Aspects of the 'Theology of Liberation,'" *Origins* 13 (September 1984); "Instruction on Christian Freedom and Liberation," *Origins* 15 (April 17, 1986): 713–28.

8. For analyses of the distinction between intrinsic and extrinsic criteria of development, see Denis Goulet, *The Cruel Choice: A New Concept in the Theory of Development* (New York, 1975), esp. xii–xv, 60–84; and Roberto S. Goizueta, *Liberation, Method, and Dialogue* (Atlanta, 1988), 3–29.

What is ultimately at stake is the locus of truth in the world and in the church: Where does one go to find God? Does one go first to the church's magisterium, or does one go first to the hungry person, the peasant, the factory worker?[9]

The transposition of social justice questions from ethics to epistemology and theological method also challenged the operative ecclesial model insofar as this shift reflected the breakdown of traditional attempts to draw clear distinctions between spiritual and secular, supernatural and natural, salvation history and temporal history, clergy and laity; attempts whose internal ambiguities became apparent in the face of the pastoral experience of the Latin American church. Seeking to preserve the autonomy of the church vis-à-vis the temporal sphere, a "distinction of plane" ecclesiology, for instance, essentially prohibited church interference in social questions except through the church's social teaching; except, in the words of Gustavo Gutiérrez, through "the mediation of the conscience of the individual Christian." The role of the clergy was thus limited to the "spiritual realm," where priests and ecclesial apostolic movements, even if primarily lay in character, were called "to evangelize and to inspire the temporal order," but only by evangelizing and inspiring individual consciences.[10]

The historical ecclesial experience of many Latin American Christians called the validity of this ecclesiology into question. In their attempts to "evangelize and inspire," lay Catholic Action movements and clergy began to feel artificially constrained by what their concrete experience, especially among the poor, revealed as overly facile, artificial, and ahistorical distinctions between the religious and the secular. When, for instance, is a priest acting as merely a Christian and when as a priest, and hence as an official representative of the church? Or when is a layperson acting as merely a Christian and when as a Christian *as such* (and hence as a representative of the church)?[11] This epistemological schizophrenia could not be sustained as more and more clergy, including bishops (e.g., Camara, Romero) and priest-theologians (e.g., Gutiérrez), and lay activists became intimately involved in and identified with the lives of grass-roots ecclesial

9. For more extended discussions of liberation theology's impact within the Roman Catholic Church, see Paul E. Sigmund, *Liberation Theology at the Crossroads: Democracy or Revolution?* (New York, 1990); Harvey Cox, *The Silencing of Leonardo Boff* (Oak Park, Ill., 1988); Arthur F. McGovern, *Liberation Theology and Its Critics: Toward an Assessment* (Maryknoll, N.Y., 1989), 197–233; and Hennelly, *Theology for a Liberating Church*, 105–17.

10. Gustavo Gutiérrez, *A Theology of Liberation* (Maryknoll, N.Y., 1973), 57. Gutiérrez discusses the transition from "New Christendom" and "distinction of planes" models to a liberation ecclesiological model (53–77). For a more detailed account of this transition and the sociohistorical crisis that occasioned it, see Silva Gotay, *Pensamiento cristiano revolucionario*, 29–136.

11. Gutiérrez, *Theology of Liberation*, 56.

communities, lives in which physical hunger and spiritual hunger exist in symbiotic relationships.[12] The rejection of the inherited, dualistic views of the relationship between faith and society, Silva Gotay points out, was thus a by-product of the active participation of many Christians in social and political movements of liberation.[13] That participation yielded, furthermore, a new awareness of the legitimating, political function historically played by the church in Latin American society:

> Under these circumstances, can it honestly be said that the Church does not interfere in "the temporal sphere"? Is the Church fulfilling a purely religious role when by its silence or friendly relationships it lends legitimacy to a dictatorial and oppressive government? . . . This principle is not applied when the question is maintaining the status quo, but it is wielded when, for example, a lay apostolic movement or a group of priests holds an attitude considered subversive to the established order. Concretely, in Latin America the distinction-of-planes model has the effect of concealing the real political option of a large sector of the Church—that is, support of the established order.[14]

In other words, in their attempts to evangelize and inspire, many Christians began to realize that the church itself was a major impediment to effective evangelization, precisely because of its political role in support of the established order. The church preached social justice while legitimating injustice. The social location or epistemological perspective of the institutional church undermined the church's spiritual mission. The preferential option for the poor thus emerged as a response to this concrete pastoral experience, and made possible a new pastoral praxis.

Perhaps the most important social manifestation of that option has been the base ecclesial communities (*comunidades eclesiales de base*, or CEBs), small, often lay-led communities of poor Christians who gather to read the Bible together, reflect on its texts in the light of their own lives, and commit themselves to living out its message in their towns and villages.[15] In the more than 80,000 CEBs throughout Latin America, the

---

12. Attempts by critics to portray the base ecclesial communities as a "parallel church" in opposition to the "institutional church" fail to account for the presence of clergy and bishops as active members of those communities; e.g., Alois Lorscheider, "The Re-defined Role of the Bishop in a Poor, Religious People (Meio Popular Pobre e Religioso)," in *La Iglesia Popular: Between Fear and Hope,* ed. Leonardo Boff and Virgil Elizondo (Edinburgh, 1984), 47–49. The relationship between the base communities and church structures is also described in Penny Lernoux, *Cry of the People* (Garden City, N.Y., 1980), 389–408.

13. Silva Gotay, *Pensamiento cristiano revolucionario,* 315.

14. Ibid., 65.

15. For a concrete example of how one such community functions, see Pablo Galdámez, *Faith of a People: The Life of a Basic Christian Community in El Salvador* (Maryknoll, N.Y., 1986).

poor, no longer merely the objects of Christian evangelization, have become the privileged locus of God's self-revelation in the world.[16] Yet in the social context of oppressive poverty, this task can never be divorced from the sociopolitical struggle; as the poor began to read the Gospel together and (in the words of the Final Document of the International Ecumenical Congress of Theology) "to announce the true God, the God revealed in Christ, the God who makes a covenant with the oppressed and defends their cause," they became increasingly aware of the tremendous disjunction between the social order that God calls for—in which the proud are scattered, the mighty are dethroned, the poor are exalted, the hungry are filled, and the rich are ostracized (Luke 1:51–53)—and the social order in which they themselves live and suffer. That God affirms their dignity as human beings and thus empowers them to work for a society in which their dignity will be respected rather than trampled. The proclamation of that God cannot be separated from the political struggle; one cannot preach a God of life and, either by action or by inaction, support social structures that purvey death.

Often, then, the common reading of the Bible and the liturgical life of the CEBs have become catalysts for more explicitly political activity, such as involvement in trade unions and agrarian reform movements, as well as the construction of clinics, schools, and the like. Phillip Berryman points out that

> the initial motivation [of the CEBs] . . . was not political. To this day many base communities are essentially pastoral and not political—at least not in any conflictive way. What has attracted attention, however, has been the political potential of these groups, especially in the most extreme circumstances, as in Central America, where base-community pastoral work prepared the soil for grass-roots organization and revolutionary struggle. . . . The social and political impact of base communities may be viewed in terms of (1) initial consciousness-raising, (2) their vision of life and motivation for involvement, (3) the sense of community and mutual aid and support they generate, (4) the experience of grass-roots democracy, (5) the direct actions they engage in, and (6) directly political effects. . . . Base communities have undeniable spin-off effects in the political process. They function in effect as cadre schools, primarily for leadership within the church. Leadership qualities developed there, however, may have spin-offs elsewhere. In Central America, the mass organizations of peasants developed out of soil prepared by church pastoral work. Often at the village level the same people who had formed the base community would become members of a

16. Torres and Eagleson, *Challenge of Basic Christian Communities,* p. 238.

militant peasant organization. In their own minds there was a direct continuity between their awakening through the gospel, their own local organizing efforts, and their decision to join a national peasant organization. One Nicaraguan organizer later said the Sandinistas regarded the base communities as "quarries" for their own organizing.[17]

The reading of the Bible within the context of oppression thus reveals to the Latin American poor a God very different from the "God" that has been preached to them for centuries. The God of the Scriptures commands not resignation but hope, not acceptance of one's "fate" as his will but resistance to oppression, not passivity but action, not a flight from the world but an immersion in the world, not submission but liberation. This God is one who, in a conflictual world, makes a preferential option for the poor—and demands the same of those who would call themselves disciples.

CATHOLIC SOCIAL TEACHING

It is impossible to understand recent movements in the Latin American church without understanding how those movements both are influenced by and go beyond the social teachings of the Catholic Church over the last century as enunciated in papal and episcopal pronouncements. This ecclesial tradition has consistently focused on the notion of human dignity as the key to a Christian social ethic. From Pope Leo XIII's encyclical *Rerum novarum,* issued in 1891, through the documents of the Second Vatican Council and Pope John Paul II's encyclicals *On Human Work, On Social Concern,* and *Centesimus annus,* the social tradition of the church has reflected an organic worldview and a concomitant insistence on the ultimate significance of all persons as integral members of the living, cosmological organism. To threaten the human dignity of any individual is thus to do violence to the whole organism.

Within this cosmology, all individuals are therefore seen as intrinsically and constitutively social. Social responsibility derives not from some contractual duty extrinsic to the individual living in society but from anthropology, from ontology itself, for to be an individual is to live in society. Just as there is no society without individuals, so there are no individuals

17. Berryman, *Liberation Theology,* 71–74. As a specific example of such grass-roots political action, Berryman tells of cases in which "people surrounded and captured a plantation owner who was treating them unjustly, took him by force to army authorities, and secured his commitment not to continue. Base communities have also been involved in land invasions" (74).

without society. Even the hermit soon discovers that he or she cannot escape "the world," for the world is not only extrinsic but also intrinsic to the individual. We carry the world within us. Likewise, my responsibility to the common good is not extrinsic, much less secondary to my rights as an individual; rather, the former is inextricably linked to the latter.

This organic cosmology has informed Catholic social teaching on everything from property rights to political revolution. In each case, the promotion of human dignity and the common good is set forth as the benchmark of authentically Christian social praxis. That praxis must reflect and affirm the dignity inherent in every person as a child of God. Moreover, the earth's resources are a common inheritance and thus must be used in such a way that they promote the good of all people. In the document on the church in the modern world, *Gaudium et spes,* the bishops at the Second Vatican Council made this point very clearly:

> God destined the earth and all that it contains for the use of all men and all people. . . . Therefore every man has the right to possess a sufficient amount of the earth's goods for himself and his family. . . . When a person is in extreme necessity, he has the right to supply himself with what he needs out of the riches of others. Faced with a world today where so many people are suffering from want, the Council asks individuals and governments to remember the saying of the Fathers: "Feed the man dying of hunger, because if you do not feed him you are killing him."[18]

Within the context of an organic cosmology, feeding the hungry is not a magnanimous action undertaken over and above the call of duty. Rather, feeding the hungry *is* our duty. To feed the hungry is not merely to undertake a charitable act but to do justice; that is, to respect another's inalienable rights as a human being. All people have a right to private property as a minimal safeguard against attempts to deny their intrinsic and irreducible value as human beings; thus the hungry person is one whose own right to private property has been violated. In his 1967 encyclical *Populorum progressio,* "On the Development of Peoples," Pope Paul VI explicitly applied this analysis to the international division of labor, which, as a consequence of colonialism and neocolonialism, has condemned whole peoples to lives of destitution and hopelessness.[19]

While consistently denouncing any system (such as communism) that subsumes the individual within the collective, Roman Catholic social

18. Austin Flannery, ed., *Vatican II: The Conciliar and Post-Conciliar Documents* (Collegeville, Minn., 1975), 975–76, GS 69.1.
19. Joseph Gremillion, ed., *The Gospel of Justice and Peace: Catholic Social Teaching since Pope John* (Maryknoll, N.Y., 1976), 387–415.

teaching has also consistently denounced any system (such as unchecked liberal individualism) that subordinates the good of the whole to the rights of a few. The latter is seen as historically prior to the former, since the failures of liberal individualism are what have created the historical conditions for the emergence of both economic and political forms of totalitarianism. "This unchecked liberalism," writes Pope Paul VI, "led to dictatorship . . . producing 'the international imperialism of money.'"[20] In his encyclical on human work, *Laborem excercens,* Pope John Paul II traces the roots of class conflict to the "practical materialism" of social and economic liberalism. By separating labor from capital and setting them in opposition to each other, economic liberalism created the social conditions that would become the seedbed of "theoretical materialism"— that is, Marxism.[21]

The mere existence of these and many other such papal texts, however, in no way guarantees their implementation. Like all historical texts, they are open to conflicting interpretations as well as to the ambiguities inherent in the process of implementation. Ricardo Antoncich specifies the problem: "Reference to the social teaching of the church enables us to determine the legitimacy of the liberating struggle undertaken by Christians. This teaching is a criterion of interpretation, or a hermeneutical criterion. But the texts themselves likewise require interpretation if their true meaning is to be found. Because the interpretation always takes place in a sociohistorical context, its validity is derived from that context: historical praxis is the criterion for interpreting the texts.[22]

The conferences of Medellín and Puebla represented attempts to read these texts within the sociohistorical context, or historical praxis, of the Latin American church. What, asked the Latin American bishops, has been the historical experience of the Latin American people? How can that experience contribute to the church's understanding of its social teaching and faith? Finally, what are the practical, pastoral implications of that understanding? Their answers changed the face of Latin American Christianity.

MEDELLÍN AND PUEBLA

The theological method implicit in the Medellín documents, and already foreshadowed in the Second Vatican Council, reflects an inductive episte-

---

20. Ibid., 395.

21. Pope John Paul II, *On Human Work* (Boston, 1981), 32–33.

22. Ricardo Antoncich, *Christians in the Face of Injustice: A Latin American Reading of Catholic Social Teaching* (Maryknoll, N.Y., 1987), 12.

mology. Vatican II asked that the church look to the "signs of the times" as *locus theologicus,* the place where God is revealed and thus where the church discovers the meaning of its faith and mission: "Nothing that is genuinely human" is alien to the church. The church's concerns are not limited to the religious realm, but include "the joy and hope, the grief and anguish" of all people, considered whole and entire, with body and soul, heart and conscience, mind and will." Furthermore, the church's concerns extend especially to "those who are poor or afflicted in any way."[23]

At Medellín, then, the Latin American church took up the challenge of discovering the meaning of its faith and mission, not in ahistorical doctrinal formulations but in its people's historical experience, in their struggles and travails, their joys and sorrows. The pastoral response of the church would then be just that, a *response* to the concrete situation of its people.

The theological method implicit in the bishops' documents involves, therefore, three distinct elements: (1) immersion in the historical struggles of the Latin American people, (2) reflection on the meaning of the Scriptures and the Christian faith in the light of those struggles, and (3) pastoral strategies for implementing those reflections, thereby strengthening the church's solidarity with the people in their struggles. Note that the meaning of the Christian faith is not posited here as a priori. The only a priori is the historical experience of the Latin American people— the "signs of the times." The meaning of the Christian faith and the meaning of God are revealed only in that history and only to the extent that Christians engage that history. The church's fundamental mission, therefore, is not to preach an ahistorical Gospel or to promote pastoral strategies deduced from doctrinal a prioris. The church's fundamental mission is to enter into solidarity with its people, to walk alongside them in their historical pilgrimage, to listen to their cries. That pilgrimage and those cries reveal the meaning of the Gospel and the meaning of a God who is an incarnate God, a historical God. This hermeneutic is already adumbrated in the first paragraph of the bishops' introduction to the final documents of the Medellín conference: "The Latin American Church, united in the Second General Conference of its Bishops, has chosen as the central theme of its deliberations Latin American man who is living a decisive moment of his historical process. In making this choice she has in no way 'detoured from,' but has actually 'returned to' man, aware that 'in order to know God, it is necessary to know man.'"[24]

23. Flannery, *Vatican II,* 903–4.
24. United States Catholic Conference, Division for Latin America, *Second General Conference of Latin American Bishops: The Church in the Present Day Transformation of Latin America in the Light of the Council, II (Conclusions)* (Washington, D.C., 1973), 34.

Having committed themselves to this theological process, the bishops begin with analyses of the sociohistorical situation of contemporary Latin Americans. That situation, they observe, is characterized by a dehumanizing poverty, a "misery that besets large masses of human beings in all of our countries" and that, "as a collective fact, expresses itself as injustice which cries to the heavens." This injustice "can be called institutionalized violence" and is rooted in an unjust social order: economic, political, and cultural structures that perpetuate underdevelopment and dependency on the "industrialized metropolises." Among the "signs of the times," however, the bishops discover not only these signs of death but also signs of life: "Latin America is obviously under the sign of transformation and development; a transformation that, besides taking place with extraordinary speed, has come to touch and influence every level of human activity, from the economic to the religious." These historical struggles for justice are "an obvious sign of the Spirit" in our midst.[25]

In this sociohistorical context, to believe in Jesus Christ is to believe in a Christ who "liberates all men from the slavery to which sin has subjected them: hunger, misery, oppression and ignorance."[26] The sociohistorical situation of Latin America is thus a *locus theologicus,* the "place" where God is revealed. The meaning of Christ for the individual Christian and for the church is mediated by the struggle against the historical manifestations of sin.

Given their social analysis and the subsequent theological reflection on the sociohistorical reality, the bishops then issue a pastoral call for the church to become a "Church of the poor," a church engaged in and in solidarity with the struggles of its people. Only to the extent that the church engages itself in those struggles will it encounter God and hence discover its identity and mission. "The Church in Latin America," write the bishops, "should be manifested, in an increasingly clear manner, as truly poor." Such solidarity implies, furthermore, that in its allocation of human and financial resources the church must give "preference to the poorest and most needy sectors."[27]

The bishops' declarations at Medellín were widely perceived as giving ecclesiastical approval to the participation of clergy and laity in movements for social change. Consequently, such movements gained momentum during the 1970s, and some of them were "radical." Participation in them, particularly if it involved Marxist social analysis, came under heavy criticism. Led by Bishop (now Cardinal) Alfonso López Trujillo of Medellín, some bishops who had played active roles at the Medellín meeting

25. Ibid., 40, 61, 140, 35.
26. Ibid., 41.
27. Ibid., 97, 191.

in 1968 now began to have second thoughts.[28] This dissension within the ranks of CELAM raised such hopes or fears, depending on one's perspective, that at its next general conference, CELAM would retract its support for a "Church of the poor."

It was thus with some trepidation that Latin Americans awaited the 1979 bishops' meeting at Puebla, Mexico. The results of that meeting seem at times ambiguous, but one decidedly unambiguous result was the bishops' reaffirmation of the preferential option for the poor.[29] Paul Sigmund underscores this point:

> The most significant single section of the Puebla Document is Part Four, much of which is devoted to the "preferential option for the poor." The bishops observe that the majority of Latin Americans are poor, indigenous peoples, peasants, manual laborers, and marginalized urban dwellers. Claiming to be following the precedent of the 1968 Medellín Conference, the bishops say, "Despite the distortions and interpretations of some, who vitiate the spirit of Medellín, and despite the disregard and even hostility of others, we affirm the need for conversion on the part of the whole church to a preferential option for the poor, an option aimed at their integral liberation."[30]

Thus, while the 1968 Medellín document spoke of a preference for the poor, the Latin American bishops did not fully articulate the notion of a "preferential option for the poor" until their 1979 meeting at Puebla. In the Puebla document the Latin American bishops define that option and explicate its social dimensions, its scriptural and theological bases, and its implications for the lives of individual Christians and the church. In a chapter devoted to the preferential option for the poor, the Puebla document reiterates the call for solidarity with the poor: "With renewed hope ... we are going to take up once again the position of ... Medellín, which adopted a clear and prophetic option expressing preference for, and solidarity with, the poor."[31]

An avowal that "the poor merit preferential attention, whatever may be the moral or personal situation in which they find themselves," is warranted and indeed required by Jesus Christ's own identification with

---

28. See Sigmund, *Liberation Theology*, 93–107.

29. See ibid., 105; Berryman, *Liberation Theology*, 43–44; Antoncich, *Christians in the Face of Injustice*, 28–32, 165–71; Enrique Dussel, "'Populus Dei' in Populo Pauperum: From Vatican II to Medellín and Puebla," in Boff and Elizondo, *Iglesia Popular*, 35–44; Enrique Dussel, *A History of the Church in Latin America: Colonialism to Liberation (1492–1979)* (Grand Rapids, 1981), 234.

30. Sigmund, *Liberation Theology*, 105.

31. Eagleson and Scharper, *Puebla and Beyond*, 264.

the poor. Consequently, solidarity with the poor "is the privileged, though not the exclusive, gauge of our following of Christ." Such solidarity is meant to benefit not only the poor but the church itself, for "the poor challenge the Church constantly, summoning it to conversion."[32]

What had been intimated in the Vatican II documents is explicitly asserted in the Medellín and especially the Puebla documents: the struggle for social justice is indeed "the privileged . . . gauge of our following of Christ." Christians and the church cannot be for the poor without first being with and of the poor.

Liberation Theology and the Preferential Option for the Poor

Just as Vatican II had given official sanction to regional bishops' conferences to address the historical situation of the local churches, and in fact had called for such meetings, Medellín and Puebla called for theological reflection on and out of the historical situation of Latin Americans. The Latin American bishops sanctioned the development of indigenous theologies.

Such theological reflection had already been taking place at the grassroots level, but the first systematic exposition of a Latin American theology did not appear until 1971, with the publication of Gustavo Gutiérrez's *Teología de la liberación*. In his first chapter Gutiérrez indicates what he perceives to be the fundamental insight of the theology of liberation: "the theology of liberation offers us not so much a new theme for reflection as a *new way* to do theology."[33] In other words, what is truly revolutionary about liberation theology is not its emphasis on the struggle for social justice—that emphasis is already evident in the tradition of Roman Catholic social teaching—but the epistemological and methodological centrality it accords that struggle. Vatican II and especially Medellín and Puebla called for Christian immersion in the struggle for justice, and Gutiérrez and other liberation theologians have articulated the epistemological warrants for that call.[34] Those warrants derive not only from Christian Scripture and tradition but, at a more basic level, from ontology and anthropology; that is, from the very nature of the person as inherently social and historical. Liberation theology thus takes the underlying assumptions of Catholic social teaching to their logical conclusion.

32. Ibid., 265.
33. Gutiérrez, *Theology of Liberation*, 15.
34. It is also important to note, however, that Gutiérrez and other Latin American theologians served as advisers to the bishops at Medellín and Puebla and thus helped shape the final documents.

The Latin American theologians' challenge to the traditional European theologies imported by the missionaries, preached from the pulpits, and taught in the schools of Latin America is based less on a different theology than on a different epistemology. Latin Americans' historical experience has revealed the contradictions inherent in the colonial theologies: the Europeans preached a God of love as they simultaneously exterminated whole populations and cultures.

While the Latin American church had inherited the theological and ethical vocabulary of the European church, with its talk of love, justice, and peace, the colonial experience demonstrated how even the loftiest ideals can be used to disguise and legitimate oppression. In other words, the history of Latin America has demonstrated the danger of ahistorical, abstract theologies that, though presumed to be eternally and universally valid, are in fact—and precisely because of that presumption—ideological instruments of oppression. These theologies have served to legitimate political oppression both directly and indirectly. Legitimation is direct when theological doctrines and symbols are used to perpetuate power-lessness, as when a hierarchical cosmology is used as justification for a hierarchical political order.[35]

Legitimation is indirect when theology is removed from the public arena to the academic ivory tower in hopes of achieving an "objectivity" unsullied by the vicissitudes of sociopolitical existence. Refusing to take a political stand lest their ideas be distorted by partisan political interests, theologians are blinded to their own implicit political, cultural, economic, racial, and gender interests. The male European academic can then pro-pound his ideas as "objective" and thus universal and invariant, while remaining blind to the biases implicit in his own inescapable historicity, which is not merely accidental but indeed intrinsic to the intellectual enterprise. The history of Latin America, and all the histories of suffering, have taught us that once a theory is presumed to be objective, it can readily be universalized and imposed as invariant, with horrific conse-quences. A particular perspective then becomes the measure of all others. Whereas the particular perspectives of liberation theology, black theology, feminist theology, and so on are clearly noted by the use of the particular-izing adjective in each case, the theologies of white male academics are

---

35. An example of such ideological distortion is the "pie in the sky by and by" theology of white preachers during the period of slavery in this country. The idea that God created some people to be masters or rulers and others to be slaves or servants was taught to "keep the niggers in their place." Slaves who rose up to challenge the social system were condemned not only for questioning the social status quo but for challenging Divine Providence and questioning the will of God. To contravene the social order would thus be to contravene the cosmological order, which presumably had been established by God and on which the social order was based.

referred to, preached, and taught as "theology," pure and simple. It is assumed that all other theologies, because of their historicity and particularity, embody particular biases. Only that theology done by white males can claim to be true theology. The histories of the victims are thus denied any value as mediators of truth, because those histories are biased and truth must be objective. And to deny the truth value of those histories is to deny the very existence of the victims, the poor.[36]

The quest for intellectual objectivity also functions to legitimate injustice inasmuch as the theologian's self-imposed silence on political questions functions implicitly to legitimate the status quo: silence is consent. Silence in the face of oppression ensures neither objectivity nor neutrality; rather, it ensures the perpetuation of the unjust status quo. The theologian, or the academic, then becomes the tyrant's silent partner.[37]

This privatization of theology is the intellectual concomitant of what the German theologian Johann Baptist Metz has called the "privatization of faith." The Enlightenment's critique of religion, the tradition of separation of church and state, and the Western liberal tradition of individualism have all combined to relegate religion to the private sphere—the individual conscience, the family, the home, the parish. Though the phenomenon of privatization is not generally part of Latin American experience per se, the privatization of religion in the Western industrial societies of the North has functioned as an ideological support for Third World underdevelopment. As religion has been removed to its "proper" place in the politically neutral private sphere, the public sphere (politics, economics) has come to be perceived as autonomous and self-regulating, operating under its own criteria of truth (cost efficiency, the law of supply and demand, realpolitik, national security) and thus immune to religious critique.[38] The "Christian values" of love, compassion, and service are thus deemed appropriate to home and parish life, but irrelevant to life in the "real world," where social and economic Darwinism rule.

36. See Roberto S. Goizueta, "Liberation Theology: Retrospect and Prospect," *Philosophy and Theology,* Fall 1988, 31. It is no coincidence that the first books that totalitarian regimes burn or at least rewrite are the history books. Such historical censorship—which in fact amounts to a form of genocide—is not exclusive to totalitarian regimes; witness the attempts to deny the existence of Nazi death camps and to romanticize the plantation system in the South.

37. One of the most tragic examples of such a silent partnership in the United States is that of the scientists who participated in the development of nuclear power during the middle part of this century. Their only concern was the pursuit of scientific truth. Only later did they become aware that what they thought were purely scholarly pursuits had been used for destructive political ends. That realization eventually led some of the most prominent scientists to become leaders in the nuclear freeze movement.

38. Johann Baptist Metz, *Faith in History and Society* (New York, 1980), 32–48. Metz rejects the old political theology, with its identification of the sacral and the secular, in favor of a new political theology, which understands that relationship as a dialectic.

Liberation theologians reject this dualistic and indeed schizophrenic anthropology. To presume that a human being lives in two distinct realms, one private and spiritual and the other public and secular, is to deny the historicity of the person. By denying the unity of history, European theologies have been blinded to their own historicity and hence to the many ways they are influenced by and reflect sociohistorically determined interests. Theology is necessarily influenced by the sociohistorical location of the theologian, for human experience is at once intellectual, spiritual, emotional, psychological, and corporeal.

It follows, then, that there can be no such thing as a politically neutral theology. If every theology is rooted in history and reflects that history, the quest for an unbiased, neutral, "objective" theology can only be illusory. Furthermore, if that history is conflictual—if it is characterized by the social conflict that is so evident when history is viewed through the victims' eyes—to say that theology is rooted in history is to say that theology necessarily plays a role in that conflict, on one side or the other, by commission or by omission. The question the theologian must ask, then, is not "Will my theology be politically biased?" but "What will be its bias?"; not "Will I take sides?" but "Which side will I take?"[39] It is at this point that liberation theologians look to the Scriptures and, reading them from the perspective of their own grass-roots ecclesial communities in Latin America, call for Christians to make a preferential option for the poor as the sine qua non of authentic Christian faith. Through the eyes of the poor, through the eyes of the victims of history, the image of history as fundamentally harmonious and ordered is revealed for the illusion it is. And through those same eyes the God of the Scriptures is revealed as a God of the poor.

Gustavo Gutiérrez discovers two overarching themes in Scripture: (1) the gratuity and universality of God's love and (2) God's preferential option for the poor.[40] At first glance, these themes appear to be mutually

---

39. Archbishop Desmond Tutu of South Africa illustrates this point: "If you are neutral in a situation of injustice, you have chosen the side of the oppressor. If an elephant has his foot on the tail of the mouse, and you say you are neutral, the mouse will not appreciate your neutrality": quoted in Robert McAfee Brown, *Unexpected News* (Philadelphia, 1984), 19. An illustration I have used elsewhere is that of the father who finds his eldest son beating up his daughter. Were the father to proclaim himself neutral and refuse to intervene, on the grounds that his equal love for his children prevents him from taking sides, his inaction would amount to implicit support for the son's injustice. Were the father to pull his son away from his daughter, his action would not indicate that he loved his son less than his daughter; it would simply mean that precisely because the father loved his children equally he must *in that context* manifest his love differently to the two of them: Goizueta, "Liberation Theology," 32.

40. Gustavo Gutiérrez, *On Job* (Maryknoll, N.Y., 1987), xi–xix; Goizueta, "Liberation Theology," 31.

contradictory. Yet our epistemological assumptions reveal them as, in fact, mutually implicit. If God's love is a real love—if it is a concrete, efficacious love—it can become manifest only in history. And if that history is conflictual, God's love is necessarily involved in that conflict, on one side or the other, by commission or omission. Just as human historicity precludes human neutrality, so the historicity of God's love precludes divine neutrality. In a historical situation of ongoing social conflict, in which the human dignity of certain groups is systematically denied, a God who was neutral would be a God who, like the "neutral" theologian, effectively condoned the conflict and the oppression.[41] In his autobiographical novel *Night,* Elie Wiesel recalls standing with other concentration camp prisoners as they witnessed the hanging of a Jewish child. "Where is God? Where is He?" someone behind me asked. . . . And I heard a voice within me answer him: 'Where is He? Here He is—He is hanging here on this gallows.'"[42] A God who is not hanging on the gallows, alongside the victims of history, is an accomplice in their victimization. To believe in such a God would be to believe in a God created in our own image, the image of bourgeois Christianity.[43]

The preferential option for the poor provides us with the lenses through which to perceive—in history, in Christian tradition, and in Scripture—God's own preferential option for the poor. In the past, refusal to take that option has resulted in emasculation of the Christian *kerygma,* or proclamation of the "truth" of faith, usually by means of a premature spiritualization or psychologization of the Christian message. A case in point is the traditional reading of Luke 4:18–19, in which the young boy Jesus reads from Isaiah in the synagogue: "The Spirit of the Lord is upon me, because he has anointed me to preach good news to the poor. He has sent me to proclaim release to the captives, and recovery of sight to the blind, to set at liberty those who are oppressed, to proclaim the acceptable year of the Lord." To the poor, this is a self-evidently radical message of justice and liberation. Yet precisely because it is good news to the poor, the message is threatening to those of us who are not poor. So we instinctively reinterpret it to make it less threatening. Witness the interpretation found in the widely used *Moffatt Bible Commentary:* "On Jesus' lips the 'good news' has a purely religious import. . . . The term *the poor* is to be taken in its inward spiritual sense . . . and similarly the expressions *captive, blind, oppressed* indicate not primarily the downtrodden victims of material force, such as Rome's, but the victims of inward repressions, neuroses, and other spiritual ills due to misdirection

41. Goizueta, "Liberation Theology," 32.
42. Elie Wiesel, *Night* (New York, 1958), 76.
43. Goizueta, "Liberation Theology," 32.

and failure of life's energies and purposes." The commentator in the equally popular *Interpreter's Bible* writes: "The captivity referred to is evidently moral and spiritual. Thought is not moving now on the plane of opening the doors of physical jails, but rather of setting men free from the invisible but terribly real imprisonment into which their souls may fall."[44]

Though it may be valid to infer such a spiritual meaning from the biblical texts, the instinctive temptation of bourgeois Christianity is to infer the spiritual meaning to the exclusion of the far more concrete and hence more threatening political meaning.[45] Likewise, when such symbols as the cross are interpreted from the perspective of the victims, their meanings are revealed in a different light. The cross no longer represents merely misfortune or bad luck, those "little crosses" we are all called upon to bear daily, but the concrete, political consequences of Jesus' singlehearted commitment to God's will. That commitment inevitably brought him into conflict with the human authorities of the time, who demanded obeisance. In other words, Jesus was crucified not because the Romans misunderstood his message but because they understood it only too well. Jesus did not "die" on the cross; he was executed as a criminal.

Jesus' execution reveals the deepest meaning of poverty. According to Gutiérrez, the preferential option for the poor encompasses three kinds of poverty: material poverty, spiritual poverty, and "poverty as a commitment to solidarity and protest."[46] Only in the light of "a commitment to solidarity and protest" against the evil that is poverty is the meaning of both material and spiritual poverty revealed. Everyone, including the poor person, is called to make that commitment as a precondition for encountering the God of the Scriptures. Consequently, the preferential option for the poor in no way romanticizes the poor, for they also are called upon to reject the dehumanizing values of their oppressors, the values of domination, which the poor all too often assimilate.[47]

The preferential option for the poor tells us nothing about the moral quality of the poor themselves, but it tells us something about God. It is not the morality of the poor that makes them the privileged mediators of God's presence. What makes them the privileged bearers of God is their sociohistorical location outside the circles of power. As outsiders, or outcasts, they transcend the dominant systems and are thus the mediators of

---

44. Quoted in Robert McAfee Brown, *Theology in a New Key* (Philadelphia, 1978), 82–83.

45. Fundamentalist or literal readings of the Gospels often incorporate literal interpretations of the very few Gospel texts that deal with sexual matters, while curiously avoiding any such interpretations of the many more texts dealing with economic matters.

46. Gutiérrez, *Theology of Liberation*, 299.

47. Sobrino, *Spirituality of Liberation*, 112.

God's transcendence. As incomprehensible anomalies in our presumably ordered society, the poor represent the God who is also an incomprehensible anomaly, a mystery. Divine transcendence is revealed through human transcendence. Divine otherness is revealed through human otherness, and no one is more "other" than the poor, the victim, the marginalized, the outcast. If, as liberation theologians aver, neutrality is not possible, then the God whom we worship and about whom we speak will either be the God of the oppressed, who transcends the dominant systems, or the God of their oppressors, who is identified with those systems.[48]

Furthermore, if Christians are called to accept "poverty as a commitment to solidarity and protest" against oppression, that commitment can be made concrete, or efficacious, only if it includes an analysis of the roots of poverty and oppression. Any attempt to apply biblical precepts to present reality must thus be mediated by social analysis. Such analysis not only illumines the conditions of the possibility of solidarity with the poor here and now; it also translates the biblical precepts from first-century language into contemporary language in order to preserve their meaning. In the early centuries, for example, the command to love the poor was usually interpreted as a command to give alms. In today's infinitely more complex global economic system, however, love of the poor must go beyond almsgiving to a commitment to changing those political and economic structures that create poverty. Christians who, in a fundamentalist fashion, merely transpose biblical precepts immediately and directly into their own modern context not only risk becoming irrelevant and ineffective; they also risk undermining the very values they seek to promote. Christians who believe they have loved the poor sufficiently when they have given to charity may actually be doing them long-term harm, for their donations in the absence of any commitment to political and economic change may serve to legitimate and indeed reinforce the very social structures that create poverty.

If neutrality and objectivity are impossible, then the preferential option for the poor must be mediated by a critical social analysis that will interpret the sociopolitical "material" of that practical option. Clodovis Boff explains that there is no such thing as a pure, unadulterated, uninterpreted "concrete reality":

> The potential distinction, and therefore the possible option, is not, then, between a theology that has recourse to socio-analytic mediation and a theology that dispenses with all interpretation of the social. The only real alternatives are a theology mediated by a *critical* reading of its proper object and a theology mediated by an *uncritical* reading of

48. Enrique Dussel, *Philosophy of Liberation* (Maryknoll, N.Y., 1985), 16–66.

the same. The first alternative outfits itself with adequate tools for its (real) approach to the (social) real, whereas the second merely apprehends the real through a reading grid of which it is unconscious. A critical reading is equipped for approaching the real, whereas a noncritical reading, unthinkingly dispensing with any mediation, actually captures only its own illusion of the real. In other words, there is always mediation—critical or acritical, disciplined or spontaneous. . . . Meanwhile, as we say, the facts do not "speak for themselves." Facts are mute. Before they can speak, they have to be questioned.[49]

The same is true of any text. The Bible does not speak for itself ("The Bible says . . ."). All that the Bible "says" is what we allow it to say, and what we allow it to say is determined by the explicit and, more important, implicit questions we bring to our reading of it.

The necessity of providing socioanalytic mediation for the option for the poor and the reading of the Scriptures, Boff goes on, thus suggests that theological scholarship must engage in dialogue with the social sciences:

> Now, if we consider the political here not as a merely speculative essence or material, but primarily under the formality of the historical, concrete praxis of concrete Christians and human beings, then we shall have to say that, owing to its particular, proper structure, the political will be knowable by the theologian only through the approach of the sciences of the social. . . . What can a theologian say, not about the abstract nature of power or society, but precisely about that altogether determinate power or society in or under which Christians and human beings generally live, struggle, and die?[50]

Whereas European theologies have traditionally used metaphysical categories to mediate Christian faith, liberation theology uses predominantly social scientific categories. European theologies have contended with nonbelievers, people who challenge the theoretical rationality of the Christian faith. Since nonbelievers attack the faith on philosophical grounds, European theologies have employed philosophical reason to defend it. The challenge of liberation theology, however, comes not from nonbelievers but from nonpersons—from creatures whose scandalous, unjust suffering contests the credibility of the Christian faith.[51]

---

49. Clodovis Boff, *Theology and Praxis* (Maryknoll, N.Y., 1987), 21. On 20–66 Boff discusses the criteria for "criticity." That discussion is crucial, but constraints of space require me to allude to it here, and refer readers to Boff's excellent analysis.
50. Ibid., 30.
51. See Brown, *Theology in a New Key,* 62–64.

Whereas most European theologies have responded to the challenges of the so-called First Enlightenment, represented by such figures as Voltaire, liberation theology has responded to the Second Enlightenment, represented principally by Karl Marx. Voltaire's philosophical attack on the credibility of the Christian faith in the light of reason called for an equally rigorous philosophical defense. Given his very different epistemology, however, Marx could reject Christianity not on philosophical grounds but only on practical grounds.[52] In such a practical critique, Marx could argue that Christianity's historical alliance with the established political powers had proved its ideas to be false. Yet, as Juan Luis Segundo observes, by rejecting Christianity and, indeed, religion on these grounds, Marx "goes against his own principles. Instead of examining the specific concrete and historical possibilities of religion and theology, he takes the easy way out of disqualifying religion in general insofar as he views it as an autonomous and ahistorical monolith. In the thought of Marx, religion is not viewed as belonging to an ambiguous superstructure. Instead it is viewed as belonging to a purely spiritual plane or, even worse, as being a merely ideal refutation of historical materialism." Segundo refers to one of the German philosopher's most famous statements on religion:

> At one point Marx writes: "Religious suffering is at the same time an expression of real suffering and *a protest against real suffering*." Now if that is the case, one would assume that Marx would proceed to infer the exact nature of the concrete spiritualized form of this protest against real suffering in each age. But instead he goes on to say: "Religion . . . is the opium of the people. The *abolition* of religion, as the illusory happiness of men, is a demand for their real happiness." Instead of "abolition," one would expect Marx to have talked about "changing" religion so that it might accentuate and eventually correct the situation being protested against.[53]

Liberation theology accepts Marx's premise, that Christianity has all too often been on the side of injustice, but rejects his conclusion, that therefore the Christian faith is necessarily oppressive and hence false. In doing so, liberation theology reveals the fundamental contradiction inherent in Marx's critique of religion and goes on to suggest that what has functioned as an ideological instrument of oppression is not the Christian faith but a distorted interpretation of it. In fact, the Christian faith has been, is, and can be a force for human liberation when it flows from the struggle for liberation rather than from an implicit or explicit commitment to the status quo.

52. See, e.g., Marx's "Theses on Feuerbach."
53. Juan Luis Segundo, *The Liberation of Theology* (Maryknoll, N.Y., 1976), 17.

Liberation theology defends the Christian faith not primarily against the theoretical atheist but against the practical atheist, who may proclaim belief in Jesus Christ but whose life denies that belief. The most dangerous enemies of Christianity are not atheists but Christians themselves. From the perspective of the poor, the major challenge to global Christianity is not the rift between believer and unbeliever but the rift between oppressor and oppressed, both of whom often claim to be Christian. From the perspective of the poor, the major challenge to global peace has been not the rift between the Christian West and the atheistic East but the rift between the imperialist powers of the North and the dependent nations of the South. The collapse of Marxism in the East, while certainly to be welcomed, serves further to mask the increasing polarization of North and South.

THE CHALLENGE TO SCHOLARLY AND INTELLECTUAL CREDIBILITY

If the preferential option for the poor is a necessary precondition for knowledge, whether one identifies that knowledge as God, faith, or simply truth, then one's historical commitment, one's praxis, is the criterion for judging the veracity of one's ideas. Orthopraxis is the criterion for verifying orthodoxy, not vice versa. Questions such as "Do you believe in God?" and "Do you know the truth?" become meaningless; the only meaningful questions are "Whose God?" and "Whose truth?"

The foundation of any accurate knowledge is what Jon Sobrino calls "honesty about the real." Consequently, a faulty epistemology can lead only to a faulty theology, spirituality, philosophy, sociology. "The poor," avers Sobrino, "show the reality of this world for what it is: sin." Though "sin is not the only reality in this world . . . unless we see flagrant sin, we shall miss the mark—if we really want to discover the truth of that reality."[54]

Liberation theologians thus insist that a scholar's credibility depends on his or her fundamental honesty or dishonesty about reality. And what determines honesty or dishonesty is the nature of that scholar's practical insertion in society. An intellectual who presumes that he or she is an isolated, atomic entity who can have access to authentic knowledge through the rigorous use of reason is blind to the self-interested bias of that "knowledge." Despite all claims to "objectivity," such an intellectual is a participant in and beneficiary of injustice. And the nature and extent

54. Sobrino, *Spirituality of Liberation*, 14–17, 30.

of that injustice is visible only to those who suffer its consequences: the poor, the outcasts, and those who, like Jesus Christ, Mohandas Ghandi, Martin Luther King, and Archbishop Romero, make a preferential option for the poor. One cannot know the truth unless one *does* the truth.

"Truth" is a verb as well as a noun. This is the scriptural understanding. When God reveals himself to Moses on Mount Sinai, that revelation takes the form not of a theological dissertation on the metaphysical qualities of God but of a list of ten commandments: if one wants to know who God is, one must live in a certain way. One can know God's will only by doing God's will. The Hebrew prophets declare that to know God is to do justice. St. John writes that the person who loves knows God, and that the person who does not love but claims to know God is a liar. The author of the Gospel of Matthew writes that the person who feeds the hungry and clothes the naked is feeding and clothing Jesus himself, since Jesus is identified with "the least of these." Conversely, the person who does not feed the hungry or clothe the naked cannot know God. In his account of the last judgment, those who are "saved" because they have responded to the needs of the poor are taken by surprise: "Lord, when did we see you hungry and feed you, or thirsty and give you drink?" (Matt. 25:37). Clearly they are not "believers." For all we know, they may be atheists. They come to know Jesus only in their responses to the cries of the poor.

Drawing upon an anthropology that understands the person as intrinsically social and going beyond the church's philosophical articulation of that anthropology in its social teaching, liberation theologians predicate that anthropology on a preferential option for the poor, a praxis that alone reveals the true meaning of human unity and community. They thus take Roman Catholic social teaching to its logical conclusions by interpreting it from the sociohistorical perspective of those conclusions themselves; namely, the struggle for social justice and human dignity. Unity and community remain abstract, obfuscatory concepts unless they are grounded in the common struggle against disunity and alienation. It is for this reason that liberation theology was developed first not in libraries but in the basic ecclesial communities of Latin America, where the Word of God is read and proclaimed in the context of that struggle.

The self-understanding of the liberation theologian, then, is similar to that of Gramsci's "organic intellectual" and is very much influenced by the pedagogical theories of Paulo Freire, for whom the teacher—here the theologian—must become, first of all, a disciple of the "students," someone who must listen before speaking.[55] Hence the theologian's participa-

55. See esp. Antonio Gramsci, *Selections from the Prison Notebooks of Antonio Gramsci*, ed. Quintin Hoare and Geoffrey Nowell Smith (New York, 1971), 5–23; Paulo Freire, *Pedagogy*

tion is at once empathic and critical, empathy serving as the necessary condition for criticism.[56] Enrique Dussel insists that, though the oppressed must initiate the liberation process themselves, the theologian must accompany that process, for the poor need "the critical consciousness of the organic intellectual" to help them discern those—often fatalistic—aspects of their self-understanding and worldview that they have assimilated from the dominant culture, which has imposed its oppressive ideology on them in order to keep them powerless.[57]

Concretely, this process has involved liberation theologians in a multiplicity of social and political projects, all direct consequences of this pedagogical process. At the heart of this process are the grass-roots ecclesial communities, whose reading of the Bible and reflection on the biblical message in the light of their sociohistorical situation becomes the catalyst for the struggle to change that situation.[58] The specific way of relating worship to social action, however, varies from community to community. "Some communities place more stress on religion; others on civic action," writes Penny Lernoux.[59] The type of civic action engaged in also varies, but such action may include the formation of peasants' organizations for self-defense against attempts by large landowners to expropriate their land, the formation of cooperatives and mutual aid societies, the formation of local democratic structures of administration, criminal justice, and housing, and the creation of "work brigades to provide jobs for the unemployed and special committees to pressure the government for schools and hospitals."[60] It is out of participation in these struggles, then, that the liberation theologian articulates a theological vision.

It is out of their experience amidst the suffering of the Latin American people that liberation theologians call all theologians and all scholars to be "honest about reality" by recognizing the practical, concrete articula-

---

of the Oppressed (New York, 1970) and *Education for Critical Consciousness* (New York, 1973). Freire's influence is analyzed in Hennelly, *Theology of a Liberating Church*, 67–80, and Berryman, *Liberation Theology*, 34–42.

56. That the theologian's praxis, or participation in the struggle for justice, is fraught with all the ambiguity of human historicity is attested to by Gutiérrez, who warns that this is "a process which can be deepened, modified, reoriented, and extended": *Theology of Liberation*, 92.

57. Enrique Dussel, *Filosofía de la liberación* (Mexico City, 1977), 105.

58. Intriguing examples of this type of communal reading are provided in Ernesto Cardenal, *The Gospel in Solentiname*, 4 vols. (Maryknoll, N.Y., 1976–82); see also Berryman, *Liberation Theology*, 45–62; Uriel Molina Oliú, "How a People's Christian Community (*Comunidad Cristiana Popular*) Is Structured and How It Functions," in Boff and Elizondo, *Iglesia Popular*, 3–9; Carlos Mesters, "The Use of the Bible in Christian Communities of the Common People," in Torres and Eagleson, *Challenge of Basic Christian Communities*, 197–210; and Lernoux, *Cry of the People*, 389–408.

59. Lernoux, *Cry of the People*, 390.

60. Berryman, *Liberation Theology*, 74.

tion of their own lives, and hence their scholarship, with the political, cultural, and economic structures of their societies. Honesty is verified less by the internal coherence of one's intellectual constructs than by the internal coherence of one's life. Without such fundamental honesty, without an experiential understanding of reality as chaos, disorder, and unjust suffering—in short, without an appreciation of the incoherence of reality—the scholar's neatly ordered, internally coherent theoretical systems and conceptual constructs will be little more than rationalizations of an illusory image of reality. Without such fundamental honesty, when scholars speak of "human existence" and "human experience," when they purvey their eloquently articulated and systematically developed theories, they will understandably be ignored, for the human existence and experience of which they speak differs radically from and therefore is irrelevant to the existence and experience of the vast majority of the world's population. Without such honesty there can be no talk of God. This point is made most poignantly by the French philosopher Simone Weil, herself a marginalized woman: "They alone will see God," she writes, "who prefer to recognize the truth and die, instead of living a long and happy existence in a state of illusion. One must want to go towards reality; then when one thinks one has found a corpse, one meets an angel who says 'He is risen.'"[61]

61. Simone Weil, *On Science, Necessity, and the Love of God* (London, 1968), 194.

12

Elites and Democracy: The Ideology of Intellectuals and the Chinese Student Protest Movement of 1989

Craig Calhoun

China's student protests of 1989 seemed to many observers to spring from nowhere on April 15, after the announcement of the death of Hu Yaobang, the former Communist Party chief. Journalists wrote of students apathetic one day and suddenly enthusiastic democrats the next. The protest movement did grow with dramatic speed, and certainly many previously apathetic students gave themselves over to it. But the image of that movement as a purely spontaneous or instantaneous response to a single event is of course an illusion.

The 1989 student protest movement built on more than a century of Chinese struggle for "science and democracy," modernization and national regeneration. More immediately, it was only the most recent in a series of struggles for democracy initiated by the 1978–80 "democracy wall" protests and carried forward especially by students in the second half of the 1980s. Indeed, it might be best to see the Chinese movement for democracy as very long, and the 1989 protests as a phase or episode rather than a movement in themselves. To locate them historically, however, is not to deny their significance. It is rather to understand them as more deeply integral to modern China. I shall address only one small aspect of these developments, the general ideology of Chinese intellectuals which stood behind and shaped the movement. This ideology is not inci-

Earlier versions of this chapter have been presented to the University of North Carolina Program in Social Theory and Cross-Cultural Studies, 1990; the Social Science History Association, 1991; and the University of Minnesota Program in History and Society, 1992. I am grateful for comments and advice from each audience. A segment of the analysis was initially published in *Praxis International*, 1990.

dental, for the movement was precisely one of an intellectual elite speaking on behalf of the Chinese people in general.

PREHISTORY TO PROTEST

Through the winter and early spring of 1988–89, groups of young teachers and students gathered on Beijing's university campuses. Six or seven might meet in a dormitory room. Sometimes, as confidence grew, a hundred would gather on a campus lawn for open discussion. In gatherings of each kind, democracy and paths for China's modernization were central themes. These themes had been on the minds of students and young teachers continuously for years. Their expression had ebbed and flowed along with the openings to popular political voices provided by periodic, temporary relaxations of repression every few years since 1979. Indeed, even before, they had been central to some of the otherwise very different discourse of the Great Proletarian Cultural Revolution.

In the late 1980s, the discussions were being pushed forward by a proliferation of intellectual voices. Waves of new publications had poured forth in response both to freedom from censorship and to publishers' profits. Prominent intellectuals such as Fang Lizhi had traveled from campus to campus speaking about the virtues of Western-style democracy and modernization. Their visits had been important not only for the spread of their own ideas but for their demonstration that someone could stand up and criticize the Communist leadership openly without being arrested or silenced. A decade before, the "democracy wall" movement had ended in sharp repression. Its most important leader, Wei Jingsheng, remained in prison, incommunicado and perhaps driven mad by solitary confinement. In early 1989, a group of prominent intellectuals led by Fang Lizhi called attention to both earlier struggles for democracy and their repression when they publicly called on the government to release Wei.

Political discussions were furthered also by the creation of institutional bases. Coffeehouses and restaurants provided space for this nascent public sphere; some even operated on campuses, leasing their facilities from the universities. Intellectuals had emulated the Shanghai of the 1920s (and the Greenwich Village of the 1950s and '60s, and the London of the 1780s) in opening an "Enlightenment Café" for discussions in a centrally located bookstore and tearoom. Even more important, perhaps, were the proliferating think tanks and research institutes. Many of them were sponsored by the government, particularly by reform factions allied with Zhao Ziyang. A few were set up by major private business corporations, such as the Stone Computer Company.[1] Others were headquartered on campuses or created as more autonomous academic institutions. They sponsored a rich and complex discourse on subjects ranging from the revitalization of traditional Chinese culture to the development of appropriate business law for China's emerging commercial sector.

Many of the young intellectuals—graduate students and junior faculty members—who led the discussions on the university campuses in the winter and early spring of 1988–89 had developed their intellectual positions and themes in the context of these institutes. They were the editors of series of books in translation, the makers of television documentaries about China's crisis, the writers of sociological analyses of public issues. Some were already well known, others had little public recognition. But they were crucial links between the emerging public discourse of China and the specific local discussions on individual campuses. Their audiences were mainly undergraduates. Many, at first, were simply the student fans of popular young teachers. They listened, and joined in discussions as disciples. But these discussions quickly grew beyond that format. Students chafed to take some direct action, not just to talk. Even in discussions, undergraduate student leaders came increasingly to the fore, voicing opinions of their own, laying out their own ideas both for China's future and for the role students could play in nudging that better future into being.

In Beijing the discussions were perhaps most intense at Beijing University, followed by Beijing Normal, People's, and Qinghua universities, but they were widespread. Each of the four major universities of the Haidian district saw substantial organizing, as did several of the more specialized schools, such as the University of Politics and Law. Outside Beijing there were few comparable centers of dissent and discussion; Shanghai offered one, Nanjing another, both on a lesser scale. Still, universities throughout China did share in the general discussion of social transformation, and there were few where the idea of democracy was not voiced. Fang Lizhi's trips, for example, took him to teacher training institutes as well as leading universities. He traversed all the major central regions of China. So, in brief, foundations were being prepared for the public protest that was to come.

That public protest was to come is not just the knowledge of hindsight. The campus discussions often turned to the question of what sort of protest could make the views of dissatisfied students and young intellectuals known. By late winter, plans were being laid for protests to take place on May 4, the seventieth anniversary of the 1919 student protest movement, which symbolized both a crucial era in China's struggle for

---

1. See David Kelly, "Chinese Intellectuals in the 1989 Democracy Movement," in *The Broken Mirror: China after Tiananmen*, ed. George Hicks (Chicago, 1990), 24–51.

democracy and modernization and the importance of students as the agents of protest and struggle.

In 1919, students from Beijing University had formed reading societies and published magazines; they had taken their message beyond the university gates to give street-corner lectures and make forays into peasant villages. Their message had turned, first of all, on the ideas of science and democracy, the need to revitalize China by transforming both culture and politics. The 1919 activists challenged Confucianism and the political inheritance of the Qing dynasty as similarly worn out, brakes on China's development. Heavily influenced by Western Enlightenment thought, they nonetheless also sought a specifically Chinese idiom for their speech and writing, and shared in a nationalist consciousness that bridled at China's weakness in world affairs and apparent backwardness. When, at the Versailles Peace Conference, China's "allies" in World War I awarded Japan sovereignty over Manchuria and key Chinese ports that had been held by Germany, the students took to the streets in public protest. They attacked the weak government that was unable to press China's proper interests on the international scene, foreshadowing 1989 in producing a partially nationalist protest against domestic rulers deemed responsible for international weakness as well as repression at home.

The May Fourth movement had been hailed by China's Communists as a major step on the path to national liberation. Its seventieth anniversary was to be the occasion of conferences, publications, and a public holiday. Twelve days before Hu Yaobang's death, students at Beijing University called on authorities to honor the May Fourth memory by encouraging free speech on campus: "This year marks the seventieth anniversary of the May Fourth Movement. As the birthplace of this extraordinary movement of democratic enlightenment, Beijing University has always held high the banners of democracy and science and marched at the very forefront of our nation's progress. Today, as Chinese commemorate the May Fourth Movement, we, students of Beijing University, the hallowed ground of democracy, continue to hope that we will be able to carry on the distinguished tradition of Beijing University." The students who petitioned the authorities through an open-letter poster were led by Wang Dan, later a key leader in the broader student movement, and one of the government's most prominent prisoners afterward. They recounted their activity: "Beginning last semester and continuing today, from activity Room 430 in Building 43 to the 'democracy lawn' in front of the statue of Cervantes, thirteen democracy salons have been spontaneously organized by students concerned with the future of the country and the Chinese nation." But party and school authorities had begun to interfere. Students called on the school to encourage, not resist democratic discussion, which would both serve the nation and "enliven the academic atmosphere." "Beijing University should serve as a special zone for promoting the democratization of politics; it should make a contribution to the progress of Chinese democracy."[2] This letter was put up on April 3, as student organizers geared up for the May 4 anniversary, which would afford what they thought to be a perfect opportunity to stage a moderate but symbolically powerful and widely noticed protest.

Intellectuals

When Chinese student protesters said in 1989 that they were acting as "the conscience of the nation," and that protest was not just a simple choice but a responsibility they had to live up to, they were speaking in line with a long tradition. Earlier intellectuals had remonstrated with emperors at great personal risk. During the declining years of the Qing dynasty, both students and older intellectuals had been in the forefront of the struggle for reform. They helped to lay part of the foundation for communism in China by reevaluating traditional culture, encouraging critical thought, and importing or developing a range of challenging ideas. Many intellectuals played key roles in the revolutionary struggle itself, or returned from safe positions abroad to help build a new China. Under Communist rule they did not fare very well. Yet, paradoxically, the vilification of intellectuals at various points under Communist rule—especially during the Cultural Revolution—reinforced the salience of the category even while it added complexity to normative evaluations of its members. The path of development since the end of Maoist rule has only enhanced this sense of a crucial role for intellectuals.[3]

2. Minzhu Han, ed., *Cries for Democracy: Writings and Speeches from the 1989 Chinese Democracy Movement* (Princeton, 1990), 16–18.
3. On the shifting fortunes and renewed prominence of intellectuals, see Timothy Cheek, "Habits of the Heart: Intellectual Assumptions Reflected by Mainland Chinese Reformers from Teng T'o to Fang Li-Chih," *Issues and Studies* 24 (1988): 31–52; Merle Goldman, *China's Intellectuals: Advise and Dissent* (Cambridge, Mass., 1981), and "Dissent Intellectuals in the People's Republic of China," in *Citizens and Groups in Chinese Politics,* ed. Victor C. Falkenheim (Ann Arbor, 1987), 159–88; Merle Goldman, Timothy Cheek, and Carol Hamrin, eds., *China's Intellectuals and the State: In Search of a New Relationship,* Harvard Contemporary China Series no. 3 (Cambridge, Mass., 1987); Perry Link, "Intellectuals and Cultural Policy after Mao," in *Modernizing China: Post-Mao Reform and Development,* ed. A. D. Barnett and R. N. Clough (Boulder, Colo., 1986), 81–102; Judith Shapiro and Liang Heng, *Cold Winds, Warm Winds: Intellectual Life in China Today* (Middletown, Conn., 1986); Jonathan Spence, *The Gate of Heavenly Peace: The Chinese and Their Revolution, 1895–1980* (Baltimore, 1981); Richard P. Suttmeier, "Riding the Tiger: The Political Life of China's Scientists," in Falkenheim, *Citizens and Groups,* 123–58; Anne Thurston, *Enemies of the People: The Ordeal of the Intellectuals in China's Great Cultural Revolution* (Cambridge, Mass., 1988); Lynn White and Li Cheng, "Diversification among Mainland Intellectuals," *Issues and Studies* 24 (1988): 50–77.

Yet it is not obvious or clear just what "intellectual" means. The category is an ideological construction, a claim about the unit among a variety of people, not simply a reflection of it. The Chinese term *zhishifenzi* is usually taken simply to mean all educated people, though that is still a fuzzy definition. During the "antirightist" campaigns and the Cultural Revolution, avoiding the label "intellectual" often made political sense. As the idea of expertise took on prestige once again in the 1980s, some provincial cadres began to claim startling numbers of intellectuals in their units because they counted everyone with a primary or perhaps secondary education. To be considered an intellectual in a village requires less formal education than to be regarded as an intellectual in Beijing. An official definition includes all those people at the middle level of expertise, equivalent to assistant engineer or above. A standard rule of thumb includes all university graduates, and "others of comparable levels." Intellectuals include writers, professors, scientists, and others who make their living by the production or dissemination of "knowledge" or "culture." But they also include doctors, lawyers, town planners, sanitation engineers, and other people with higher education. Especially at the more elite end, this notion of "intellectuals" reflects a process of class formation through which intellectuals have come to share a variety of ideas and interests, and a common sense of themselves and their role in China.

Chinese students constitute a specific, generationally defined segment of the more general class of intellectuals. The protesters of 1989 had strong identities as budding intellectuals and as students in particular. They were different from other intellectuals not only in their youth and the lesser development of their ideas and skills, but in the fact that they had no families to support or jobs to risk (at least in the immediate sense). They were therefore understood to be freer than their elders to act through public protest as a "conscience to the nation." In this understanding of themselves, the students echoed older Chinese precedents, most notably the student and intellectual movement of May 4, 1919, whose anniversary they celebrated in the second of 1989's really large marches. Of course, the student "fraction" of the intellectual class also had its own complaints: crowded, poorly constructed dormitories, inadequate stipends, a shortage of good jobs after graduation, and so forth.

More senior intellectuals had exerted enormous influence on students through their writing, public speaking, and teaching in recent years. During this prehistory, and to a lesser extent during the protests themselves, more established intellectuals offered advice, tried to protect young activists, and pushed for change in quieter ways (though a special respect was paid to those elders who did put themselves on the line in public protest). But protesting students did not simply follow the lead or advice of older intellectuals. Indeed, most established intellectuals urged caution throughout the movement.

The younger generation had its own orientation. Its members—who of course had heterogeneous views of their own—absorbed some aspects of their elders' ideology more than others, and recombined elements in new mixes. In particular, the older generations, from the young to the very senior, were shaped profoundly by their response to the Cultural Revolution. Though these intellectuals did not, for the most part, reach the same conclusion as China's aging leadership, they did share the fear of widespread turmoil. They often argued that students were going too far and should pull back, not just because the government might crack down, as indeed it did, but because order might disintegrate. Many of these older intellectuals, including the most prominent among them, Fang Lizhi, were very radical in their critique of Communist rule. But their call ultimately was for a kind of reform in which the best-trained, most elite experts would advise the government, not for a mass mobilization of the Chinese people. Only a few of these prominent older intellectuals could find anything good to say about the Great Proletarian Cultural Revolution. Liu Binyan is distinctive in being able to praise the democratic, antibureaucratic ideals of the Cultural Revolution at the same time that he shows how those ideals were negated by the party apparatuses and cliques that maintained power during it.[4] The Cultural Revolution was not the same sort of personal experience for most students in the protest (most of the main leaders were quite young—twenty-two years or younger). The point is not that they supported the Cultural Revolution, or learned very directly from it, but that memories of it did not damn for them the idea of participatory democracy. They were often elitist in their own ways, but they were far more willing to risk turmoil and to call for mass participation as a solution to the evils wrought by established authorities.

"Science and Democracy"

In the early twentieth century, intellectuals developed personifications of science and democracy as part of their effort to spread enlightenment among the less educated in China (and thereby strengthen the nation both domestically and internationally). "Mr. Science" and "Mr. Democracy" (often presented not through the full Chinese terms but through single syllables equivalent to "Mr. Sci" and "Mr. De") were widely touted as solutions to China's problems. These problems were many and varied, but were perceived centrally in terms of modernization and relations with

4. Binyan Liu, *Another Kind of Loyalty* (New York, 1990).

the West. Thus the protest of May 4, 1919, was sparked by China's abuse at the hands of its nominal allies in the Versailles Treaty negotiations, which ceded large tracts of China to Japanese control. Political weakness was seen simultaneously in terms of a corrupt, declining dynasty and of failed modernization and lack of national strength. Similarly, China's poverty had become an increasing concern, and the importance of both "Mr. Science" and political reform lay substantially in paving the way for economic modernization and improvement in material standards of living. Finally, as the Enlightenment imagery suggests, May Fourth intellectuals worried about the cultural state of the nation. Illiteracy and in general a low level of cultural attainment among the mass of the population formed part of the story. Beyond it, though, was a critique of traditional Chinese culture, from the binding of women's feet to the emphasis on stultifying rote learning. China, it seemed, needed not only more culture but a different culture.

The struggles of China's late nineteenth-and early twentieth-century intellectuals were rooted in the development of China's first public sphere.[5] Whereas in imperial China, intellectuals had generally been incorporated into the state, the decline of the Qing dynasty, the rise of quasi-autonomous merchant elites, and the impact of Western incursions all provided opportunities for greater autonomy. Growing literacy helped to create a market for publications. For the first time intellectuals addressed themselves not to emperor and court but to the public, conceptualized under the term *gong*. The intellectuals who rose to prominence in this early public sphere were partisans of nationalism and modernization. They defended the idea of a China integrated by its culture in an era when the government was weak and divided and when foreigners were a permanent menace. They sought modernization because it seemed to offer the only means to attain a strong and prosperous China. In 1919, the weakness of China's new but corrupt republican government in the face of betrayal by China's Western allies at Versailles sparked the country's first major student protests, recalled as the May 4 movement because of a day of carnage.

---

5. The term "public sphere" comes from Jürgen Habermas, *The Structural Transformation of the Public Sphere: An Inquiry into a Category of Bourgeois Society*, trans. Thomas Burger with the assistance of Frederick Lawrence (Cambridge, Mass., 1989); see the discussion in Craig Calhoun, ed., *Habermas and the Public Sphere* (Cambridge, Mass., 1992). The term has been introduced into the analysis of early twentieth-century China especially by William T. Rowe, "The Public Sphere in Modern China," *Modern China* 16 (1990): 309–29, and Mary Rankin, "The Public Sphere in Modern China," *Etudes Chinoises*, 1991. For applications to 1989 see David Strand, "Protest in Beijing: Civil Society and Public Sphere in China," *Problems of Communism* 39 (1990): 1–19, and Craig Calhoun, "Tienanman, Television, and the Public Sphere: Internationalization of Culture and the Beijing Spring of 1989," *Public Culture* 2 (1989): 54–70.

In the late winter and early spring of 1989, many of China's intellectuals had resumed the May Fourth struggle. They held "democracy salons" and open lectures on university campuses, wrote essays, debated the merits of reform proposals, and laid plans for a celebration of the seventieth anniversary of the May Fourth movement. Though neo-Confucians were increasingly prominent in Beijing, for the most part the activists' ideology shared a good deal with that of the European Enlightenment. One poster of April 30, for example, declared that its author was "attracted with a magnetic force by justice and the luminous appeal of reason."[6] Another poster, headed "Hold Up the Banner of Reason," proclaimed that "knowledge is power."[7] A committee was established to promulgate a "Chinese Declaration of the Rights of Man."[8] The Western ideology of human rights was repeatedly invoked. One wall poster I saw during the 1989 student protest saw this ideology as the essential contribution of Western thought to the discourse; after a listing of more authoritarian views from Chinese tradition and the Communist Party, it concluded simply: "Believe in human rights—foreigner." Similarly, a key open letter of February 13 read: "We believe that on the occasion of the fortieth anniversary of the establishment of the PRC and the seventieth anniversary of the May Fourth Movement, the granting of an amnesty, especially the release of political prisoners like Wei Jingsheng, will create a harmonious atmosphere conducive to reforms and at the same time conform with the world's general trend that human rights are increasingly respected."[9]

In early 1989, intellectuals were beginning to organize themselves and to speak more forcefully in challenge to the government than at any time in the history of the People's Republic of China. The petitions to free Wei Jingsheng and other political prisoners were the focus. As Perry Link comments: "Although the petitions failed to free any prisoners, their very considerable significance was to mark the first time in Communist Chinese history that intellectuals have, as a group, publicly opposed the top leader

6. Jean-Philippe Béja, Michel Bonnin, and Alain Peyraube, *Le Tremblement de terre de Pékin* (Paris, 1991), 121.

7. Han, *Cries for Democracy*, 140–43.

8. Lichuan Chen and Christian Thimonier, *L'Impossible Printemps* (Paris, 1990), 106–8.

9. Translated in Chen-pang Chang, "The Awakening of Intellectuals in Mainland China," *Issues and Studies* 25 (1989): 1–3. Chang comments that this letter "marks the first time since the founding of the Chinese Communist regime that mainland intellectuals have dared to publicly raise their collective voice despite the possibility that they might be subjected to persecution as a result. It signifies a growing independent political activity among mainland intellectuals" (1). Individuals had dissented before, of course, and sometimes paid a high price for doing so, but the collective sponsorship of this letter is noteworthy. It is worth noting also that the letter was signed by intellectuals of all three of China's main generations, old, middle aged, and young.

on a sensitive issue."[10] Two initial petitions drew a stern warning that things must go no further; the intellectuals responded with a third petition. This one was pointedly signed by forty-three scholars, precisely one more than had signed the second petition. These intellectuals built on the heroic efforts of such figures as the physicist Fang Lizhi (perhaps China's closest analogue to an East European–style dissident, a form not generally characteristic of the Chinese scene) and the investigative journalist Liu Binyan. Crucially, though, they defied the government as an organized group, not simply as courageous individuals.

The public declarations of senior intellectuals inspired students involved in the free-wheeling "democracy salons" and open discussion sessions on the major campuses. Many of the later student leaders were among those most involved in the discussions of the winter and early spring. They transmitted ideas as they in turn gave speeches to their fellows. They did have a base on which to build. Crucial to the provision of this base was the relative freedom of publication that China had begun to enjoy. Thus Fang Lizhi's speeches not only reached thousands in his immediate audiences but were transcribed and published widely. Freedom to publish combined with increasing freedom to travel to encourage common attitudes on campuses all over China (though not necessarily off campuses, let alone outside urban areas). The publications that played important roles were of several kinds. Academic journals printed analyses of China's crisis and proposals for reform. Even many university-sponsored and putatively purely scholarly journals in China were devoted not to ivory-tower academic pursuits but to concrete discussion of the contemporary situation. Beyond them were intellectual journals such as *Seeking Facts* (the former *Red Flag*) and newspapers such as the *People's Daily* and the *Guangming Daily* (the so-called intellectuals' newspaper). Both elite literary magazines and their popular cousins carried commentary on current events as well as essays and fiction dealing with themes of public concern. Basic concerns about Chinese society and the appropriate stance to take toward it were spread in a variety of ways, and translated from a sophisticated intellectual discourse into a more popularly influential idiom of dissent.

Popular music was also a very important medium for transmission of political dissent. Singers did not attempt to develop major social analyses in their lyrics, of course, but they did give expression to feelings that moved many others. When Cui Jian, for example, sang "Nothing I Have," he expressed something of the sense of social and cultural bankruptcy that many Chinese students felt. His songs in particular gave encapsulated,

10. Perry Link, "The Chinese Intellectuals and the Revolt," *New York Review of Books*, July 15, 1989, 34–41.

often repeated expression to grievances and desires; the very style of much of the music combined Westernization with countercultural critique. Another popular singer's simple lyric, "Follow your own feelings," summed up one of the powerful urges, even moral mandates, for Chinese students. Film and the performing arts played similar roles.[11] Perhaps most important, the proliferation of gathering places, from private restaurants to the short-lived coffeehouses, and above all the willingness of administrators to treat the elite university campuses as quasi-autonomous provided something of the material basis, the "free spaces" for a nascent public sphere.

THE VARIETIES OF INTELLECTUALS

Chinese intellectuals in 1989 did not speak with one voice, of course. There were differences even among the supporters of the protests. One continuum seems particularly important. At one pole, the emphasis was on a discourse between experts and government. At the other, it was on a public discourse, among intellectuals and potentially among the people in general. For those who addressed the public, there was a second continuum between those who emphasized a crisis of signification, of culture, and others who placed the accent on political institutions.

It is no surprise that these positions correspond, at least in part, to various intellectual specializations. For convenience, we can follow the Chinese adaptation of Western categories and speak of (1) scientists and technical workers, of whom Fang Lizhi is the most prominent; (2) social scientists and advisers to government and party reformers, of whom Yan Jiaqi, Su Shaozhi, and Li Zehou are the best known; and (3) literary intellectuals, including such journalists as Liu Binyan, such critics as Liu

---

11. Perhaps the most remarkable instance in these media in 1988 was the television series *He Shang* (*Yellow River Elegy;* see Frederick Wakeman, "All the Rage in China," *New York Review of Books,* March 2, 1989, 19–21; Calhoun, "Tienanmen, Television"), a stylish meditation on Chinese culture organized around a montage of footage on the Yellow River. Instead of praising the Yellow River as the cradle of Chinese civilization, the series criticized its frequent floods and the soil erosion that gave it its color. Implicitly, it showed Chinese culture as flawed at its roots and in need of radical reform. It visually likened China to primitive Africa and such "dead" cultures as that of ancient Egypt. Glamorous shots of skyscrapers represented the attractions of the West, and a recurring motif was the muddy Yellow River flowing into the bright-blue sea. This was an even more radical—and remarkably popular—critique than such films as *Red Sorghum* and *Yellow Earth,* which presented implicit or explicit critiques of either the Cultural Revolution or more general and ongoing aspects of the Chinese system. The authors of *He Shang* were prominent younger to early-middle-aged intellectuals.

Zaifu, and such creative writers as Bei Dao and Liu Xinwu.[12] Each of
these groups had its distinctive social and institutional bases. Fang Lizhi's
main audiences were at Beijing University and the Chinese University of
Science and Technology. The social scientists were based especially at the
Chinese Academy of Social Sciences, though some were also scattered
through party and quasi-private think tanks. Some literary intellectuals
were on the faculties of universities, or housed in such institutions as the
Academy for Chinese Culture, but they were most distinctively writers
for increasingly open newspapers and magazines, including a host of new,
substantially independent publications and book series; they were also
engaged in efforts to develop a sort of coffeehouse and salon culture
outside of Beijing's official institutions.[13] Each of these three groups also
had its distinctive views and lines of argument on China's current situation; though these discourses sometimes overlapped, of course, they also
had their own internal heterogeneity.

Natural Scientists

Relatively a few natural scientists were among the most visible leaders
of protest. They tended to emphasize freedom to pursue their own scientific and technical work, and the economic contributions that work could
make to China's modernization and prosperity. Their emphasis was on
the first term in the old May Fourth slogan, "Science and democracy." In
the same sense, though, the ideology of science colored the notion of
democracy far beyond the ranks of scientists. When scientists considered
democracy, they tended to identify it very strongly with the rational,
efficient management of government by people of trained expertise. Their
most general concern was with the modernization of China. While most
pursued this project directly in their scientific careers, a few offered
broader critiques or programs for remaking China in the image of science.
Thus Wen Yuankai, a former vice-president of the Chinese University of
Science and Technology (CUST), wrote a widely read book titled *Reform
and Remolding of National Character*.

12. And at the same time that, for convenience, we may see the intellectual field organized
into the traditional categories of natural scientists, social scientists, and literary intellectuals,
we must realize that this categorization draws on folk constructs that may misrepresent
much of the actual organization. See, for comparison, Pierre Bourdieu's arguments about
the need to break with such folk categorizations of the French academic field, and with the
self-interestedness of most of the analysts who deploy them, in *Homo Academicus* (Stanford, 1987).

13. The best-known effort in this area, the Enlightenment Café, was a project especially
of the more radical Westernizers. Its main protagonists were literary intellectuals, but it
included Fang Lizhi among its sponsors and somewhat cross-cut occupational categories.

Another former vice-president of CUST, Fang Lizhi, became the most influential of these scientists and indeed of all spokespeople for Chinese intellectuals. His arguments are heavily colored by an ideology of science, but also have a resonance far beyond the ranks of scientists; he thus transcends the category in which he is placed here. Fang will get more attention here than any other individual, both because of his enormous influence and because his speeches are so frequently concerned with the question of what role intellectuals should play in Chinese society. Fang was also unusually radical in his positions. For example, natural scientists in general tended to be strong supporters of Westernization, but Fang went further to embrace even condemnation of the government: "Talking about China's modernization, I personally like the idea of Westernization at full scale."[14] What Fang thematized about the West, however, was quite specific—an idealized notion of science, an empiricist discourse of truth, democracy as embodied in conventional electoral institutions, and above all an account of modernity as an evolutionary ideal more or less independent of cultural particularity.[15]

Like other scientific and technical researchers, Fang sought institutional arrangements to make practical contributions without the distortion or impediment of corrupt and ideological leadership: "As an intellectual, one should be a driving force for society. One major aspect of the effort to push the society forward is to do a better job in our professional field so that we can give more to society. . . . Our social responsibility, so to speak, is for each of us here to work for a better social environment that will allow our intellectuals to make good use of their talent and work more efficiently. . . . One important sign of a developed society is that intellectuals have a say in social development and enjoy considerable influence."[16] Fang illustrated the influence he imagined intellectuals to have in the West with a story of attending a scientific conference in Rome at which both the Italian president and the pope listened to the scientists. The contrast to senior Chinese leaders, who never meet with even the most eminent scientists or take an interest in scientific work, was telling

14. Lizhi Fang, "China Needs Modernization in All Fields—Democracy, Reform, and Modernization" (speech of November 18, 1986), *Chinese Law and Government* 21 (1988): 87.

15. This element of Fang's vision was distinctive in a discourse where nationalism played a major role. Fang spoke out against nationalism as a guiding force in Chinese reform, arguing that "patriotism should not be our top priority," and that feelings of national pride were likely to block the way to progress. Liu Binyan and others objected, arguing that patriotism was still one of China's most precious resources (Link, "Chinese Intellectuals," 40). On this point, Liu seems to come closer to sensing where the strength of feeling motivating radical protest came from in 1989.

16. Lizhi Fang, "The Social Responsibilities of Young Intellectuals Today" (1986), *Chinese Law and Government* 21 (1988): 68–74.

to Fang and his listeners on several levels. The Italian president, for example, sat in the front row, not on stage: "The president himself must sit down there because he was a citizen like all of his compatriots." Even more impressive was the interaction with the pope:

> The following day, we had a scientific popularization meeting with the Pope in a church. We scientific researchers took pains to explain scientific knowledge to him because we wanted him to believe in our research. Since he represents the power of God, . . . we sat before him. . . . But we and the Pope sat face to face. Thus, we explained our latest discoveries to him. These two meetings impressed me deeply, very deeply! I learned what position knowledge has attained in the modern age. After we finished with our explanations, the Pope made a speech to thank us. . . . What he said [was] concerned chiefly with scientific knowledge. He said he understood our explanations about the Halley's Comet, cosmic dust, black hole, and the universe. His speech contained almost nothing irrelevant to science. . . . After these two meetings, I came to the conclusion that in those developed, democratic countries, knowledge has an independent position. It has its own value and independent position. Moreover, everyone must understand the importance of knowledge. Everyone, from those who occupy high positions such as the president of a nation and the Pope to ordinary people, must understand this. . . . If one wants to be a noble man or a man in a high position, one must not be ignorant. Therefore, I feel that there is truly a great difference between those nations and ours.[17]

Having leaders who couldn't understand their work and didn't care to was obviously bad for intellectuals. But Fang emphasized that it was also bad for society as a whole. Repeatedly, Fang argued in a fashion indebted to Daniel Bell and his popularizers Alvin Toffler and John Naisbitt (both of whose books are widely read in Chinese translation) that modern technology has made knowledge, rather than labor or other material means of production, basic: "Intellectuals, who own and create information and knowledge, are the most dynamic component of the productive forces; this is what determines their social status.[18]

17. Lizhi Fang, "Intellectuals and the Chinese Society," *Issues and Studies* 23 (1987): 127–28.

18. Lizhi Fang, "Intellectual and Intellectual Ideology" (interview with Dai Qing), *Beijing Review*, December 15, 1986, 16–17. Elsewhere Fang made a similar argument for "white-collar workers," explicitly appropriating that Western term but changing its connotation substantially: "By white-collar workers, we refer to people who have attained a comparatively high cultural level and are well-versed in art, knowledge and technology": "Intellectuals and the Chinese Society," 129. Yet in a later speech, "Intellectuals Should Unite" (1987), *Chinese Law and Government* 21 (1988): 96–102, Fang made the distinction

Like other reform-oriented Chinese intellectuals, Fang spoke frequently of democracy. His emphasis, however, was not egalitarian. Rather than mass participatory institutions, he advocated a government by experts. At the extreme, it seemed as though he would like to see government by physicists. Thus he argued: "It's up to the intellectuals as a class, with their sense of social responsibility, their consciousness about democracy, and their initiative to strive for their rights, to decide whether the democratic system can survive and develop in a given society."[19] Fang did not argue that the decision on whether democracy would survive might more properly—more democratically—belong to the society as a whole. He clearly thought the society was not ready: "You can go travel in the villages and look around; I feel those uneducated peasants, living under traditional influence, have a psychological consciousness that is very deficient. It is very difficult to instill a democratic consciousness in them; they still demand an honest and upright official; without an official they are uncomfortable."[20] Fang's conception of democracy was not essentially participatory. It turned on *(a)* human rights, *(b)* the importance of honest, expert officials, and *(c)* the responsibility and right of intellectuals to criticize the government.

Though Fang was a major voice for human rights in China, like many intellectuals he hesitated before such radical implications of the ideology as granting the "uneducated" equal standing in public discourse with intellectuals. Like most students I talked to during the protest movement, he did not consider democracy to be inherently a process of education

(relatively rare in China) between narrow expertise and broader social consciousness—a distinction actually closer to the typical claims of the literary intellectuals: Westerners "believe those who know nothing but their own professions are not intellectuals but technicians or experts, and they think that intellectuals must bear some social responsibility. I think we as intellectuals should also have such a belief, because at least we still want to see China as a winner in the fight for its survival instead of a loser to be phased out by human history" (101–2). The way scientific and technological advance has made intellectuals (in the broad Chinese sense) the leading force in society is a theme Fang repeats in many speeches. That his interview with Dai Qing was published in the government-run *Beijing Review* should remind us that Fang's views were not isolated, and not without some support in at least the reform branches of the Communist Party. This interview was published only a month before Fang was relieved of his post as vice-president of CUST and expelled from the party. In several speeches, Fang suggested that a good Marxist account could be given for why intellectuals were the most advanced class (e.g., "Intellectuals and the Chinese Society," 128–29); this stance obviously did not make his arguments substantially more appealing to the authorities.

19. Lizhi Fang, "Intellectuals and Chinese Society" (speech of November 15, 1986; alternative translation of 1987), *Chinese Law and Government* 21 (1988): 75–86.

20. Translated in Richard Krauss, "The Lament of Astrophysicist Fang Lizhi: China's Intellectuals in a Global Context," in *Marxism and the Chinese Experience*, ed. Arif Dirlie and Maurice Meisner (White Plains, N.Y., 1989), 294–315. These words are from the same speech as Fang, "China Needs Modernization."

through participation in political activity. Education was something intellectuals would offer to peasants, workers, and soldiers; democratic discourse was by and large a right of the educated.

Fang stressed that democracy should not mean simply a relaxation of controls (as the Communist Party seemed sometimes to imply) and that it ought to flow from bottom to top (even if he was a bit inconsistent in deciding just where the social "bottom" lay). "What is the meaning of democracy? Democracy means that every human being has his own rights and that human beings, each exercising his own rights, form our society. Therefore, rights are in the hands of every citizen. They are not given by top leaders of the nation. All people are born with them."[21] Thus Fang argued persuasively that students ought not to believe the party's claim to have "given" them an education. Their education, he suggested, was a right. If it was anyone's "gift," the donors were their parents, who had labored hard to provide for them.[22] On the one hand, this argument scored an excellent point against the party's (in this case highly traditional) claim as authoritarian benefactor. On the other hand, it ignored the extent to which educational opportunities remained class-stratified in the China of the 1980s; virtually none of the university students to whom Fang spoke were from peasant families and few were the children of ordinary workers.

Similarly, Fang did recognize the importance of critical discourse to the development of a democratic public sphere:

> I hope we may all benefit from this interchanging discussion method. I don't want you to listen to me only. . . . I think, if I have said something wrong, you may refute me. Thus, we shall advance toward democracy. I must stress this. I insist on expressing my own opinion. When I see something wrong, I say it. If my criticisms are incorrect, you may always refute me. This [expression of one's own opinion] may be gradually realized when "both sides are not afraid of each other." I think, democracy is still far away, but at least, outspoken criticisms may create a democratic impression. I mean, we intellectuals are able to play a certain role in democratization.[23]

21. Fang, "Intellectuals and the Chinese Society," 137. "Democracy has a very clear definition, which is different from just relaxing a little bit here and there in a controlled society. What democracy means is the basic rights of the people, or human rights": "China Needs Modernization," 89.
22. Fang, "Intellectuals and the Chinese Society," 139; "Intellectuals and Chinese Society," 84.
23. Fang, "Intellectuals and the Chinese Society," 135; "Intellectuals and Chinese Society," 80.

But, ultimately, Fang linked democracy very closely to science; "science and democracy are running parallel."[24] In the tradition of May 4, 1919, science meant first rationalism as against tradition. Fang railed against China's feudal heritage as much as against communism; indeed, he saw the two as closely linked. His individualism entailed rejection of both Confucianism and communism, which shared a definition of personhood in terms of social relations and obligations to others.[25]

"Seek truth from facts" is an old Maoist epigram that Deng Xiaoping made emblematic of the pragmatism of the reform era. For many intellectuals, however, including Fang, it had a more profound if ultimately ambiguous meaning. On the one hand, "Seek truth from facts" could refer to the ideology of empiricist science, and this is a powerful part of Fang Lizhi's rhetorical claim to attention. On the other hand, the same saying could refer not to external verification of factual evidence but to an extreme subjectivism by which the "facts" are understood to be those of irrefutable personal experience. This is a more important rhetorical trope for many of the literary intellectuals of the 1980s, especially for creative writers, but it is not insignificant for Fang as well. "I cannot control myself," he said in one speech, "I feel that if I don't speak out, I shall neglect my duty as a citizen of this nation."[26] Fang frequently insisted on the importance of talking about his own experience. He adopted what Theodor Adorno called "the jargon of authenticity."[27] But this was not just a part of Fang Lizhi's rhetoric, it was also a powerful component of the intellectual complaint against Communist rule. Along with many others, he sought an end to the thousand daily ways in which protecting oneself from the regime meant compromising one's values and sacrificing one's sense of integrity.

Fang saw the need for honest self-expression as especially important for scientists:

> Scientists must express their feelings about anything in society, especially if unreasonable, wrong and evil things emerge. . . . Since physicists pursue the unity, harmony and perfection of nature, how can they logically tolerate unreason, discordance and evil? Physicists' methods of pursuing truth make them extremely sensitive while their courage in seeking it enables them to accomplish something.
>
> Let's take a look at the events of the postwar years. Almost invariably

24. Fang, "China Needs Modernization," 92.
25. Cf. Krauss, "Lament," 297.
26. Fang, "Intellectuals and the Chinese Society," 125.
27. Theodor Adorno, *The Jargon of Authenticity,* trans. Knut Tarnowski and Frederic Will (Evanston, Ill., 1973).

it was the natural scientists who were the first to become conscious of the emergence of each social crisis.[28]

Here Fang is mobilizing two of his favorite rhetorical tropes at once: his claim to speak from the privileged standpoint of science and his claim to special insight because of his knowledge of the West. The rhetoric of science is not just window dressing. It is closely linked to Fang's basic self-understanding and his conception of democracy and modernization. It is important to see how Fang sets his priorities and how he conceptualizes democracy, for his account of the Chinese situation and the role of intellectuals was among the most directly influential on the student protesters of 1989. And in the conclusion to one of his most famous and widely circulated speeches, here is how he orders and sums up his points: "We should have our own judgment about what is right, good, and beautiful in our academic field, free from the control of political power, before we can achieve modernization and true democracy, and not the so-called democracy."[29] This is the call of an academic scientist, one who sees democracy primarily in terms of rationality, not participation, and as crucially dependent on the leadership of specialized elite intellectuals.[30] There is nothing inherently objectionable here. Surely few of us would disagree with statements such as this one: "What I pursue is a more reasonable society that is pluralistic, nonexclusive, a society that incorporates the best in the human race."[31] Yet one has to consider also that Fang almost never mentions peasants or workers as significant or desirable forces in society, that his conception of freedom is couched almost entirely in terms of intellectuals' rights to carry on their work and to criticize the government, and that his notion of democracy is overwhelmingly a call for rational, scientific leadership, for modernization in the May Fourth sense, not for anything like "government of the people, by the people, for the people."

28. Fang, "Intellectual and Intellectual Ideology," 16–17.
29. Fang, "China Needs Modernization," 93.
30. As Richard Krauss sums up, perhaps a bit harshly, "I find that Fang is less an advocate for democracy than a spokesman for a group of intellectuals who are resentful that they do not have greater privileges in China today": "Lament," 295. For a more admiring view, see Perry Link, "The Thought and Spirit of Fang Lizhi," in Hicks, *Broken Mirror,* 100–114. Of course, Fang has a very exalted view of these intellectuals: "Generally speaking, people, who have internalized the elements of civilization and possess knowledge, have hearts which are relatively noble, their mode of thought is invariably scientific and they therefore have a high sense of social responsibility or even self-sacrifice. . . . Their point of departure is not their personal interests, but social progress": "Intellectual and Intellectual Ideology," 17.
31. Fang, "Social Responsibilities," 73.

Social Scientists

Social scientists by and large agreed with Fang's criticisms. Many went further, however, in developing specific views about market reforms and other economic policies, even advocating increasing private ownership and stock trading.[32] Social scientists were also much more likely to add a specifically political argument about reform of the Communist Party, loosening of central controls, or even free, multiparty elections. Some social scientists, such as Su Shaozhi (director of the Institute of Marxism–Leninism–Mao Zedong Thought at the Chinese Academy of Social Sciences) and Zhang Xianyang (of the same institute), tried to develop a more intellectually serious Marxist theory suitable to China's reform and modernization.[33] Their attempts to revitalize Marxism did not necessarily make these intellectuals less radical (or safer in the eyes of authorities). Su publicly endorsed the students' protest and is now in exile.

Closely related but somewhat more prominent in 1989 was a second group that tried to work within the party framework, this time with much less reference to Marxism. Yan Jiaqi, former director of the Institute of Political Science of the Chinese Academy of Social Sciences, was among the most visible of this group. One of Zhao Ziyang's closest advisers, he helped to coordinate the activities of the various think tanks that developed policy analysis and proposals for the party reformers.[34] Econometricians, demographers, and others often saw themselves as essentially applied scientists whose role was to further the cause of China's modernization. Many had views very similar to Fang's, not just on the failings of the Chinese government but on the nature of democracy and on modernization as a process best directed by experts. They might place less emphasis on institutional autonomy than the physical and biomedical scientists did, though, and often worked closely as advisers to various party and government sectors. Social scientists were apt to be both more closely involved with concrete reform activities (such as rewriting laws governing

32. See Orville Schell, *Discos and Democracy: China in the Throes of Reform* (New York, 1988), 44–55.
33. Among other contributions, Su encouraged a return to serious study of Marx's original texts, as distinct from the Soviet-style summaries reflecting the party's position at any particular moment. See Shaozhi Su, *Democratization and Reform* (Nottingham, 1988).
34. Now in exile, Yan has emerged as a key leader of the democratic movement in the Chinese diaspora. Wan Runnan, general manager of the Stone Computer Corporation (China's largest private company), and Cao Shiyuan, president of the Stone Corporation's Institute of Social Development (a remarkable private think tank), also fitted into this group, as did a great many of China's economists. Cao was arrested after the June massacre and remains in prison.

private companies) and were more often vocally critical of the conservative forces in the government.[35]

Social scientists with technocratic visions were not necessarily moderate in their views on reform. They might want vast changes, but changes in which professionally trained elites played crucial managerial roles, and in which popular democratic decision making was a negligible factor. The one-child policy of the early to mid-1980s, for example, was a radical reform. It reversed Mao Zedong's Marxist anti-Malthusianism with an image of inevitable competition for limited goods, and it flew in the face of traditional Chinese values. Its proponents made extensive use of projections based on Western demographic techniques and argued for the need to gather better statistics and train more demographers to analyze them. The policy could simply be decided upon when expert analysis convinced top government and party officials; it did not require mass democratic consideration and indeed was considered to be too important to trust to such procedures even if they had been considered.

Similarly, many of the major economic reforms involved attempts to transform the economy from the top down. Deng argued explicitly that it was possible to pick various economic reforms from the capitalist world without adding democratic political institutions. Even in the political realm, many reformers were more interested in improving administrative efficiency than in promoting popular participation. They focused, for example, on increasing the education and training of middle-level cadres. Indeed, many of these intellectuals were themselves recent recipients of foreign educations who had been promoted over more senior colleagues to positions of considerable influence. Of course there was enormous room for variation here. Arguments for decentralization of economic decision making could be taken as implying the need for private ownership of firms, or not; as implying the need for democratic institutions within those firms, or not; as implying the need for similar decentralization or democratization of political decisions, or not. Some reformers argued (not unlike the USSR's Mikhail Gorbachev) that the strong authority of the party center was necessary to carry out the radical transformation of the economy, even though a policy goal of that transformation was to lessen reliance on central planning. Gorbachev, however, emphasized the need for political openness and restructuring to coincide with or even pave the way for economic change. The Chinese leadership resolutely maintained the strict priority of economic matters. Perhaps as a result, even in the

35. Very few social scientists of any note actually spoke out against radical reform. Some conservatives in the government did try to promote the work of He Xin, a youngish but prolific researcher at the Chinese Academy of Social Sciences, precisely because he was critical of radical reform; after June 4 he became even more visible, but not more popular or typical.

crisis of the late 1980s, China's economy never fell into the shambles of its Soviet counterpart. But perhaps the crucial reason for the difference was that Gorbachev saw political reform as the only way for him to bring adequate pressure to bear on factory managers and economic planners entrenched in the Soviet bureaucracy, while China's enterprise managers and planning bureaucrats did not have any substantial basis for resistance or challenge to the central government's directives. Moreover, Deng does not seem to have faced such deep challenges on this aspect of his reforms as Gorbachev did.

By Chinese categorizations, many journalists were also social scientists, including notably Wang Ruoshui, former editor of the *People's Daily*. These journalists not only wrote social commentary themselves, they managed the major organs of widespread public dissemination of ideas. Qin Benli (editor of the *World Economic Herald*) achieved fame in the West when demonstrations followed the decision of Jiang Zemin and the Shanghai government to close his paper down a few months before the 1989 student protest movement began. Influential economic analysis was as likely to appear in his paper as in professional journals. Qin also figured among a substantial group of social scientists who had major impacts as purveyors and translators of Western thought for Chinese consumption. A number of book series had been founded in the late 1980s, for example, including notably the *Toward the Future* series in Sichuan, edited by Jin Guantao, Bao Zhunxin, and Xie Xuanjin. Bao was also a member of the Institute of History at the Chinese Academy of Social Sciences. Jin was widely quoted as having suggested that "the experiment and failure of socialism is one of the main inheritances of humankind in the twentieth century." Xie was co-author, with the Beijing Normal Institute lecturer Wang Luxiang and the journalist Su Xiaokang, of *He Shang (Yellow River Elegy)*, the remarkable television film series that galvanized viewers across China with its portrayal of Chinese culture as trapped in cycles of self-destruction and unable to meet the challenge of international competition.[36]

Counterposed to these radical Westernizers was a group that was dedicated to revitalizing traditional Chinese culture and found the basis for dissent and reform in a distinctively Chinese heritage. Li Zehou was officially a philosopher at the Chinese Academy of Social Sciences but was best known as a historian who had written influentially on traditional Chinese aesthetics and on "the six generations" of modern Chinese intel-

36. See n. 11 above. Two other particularly influential members of this grouping were Ge Yang, editor of *New Observations,* and Liu Xiaobo, a popular Beijing Normal University lecturer who was among the intellectuals who began a hunger strike near the end of the occupation of Tiananmen Square in May.

lectuals.[37] Liang Congjie, editor of a magazine called *Intellectuals,* the historian Pang Pu, and the philosopher Tang Yijie of Beijing University were also prominent. Their reconstruction of traditional Chinese culture explicitly focused on the important role allocated to intellectuals. The newly founded International Academy of Chinese Culture provided them with a base and brought young scholars from all over the country to its headquarters near People's University. This last group held perhaps the greatest prestige in the intellectual community, but it was the Westernizers who commanded the most widespread popularity.

Literary Intellectuals

The category of literary intellectuals can cover a variety of kinds of writing in China. Foremost, perhaps, were the creative writers—poets, novelists, and some essayists (generic distinctions are not always clear or always demarcated exactly as we find them in the West). Second, were the literary critics. Third, but very prominent, were the investigative reporters.

Chinese radicals and reformers had long seen literary efforts as central to the basic changes they wanted to produce. As Liang Qichao wrote in 1902: "To renovate the people of a nation, the fictional literature of that nation must first be renovated . . . to renovate morality, we must renovate fiction, to renovate manners we must first renovate fiction . . . to renew the people's hearts and minds and remold their character, we must first renovate fiction." In the Chinese case, reform of the very language itself was crucial because the classical language was so inextricably tied up with Confucianism and imperial rule. Yu Pingbo, a veteran of the May Fourth protest, wrote in a commemorative poem on the sixtieth anniversary in 1979, "We did not worry if our words were sweet or bitter / We just wrote in the newly born vernacular."[38]

Poetry and fiction had become controversial again in reform-era China. Authors had experimented with new styles, from a sort of vague, evocative poetry that came to be known as "misty" to stream-of-consciousness

37. See Zehou Li and Vera Schwarcz, "Six Generations of Modern Chinese Intellectuals," *Chinese Studies in History* 17 (1982–83): 42–57.

38. Quoted in Vera Schwarcz, *The Chinese Enlightenment: Intellectuals and the Legacy of the May Fourth Movement of 1919* (Berkeley, 1986), 33, 20. This use of language is not unique to China. Writing in the vernacular rather than in Latin was one of the crucial developments that paved the way for the European Enlightenment; it is worth reminding ourselves that a figure as modern as Thomas Hobbes was a pioneer in this regard. And in the European Enlightenment, and in the development of modern consciousness more generally, literature played a central role. Similarly, in nationalist and other radical movements throughout the Third World, literary production may be the central means by which elite intellectual ideas are circulated and introduced into broader discussions.

novels. The most important common thread was a new preoccupation with individual experience and especially its distinctiveness—a theme previously forbidden in Communist China. When poets such as Bei Dao, Shu Ting, and Jiang He began to write the new sort of poetry, particularly in the journal *Today,* founded during the 1978–80 democracy movement, it was widely understood to carry simultaneous political, cultural, and personal messages. In Shu Ting's famous 1982 poem, "The Wall," for example, her opening and closing verses read:

> I have no means to resist the wall,
> Only the will.

> Finally I know
> What I have to resist first:
> My compromise with walls, my
> Insecurity with this world.[39]

As factory worker as well as a poet, Shu was initially celebrated in part for the particular female strength she brought to her writing. More recently she has been criticized for making accommodations with the literary and party establishment. This complaint itself suggests the extent to which followers of the new poetry want a radical authenticity from their writers.

Older poets such as Ai Qing attacked the new poetry, likening it to an intellectual version of the Red Guards, even calling it the "Beat and Smash Poetic School." Indeed, it did have roots in the Cultural Revolution, in both the intensity of commitment and later disillusionment of young participants and the wounds with which so many Chinese people were left. It was this poetry, more than any directly political texts, that established the crucial link between the protesting Chinese students of 1989 and their forebears of 1978–80.[40] The Beijing University critic Xie Mian became a minor hero for standing up against the old poets and defending the "misty" poems as an authentic and important part of modern Chinese literature. Protesting students in 1989 frequently quoted Jiang He's

---

39. Geremie Barmé and John Minford, eds., *Seeds of Fire: Chinese Voices of Conscience* (New York, 1990), 18.

40. This linkage is confirmed implicitly by Shen Tong's autobiography: Tong Shen with Marianne Yen, *Almost a Revolution* (New York, 1990). The 1979–80 "democracy wall" protests were the most important of the earlier popular struggles of the reform era. They were mounted largely by intellectually alert young workers and veterans of the Cultural Revolution, including Wei Jingsheng, Wang Xizhe, and Xu Wenli. One dimension of their protest was a call for China to live up to some of the democratic ideals that had been promulgated in the early years of the Cultural Revolution, but that seemed to have been betrayed by both the later Cultural Revolution and successor regimes.

"Motherland, O My Motherland" and Bei Dao's "The Answer," particularly the stanzas reading:

> Baseness is the password of the base,
> Honour is the epitaph of the honourable.
> Look how the gilded sky is covered
> With the drifting, crooked shadows of the dead.
>
> I come into this world
> Bringing only paper, rope, a shadow,
> To proclaim before the judgment
> The voices of the judged:
>
> Let me tell you, world, I—do—not—believe!
> If a thousand challengers lie beneath your feet,
> Count me as number one thousand and one.
>
> I don't believe the sky is blue;
> I don't believe in the sound of thunder;
> I don't believe that dreams are false;
> I don't believe that death has no revenge.[41]

One marcher I saw on May 4 carried aloft a sign with no words, simply a piece of paper, a bit of rope, and a cut-out shadow.

Novelists and short-story writers of the same era were perhaps less radical and struck less often to the very heart of their Chinese readers, but they were also influential. "Exploring" writers such as Jiang Zilong, Chen Rong, and Liu Xinwu (editor of *People's Literature*) also took up the implicit critique of the Cultural Revolution and surviving "leftist" tendencies, and also tried to rehabilitate a certain individualism. In his "Black Walls," Liu has his protagonist paint the apartment entirely black, only to confront the puzzlement and ultimate hostility of his neighbors. The point is made apparent even by an orthodox literary critic who claims he cannot find it: "A certain fellow by the name of Zhou—a man recognized as being a little 'odd'—paints the walls and ceiling of his apartment black without providing the slightest explanation. An egotistical 'indulgence' of this nature can hardly be seen as normal or acceptable . . . the problem, however, is that the author . . . regards the 'abnormal' as 'normal,' and is critical of the attempted suppression of Zhou's desire to

---

41. Barmé and Minford, *Seeds of Fire*, 236. Bei Dao's poetry was only occasionally political, though its iconoclastic individualism made it nearly always fairly radical and moving to young people. Though he is not personally flamboyant in the same way, and his style is not the same, his artistic stance is in some ways reminiscent of Xu Zhimo's seventy years before.

express his quirky individuality. . . ."[42] The stifling of individuality was linked to the stifling of artistic and literary creativity. As Wang Ruowang put it, turning a government condemnation on its head, "we should say that those people who opposed the freedom of creativity are themselves the greatest source of contamination in spiritual pollution."[43]

Literary critics such as Liu Zaifu and Liu Xiaobo (as well as Xie Mian) played important roles in China. Not only did they help to elucidate themes in literature and act as arbiters of taste and reputation, they engaged in the ongoing project of linking contemporary literature to Chinese culture. Critics were also at the center of debate over that culture. Whereas Liu Zaifu sought both to reform Marxist criticism from within and to emphasize the continuing importance of the old Chinese literary tradition, Liu Xiaobo was more of an enthusiastic Westernizer and a radical (indeed, he was something of a self-conscious enfant terrible).[44] In this context, "traditional" means seeking a good balance of emotion and rationality, with stress on the collectivity and the social responsibility of the artist. "Radical," by contrast, means a focus on the expression of personal feeling, individuality, auratic art (to borrow Walter Benjamin's term), the autonomy of artistic production and its potential independence of national particularity in the modern metropolitan culture.[45]

Something of this tension was played out in differences between the creative writers and the investigative reporters. The reporters were positioned between social scientists and literary intellectuals (though in China even literary critics were often housed in the Academy of Social Sciences). The Communist Party, which long held that social reportage (and sometimes only social reportage emphasizing the morale-building good side of socialist society) was the main responsibility of writers, saw reporters as central to literature. Younger writers were more likely to disagree, wishing to claim that turf for art. In 1989 the younger writers Su Xiaokang and Dai Qing were attracting more and more readers (Su was one of the co-authors of *Yellow River Elegy* and had close ties in academic circles; he was also a lecturer in the Beijing Broadcast Institute). Much more famous, Wang Ruowang and Liu Binyan were the senior statesmen

42. The story is translated in Barmé and Minford, *Seeds of Fire,* and the criticism reprinted on 29. The critic goes on to suggest that in this story Liu "has revealed that he lacks a firm basis in life, and that he is out of step with the world around him."

43. Yuqian Guan, "Wang Ruowang Discusses Literary Policy and the Reform," *Chinese Law and Government* 21 (1988): 44.

44. See Geremie Barmé, "Confession, Redemption, and Death: Liu Xiaobo and the Protest Movement of 1989," in Hicks, *Broken Mirror,* 52–99.

45. It is thus no accident that Liu Xiaobo's participation in the 1989 protests makes him seem so akin to nineteenth-century European romantics and yet strikes a chord in many Chinese. As Barmé puts it, "Liu Xiaobo expressed the desire for people to participate in protest as part of a civil action of redemption": *Seeds of Fire,* 76.

of this group, long-standing Communists who wielded considerable influence as writers in official periodicals. Both Wang and Liu had been attacked repeatedly as rightists and periodically accepted discipline (including, in Liu's case, temporary expulsion) by the party throughout their careers. Even in their most critical writings, they are remarkable for retaining a commitment to some of the ideas that had made them Communists in the first place. In one of his articles, for example, Liu spoke of "another kind of loyalty" to the party, one that put ideals and the interests of the people ahead of the dictates of the bureaucracy and discipline of the hierarchy.[46] He tied his efforts to the reform branch of the Communist Party, exemplified by Hu Yaobang. After the fall of the Gang of Four, the project of rediscovering the forward momentum of Chinese liberation seemed urgent, and seemed also to depend on uncovering the various ways in which old "leftists" clung to power despite rectification campaigns.

From 1979 on, Wang became increasingly bold and unrepentant when his views were, as he admitted, "heterodox."[47] He was one of the few writers willing to look seriously at the implications of policies based on Deng's slogan "To get rich is glorious." Class polarization, he argued, was an inevitable consequence of the policies being pursued. Wang argued not for reversal of the reforms but for taking their consequences seriously: "If we go on emphasizing that we don't want inequalities to develop, we may as well attack the economic reforms and turn everything back to the egalitarians. Let them carry on their highly authoritarian management. Let them decisively and fearlessly cut down to size those who were so bold as to get rich sooner than others."[48] Ultimately Wang was dismissed from the party for his refusal to recant such views; Deng was determined to maintain an egalitarian myth even as he opened up a market economy with hints of capitalism. Yet this was a serious problem. One of the main ideological problems China faced in the spring of 1989 was that the government had not developed a rationale for economic inequality or permitted a public discourse from which one might have emerged. Nearly all serious and novel inequalities of wealth looked to many ordinary people like corruption.

Even more famous than Wang was (and is) Liu Binyan. The two played enormously popular roles as gadflies and consciences of the nation. Liu specialized in documenting the corruption of local Communist Party officials and the failure of the party hierarchy to do anything about it. As he was himself a party member and was writing in an officially controlled

46. See Schell, *Discos and Democracy;* Binyan Liu, *Another Kind of Loyalty.*
47. Guan, "Wang Ruowang."
48. Quoted in Schell, *Discos and Democracy,* 173.

press, his exposés sometimes carried more weight than those in Western papers; people sought him out to try to get their problems resolved. He maintained voluminous files on investigations all over China, often working with teams of assistants. When he felt he had documented a wrong that needed to be righted, he might send a file directly to a senior party official, such as Hu Yaobang, as well as (or instead of) publishing an article about it. Of course Liu was not always successful, and often his articles backfired, bringing retaliation rather than redress to those whose grievances he documented.[49] Liu had been writing much the same sort of report for more than thirty years when he was finally expelled from the party in 1987.

Liu Binyan joined the Communist Party as a teenager, five years before the 1949 revolution. He was active in the underground struggle first for the liberation of China from Japanese occupation and then for Communist victory over the Guomindang. After the war, he returned to his plans for writing. "I wanted to use my pen to slash the pall hanging over China, to dispel the gloom and open up the mental horizons of the people."[50] Unfortunately for Liu, he thought that dispelling the gloom depended on honest reporting of the causes of China's problems. In one of his first major articles, Liu told of two engineers. One had built bridges entirely according to party directives, and failed to take emergency measures when floods came early in 1954. The floods washed away the bridge support his team had built. The other engineer refused to wait for orders from above, changed the plans, and saved his construction team's work. The party promoted the first man and demoted the second. And so it has been for Liu, though he continues to exhibit the second sort of loyalty, along with his incorrigible optimism. Liu lost some twenty-two years of his life to labor reform among the peasants and other punishments. Condemned as a rightist, he had been rehabilitated only a few months when the Cultural Revolution broke out in 1966 and he was again attacked. Yet the Cultural Revolution began with a promise to democratize China. Even in the midst of his sufferings, Liu could see positive potential in its attack on bureaucratism, corruption, and special privileges for party leaders. Though he was one of the most resolute and effective opponents of those who came to power during the Cultural Revolution, Liu is set apart from other intellectuals by his ability to see something important in its ideals. In this quality, as in the fact that he had genuinely been a revolutionary, Liu is quite different from Lizhi, for example. He still believes in the ideals that motivated him to become a Communist. He is not just

49. See Binyan Liu, "Self-Examination" (1986), *Chinese Law and Government* 21 (1988): 14–34, and *Another Kind of Loyalty*.
50. Liu, *Another Kind of Loyalty*, 52.

a spokesman for intellectuals, but a man who clearly cares about all sorts of ordinary people; he wants their freedom and their democracy as well as his own.

Liu maintained his investigative reporting in the face not only of party pressure but of a changing fashion among writers. "In recent years, with the exception of a very small number, writers with a similar set of experiences as mine have turned their attention to subjects that are less politically or socially sensitive, devoting themselves to the pursuit of art. Consequently, even more than ever I have stood as the odd man out."[51] Later, "fewer and fewer Chinese writers think they should use their writing to help the Chinese people to reorganize society. One common view is that it would destroy the artistic purity of their work and cause it to lose the value of timelessness."[52] Liu regarded those writers and artists who turned away from "reality" as people whose sense of mission had never been strong, and who turned to commercialism, the ideology of art for art's sake, or the pursuit of a Nobel prize partly out of timidity in the face of hostile authority.[53] As far as he was concerned, the purpose of writing, for a person of conscience, was social improvement. At a conference in California in April 1989, Liu (already living in the United States) clashed with the modernist writer Bei Dao over just this issue. Perry Link sums up their exchange:

> "Our job is to tell the truth," said Bei Dao, "and if we don't we indeed *are* inferior to bean curd vendors, who do their jobs quite well." But there was no consensus on how much an intellectuals' independence should be devoted to social action as opposed to pure scholarship or art. "I see a terrible incongruity," said Liu Binyan. "On one side, 500,000 people massed in Tiananmen Square; on the other, in our literary magazines, essentially a blank—*avant-garde* experiments, read only by a few, understandable sometimes by none."
>
> Bei Dao bluntly disagreed. "True art does not ask about its own 'social effects.' We will understand this problem more adequately only when we understand why foreign writers, unlike Chinese writers, sometimes commit suicide. . . . It's because they're concerned with life itself, not social engineering."[54]

Liu Binyan's style is simple and straightforward, often a flat statement of telling facts punctuated by occasional condemnations in the strongest

51. Liu, "Self-Examination," 33.
52. Binyan Liu, with Ruan Ming and Xu Gang, *"Tell the World": What Happened in China and Why* (New York, 1989), 25.
53. Liu, *Another Kind of Loyalty*, 171.
54. Link, "Chinese Intellectuals," 40.

terms. No readers were ever likely to miss the point of his articles, even when references were oblique out of political necessity. And his pieces were simultaneously reports for the party and publications for the people. He was, in a sense, the sort of socially responsible writer that Communist activists said they wanted, and praised until they were in power and had to bear the brunt of the criticism. To label Liu a bourgeois individualist was merely to say that he insisted on civil rights and liberties, including the rights of the victims of party excesses and his own right to publish the truth as he saw it. The new poets and younger fiction writers, however, have often expressed something much more akin to the "bourgeois individualism" of the West, with emphasis on self-expression as an end in itself and an understanding of art as the product solely of inner consciousness.

It is nonetheless important to realize that the sense of Chinese cultural crisis and a concern for the fate of the nation did drive these younger, less political writers as well. Liu Binyan, for example, reports on the young scholar Liu Xiaobo: "After Yaobang died, Liu published an article in the *China News Daily,* a Chinese-language New York newspaper, in which he said he did not think much of the student movement. His opinions were unusual: For instance, he thought Hu Yaobang was only the leader of the Party, and that we should not honor him so. Instead, we should honor Wei Jingsheng, who had been imprisoned by the Communist Party ten years earlier for fighting in the Democracy movement."[55] Nonetheless, Liu Xiaobo did return to Beijing, and he was one of the intellectuals who caused a stir by announcing a hunger strike of their own at the monument to the people's heroes only days before the massacre. He was arrested and reportedly tortured.

The work of Liu Binyan and similar investigative reporters no doubt loomed much larger in the minds of the broad mass of the Chinese people than the experimental, often obscure poetry and fiction of the 1980s. Yet in the student movement the two influences merged. Students responded both to a straightforward account of the corruption of the Communist regime and to a more nebulous sense of cultural crisis—and potential. They responded both to simple logical arguments for civil liberties and human rights and to more mystical literary expressions based on a claim to those rights. They responded also to the physical presence of older intellectuals. As Liu Binyan remarks: "Literary critics could be seen shouting in streets and alleys, calling people to block army vehicles; famous writers ran around in a sweat, buying urinals for students. Scholars of the Chinese Academy of Social Sciences were also very active. Groups of people from many research institutes came to join the movement. Univer-

---

55. Liu et al., *"Tell the World,"* 25.

sity professors plunged in, also abandoning their usual discreet and retir-
ing behavior."[56] The student protest movement had taken older
intellectuals partly by surprise. A few retired to their apartments, but a
great many came forward to support the students. Though these intellectuals gave advice, they did not run the movement behind the scenes, as
some observers have charged (and a few intellectuals have claimed). Their
greatest influence was through the ideas that shaped the students' consciousness.

REPRESENTING THE NATION

Students' demands initially reflected their particularistic concerns rather
closely: for recognition of an autonomous students' association, improvement of a variety of conditions in universities, and more choice and meri-
tocracy in the assignment of graduates to jobs. Yet once the protest took
root, a variety of deeper, longer-range ideas came to the fore. Grievances
specific to students and intellectuals flowed together with a discourse
about democracy, modernization, and China's cultural crisis.

At first students sounded much like Fang Lizhi. His views both shaped
and reflected a very broadly shared orientation. Thus students saw the
project of democracy through lenses colored by class. When they spoke
of the relation of education to democracy, for example, they always spoke
of the need for educated people, such as themselves, to "educate the
masses of people." They did not speak of democracy as itself a process of
public education as well as of self-government. At the same time, the
basic self-identification of the students in Tiananmen Square—not just
their intellectual self-categorization but their lived identity—was transformed, and was for a time radicalized. Their consciousness expanded
beyond class concerns to include national ones and in important ways
universal ideals. The movement itself helped to liberate their thoughts
from concern over where they would work after graduation and turn
them toward the questions of China's future. This broadening of horizons
still encompassed practical concerns of the kind stressed by Fang and
various social scientists, but it also opened up a more radical, emotionally
inspiring vision, provided largely by literary intellectuals. The students'
protest was a moral declaration, an act of "value rationality," in Max
Weber's sense, not just an attempt to achieve specific reforms.

It was this only half-explicit vision that made sense of the risks students
took, the sacrifices they made. In the same way, when the ordinary people

56. Ibid., 25–26.

of Beijing rallied to protect the student hunger strikers on May 19, they did so not only because the students were speaking for ideals they shared but because they saw the act of refusing sustenance and courting government reprisals as proof that the students were not just seeking personal gain but sacrificing themselves for the people as a whole.[57] In the midst of the struggle it became possible to identify emotionally with a general category—the Chinese people—which under more ordinary circumstances would be rent by numerous divisions. Despite their own elitism, students were in many ways much more committed to democracy than most older intellectuals. Repeating the old May Fourth slogan, "Science and democracy," the older generation always seemed to put the emphasis on "science," while the younger generation put it on "democracy." To many of them, at least, democracy meant not just administrative reform or proper respect for expert advice, but genuine participation.

This is the source of the radicalism—and indeed the arrogance—of students' demand for high-level dialogue. From early in the protests, students had called for a "dialogue among equals" with top policy-making officials. They were disappointed that they were able to have this dialogue only with Yuan Mu, the spokesman of the State Council, and that he did not treat them as equals. Later, when Li Peng did speak with students, they challenged him directly for making a (rather haughty) speech and not truly engaging in a dialogue. Yet, from the standpoint of Chinese history, the fact that the students were able to get even this approach to dialogue was quite remarkable. The call for such a dialogue was only apparently a mild demand; in fact, it asked for a very radical act of political symbolism. On the one hand, it reflected the students' very high opinion of their own importance as young intellectuals (and echoed Fang Lizhi's emphasis on how Western leaders listen to scientists). On the other hand, this call for dialogue reflected on egalitarian ideology and offered echoes of young Red Guards interrogating senior officials in the 1960s. Of course the student protesters had no intention of acting like Red Guards, but others quickly noted the similarities. Undergraduates thought nothing of summoning the president of my university out to a rather forced dialogue one morning in May, but even some Ph.D. candidates were old enough to be reminded of the Cultural Revolution and were slightly

---

57. Here, as so often, 1989 directly echoed 1919. In the first article to speak of the May 4 protest as a "movement," Luo Jialun wrote on May 26, 1919: "This movement shows the spirit of sacrifice of the students. Chinese students used to be eloquent in speech and extravagant in writing, but whenever they had to act, they would be overly cautious. . . . This time, and only this time, they struggled barehanded with the forces of reaction. . . . The students' defiant spirit overcame the lethargy of society. Their spirit of autonomy [*zijeu*] can never be wiped out again. This is the spirit which will be needed for China to be reborn" (quoted in Schwarcz, *Chinese Enlightenment,* 22).

chilled by the action. One argued with the students at the edge of the crowd, but they dismissed his views.

Underlying some of these tensions are varying conceptions of the intellectual's role in Chinese society. I met no students in 1989 who were prepared to defend a strong ideal of "redness" and party discipline. The opposition of professional-technical expertise to personal-literary expression carried a good deal of weight, however. Linked to this dichotomy is the difference between analyses of China's current predicament which focus on purely economic issues, those that complement this focus with emphasis on political reform, and those that go beyond either of these notions of reform to emphasize the need to confront a basic crisis in Chinese culture.

Though most Western observers overlooked it, this sense of crisis permeated the concerns of students involved in the spring protests. It linked the China of 1989 to that of 1919 as surely as the slogan "Science and democracy," the rhetoric of modernization, or the concern with how to gain wealth and power in the world. Indeed, the sense of cultural crisis was linked to all these things. It was born in large part of China's relations with the Western world, the uncertainty about whether China's weakness should be blamed on something intrinsic to Chinese culture or character.

To understand the intellectual orientation and the strength of feeling that lay behind the willingness of so many of China's brightest young people to become martyrs, one has to go beyond the conventional Western focus on capitalism and democracy. Some party leaders, to be sure, wanted economic reform without political change or threats to their power. They pursued the virtually impossible line of trying to import Western technology, economic thought, and bits of business practice without accepting any of their political or cultural corollaries.[58] Many reformers were interested primarily in the same economic goods, but even in pushing for purely technocratic economic solutions they saw some need to streamline administration and reform the structure of power. Like nearly everyone, student, professional, intellectual, worker, or peasant, many of these reformers saw the need to do at least something about corruption. More radical reformers—and most of the students in Tiananmen Square—added political democracy to their demands. They meant, first, civil rights and liberties: freedom of speech, freedom to publish, freedom of association. Beyond these basic demands, elections and other forms of participation were possibilities that some students desired with

---

58. Here they echoed the longstanding *ti-yong* distinction, by which Chinese leaders had suggested that the "essence" of Chinese culture could be preserved amidst imported Western technology and other material advances.

varying degrees of urgency. A government that was truly interested in the will of the people and willing to listen to their views and needs (especially as interpreted by intellectuals) was a more basic desire.

All of these goals motivated student protesters. But they are not adequate to explain the depth of emotions in the square or the capacity of students to identify with the Chinese nation. Behind or beyond these various practical goals was a concern for just what it could mean to be Chinese as the twenty-first century approached. This compelling question of personal identity was resolved no more adequately by pursuit of Westernization than by appeal to traditional Chinese culture. This question linked the individual to the social in ways few students could articulate explicitly. But it is important that all the expressive individualism of youth in the 1980s was not *just* selfishness (though goodness knows it was often that as well). It was also an attempt to rethink identity and options for human action. Students could turn from apparent selfishness to self-sacrifice partly because external conditions changed, but also because their own discourse, even at its most individualistic, was not just about themselves but about China.[59]

The students who protested in Tiananmen Square were young or budding intellectuals. They saw China's problems through lenses that focused attention on their own role. But they were concerned about China's fate, and saw the existing government policies as denying them not only privileges and income but a proper chance to help the country meet its challenges. Technological improvements and economic reforms certainly required intellectual expertise, and students felt that the government did not invest enough in preparing them for this role or in rewarding them for taking it on. More basically, democracy required a public discourse, and students saw intellectuals as playing the most central role in this

59. I do not mean to imply that I support the radical individualism of many Chinese students; I found myself frequently in arguments on this score in Beijing. I think the individualism they adopted rather uncritically from the West, built on indigenous foundations, is a very problematic ideology, not least because it reproduces rather than overcomes the dualism of individual and society. What I want to stress is that however problematic the rhetoric, the concern was still substantially social. This individualism led in many cases to a focus on negative liberty to the exclusion of positive; it could sound very much like the "possessive individualism" of the West, and perhaps it could have ended up there. But the individualism did not rest on Western social foundations; it gained its definition in struggle with others, and it was crucially valorized by the crisis in Chinese culture which undermined all more manifestly social definitions of self. A version of this problem had existed in 1919. Far from solving the problem, the Communist regime exacerbated it, and in the process discredited Marxism so that it could not act as a viable counterbalance to Western individualism. The protest movement itself offered nobler possibilities for personal identity, at least for a time, but I think also in ways that permanently transformed some participants.

arena, as watchdogs for government accountability, proposers of policies, and interpreters of the demands and desires of the less articulate masses. Finally, the sense that China was racked not just by material underdevelopment but by cultural crisis seemed more than anything else to call for contributions that intellectuals alone could make.

Contributors

JANE BURBANK is Professor of History at the University of Michigan.

CRAIG CALHOUN is Professor of Sociology and History at the University of North Carolina at Chapel Hill.

ELLEN C. DUBOIS is Professor of History at the University of California, Los Angeles.

GEOFF ELEY is Professor of History at the University of Michigan.

JAMES EPSTEIN is Professor of History at Vanderbilt University.

LEON FINK is Professor of History at the University of North Carolina at Chapel Hill.

MARY O. FURNER is Professor of History at the University of California at Santa Barbara.

ROBERTO S. GOIZUETA is Associate Professor of Theology at Loyola University of Chicago.

THOMAS C. HOLT is James Westfall Thompson Professor of History at the University of Chicago.

LLOYD KRAMER is Professor of History at the University of North Carolina at Chapel Hill.

STEPHEN T. LEONARD is Associate Professor of Political Science at the University of North Carolina at Chapel Hill.

DONALD M. REID is Professor of History at the University of North Carolina at Chapel Hill.

Index